# INFORMATION SYSTEMS: A STRATEGIC APPROACH

*G. VAUGHN JOHNSON*

*University of Nebraska at Omaha*

*Mountain Top Publishing*

*Omaha, Nebraska*

*To my grandfather, Junius E. Payne*

*Production*: Susan Hansen
*Editing*: DeAnne Jensen
*Illustrations*: Susan Hansen
*Design*: Jami Spittler, Upstream Design
*Cover Designer*: Jami Spittler, Upstream Design
*Typography*: Petersen Type-Tech, Inc.
*Printing and Binding*: Walsworth Press Co. Inc.


Printed in the United States of America

Library of Congress Cataloging in Publication Data
Johnson, G. Vaughn
Information Systems: A Strategic Approach
89-064495
ISBN 0-9625533-0-1

Mountain Top Publishing
12520 Poppleton, Omaha, Nebraska 68144

**Chapter 1** INFORMATION SYSTEMS: AN ERA OF CHANGE 1

Overview and Objectives 2
The Concept of Systems 2
Information Systems 5
Types of Information Systems 8
Information Characteristics 12
Information Characteristics by Type of Information Systems 14
Organizational Information Requirements 17
An Era of Innovation in Information Processing 18
An Era of Discontinuity 23
The Changing Focus of Information Systems 27
Guidelines for Managers 31
Guidelines for MIS Professionals 32
Key Terms 32
Review Questions 33
Case Study 33
Suggestions for Further Reading 35

**Chapter 2** INFORMATION - A STRATEGIC RESOURCE 37

Overview and Objectives 38
Strategic Uses of Information Systems 38
Applying Information Technology for Competitive Advantage 42
Characteristics of Strategic Information Systems 44
Implication for Development of Strategic Information Systems 49
Cleaning Up the Mess in the Back Room 50
Corporate Culture and Information Technology 51
Executive Leadership 55
Realizing the Productivity Promise of the Computer 60
Guidelines for Managers 61
Guidelines for MIS Professionals 61
Key Terms 61
Review Questions 62
Case Study 62
Suggestions for Further Reading 63

**Chapter 3** INFORMATION RESOURCE MANAGEMENT 65

Overview and Objectives 66
Introduction 66
Goals of IRM 67
Requirements for IRM Success 68
Approaches to Information Systems Development 73
Developing an Enterprise Model 78

Enterprise Modeling Implementation Issues 82
Information Resource Management Deliverables 85
The Misuse of Database Technology 86
Guidelines for Managers 88
Guidelines for MIS Professionals 88
Key Terms 89
Review Questions 89
Case Study 89
Suggestions for Further Reading 91

**Chapter 4** INTEGRATED DATABASE MANAGEMENT SYSTEMS 93
Overview and Objectives 94
Introduction 94
Advantages of Database Processing 97
Integrated Database Management Systems 99
Types of Database Management Systems 101
Database Terminology 107
Performance Issues in Relational Database Management Systems 110
Alternative Relational DBMS Architectures 113
Workstation DBMS Directions 113
Additional Benefits of a Database Environment 114
Costs of Database Management Systems 115
Keys to Success With Database 116
Emerging Computing Environment 117
Guidelines for Managers 119
Guidelines for MIS Professionals 119
Key Terms 119
Review Questions 120
Case Study 121

**Supplement to Chapter 4** STRUCTURED QUERY LANGUAGE - SQL 123
Introduction 124
SQL Commands 124
Strengths and Limitations of SQL 138

**Chapter 5** DATA ADMINISTRATION 141
Overview and Objectives 142
Application Focus Versus Information Focus 142
Data Administration 148
Data Dictionary 151
Data Element Naming Conventions 156
Benefits of Data Administration 158
Costs of Data Administration 158

Database Controls 160
The Impact of Data Administration on Information Quality 162
Auditing Considerations in Data Administration 163
Guidelines for Managers 164
Guidelines for MIS Professionals 164
Key Terms 165
Review Questions 165
Case Study 166
Suggestions for Further Reading 167

**Chapter 6** Systems Analysis and Design 169
Overview and Objectives 170
The Process of Systems Analysis 170
Traditional Systems Development Life Cycle 172
Four Generations of Systems Analysis Tools 174
Structured Systems Analysis Tools 182
Guidelines for Managers 189
Guidelines for MIS Professionals 190
Key Terms 190
Review Questions 190
Case Study 191
Suggestions for Further Reading 192

**Chapter 7** Software Development Issues 193
Overview and Objectives 194
Software Development Methodology 194
Problems Related to Current Methodologies 196
The User's Role in Software Development 199
Assumptions of Traditional Systems Analysis 201
Problems with Traditional Systems Analysis 202
What Do We Need in Software Development Methodologies 203
Alternatives to Conventional Software Development 205
Selection of a Software Development Method 210
A Comparison of Alternative Approaches to Software Development 212
Guidelines for Managers 214
Guidelines for MIS Professionals 214
Key Terms 214
Review Questions 215
Case Study 216
Suggestions for Further Reading 217

**Supplement to Chapter 7**

PROGRAMMING LANGUAGES: FOUR GENERATIONS 219

Overview and Objectives 220
Four Generations of Programming Languages 220
First Generation: Machine Language 221
Second Generation: Assembly Language 222
Third Generation: High Level Language 223
A Taxonomy of Fourth Generation Software 227
Procedural Versus Non-Procedural 233
Compilers Versus Interpreter 237
The Impact of Fourth Generation Languages 238
Disadvantages of 4GLs 242
The Future of 4GLs 246
Guidelines for Managers 246
Guidelines for MIS Professionals 246
Key Terms 246
Review Questions 247

**Chapter 8**

COMPUTER AIDED SOFTWARE ENGINEERING (CASE) 249

Overview and Objectives 250
Introduction 250
Variations of CASE 252
Components of CASE 256
Emerging Directions of CASE 258
Software Development Methodology and CASE Tools 260
Advantages and Limitations of CASE 263
CASE Versus 4GLs 267
The CASE Database Connection 269
Guidelines for Managers 269
Guidelines for MIS Professionals 269
Key Terms 270
Review Questions 270
Case Study 270
Suggestions for Further Reading 272

**Chapter 9**

INFORMATION ENGINEERING 273

Overview and Objectives 274
Introduction 274
Stages of Information Engineering 275
A Data Driven Methodology 277
Information Engineering Diagramming Tools 280
Action Diagrams 283
Linking Database Design to Activity Diagramming 288

Information Engineering Facility 290
Managing Information Engineering Systems Development 296
Guidelines for Managers 297
Guidelines for MIS Professionals 298
Key Terms 298
Review Questions 298
Case Study 299
Suggestions for Further Reading 300

Chapter 10 DISTRIBUTED PROCESSING 301
Overview and Objectives 302
Introduction 302
Distributed Processing Network Alternatives 302
Forces Behind Distributed Processing 304
Connectivity 307
Distributed Networks with File Servers 312
Distributed Networks with Database Servers 312
Distributed Database 316
Guidelines for Managers 321
Guidelines for MIS Professionals 321
Key Terms 322
Review Questions 322
Case Study 323

Chapter 11 TELECOMMUNICATIONS AND NETWORKING 325
Overview and Objectives 326
Introduction 326
Telecommunications Fundamentals 328
Environmental Changes in Telecommunications 329
Local Area Networks 334
Wide Area Networks 344
Network Administration 346
Guidelines for Managers 347
Guidelines for MIS Professionals 348
Key Terms 348
Review Questions 349
Case Study 349

Chapter 12 MANAGING END-USER COMPUTING 351
Overview and Objectives 352
Introduction 352
Managerial Approaches to Personal Computing 356
The Information Center 360
Linking Information Centers and MIS 361

| | | |
|---|---|---|
| | Benefits of End-User Computing | 364 |
| | Personal Computer Workstations | 365 |
| | Managing End-User Computing Development | 369 |
| | Guidelines for Managers | 370 |
| | Guidelines for MIS Professionals | 370 |
| | Key Terms | 370 |
| | Review Questions | 371 |
| | Case Study | 371 |
| | Suggestions for Further Reading | 372 |
| **Chapter 13** | DECISION SUPPORT AND EXPERT SYSTEMS | 373 |
| | Overview and Objectives | 374 |
| | Decision Support Systems | 374 |
| | Model Building | 376 |
| | Semistructured Decisions | 377 |
| | Decision Support Usage Patterns | 379 |
| | Executive Information Systems | 380 |
| | Types of Decision Support Tools | 381 |
| | Financial Planning - A Case Study | 385 |
| | Expert Systems | 390 |
| | Development of Expert Systems | 394 |
| | Applications of Expert Systems | 395 |
| | Guidelines for Managers | 398 |
| | Guidelines for MIS Professionals | 398 |
| | Key Terms | 399 |
| | Review Questions | 399 |
| | Case Study | 400 |
| | Suggestions for Further Reading | 401 |
| **Chapter 14** | OFFICE AUTOMATION: IMPROVING WHITE COLLAR PRODUCTIVITY | 403 |
| | Overview and Objectives | 404 |
| | White Collar Productivity | 404 |
| | Office Automation Components | 406 |
| | Management Concerns in Office Automation | 417 |
| | Guidelines for Managers | 421 |
| | Guidelines for MIS Professionals | 421 |
| | Key Terms | 421 |
| | Review Questions | 422 |
| | Case Study | 422 |
| **Chapter 15** | MANUFACTURING INFORMATION SYSTEMS | 425 |
| | Overview and Objectives | 426 |
| | The Current Manufacturing Environment | 426 |

Simplicity - The Key to Improved Production Performance 431
Automation - New Manufacturing Technologies 437
Integration - Linking Islands of Automation 440
Use and Misuse of Computers in Manufacturing 443
A Contingency View of Automation 446
The Advantages of the Factory of the Future 446
Guidelines for Managers 449
Guidelines for MIS Professionals 449
Key Terms 450
Review Questions 450
Case Study 451
Suggestions for Further Reading 452

**Chapter 16** COMPUTERS AND SOCIETY 453
Overview and Objectives 454
The Post Industrial Society 454
Impact of Information Technology on Enterprise 457
Management of Technology 463
Computer Crime and Malicious Mischief 464
Information Ethics 467
Key Terms 470
Review Questions 470
Suggestions for Further Reading 471

**Appendix** DATABASE DESIGN 473
Overview and Objectives 474
Introduction 474
Conceptual Database Design 475
Normalization 481
Bubble Charting 482
A Three Step Normalization Process 494
Canonical Synthesis 499
Guidelines for Managers 505
Guidelines for MIS Professionals 506
Key Terms 506
Review Questions 507
Case Study 508

REFERENCES 511

INDEX 525

# Preface

The application of information technology in business is entering a period of rapid change. New technologies including the microprocessor, relational database, networks, optical disks and computer assisted software engineering (CASE) are creating an era of innovation. This period of turmoil creates both opportunities and risks.

Information technology is frequently poorly managed, particularly by managers who do not understand its capabilities. Strategic information systems have given some firms a competitive advantage by (1) lowering costs, (2) improving customer service and (3) spawning new businesses. To manage information technology managers must be informed and provide a leadership role.

Executive leadership is required to identify strategic opportunities and to stay the course during the implementation process. Understanding the technology is essential for executives to have the commitment necessary to persist during periods of adversity and opposition.

The emphasis in business information systems is shifting from efficiency to effectiveness; from cutting costs to increasing revenue; from automating clerical tasks to developing systems that provide a competitive advantage.

Managers need to recognize that information is a resource that must be managed. Managing information as a resource suggests some of the following actions:

- Improving the response to strategic opportunities by improving software development productivity and shortening lead times.
- Improving the quality of information by getting the firm's data house in order.
- Making end-users more self sufficient by making the corporate database more accessible.
- Actively investigating new information technology using an Advanced Technology Group.

# To the Instructor:

*Information Systems: A Strategic Approach* is designed for upper-division undergraduates and MBAs. It is written for the non-technical student who has completed an introductory course in computers and information processing systems. While MIS majors will be familiar with much of the information technology discussed in the text, they will find it provides a strategic framework for the application of this technology.

The textbook has two features that add interest and realism. These are Issues and Controversies and When Things Go Right/When Things Go Wrong. Issues and Controversies presents controversial views. These views have been carefully selected to relate to the text materials. When Things Go Right/When Things Go Wrong are short case studies of organizations which are applying information technology. Sometimes with great success and others with notable failure.

Included at the end of each chapter are suggestions for further reading. These are selected references which will provide greater depth for the motivated student.

A case study is included at the end of each chapter to provide an opportunity for students to think about and discuss the issues contained in the chapter.

The more technical material is incorporated in the textbook as chapter supplements or the Appendix. If the instructor desires to use this material it can be assigned like a regular chapter. No continuity will be lost if the material is omitted.

Students and instructors are encouraged to communicate directly with the author any suggestions for improvement.

# Acknowledgments

This textbook is the product of a team effort. A special acknowledgment is due to several individuals who played a key role in the development of this text. Foremost among these is Susan Hansen. She developed all the diagrams and produced the book using page composition software. Her persistence and enthusiasm were contagious.

My daughter, DeAnne Jensen, provided copy editing assistance for the entire book. She edited the book for structure, substance and style. She made numerous suggestions which clarified the text and improved the manuscript.

The author wishes to acknowledge the assistance of several graduate research assistants. Judy Deggendorf, in particular, went above and beyond the call of duty. Her dedication was appreciated.

Thanks also to Jackie Lynch who typed the entire manuscript through many revisions. She was always willing and produced quality work in a timely fashion.

I also wish to express gratitude to my wife Sandy who had faith in my ability to finish this project. My sons, Steve, Mike and Scott encouraged me to *go for it*.

# 1

# Information Systems: An Era of Change

*"The history of Information Technology can be characterized as the over estimation of what can be accomplished immediately and the under estimation of long-term consequences."*

*Paul A. Strassmann*

## Overview and Objectives

THIS CHAPTER EXAMINES THE CURRENT STATE OF INFORMATION systems and how new technology is bringing about a period of change. Historically, information systems have been used primarily for transaction processing applications. Technological developments have made decision support systems and office automation realities. These developments have also created the end-user computing era and enhanced the possibility of using information technology for competitive advantage.

After looking at the current state of information systems we will examine the impact of these changes on information systems departments, information systems professionals, and software development methodologies. Along the way we will identify the emerging trends in information systems.

AFTER READING THIS CHAPTER YOU SHOULD BE ABLE TO:

- Discuss the two major types of transaction processing.
- Explain decision support systems and office automation.
- Explain how information requirements for transaction processing differ from decision support applications.
- Identify the major technological developments and their implications.
- Discuss the impact of these technologies on information systems departments.

## The Concept of Systems

A SYSTEM IS COMPOSED OF TWO OR MORE INDEPENDENT PARTS that can be distinguished from their environment by a boundary. Obviously, this definition will apply to a wide variety of objects in the world we live in, including a cell, an automobile, a restaurant, and a set of accounting procedures.

Systems can usually be divided into subsystems. For example, an automobile is made up of a cooling subsystem, an exhaust subsystem, a braking subsystem, an electrical subsystem, and a power-train subsystem.

Systems can be classified as open or closed depending on how they interact with their environment. Typically, open systems such as biological systems must respond to changes in the environment to survive and grow. They are capable of altering their structure and function. Animals, for example, can derive their energy from a broad variety of foods. Closed systems, on the other hand, exhibit stable structure and continuity. They are not capable of adjusting their structure or function.

## CHARACTERISTICS OF SYSTEMS

All systems, whether open or closed, have a number of characteristics in common.

1. Systems are integrated.

   The parts of a system are designed to harmonize and work together. Because this integration focuses on an overall objective rather than the performance of each part, a system can achieve synergism—the whole is greater than the sum of the parts. In basketball, for example, a team can accomplish more collectively than five players focused on individual performance.

2. Systems must be adjusted.

   Systems require adjustment to respond to changes in their environment. Over time a system left to its own devices will run down and become disorganized. This tendency toward disorder is referred to as *entropy*. Open systems escape the effects of entropy by responding to change: adjusting their structure and function. Closed systems, which have a stable structure and function, require outside intervention to make adjustments in structure and function.

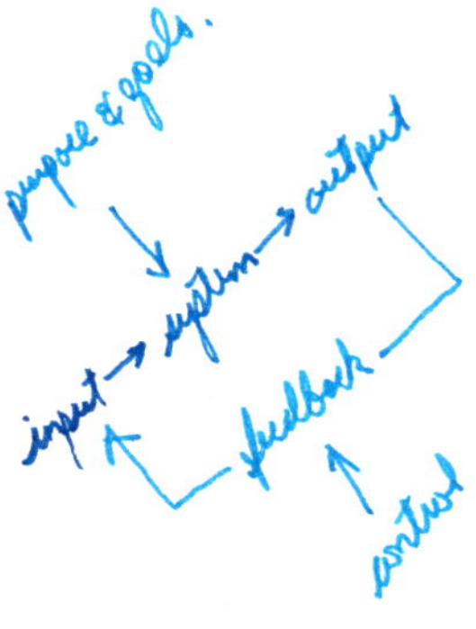


3. Systems are goal oriented.

   The structure of a system is designed for a specific function. The component parts work together to achieve this purpose or objective. This suggests that different objectives require different systems.

4. Systems require feedback.

   Feedback is information about system performance. It is required to determine the necessary adjustments. The need for feedback is increased if the environment is experiencing rapid change.

5. Systems transform inputs into outputs.

   All systems perform a transformation process. Inputs are changed to outputs.

The efficiency of a transformation process may be measured by comparing the cost of inputs with the value of outputs. Efficiency is concerned with resource utilization.

Effectiveness, on the other hand, is concerned with the appropriateness of the transformation process. Is the organization doing the right things in the transformation process? Recently there has been more emphasis on the effectiveness of information systems. This is an attempt to fit information systems into the firm's overall business strategy.

## ORGANIZATIONS AS SYSTEMS

Organizations can be described as systems. Some organizations exhibit properties characteristic of closed systems. These organizations are bureaucratic in nature, tending to have a high degree of centralization, extensive rules and regulations, narrow spans of control, and many levels of organization. They exhibit stable structure and function.

Other organizations display many of the properties of open systems. Burns and Stalker have referred to open systems models of organizations as organic. Organic organizations are adaptive in nature, exhibiting properties of growth, change, decay and death.

Organizations that must survive in a changing environment clearly have greater need for information about that environment than organizations living in a stable environment. These organizations also need to have more feedback concerning their own performance. The need to monitor their performance is necessary since organizational survival hinges on successful adaptation. Information reduces the uncertainty of a changing environment. A representation of organizations as systems is shown in Figure 1.1.

One authority has suggested that the degree of uncertainty in a situation can be measured by:[1]

1. the diversity of outputs produced by the organization,
2. the number of inputs utilized,
3. the level of goal difficulty.

Feedback reduces organization uncertainty. Organizations have a unique capability different from most systems in their ability to anticipate future changes.

FIGURE 1.1 *The Organization as a System*

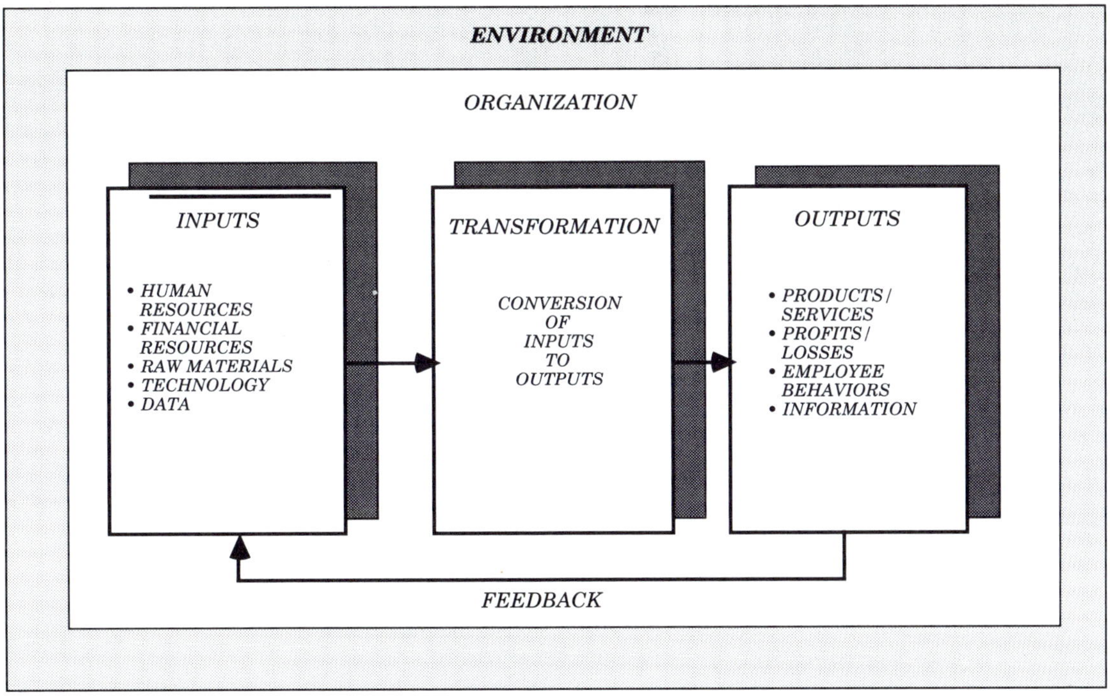


## Information Systems

AN INFORMATION SYSTEM IS DESIGNED FOR COLLECTION, transmission, processing, storage and retrieval of data. The objectives of information systems are complex but include: 1) improving productivity, 2) monitoring organizational performance, 3) providing the information required for planning and decision making, and 4) supplying a competitive advantage.

### INFORMATION SYSTEMS TRANSFORM INPUTS INTO OUTPUTS

Information processing is a transformation process which transforms data (input) into information (output). The difference between data and information is a source of much confusion. Information is facts in context whereas data are the raw facts, such as numbers, letters and symbols that are used to produce information. If I were to hand you a slip of paper with the number 95 written on it what would you have - a golf score or an exam score? The number 95 is raw data.

But if I were to tell you that it represented your score on the first exam then you have information.

Information, as was indicated earlier, reduces uncertainty. Knowing your exam score removes any feeling of doubt and clarifies what was previously ambiguous. It also assists in decision making with vacillation often giving way to decisiveness.

## INFORMATION SYSTEMS ARE INTEGRATED

Integration refers to the parts of a system working together. These parts may be both human and machine. Information systems need not be automated. Computer information systems consist of hardware, software, database, networks, methodologies, and personnel. These components are described below:[2]

| COMPONENT | DESCRIPTION |
|---|---|
| Hardware | Equipment that performs one of the follow ing functions:<br>1. Input or data entry<br>2. Output<br>3. Secondary storage of programs and data<br>4. Central processing unit (CPU)<br>5. Communications |
| Software | The detailed instructions that control the computer. Software consists of two major types:<br>1. System software<br>2. Application software |
| Database | Data stored by the computer system for use by application programs. Ideally a database is data designed for sharing across application boundaries. |
| Networks | Networks refer to communication networks which enable computers to be linked together to share resources and exchange data. |

| COMPONENT | DESCRIPTION |
|---|---|
| Methodologies | Prescriptions of how certain tasks should be performed. Methodologies include principles, practices and procedures applied to information systems. They are specifically related to the following:<br>1. Software development<br>2. Instructions to users<br>3. Data entry |
| Personnel | Information systems professionals including data entry personnel, computer operators, programmers, analysts, data administrators, information center consultants and managers. |

Historically, the integration of information systems was accomplished by careful selection of the component parts, an overall plan, and organizational standards and procedures. One of the weaknesses of the information technology of the 1970s is the difficulty of integrating information from two or more applications. Integration is very difficult or impossible to achieve in a file processing environment. The source of the difficulty is incompatible data formats and no provision for sharing data from different applications. It is highly desirable to have the flexibility necessary to integrate information in unanticipated ways both for current systems and future applications. New database technology makes this possible.

The emerging approach to integration involves designing the database for sharing data across application boundaries. The database becomes the focal point for integration of the information system.

## INFORMATION SYSTEMS MUST BE ADJUSTED

Information systems operate in the context of an organization. Organizations and their information requirements change for internal and external reasons. Some of these changes include: growth, organizational structural change, changes in the law and government regulations, and changes in the organization's products or services.

Information systems work best in a stable environment, but this ideal is seldom realized except for relatively brief periods. Software maintenance, which is the adjustment of software to change, is frequently the dominant activity of information systems departments. Unfortunately maintenance often crowds out new application development.

### EFFICIENCY VS. EFFECTIVENESS

Information systems should be designed to contribute to organizational success. Historically, most information systems have been designed for automation of clerical functions. The objective of these systems is usually labor cost savings. This type of objective is focused on efficiency or conserving resources. An emerging focus is to design information systems to assist the organization to be more effective, to assist it in meeting its overall objectives.

## Types of Information Systems

INFORMATION PROCESSING APPLICATIONS IN BUSINESS CAN BE divided into three categories (1) transaction processing, (2) decision support systems, and (3) office automation. In the past most information systems in business have been transaction processing systems.

A transaction is an act of *doing business;* for example, goods and services are purchased and sold, an employee is paid, cash is received and paid out. Transaction processing is concerned with the capturing, accumulating, maintaining and reporting of transaction data.

### TRANSACTION PROCESSING SYSTEMS

Transaction processing systems come in two varieties: (1) batch processing systems and (2) on-line transaction processing systems (OLTP). The earliest form of commercial computer systems were batch processing systems. Transactions were processed a batch at a time. Typically, this involved several steps in data preparation including:

1. The collection of transaction documents for a given period.
2. Data entry to transform paper documents to machine readable input.
3. Sorting of transactions to correspond with the sequence of a master file.

Batch processing of transactions was possible after these data preparation steps were completed. The advantages of batch processing were its simplicity and its minimal use of the computer. The second advantage is questionable in view of the change in relative costs of personnel versus computer hardware over time. Computers are now relatively inexpensive. Figure 1.2 illustrates batch processing.

FIGURE 1.2

*A Traditional Batch Processing System*

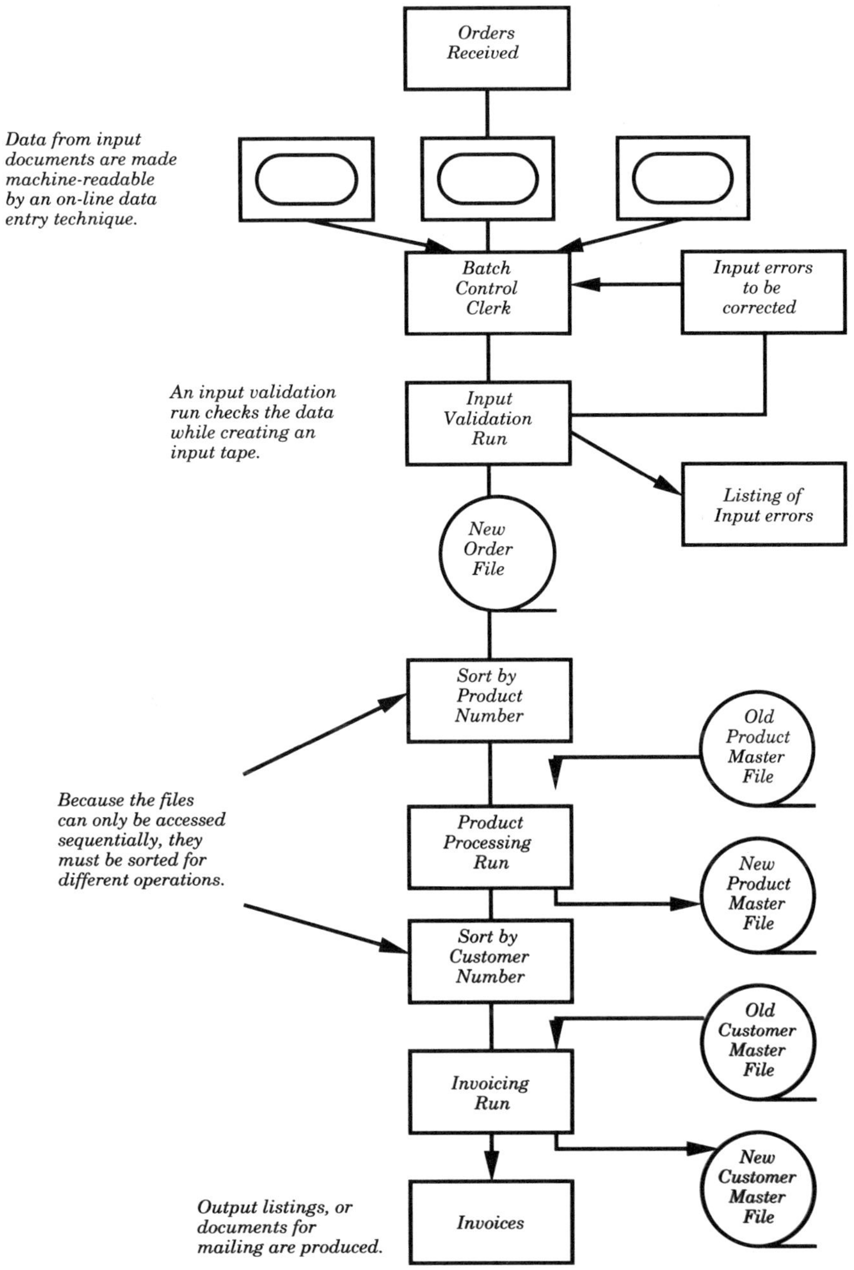

Batch processing has two major disadvantages (1) the labor required for data preparation is extensive, and (2) the information available from a batch processing system is not up-to-date.

The need for timely information in some applications has created the need for on-line transaction processing (OLTP) systems. The use of automatic teller machines (ATMs) in banking would be typical. On-line transaction processing might be defined as multiple users of a central data storage facility doing on-line inquiries and updates.

The need for timely updates of customer account balances for ATM applications is required to prevent accidental or intentional withdrawals which exceed account balances. ATM systems have grown rapidly, fueled by lower hardware costs and their acceptance by consumers.

The cost per transaction has dropped dramatically in recent years for on-line transaction processing systems. This development is the result of less expensive disk drives, telecommunications, central processing units and other computer components. The result has been very rapid growth in OLTP systems.[3] An example of an OLTP system used for order-entry is shown in Figure 1.3.

The cost of on-line transaction processing is expected to drop dramatically in the next decade due to the introduction of database server architectures. These systems incorporate low cost microcomputers in networks that perform transaction processing. This development is discussed in greater detail in the chapters on database and distributed processing.

The advantage of OLTP systems is that they bypass the costly data entry function and provide up-to-the-minute information. A point of sale (POS) terminal connected to a computer in a retail store illustrates these advantages. The terminal scans a UPC label, automatically determines a price, and prints an item description. In addition, the quantity on hand is adjusted for each item purchased. This process may also include a decision on the customer's credit worthiness, which is determined by the computer. If credit is granted, credit records are updated.

The special requirements of OLTP systems has created a specialized market for computer systems which are fault tolerant. A fault tolerant computer system is designed to continue to operate in spite of component or power failures. These specialized computers have found a niche in ATM applications as well as other OLTP systems.

While the original installations of OLTP systems were primarily POS systems in retail stores and electronic funds transfer systems (EFTS) for banks, the emerging markets are for what are termed "blue collar" applications. The automation of the factory is expected to be one the largest markets of OLTP systems in the next decade.[4]

Until quite recently, transaction processing was the focus of automated information processing in business. New developments in computer technology have made decision support systems, office automation, and factory automation practical.

FIGURE 1.3
*An On-Line Transaction Processing System*

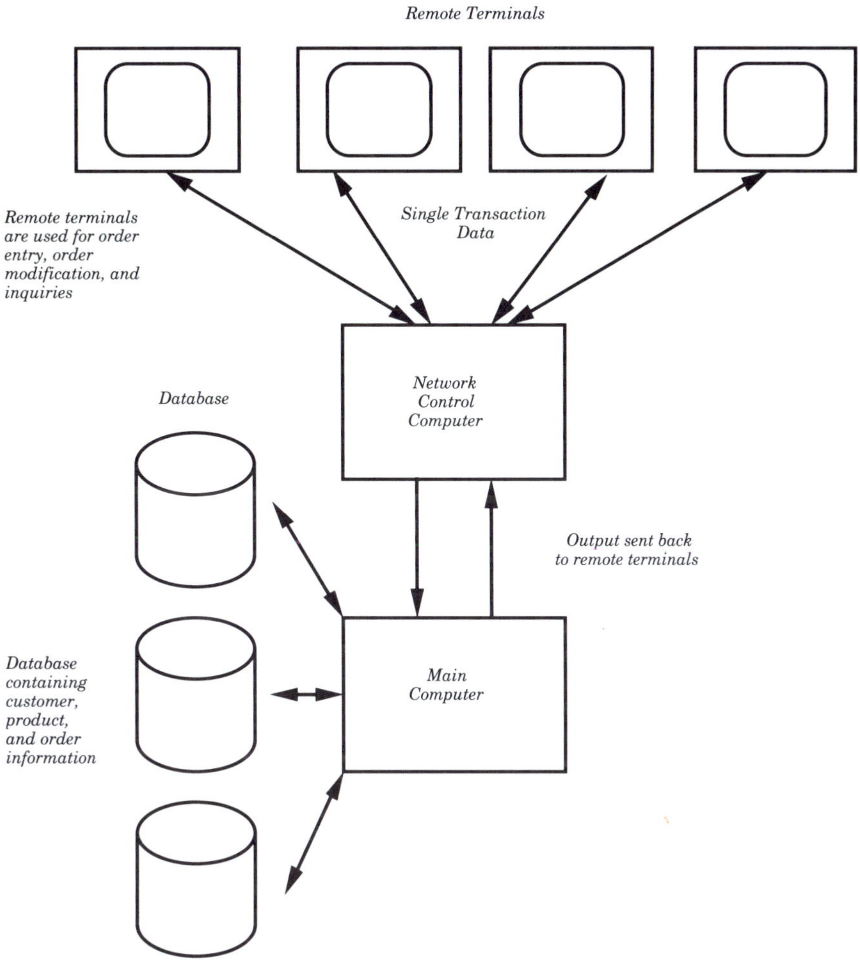

## DECISION SUPPORT SYSTEMS

Decision support applications provide information for management decisions. Typically, decision support systems are interactive, and provide easy access to analytical software and data. The term "interactive" means that the user enters a command on a keyboard and the computer responds with messages or output on a display screen.

Decision support systems are used at irregular intervals *as required by* the end-user. End-users are usually managers and professionals. Transaction processing systems, in contrast to decision support systems, provide reports on a *regular basis*. Whereas transaction processing is something done by information systems professionals, decision support applications are an end-user activity.

Decision support applications are characterized by using a computer and a decision maker as a team. The team builds on the strengths of each. The computer utilizes its computational speed and accuracy coupled with its ability to recall and access detailed information very quickly. The human contribution to the team is creativity and intuition. Human beings have an unexcelled capability to visualizing relationships and asking "what if" questions.

For decision support systems, users frequently build symbolic models. These symbolic models are simple mathematical relationships. An example would be a ratio—cost of goods sold is 60% of sales. Most students have experience with model airplanes and model cars. Physical models of airplanes and automobiles are used by manufacturers for testing prior to actual production. The advantage of building physical models is that it enables an organization to visualize and test a model prior to actual production. Symbolic models serve a similar function in decision support applications. The assumptions of the model builder can be tested against experience and the plausibility of the outcome.

The personal computer is at the focal point in implementing decision support and office automation application. In the past few years, personal computers have conditioned millions of managers and professionals to the use of a keyboard and CRT display. Many of these personal computer users have become adept at using software packages such as Lotus 1-2-3 which is a decision support package used for financial planning. Many have also become skilled at word processing using packages such as Word Perfect.

The stand-alone personal computer is a partial solution. The task that remains is to tie personal computers together into an integrated network for communications, storage, and retrieval. A network also permits users to share expensive printers, graphics terminals, and software. Finally, since most transaction processing takes place on large computers (mainframes), it is quite desirable to interface personal computers to mainframes to gain access to the data stored there.

### OFFICE AUTOMATION

The concept of office automation involves automating the processes of creating, filing, storing, and retrieving documents. It also involves communications systems that transmit electronic messages in lieu of paper or voice messages.

Office automation, like factory automation, currently exists as isolated islands of automation. The task of integrating these islands of automation with each other and providing easy to use interfaces to the transaction processing and decision support systems is yet to be accomplished.

### FACTORY AUTOMATION

The development of computer integrated manufacturing (CIM) systems will be a major strategic opportunity for the 1990s for manufacturing firms. These systems will require a joint effort between MIS professionals and manufacturing engineers. Managers need to be more knowledgeable about the benefits of CIM and how factory automation can provide a firm with a competitive advantage.

## Information Characteristics

INFORMATION SYSTEMS SHOULD BE TAILORED TO MEET THE REquirements of a particular application. Information systems designers should be aware of various information attributes. These are discussed below:

TIMELINESS: Timeliness refers to the time value of information. Old information has lost most of its value. Airline reservation systems, automatic teller systems (ATMs) used in banking and point of sale terminal systems (POS) used by department stores and grocery stores require a high degree of timeliness. For example, an

ATM system in a bank requires nearly instant update of a customer's account to prevent a customer from withdrawing cash from an account with a negative balance.

SCOPE: Scope refers to the breadth of the application. A payroll system is narrow in scope encompassing a single function. A merger study would be much broader in scope including many functions such as marketing, financial, and human resource considerations.

SOURCE: Source refers to the origin of data. Market share data, population characteristics, and economic projections would be derived from external sources; while production costs and sales by product line are from internal sources.

TIME HORIZON: Most financial reports are historical documents reporting what has occurred. Historical reports are more useful for control—identifying problems and taking correction action—than for planning. Planning requires a futuristic perspective. A budget is a common planning document.

FREQUENCY OF USE: Transaction processing systems continually collect transaction data and provide scheduled routine reports which summarize these transactions. Decision support systems are used as required (ad hoc). The typical use of decision support systems is irregular but intensive during the period of use.

LEVEL OF AGGREGATION: Lower level managers typically need detailed information about their functional responsibilities. They need cost or sales data by product, time period, or subdivision. Top management is more concerned with trends and overall performance and is usually satisfied with summary data.

ORGANIZATION: Organization refers to the extent to which information is structured for end-users. Periodic reports are highly structured whereas ad hoc queries have little if any structure.

## Information Characteristics by Type of Information System

TRANSACTION PROCESSING SYSTEMS PROVIDE INFORMATION TO managers with distinctly different characteristics than decision support systems. As indicated in Figure 1.4, the information provided by transaction processing systems tends to be more specific, immediate, and internal.

FIGURE 1.4 *Information Characteristics by Types of Information System*

| INFORMATION CHARACTERISTIC | TRANSACTION PROCESSING SYSTEM | DECISION SUPPORT SYSTEM |
|---|---|---|
| *Source* | *Internal* | *Internal and External* |
| *Scope* | *Single Function* | *Cross Functional* |
| *Timeliness* | *Important* | *Unimportant* |
| *Time Horizon* | *Historical* | *Future* |
| *Frequency of Use* | *Continuous* | *Ad Hoc* |
| *Organization* | *Highly Structured* | *Loose* |
| *Level of Aggregation* | *Detailed* | *Summary* |

The information requirements of lower management are often met by transaction processing systems. In contrast the information needs of top management are best addressed by a decision support system. This relationship is illustrated in Figure 1.5.

FIGURE 1.5 *Information Source by Level of Management*

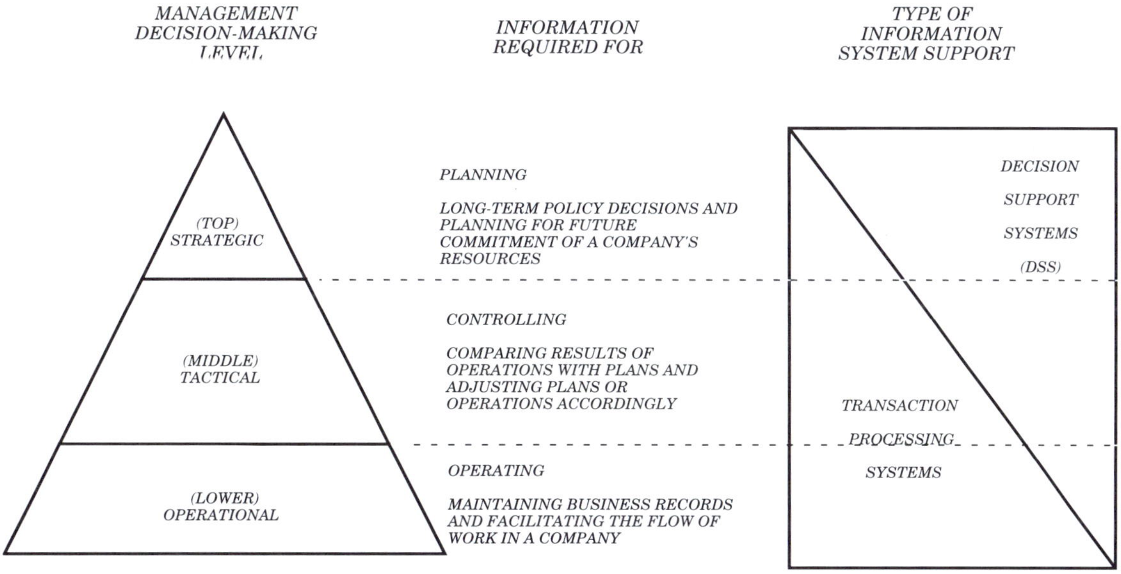

Figure 1.5 may give the impression that top management as a group is directly involved with decision support systems. While direct involvement of top management is growing, most of the information for top management is usually provided by middle managers. Middle managers typically interact with decision support systems as intermediaries for top management.

Decision support systems are a synergism between a manager and a computer. These systems concentrate on a middle ground of semi-structured problems that are not so structured that they can be solved by the computer acting alone but not so unstructured that the solution is a human judgment without quantitative analysis. This is illustrated in Figure 1.6.

FIGURE 1.6
*Decision Support Systems*

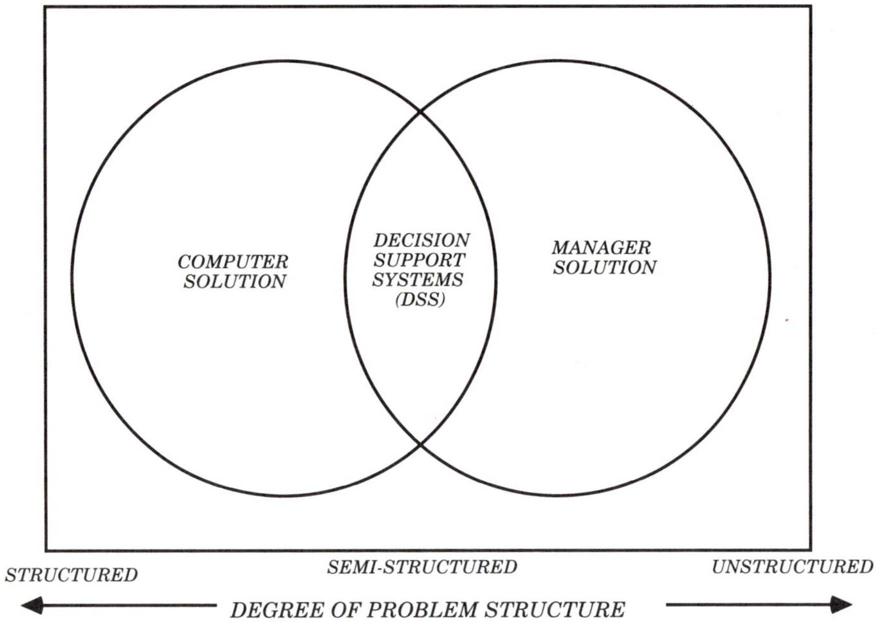


Some top managers are enthusiastic users of personal computers and terminals, but they are the exception rather than the rule. However, a new generation of managers with greater computer skills, resulting from their educational backgrounds and experience, are poised to move into the executive suite.

## Organizational Information Requirements

ORGANIZATIONAL INFORMATION REQUIREMENTS CAN BE broken down into four categories.[5]

1. **Monitor** — Routine systems that monitor transactions and produce summary reports on a regular schedule.
   financial accounting systems
2. **Exception** — Systems that produce reports which compare actual performance with expected performance.
   management accounting systems
3. **Inquiry** — Systems that allow end users to access computer data and format reports.
4. **Analysis** — Systems that allow end users to analyze data to support decision making. These systems may use analytical models and software packages such as IFPS, SAS, and LOTUS 1-2-3.

The first two categories of information, monitor and exception, can be provided by a well designed accounting system. Monitor information is provided by financial accounting reports such as income statements and balance sheets. Exception reports are usually provided by management accounting systems. Typical management accounting reports would include budget performance reports and product cost reports. These reports require organizational standards such as budgets and standard product costs for comparison purposes. These two categories, monitor and exception, are closely related to transaction processing systems.

Computer based inquiry and analysis systems give these two categories a new dimension. Historically, this type of information was derived from routine reports and manual ad hoc information gathering. Today, computer systems make it possible to automate the process of information gathering. Systems of this type generate information useful for management problem identification and problem solving. If, for example, a manager wants to project the future sales and profits of a new product or to determine the relative profitability of existing products, a financial planning package such as Lotus 1-2-3 would be quite useful.

A study at the Sloan School of Management at MIT projects future demand for these four categories of management information systems as follows:[6]

12 times as many analysis systems as are currently installed
4 times as many query systems
1.5 times as many exception systems
1/4 as many monitor systems

These figures indicate a need for greater emphasis on analysis and query systems useful for management decision making. Routine monitoring systems are being de-emphasized.

## An Era of Innovation in Information Processing

THE APPLICATION OF COMPUTERS IN BUSINESS ORGANIZATIONS recently passed its thirty-fifth anniversary. During these thirty-five years, computers have passed through four distinct generations. Technical advances in semi-conductor technology, the miniature silicon chips that are the building blocks of modern computers, are largely responsible for increasing the computers' capabilities while simultaneously lowering their cost. The price of computers has declined about 20% per year over a span of 20 years. Since 1955, computer prices have declined by a factor of 1000[7]

### MINIATURIZATION: THE COMPUTER ON A CHIP

The original digital computer, Eniac, occupied 1500 square feet and weighed 30 tons. In an interview a few years ago, one of the developers of Eniac, the late John Mauchley, indicated that his new desktop Radio Shack personal computer had considerably more computer power than Eniac.[8] This simultaneous increase in the power of personal computers and miniaturization is made possible by a single silicon chip.

Personal computers which are built around the "computer on a chip" are changing the business computing environment. A small silicon chip known as a microprocessor incorporates the entire electronic circuitry of a computer on a single chip. In addition to personal computers, microprocessors are also being used in a variety of other products including calculators, automobiles and robots.

The development of microprocessors of increasing processing capability is indicated by data found in Table 1.1.

TABLE 1.1
*Microprocessor Evolution*

| PRODUCT | YEAR OF APPEARANCE | BIT SIZE | APPLICATION |
|---|---|---|---|
| Intel 4004 | 1971 | 4 | Simple calculator |
| Intel 8080 | 1976 | 8 | Hobby computers |
| Intel 8086 | 1979 | 16 | IBM personal computer |
| Motorola 68000 | 1979 | 16/32 | Multiuser computer systems |
| Intel 80386 | 1986 | 32 | Mainframe computer applications |
| Intel 80486 | 1989 | 32 | Large mainframe computer applications |

During the 1960's the cost per unit of computing declined rapidly as the size of the computer increased. This relationship became known as Grosch's Law. Large firms, recognizing the economies of scale in large computers, purchased computers larger than was required for their own needs and attempted to sell time to other users to help pay for their machines. With the coming of the new microprocessor technology in the 70's large computers lost their cost-per-unit advantage.

Today microcomputers, computers based on microprocessors, have repealed Grosch's law. Microcomputers, including personal computers, provide the lowest cost per unit of computing of any size computer. Microprocessors, which can be mass produced at relatively low cost and are the most important component of personal computers, make this low cost processing possible. Furthermore, the most technologically advanced computers today are microcomputers.

A recent study compared the purchase price of computers with the number of instructions they could process in a second. Processing speed was measured in millions of instructions per second. The average results by computer size category are shown below:[9]

TABLE 1.2
*Computer Size vs. Cost Per Million Instructions Per Second*

| COMPUTER SIZE | MIPS/$100,000 |
|---|---|
| Microcomputers | 8 |
| Minicomputers | .5 |
| Small mainframes | .25 |
| Large mainframes | .22 |
| Super Computers | .25 |

These figures clearly show that microcomputers provide much greater processing per dollar invested than all other computer categories. The figures clearly show that Grosch's Law has been reversed.

The implications of these developments are far-reaching. Microcomputers will continue to grow in processing power. Costs per unit of computing will continue to decline. Several years ago IBM demonstrated that it could put the central processing unit of a System/370 computer on a single chip. Digital Equipment Company has developed a microcomputer version of its popular VAX super mini-computer as a desktop computer. Furthermore, it is estimated that microcomputer versions of larger computers could be manufactured for approximately one tenth the cost of the large machine.

## STORAGE MEDIA

Storage is required in a data processing system because of the limited memory capacity of computers. Computer programs and data not being used are stored in the computer's equivalent of a file cabinet, the magnetic disk. Magnetic disks are used to store numerical and alphabetical data but generally not images.

The cost of storing data on a magnetic disk has declined rapidly since its introduction in the late 1950's. This is indicated by Figure 1.7.

Magnetic disks will continue to serve as the primary storage media for data in the foreseeable future. Alternatives to magnetic disks are more expensive and less flexible. Furthermore, research developments have continued to enhance disk capacity by increasing the density of data on a disk and decreasing the data access time.

While magnetic disk devices continue to be the preferred method for storing numeric data, they have limitations. The cost and limited storage capacity of magnetic disk media make them impractical to store images. Organizations that need to store images are currently relying on older methods for preserving images of documents.

Images of paper documents are preserved for reference purposes. Many banks microfilm checks. Hospitals microfilm medical records. Universities microfilm student records. Libraries microfilm newspapers, rare documents and journals. Images are preserved to conserve space, duplicate scarce materials, and improve access to voluminous materials. To store images that can be accessed and displayed by a computer in a fraction of a second, a new technology is required.

FIGURE 1.7
*IBM Direct Access Storage Device Costs*

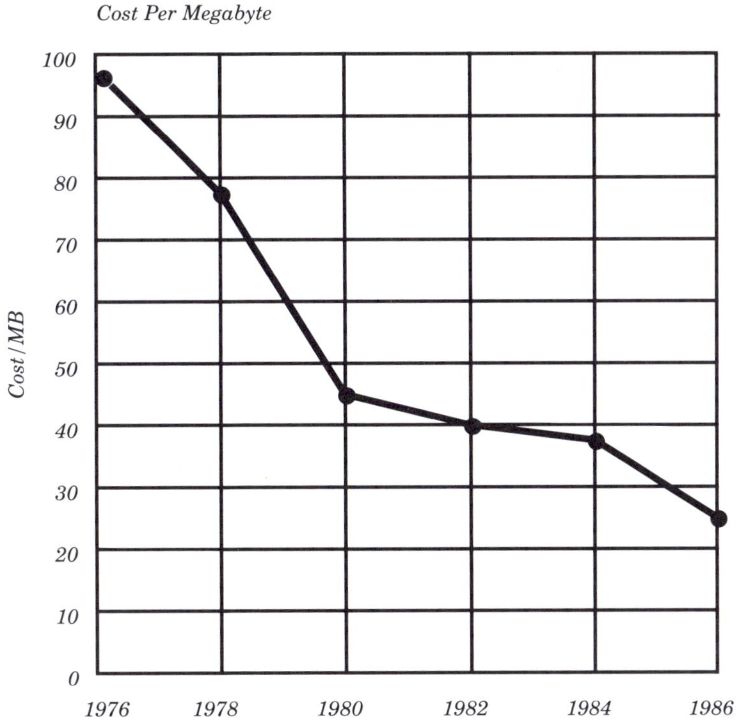


Optical disks represent a new method for storing both data and images. Optical disks, initially developed for a consumer product, the video disk player, and now being used for digital stereo may represent an ideal storage medium for many business applications. In the future optical disks will be the preferred medium for word processing applications and serve as the storage medium for electronic filing cabinets. Projected cost comparisons of alternative storage technologies are shown in Table 1.3.

TABLE 1.3
*Forecasted Cost Comparisons of Storage Technologies[a] (millicents per bit)*

| | 1987 | 1992 | 1997 |
|---|---|---|---|
| Semiconductor (RAM)* | 7-100 | 2-40 | .5-10 |
| Magnetic Disk | 12 | 03-.06 | 01-.03 |
| Optical Disk | 05-.01 | 01-.02 | 001-.003 |

*Semiconductor storage costs varies with the speed of the devices.

[a]U.S. Department of Commerce, "Future Information Processing Technology-1983" (Washington, D.C.: National Bureau of Standards, 1983), p. 51.

Optical disks currently on the market will store about 250 million characters, approximately the same number as the Encyclopedia Britannica. The Bible would require about 2.5 million characters.

This technology will make it possible for computers to be able to store and quickly retrieve images, extending the application of computers in the office and making it possible to have an enormous store of information readily available. When this development is coupled with advances in communications technology the possibilities are dramatic and exciting. Access to rare documents stored in libraries in distant locations becomes feasible.

## DEVELOPMENTS IN TELECOMMUNICATIONS

The development of communication technology has proceeded on several fronts, including communication satellites, local area networks, fiberoptics, and packet switching networks. These technological developments have been accompanied by deregulation of the telephone industry, which insures that the telephone industry, which has been stable over a long period of time, will be dynamic as new competitors offer new services to individuals and business firms.

The telephone industry has historically been regarded as a mechanism for transmission of a voice over a network of copper wires. The development of microwave and communications satellites has made it possible to provide voice, video and data communication services over long distances without the necessity of a point-to-point cable connection. The transmission of high-speed data and images is made possible by the wider band width of the newer communications media. Wider band widths refers to greater capacity. Whereas a voice grade telephone line is limited to about 2400 BAUD (approximately 300 characters per second), new developments make it possible to transmit billions of characters per second.

Giant satellites, made possible by the payload capacity of the space shuttle, will dramatically lower the cost of satellite receiving and transmitting stations. The lower costs of the earth stations is a result of the increased power of the new satellites which reduces the required size of earth stations.

### DATA BASE MANAGEMENT SYSTEMS

Business experience with data base management systems has been mixed. Early data base management systems were complex and difficult to use. However, new concepts in data base technology are now available. These new systems are referred to as *relational* data base management systems: based on a sound theoretical foundation, they are clearly superior to earlier data base concepts.

The relational data base has made it possible to develop new concepts in programming known as 4th generation programming languages. This development is feasible because a relational data base rigorously defines the relationship between data items.

Fourth generation languages (4GL) make use of a relational data base capability referred to as *automatic navigation*. Suppose you are visiting in New York City and want to see the Broadway production of the play "CATS." Hailing a taxi you tell the driver to take you to the play "CATS". You assume the taxi driver knows how to get around NYC and knows the theatre where "CATS" is playing. If the driver is less knowledgeable you may have to give him/her more explicit instructions. Fourth generation languages are like a knowledgeable taxi driver. They eliminate most of the instructions of how a task is to be accomplished and focus on what is to be done.

A development closely related to 4GLs is CASE (computer aided software engineering). CASE uses graphical specifications to represent the logic of programs. Once the specifications are completed an integrated CASE product can generate the computer code corresponding to the specifications. CASE represents an extension of 4GLs.

## An Era of Discontinuity

INFORMATION SYSTEMS MANAGERS AND PROFESSIONALS HAVE recently been confronted with several powerful winds of change. These forces are like technology driven discontinuities. This new technology brings a wave of challenges to information systems professionals because it renders much of their knowledge base and skills obsolete; it challenges managers to use the new technology for competitive advantage, and finally it challenges organizations to implement this new technology effectively.

Some of these discontinuities have been described as follows:[10]

## THE PROLIFERATION OF INCOMPATIBLE COMPUTER SYSTEMS

During the 1970's, information processing was centralized and under the control of information systems professionals. Data center factories were created to process data 24 hours a day. The systems were designed for stability and reliability of operation. Economies of scale supported using very large computers for information processing.

Today the information systems running in most organizations are far more complex. Information processing typically consists of a three tiered hierarchy of mainframes; minicomputers doing departmental or single function applications (such as order entry); and personal computers. Each level in the hierarchy has different selection of languages, application development tools, data base management systems, and commercial application packages. The complexity of this structure is compounded by a lack of compatibility between different levels of the hierarchy. This incompatibility is the result of computers developed with different operating systems and architectures—frequently by different vendors.

The information systems manager knows that the proliferation of incompatible hardware and software will create difficult support and integration problems if the firm attempts to move to a network environment. He also knows that end-users are careless about documentation and testing of software neither do most understand the need for data security and consistency.[11]

## THE END-USER REVOLUTION

The personal computer is part of a revolution toward end-user computing that has swept corporate America. End-user computing is computing done by end-users without professional assistance. More end-users have turned away from their information systems departments, which have come to be seen as unresponsive to users at best—or at worst, totally incompetent. Their backlog of new applications is discouraging to end users, who often see the personal computer as a way around the road block.

The loss of power that this end-user revolution represents for the information systems manager can be measured in corporate budgets. At Xerox, for example, over 40% of the total budget in recent years is devoted to direct support of end users compared with virtually nothing just 10 years ago.[12] Explosive growth in the demand for personal computers, software packages, and easy-to-use languages are limiting other information systems initiatives.

End-user experience with user-friendly software and application development packages on personal computers have made end-users more knowledgeable about computing and less tolerant of application backlogs. In short, in the personal computer era end-users are more knowledgeable and demanding. Initially the end-user revolution demanded freedom from the control of information systems departments, now the pendulum has swung in the other direction.

## THE DEMAND FOR INTEGRATION AND NETWORKING

End-users are beginning to understand the limitations of a free standing personal computer. They are demanding access to data stored on large mainframe computer systems. This will require the creation of network encompassing personal computers, minicomputers, and mainframes which is a challenging task considering the problems of incompatibility discussed earlier. Making this network easy to use is even more challenging.

The vision of using the personal computer as a managerial work station in an office automation system is also growing. The concept of a managerial work station is similar to that of an engineering work station. The purpose is to enhance the productivity of managers and non-technical professionals.[13] A personal computer is transformed into a managerial work station when it is connected to a network allowing it to interface with a mainframe and its data base.[14]

## NEW METHODS OF APPLICATION DEVELOPMENT

During the 1960s, application development was a "seat-of-the-pants" process. During the 1970s, formal application development methodologies were developed. These methodologies required extensive analysis and documentation of proposed software applications. The specification process was long and tedious and had a distinctly bureaucratic flavor. The resulting solution frequently required much adjustment upon implementation, frustrating users and MIS professionals alike.

End users have discovered that there are several alternatives to the old methodologies. One of these alternatives is developing the application themselves using tools like FOCUS and NOMAD2. Programming in these languages is greatly simplified compared with earlier third generation languages. These fourth generation languages were designed for end-users.

End users have discovered that personal computer packages like Lotus 1-2-3 make them less dependent on information systems professionals. They have learned that self development means they no longer have to wait in the application development queue. They, in effect, go to the head of the line without having to wait for information systems professionals to get to their project.

Enlightened systems professionals have recognized the benefits of the new methods of application development and are beginning to use 4th generation languages and CASE tools for new applications. They are also developing data bases that enable end-users to access data themselves with powerful query languages such as SQL.

The MIS staff is beginning to use 4GLs and CASE tools for building prototypes of new systems. A prototype is a working model which gives the look and feel of a real system. These prototypes are then improved in successive steps until a working system is obtained.

The new methods of software development are data driven instead of process driven. The essential difference between a data driven and a process driven approach is the priority given to program logic versus data structure. A process approach develops the logical structure of programs first and then gives attention to the data structure. The data driven approach reverses the sequence by giving first priority to data structure. The data structure is independent of individual applications and can be used for many different applications.

These developments are the result of technological change that has created new alternatives for software development. These changes have come so rapidly that the management and economic implications of these developments are not yet fully recognized by either MIS professionals or managers.

## The Changing Focus of Information Systems

CASE: Computer Assisted System Engineering

COMPUTER APPLICATIONS IN BUSINESS ORGANIZATIONS HAVE been focused almost exclusively on transaction processing during the first thirty years of commercial computing history. Transaction processing systems include such applications as customer billing, order entry and payroll processing. The objective of transaction processing applications is to automate clerical activities. Transaction processing systems typically provide more accurate and timely information while lowering the costs of clerical labor as compared with the manual systems they replaced.

Some observers might feel the opportunities for further applications of transaction processing are limited. However, new applications such as Electronic Funds Transfer Systems (EFTS) are merely refinements of old transaction processing systems that required considerable data entry labor. These new systems enable users to perform banking functions at a remote terminal (automatic teller) or a touch tone telephone. By capturing the data at the time the transaction occurs, these new systems bypass the manual data entry function which required a data entry clerk to key-in information from a paper document to the computer.

Furthermore thousands of small business firms have never used computers to automate their transaction processing. Introducing computers to this group of customers has been made possible by the development of small inexpensive computers that can meet the transaction processing needs of the small business.

### PREOCCUPATION WITH TRANSACTION PROCESSING

Transaction processing applications consume approximately 80% of commercial computing time today. Developing and maintaining these transaction processing applications is the primary focus of the information processing staff, consuming 50% to 80% of the data processing staff programming resources. Because of the pressures of maintaining the transaction processing system, decision support applications tend to get low priority.

The term "maintenance" may be confusing since, strictly speaking, computer programs don't wear out. They do, however, require modifications due to changes in the organization, changes in tax laws and regulations, and new features which are desired by end users.

The difficulty of keeping up with the maintenance of existing applications leads to backlogs of new applications. Backlogs in a typical organization would occupy the existing staff from several months to several years. This backlog of new applications is frustrating to end users and may lead to conflict between end users and information systems professionals. These and other problems are highlighted in "When Things Go Wrong."

**When things go wrong**

## Problems of Computing as Seen by Users and Management

**Users cannot obtain applications when they want them. There is often a delay of years.**

**It is difficult or impossible to obtain changes that managers need in a reasonable amount of time.**

**The programs have errors in them or sometimes do not work.**

**Systems delivered often do not match the true user requirements.**

**It is difficult to understand DP (data processing) and communicate precise requirements.**

**Specifications on which users have to sign off, are difficult to check and are usually full of inconsistencies, omissions, and errors.**

**Systems cost much more to develop and maintain than anticipated.**

**Because of the long time required to obtain results, the most important decision-support systems are never implemented. The support is needed more quickly than the time needed to create the programs.**

James Martin, An Information Systems Manifesto, ©1984, pp. 4. Reprinted by permissions of Prentice-Hall, Inc., Englewood Cliffs, N.J.

Managers, impatient with the Information Systems department's inability to provide them with information quickly, may explore other means of obtaining the information they desire. Two common solutions are to acquire a personal computer or a departmental minicomputer to meet their information needs.

New technology makes it appropriate to give greater attention to the information needs of managers. Whereas in the past, managers' information needs were derived from transaction processing reports or from manually gathered external data, it is now possible for managers to get the information they need directly. This can be done with new fourth generation tools such as query languages. It is important to note that a foundation of accessible transaction data is a necessary prerequisite for decision-support systems and user based computing.

## EMERGING FOCUS - DECISION SUPPORT SYSTEMS AND USER BASED COMPUTING

Decision support systems are designed to assist managers in obtaining information that is desired for decision making. The requirement can be met by tools that are easy to use and that are capable of getting results quickly.

Personal computer sales may be one measure of the demand for decision support applications. These computers, which are used almost exclusively for decision support applications in large organizations, have permanently altered the business computing environment.

Another indicator of the trend towards decision support systems is shown in figures from an MIT study of thirteen major corporations. Existing applications were approximately 80% transaction processing systems. However, in examining the development backlog, only 43% were transaction processing applications and 57% were decision support applications.[15]

The emerging focus goes beyond decision support systems that are designed to satisfy managers' information needs. It includes user based computing using fourth generation software tools. The power and simplicity of fourth generation languages makes it possible for users to create their own applications.

## COMPETITIVE USES OF INFORMATION SYSTEMS

Information systems traditionally had an internal focus concentrating on automating basic clerical functions. Many organizations are beginning to recognize opportunities to use information systems for competitive advantage.

American Hospital Supply Corp. has developed an order entry and distribution system which links them with 4000 customers. *Fortune* magazine reported that this development had a major impact on increasing their market share. The strategic use of information systems is the focus of Chapter 2.

## A New Breed of Information Systems Managers

The changes described in this chapter requires a new breed of information systems managers. It requires someone comfortable with new technology and yet able to relate that technology to new business opportunities: in short, an *entrepreneur*. It also requires a manager that is skilled in relating to various groups and managing professionals. Ultimately it is human factors that determine the effectiveness of information systems.

## Trends in Information Processing

The information processing industry is clearly in a state of transformation as indicated below:

TABLE 1.4
*Transitions in Information Processing*

| | Recent Practice | Trend Towards |
|---|---|---|
| Computers | Large Centralized Computers | Microcomputers<br>Personal Computers<br>Distributed Processing |
| Programming | Cobol<br>Fortran<br>Basic<br>File Processing<br>Professional Programmers | CASE<br>4th Generation Languages<br>User based computing<br>Specialized applications packages<br>Query Languages |
| Processing | Transaction processing | Decision Support Computing<br>Office Automation |
| Storage Media | Magnetic disk | Optical disk |
| Communications | Data communication over phone lines | Integrated voice, data and image communication networks |
| MIS Professionals | Programmers<br>Systems Analysts | Information Center Consultants<br>Data Administrators<br>Network Administrators |
| Objective | Efficiency | Effectiveness |
| Software Development Methodology | Process driven | Data driven |

The details of this transition are described in succeeding chapters.

## Guidelines for Managers

MANAGERS SHOULD NO LONGER BE SATISFIED WITH INFORmation systems departments that experience application backlogs, programs with errors, and applications that cost more than originally anticipated. They should insist that information systems departments use new technology to improve their own productivity. They should also give full organizational support to end-user computing by providing training, software and consultation. End-user computing must be *managed* if it is to be integrated with other information systems.

James Martin, a noted computer expert, has published *An Information Systems Manifesto*. A manifesto can be defined as a public declaration of initiatives, objectives, opinions or motives—usually the rationale behind controversial or revolutionary change. Martin's Manifesto for top management is found in Issues and Controversies. He advocates using the power of the computer to develop software, an idea he refers to as Information Engineering. This concept is discussed in Chapter 9.

## Issues and Controversies

### A Manifesto for Senior Management

**Understand how your organization ought to change as it becomes a fully electronic enterprise. Electronics are changing products, services, fabrication techniques, selling techniques, decision making, flows of information, mechanisms of control and management structures.**

**Understand that a revolution is taking place in DP but that many DP departments are not moving fast enough to the higher productivity techniques. There is often psychological or political resistance to the new methods, which management needs to overcome. Ensure that your organization is migrating away from slow methods and can respond to information needs by using fourth-generation languages, information center techniques, flexible data bases and the maximum automation of the DP function as described in this book.**

**Ensure that decision makers at all levels have the tools they need for making the best possible decisions. Ensure that the necessary information resources are available to them. To achieve this, ensure that information engineering is done throughout the enterprise.**

**Information engineering needs top-down management of information resources, through data modeling and strategic planning of networks. These**

**essential aspects of managing a computerized corporation have often failed because of organizational and political factors. They have been managed at too low a level. Top management must understand the need for them and ensure that an appropriate information infrastructure is built.**

James Martin, An Information Systems Manifesto, ©1984, p. 18. Reprinted by permission of Prentice-Hall, Inc., Englewood Cliffs, N.J.

## Guidelines for MIS Professionals

THE NEW TECHNOLOGY DESCRIBED IN THIS CHAPTER REPRESENTS either a threat or an opportunity to MIS professionals. It is a threat to information systems professionals who resist the new and more flexible technology which promises significantly improved productivity. They will find that their existing skills will decline in value over time. Information systems professionals who embrace the new technology will make themselves more valuable. They should be able to build applications more quickly and meet the expectations of end-users.

## Key Terms

Systems
Subsystems
Inputs
Outputs
Efficiency
Effectiveness
Feedback
Information Systems
Integration
Transaction Processing
Batch Processing
On-Line Processing
Decision Support Systems (DSS)
Personal Computer
Office Automation
Networking
Microprocessors
Magnetic Disks
Optical Disks
Data Base Management Systems
4th Generation Programming Languages
Automatic Navigation
End-User
Query Languages
Maintenance
Process Driven
Data Driven

## Review Questions

1. Give three examples of interactive processing systems.
2. A program that creates a cost-benefit model is an example of which type of information processing application?
3. Name five characteristics of information that the manager should consider.
4. Give an example of a transaction processing system with which you are familiar.
5. List the four catagories of organizational information requirements.
6. What are the advantages and disadvantages of batch processing?
7. Compare and contrast process-driven and data-driven methodologies.
8. Use the concept of an open system to explain why decision support systems are so important to upper-level managers.
9. Is a telephone bill an example of data or information? Explain.
10. How is new technology bringing about a period of change in today's information systems?

## Case Study

### AMERICAN EXPRESS COMPANY

Currently, the American Express Company has four types of interrelated businesses: travel-related services, international banking, investments and insurance. All of these businesses are global, are service-oriented, and rely on extensive application of computer and telecommunications.

American Express Travel Related Services Inc. - TRS - is responsible for the best known American Express products and services. These include:

- The American Express Card, with over 17 million current cardmembers, more than 1 million charges each business day in 26 currencies, and 150 million card authorizations processed annually.
- American Express Tavelers Cheques offered in 7 currencies at 60,000 international locations, with nearly $2.5 billion outstanding and 325 million cheques cleared annually.
- Money orders sold through 18,000 outlets.

- Credit card processing and authorizations for approximately 16 million accounts at more than 5,000 financial institutions, with over 350 million transactions processed annually.

The information processing and communications of all American Express businesses are done by a worldwide data processing and telecommunications operation. It is comprised of 16 major information-processing centers, 10 worldwide data and timesharing networks, and some 7,000 employees in systems and telecommunications. The management of this technology parallels the operation of American Express itself. It is global and service-oriented. The entire operation is "market driven" rather than "technology driven," and corporate management takes care to see that it stays that way.

Technology plays two important roles within the business units. The first is the day-to-day operation, with its high volume of intensive transaction processing and record keeping. That operation can be likened to a factory where even a one-hour disruption of service impairs the performance of the business units. The second can be defined as strategic. As an example of a strategic product is Funds Access Services, which gives holders of the American Express Card greater access to funds when they're away from home.

The technology used by American Express comprises a wide variety of processors, software, and telecommunications equipment. It extends from corporatewide networks down to the desktops of many of its employees, where the first link in the information-processing chain is forged with the personal computer.

Micros are used by staff personnel throughout the company. Planners use them to analyze trade-offs, for example, "in setting up new service centers, in buying versus leasing office space, budgeting, and even consolidating information for tax returns."

The company is also working with development tools from several artificial-intelligence systems vendors to create expert system for salespeople.

Among the other emerging technologies American Express is exploring is image processing; specifically, optical disk technology. The company feels it can be used to improve the American Express Card's country-club style billings, in which copies of signed receipts instead of just an itemized statement, are returned to the cardholder with his bill.

Any new such undertaking requires extensive planning, notes company executives, observing that "the shorter the distance between the line management and the systems expert, the better that planning works." The planning also requires cooperation among the various business units, which are continually looking for ways to share technology.

That kind of effort, and the planning for the company's systems use in general, is a benefit of American Express's policy of installing information systems executives at top levels in the corporation. The senior information systems executive at Shearson, for example, is a member of the highest internal management board. At Travel Related Services, too, the top systems and telecommunications officer reports to the president.

The subsidiary also has a governing executive committee, on which this officer serves.

1. Discuss the difference between "market driven" versus "technology driven" approach to information systems operations.
2. Give an example of a transaction processing system at American Express. A decision support system? Office Automation?
3. Do you think the major objective of American Express' information systems is one of efficiency or effectiveness? Why?

## Suggestions for Further Reading

Benjamin, Robert I. et al., "Changing Role of the Corporate Information Systems Officer," MIS Quarterly, September 1985, pp. 177-188.

*The authors make three predictions about the new directions CIO's are taking in organizations. These predictions concern decentralization of line responsibility, more staff-oriented responsibility, and increased responsibility for information policy and strategy. The predictions are supported by the results of a survey of twenty-five large organizations. Results of the survey are included.*

James Martin, An Information Systems Manifesto (Prentice-Hall, 1984)

*The author writes a provocative book which suggests that a revolution in business information systems is in progress. He examines the current data processing environment and concludes that a vast change in productivity is required. The solution is the automation of automation, or using the computer to generate software from specifications.*

# 2

# Information - A Strategic Resource

*"Clearly, it is time for top management to get off the sidelines. Recognizing that information is a strategic resource implies a clear need to link information systems to business strategy...Senior executives are increasingly feeling the need to become informed, energized and engaged in information systems."*

*John F. Rockart and Adam Crscenzi*

## Objectives and Overviews

IN THIS CHAPTER WE DISCUSS THE USE OF INFORMATION technology for competitive advantage. Information systems, which have traditionally been regarded as supporting functions, are becoming strategic weapons. Using information for competitive advantage requires two fundamental shifts in its oversight: (1) management must assume a more active role in planning information systems, and (2) managers must identify opportunities to use information technology for competitive advantage.

AFTER READING THIS CHAPTER YOU SHOULD BE ABLE TO:

- Discuss some examples of the use of information as a competitive weapon.
- Explain the objectives for achieving competitive advantage with information technology.
- Discuss the two major factors limiting application of information technology for strategic uses.
- Explain some characteristics of information systems used for competitive advantage.
- Explain some specific things managers must do to manage information technology more effectively.

## Strategic Uses of Information Systems

THE TRADITIONAL VIEW OF INFORMATION SYSTEMS IS THAT their role in the organization is a supporting one. Information systems were considered to be clerical processing systems with little impact on organizational success or failure. Most managers of information systems departments accepted this supporting role and consequently focused on existing transaction processing systems and the associated information flows, data bases, and the production of reports required to support the organization's operations. Now, however, many organizations are beginning to use information technology to create a competitive advantage, to spawn new businesses, and to alter the competitive environment. More and more, information systems are being viewed as a strategic resource, a development which requires managers to become informed and involved.

Firms that recognize the information revolution sweeping through our economy will capitalize upon it. Dramatic cost reductions in information processing are changing the competitive landscape. These reductions impact the cost of obtaining, processing, and transmitting information and create new business opportunities.

The emerging view is that information systems can be used very effectively as a competitive weapon. Specifically, they can provide the following benefits:

1. Lower costs
2. Increased revenue
3. Improved quality of product or service
4. Improved responsiveness to customers (better service)

A few examples will illustrate these benefits.

## AIRLINE RESERVATION SYSTEMS

American Airlines and United Airlines have developed the two leading computerized airline reservation systems. American's system is known as Sabre and United's as Apollo.

Both of these systems are marketed to independent travel agencies which sell approximately 90% of all airline tickets. The catch is that Sabre and Apollo give preference to American and United flight listings. For example, if a reservation agent requests a listing of flights from New York to Dallas, the system will present the flight listings of American or United before showing any other airlines' flights.

The advantage of this system is additional revenue to the preferred carrier. The magnitude of the competitive advantage can be further appreciated by the fact that these two systems dominate the airline reservation systems market together having an approximate 80% market share.[1]

## MCKESSON CORPORATION

McKesson Corporation has also used its information system as a formidable competitive weapon. This organization, which has been known in the past as Foremost-McKesson and McKesson-Robbins, dealt in drug and food distribution. More recently, it has disposed of its food business to concentrate on distribution of a variety of products. The president of the corporation said in the 1983 annual report:

> Perhaps the single greatest advantage that the McKesson distribution companies enjoy has been - and will continue to be - in computer technology, where our size and diversity have enabled us to achieve the necessary critical mass. Our data processing resources now involve 550 people and an annual budget of more than $65 million. We intend to continue the proliferation of this technology among our current distribution businesses and to seek out opportunities to apply it to other distribution-related businesses. This shift in emphasis - making value added distribution our primary thrust with a secondary thrust in certain proprietory product areas - reflects the facts as they are today.[2]

Examples of McKesson's new marketing thrust are as follows:

COSMCK/ECONOSCAN - This is a computer based inventory and ordering system for druggists, supermarkets, and mass merchandisers. It is designed to assist retailers to stock, price-label, rotate, and display merchandise. Econoscan is a hand-held scanning device that reads product labels from shelf merchandise and transmit inventory and order information over a telephone line to a McKesson distribution center. Overnight, the order is filled and shipped in containers arranged to correspond with shelf displays.

PHARMACEUTICAL CARD SYSTEM - PCS is a prescription drug claim processing system sold to 45,000 pharmacies. It is designed to document the prescriptions of card holders. Claims are submitted automatically to third party health reimbursement agencies. A spin-off of this system, which exemplifies the strategic vision of McKesson, is the Pharmaceutical Data Services (PDS) unit, which analyzes retail drug prescriptions and prepares marketing reports. These reports are marketed to drug manufacturers, financial institutions, and various government agencies.[3]

These examples illustrate how McKesson uses information systems as a competitive weapon. Top management of McKesson has created an environment where information technology is considered a vital strategic weapon. Some additional examples are shown in Table 2.1.

**TABLE 2.1**
*Strategic Information Systems*

| FIRM | DESCRIPTION |
|---|---|
| Banc One | Since 1967 this relatively small Columbus, Ohio, bank has acquired about 50 smaller banks. It has developed several computer systems which it installs in acquired banks. The credit card processing system earns about $50 million a year. It also has an automatic teller machine network which it has used for over 15 years. In conjunction with Merrill Lynch it developed Cash Management Account and became the nation's third largest VISA processor. Strategic information systems have helped Banc One grow from a small local bank with $150 million in assets to a regional bank with assets of over $15 billion.[a] |
| Gannett Co. | This innovative company is using satellite transmission technology to transmit 4 color images of *USA Today* to 30 U.S. printing plants and plants in Zurich and Singapore. Editorial content is prepared in Washington, D.C. offices and transmitted to plants from a Western Union Satellite.[b] |
| Allen-Bradley | This company has become a world-class manufacturer of contactors (devices that stop and start electric motors), relays and printed circuit boards. Allen-Bradley's success with computer integrated manufacturing (CIM) has spawned a system integration and consulting business that is world-wide in scope and which includes Digital Equipment Corp. as a partner.[c] |
| Hannaford Brothers | Owners of Shop 'n Save grocery stores. Have used bar code scanning data to analyze profit contribution of 17,000 items sold in 65 different stores. Data has allowed them to make informed decisions on issues |

| FIRM | DESCRIPTION |
|---|---|
| | such as which brands of pickles to carry and how to price them. Result has been an increase in net margin from industry average of 1.0% to 1.8%.[d] |

Sources: [a]Jerome D. Colonna, "Holding Firm Banks on Several Systems," Information Week, (May 26, 1986), pp. 40-41.

[b]Robert Budag, "Other Firms Using Systems Strategically," Information Week, (May 26, 1986), p. 60.

[c]Dennis Livingston, "Pulling It All Together," Mini-Micro Systems (September 1988), pp. 110-117; Gene Bylinsky, "A Breakthrough in Automating the Assembly Line," Fortune (May 26, 1986), pp. 64-66.

[d]Gary Geipel, "At Today's Supermarket, the Computer is Doing it All," Business Week (August 11, 1986), p. 64.

## Apply Information Technology for Competitive Advantage

PORTER AND MILLER HAVE SUGGESTED THREE BASIC OBJECTIVES for a firm to achieve competitive advantage with information technology.[4]

1. It must alter the industry structure.
2. It must improve its position in the industry with its existing businesses.
3. It must create new business opportunities.

### ALTER INDUSTRY STRUCTURE

To alter the industry structure an organization must use information technology to shift the competitive balance in its favor. This can be accomplished by changing the way the firm does business so it can gain competitive advantage.

For example, American Hospital Supply (AHS), a division of Baxter, places order entry terminals in hospital purchasing departments to link its customers with an order entry system on AHS computers. This system is successful because it simplifies the ordering process for customers and reduces costs for both the customer and AHS. This system is described in When Things Go Right.

**When things go right**

## American Hospital Supply's - ASAP

**Over the last decade American Hospital Supply Corp (AHSC) has grown from $1 billion in annual revenue to $3 billion. This has been accomplished without having to add a significant number of personnel to its sales force. One of the primary reasons for this success is attributed to ASAP, an automatic order entry system developed by American. About 4,500 hospitals and other medical facilities have terminals connected to AHSC computers. When a customer transmits an order over ASAP, a confirmation is sent back to the customer and the order is transferred to one of American's 66 distribution centers. The customer knows in less than two minutes which items American has in stock and at what price. From the distribution center, the order is filled and trucked to the customer. American guarantees 95% availability.**

**Some competing firms have order entry systems that are easier to use but are not tied to their inventory system. These systems will accept orders for items not in stock.**

**American is attempting to enhance the system by electronic invoicing and electronic funds transfer. This concept has met some resistance from hospital finance departments. Some other recent enhancements to the system include the ability to interface with bar-code scanners and personal computers.**

**This system originated in the early 1960s but the number of hospitals using it has doubled in the last five years. Most recent figures show that American processed 46% of its total orders over ASAP, compared with 31% in 1981.**

Adapted from, "AHSC On-Line System Ships Supplies ASAP," Information Week, May 26, 1986, pp. 35, 38.

## IMPROVE COMPETITIVE POSITION

To improve its position with its existing businesses an organization must identify a means of using information technology to reduce costs, differentiate its products or services or extend the scope of its current business. The Dow Jones firm is an especially good example of the latter.

Dow Jones, publisher of the *Wall Street Journal*, has reduced the costs associated with image processing and transmission to the point that it is able to transmit an image to a remote printing plant and print and distribute a newspaper at a competitive price. As a result, the firm has expanded into the national and international markets while still is able to control its centralized editorial operations. Dow Jones recognized the potential of using information technology for competitive advantage.

### SPAWN NEW BUSINESS

The third objective is to spawn new businesses with information technology. This can be done in several ways, including selling information that is a by-product of the current business, exploiting excess capacity to develop a new business, or developing a new product or service that is related to the firm's current business and made possible by information technology.

McKesson Corporation's pharmaceutical card system is a by-product of its order-entry system. The system also develops a data base of retail prescription sales that is sold to pharmaceutical firms and government agencies. Several supermarket chains with bar code scanning systems have developed applications that analyze consumer buying habits. This information is being sold to market research firms.[5] What these firms have in common is ingenious and creative approaches to exploiting the full potential of their management information systems.

## Characteristics of Strategic Information Systems

THERE ARE SEVERAL CHARACTERISTICS THAT ARE COMMON TO many strategic information systems. One of the most common characteristics of these systems is that they tend to transcend a firm's boundaries.

### THE EXTENDED ENTERPRISE

The traditional view of the firm has been a pyramid which defines a top-down hierarchy and a sequence of decision making levels from strategic planning to operations. This is illustrated in Figure 2.1.

During the 1960s and 1970s, this was the context in which information systems were developed. At the lowest level were the transaction-based systems such as order entry, accounts payable, accounts receivable, payroll and general ledger. These systems provided the foundation upon which the information requirements of the organization were built. The information requirements of top management, however, frequently could not be met by distilling the transaction reports. To meet these information requirements ad hoc information gathering was often required, frequently from sources outside the firm.

FIGURE 2.1
*The Traditional View of the Enterprise*

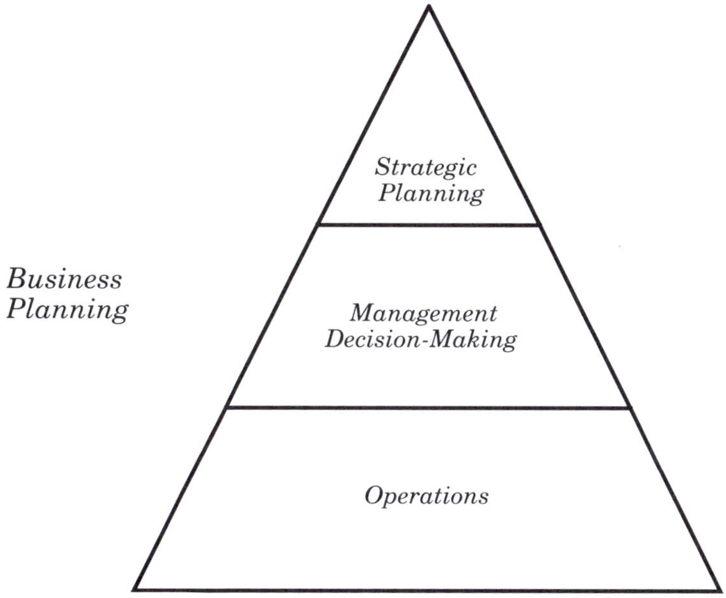


[a] *Donald A. Marchand and Forest W. Horton, Jr., Infotrends (New York: John WIley and Sons, Inc., 1986), p. 77.*

The new view of the organization has been referred to as the extended enterprise. It is illustrated in Figure 2.2.

This view recognizes the advantages of thinking strategically by extending the boundaries of the enterprise to include suppliers, dealers, and customers. It addresses not only the internal information needs of the firm, but also the informational interactions with these external groups.[6]

Some of the most dramatic and potentially powerful uses of information technology for competitive advantage involve networks that extend beyond a given company's boundaries. Systems shared by two or more firms have significantly enhanced the productivity, increased the market share and improved the flexibility of several companies. These networks are designed to join a buyer and a seller with the objective of making a sale of goods or services.[7]

The airline reservation systems link an airline to travel agents, other airlines, hotels, and car rental firms. The Sabre system developed by American Airlines has changed the rules of competition in the airline industry. Some of American competitors face a significant barrier to duplicating this system. In the mean time, American has found that it gained 12 to 20 percent market share in travel agencies equipped with its reservation systems.[8]

These are legitimate public policy issues that involve interorganizational information systems. To what extent should the government be concerned with an unhealthy dependence on the part of the customers or competitors using such systems. The anti-trust issues of extended enterprise information systems are still being resolved in the courts.

The use of information systems extending beyond company boundaries has created the need for developing standards, protocols, and product codes. Whereas the government has historically initiated standards, more recently industry groups have taken the initiative. For example, the creation of the universal product code (UPC) in the grocery industry and the magnetic strips on credit cards used in automatic teller machines (ATMs) were industry developed standards.[9]

FIGURE 2.2
*The Extended Enterprise*

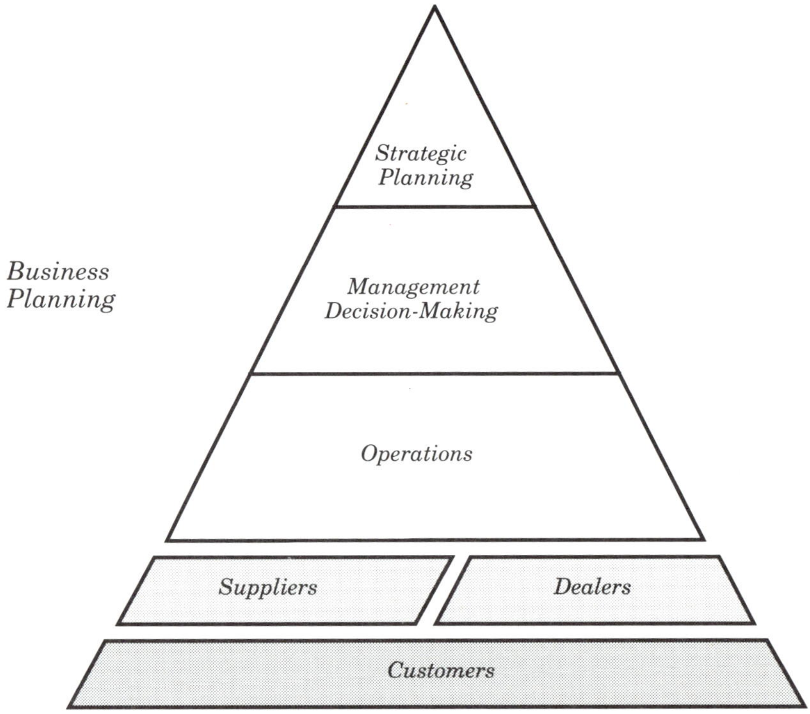


[b] *Ibid., p. 79*

## EFFECTIVENESS ORIENTATION

The major economic consequences of airline reservation systems are not found in lower transaction costs. The real impact of these systems is found in the convenience for customers in making reservations and the confidence the customer has in shopping for the best combination of fares and departure times for a trip. The effects of customer convenience far exceed the effects of administrative cost reduction.

Strategic uses of information technology must have an external focus on customers, clients, or suppliers. Information technology is used to improve existing services or to develop new ones.

Airline reservation systems represent what Strassman refers to as an "information middleman." A customer can contact an agent for an airline and complete the entire process of booking and paying for airline, hotel, and rental car reservations. This complex transaction may involve several different departments within an airline as well as external organizations, but all of this is transparent to the customer. The burden of coordinating with the airline and its various functions as well as other organizations is left to the "information middleman" as represented by the reservation system. The ease of coordinating a customer's needs is increased because responsibility is assumed at a *single point of contact*.[10]

## SOURCE DATA AUTOMATION

One of the major ways of cutting costs is to eliminate the expensive data entry function. This method is applied in both point of sale (POS) terminals used in grocery and department stores as well as automatic teller machines (ATMs) used by banks.

Banks have found that automatic teller machines are far less costly than their human counterparts. Citicorp, the leader in ATMs, has built a retail banking empire of more than 11,000 ATMs in 45 states. Consumer deposits handled through the ATMs provide a source of revenue at a lower cost than accounts handled by tellers. The ATMs located in airports, colleges and supermarkets throughout the country enable customers to make deposits, and withdrawals or transfer funds from one account to another.

ATM's are but one example of source data automation that cuts data entry expense. Bar code scanners, which are a component of POS terminals, are used in grocery stores for pricing merchandise as well as for inventory control. They are also used as an input device for automated package sorting by Federal Express. The Federal Express system reads a bar code label attached to a package which has information about its destination and automatically sorts the package by placing it on the proper conveyor belt leading to a plane loading dock.

An added bonus of automating data entry is the quality of the data. A Department of Defense study showed that the error rate for machine scanning of bar codes was 1 of 3,000,000 compared with 1 in 300 for manual entry.[11]

As the costs of this technology continue to come down it is easy to visualize additional applications. Financial institutions that issue credit cards are beginning to use source data automation to cut data entry costs as well as to avoid granting credit to poor credit risks.

## FOSTERING LONG TERM DOMINANT MARKET POSITION

A beneficial theme common in the strategic use of information systems is that they foster long-term business relationships with customers. Customers are effectively "locked into" long term commitments. Customers using American Airlines' Sabre System or America Hospital Supply's ASAP become accustomed to using these systems. The requirement to learn a new system becomes a barrier for competitors attempting to displace these systems. New systems will have to offer significant advantages to overcome this hurdle.

Not only do these systems foster long term business relationships, they tend to foster a near-monopoly situation. As one executive aptly described strategic information systems, "They destroy your customers' interest in competitive products."[12]

While only a few of these systems tie a customer to a single supplier, most of them exhibit some "tilt" towards the developers of the system. Eventually these pioneer systems may be replaced by more comprehensive systems without bias. In the meantime, there are significant advantages to being first.

## EXTENDED DEVELOPMENT PERIOD

Succeeding with strategic uses of information technology requires a long term commitment. Today the benefits of the American Airlines

Sabre system are obvious. It took a commitment of 15 years, however, to build the system. Similarly, American Hospital Supply's ASAP has been very successful since 1981, but it had its beginnings in the early 1960s.

The extended period of development may also be compounded by a system's slow acceptance in the market place. Citicorp found that, initially, customers were reluctant to use its ATM system. Gradually, the ATMs won customers over with the realization the machines were fast, accurate, easy to use, and available 24 hours a day.

The payoff from these three systems has been substantial. The developers have enjoyed dominant market positions. It is unlikely, however, that investment in similar systems would be acceptable to most corporations. The technological and market risks of systems associated with an extended development period would make them unlikely investment projects. It required a conviction by the management of these three firms to stick with these projects. Today, however, some of their competitors are faced with the task of duplicating these systems, not knowing if they will achieve the same level of success in the market place.

New developments in CASE technology may alter this pattern of extended development for strategic information systems. Some authorities believe that small firms using this technology will be able to develop strategic information systems in a fraction of the time and cost of earlier strategic systems.[13]

## Implications for Development of Strategic Information systems

COPELAND AND MCKENNEY EXAMINED THE DEVELOPMENT OF airline reservation systems and have identified three patterns that relate to strategic uses of information systems.[14] The first of these is task/technology congruence.

### TASK/TECHNOLOGY CONGRUENCE

The lesson to be learned from the airlines is that technical competence is a necessary requirement for obtaining strategic advantage with information systems. Too often the advocates of strategic information systems focus on market opportunities and imply that strategic vision is a sufficient condition for developing them. The history of airline reservation systems suggest that firms are more likely to be successful with technological competence than managerial vision.

## IMPORTANCE OF INTELLIGENT PERSISTENCE

Developing competitive advantage with information technology depends on intelligent persistence—a combination of learning by doing and opportunism—more than extraordinary vision. Persistence yields valuable experience which is not easily obtained by rivals. Competitors can purchase technology but the advantage obtained by consistent exploitation of opportunities revealed in the evolution of strategic systems should be sustainable.

## ROLE OF SCALE ECONOMIES

Copeland and McKenney believe the development of airline reservation systems shows consistent economies of scale. That is large airlines enjoyed lower processing costs with their large processing capacity than their smaller rivals.

* Such an argument was undoubtedly true during the 70's and 80's but ignores the development of the microprocessor and of CASE technology. Schussel has argued that CASE technology will enable a small or medium sized firm to develop strategic information systems that would have cost hundreds of millions of dollars in the 60's and 70's.[15]

## Cleaning up the Mess in the Back Room

current computer operations

THE VISION OF USING INFORMATION TECHNOLOGY FOR COMpetitive advantage is an exciting prospect. There is, however, the reality of the "mess in the back room." The back room refers to current computer operations.

It is inconceivable that a department mired in disorder and operating ineffectively would be called upon to develop strategic information systems. Before information systems executives will be given critical new responsibilities, they must get their own departments operating effectively.

Some respected industry experts recently made this observation:[16]

> Consider for a moment what is all too frequently the norm for the information processing organization. First,

> in spite of inevitably rising budgets for hardware and software, few information systems groups can point to any real productivity gains. Application backlogs continue to mount, but few organizations are successfully doing anything about it. A surprising number have lost the initiative in the realm of personal computers and find themselves outstripped in their use by the finance and manufacturing groups. Computer operations in many corporations continue to be a never-ending fire drill.

These comments suggest that, all too frequently, information systems departments are inward looking and defensive. Repeatedly, projects are completed late and over budget. The pressures of maintaining the existing systems make information systems departments react negatively to change as represented by new applications or new technology.

Many observers attribute these weaknesses to poor management. They would suggest that the "Peter Principle" is operative in information systems departments. The "Peter Principle" simply means that managers are promoted until they reach the level of their incompetence.

There is some validity to the view that information systems executives are primarily from technical backgrounds with little or no managerial training and experience. However, the problems in information systems departments are too widespread to attribute them to incompetence on the part of information systems executives. These problems are inherent in an inflexible information systems technology, which must be replaced by a newer and more flexible technology. This change, however, will require a willingness, on the part of the organization, to evaluate new ideas.

## Corporate Culture and Information Technology

CORPORATE CULTURE IS A SET OF VALUES, UNWRITTEN RULES, and customs that govern behavior in an organization. These behavioral prescriptions represent organizational values and are mechanisms for encouraging "correct" behavior. Well defined corporate cultures can help an organization succeed by reinforcing strategically appropriate behavior. An informal culture can be far more effective than a set of formal controls in guiding behavior toward what is best for the firm.

Linder has identified five dimensions of corporate culture that are related to adoption of information technology and methodology. These dimensions are shown below in Table 2.2.

TABLE 2.2
*Dimensions of Corporate Culture*

| | |
|---|---|
| ENTREPRENEURIAL | CONSERVATIVE |
| Risk-encouraging | Risk-averse |
| Informal | Formal |
| Decisive | Deliberate |
| Results-oriented | Process-oriented |
| Aggressive | Defensive |
| CLEAR LINES OF AUTHORITY | AMBIGUOUS AUTHORITY |
| Functional or divisional | Matrix |
| Profit and loss responsibility | Cost and revenue centers |
| Hierarchical | Consensual |
| COOPERATIVE | COMPETITIVE |
| Team-oriented | "Macho" |
| Collaborative | Individualistic |
| Reward-oriented | Censure-oriented |
| Merit-based | Power-based |
| LED | MANAGED |
| Long-term goals | Short-term objectives |
| Clear, enduring mission | Mixed messages |
| Big picture-oriented | Detail-oriented |
| Creative | Analytical |
| ETHICAL | AMORAL |
| Visible ethics policies | Tacit acceptance of unethical behavior |
| Ethical leadership & supervision | Hiring for cultural fit |
| Internal checks and balances | No attention to reconciliation between systems |

Source: Jane Linder, "Harnessing Corporate Culture," Computerworld (September 23, 1985), p. ID2. Copyright 1985 by CW Publishing Inc., Framingham, MA 01701 - Reprinted from Computerworld.

## ENTREPRENEURIAL VS. CONSERVATIVE

Four of the dimensions seem particularly relevant to information technology implementation. Entrepreneurial firms encourage risk taking and are informal, decisive, and aggressive. They place a high value on results.

Conservative firms are quite different; they tend to avoid risk, and are slow and deliberate in their decision making processes. They focus on procedures, being more concerned with *how* something is done than with *what* is accomplished.

Entrepreneurial firms are comfortable with new technology. their willingness to experiment with state-of-the-art, unproven technologies provides a stimulating environment to information systems professionals. It may also lead to high payoff projects that, in turn, bring about competitive advantages.

The experimental nature of some new software development methodologies such as prototyping seem particularly well suited for entrepreneurial organizations. The conservative organization, on the other hand, will feel more comfortable with current technology and accepted procedures in developing new systems.

Projects are justified in conservative firms based on savings and return on investment. Entrepreneurial firms are comfortable with high-risk projects aimed at increasing revenue.

## COOPERATIVE VS. COMPETITIVE

Cooperative organizations have a team spirit. For example, Delta Airlines is known for its family feeling. Senior mentors in cooperative organizations cultivate and nurture subordinates to prepare them for succession. Cooperative organizations are good candidates for database applications which share data across departmental and functional boundaries. New technologies, which make data more accessible to users, are appropriate for a cooperative culture.

Competitive organizations tend to be dominated by "stars." Law firms and consulting organizations are typically competitive. Information systems in competitive cultures are "owned" by a department. This tends to lead to free standing systems that are often quite difficult to integrate.

Data security is a high priority in the competitive environment. Organizational wide standards, data administration and data sharing will be very difficult to implement in competitive cultures.

## LED VS. MANAGED

Managed organizations are run by the numbers. They pursue short term goals which are subject to frequent change. Long term projects are suspect.

Managed organizations frequently have information systems departments that are floundering. They may adopt new technology but abandon it when difficulties arise. To solve the information systems department's problems they may use extensive consulting services and/or purchase software without doing an adequate job of evaluation. These departments usually lack priorities and are poor candidates to develop strategic information systems.

An organization that is *led* has managers that do their homework. It has a clear sense of direction that is communicated throughout the organization. It pursues long term objectives and persists in these goals even when frustrated in the short run.

## MORAL VS. AMORAL

Moral firms tie the purposes of the organization to human values. These organizations are clear about what they stand for and serious about shaping values. They consciously seek to transmit a corporate culture from one generation of employees to another. These firms are unashamed collectors and tellers of stories, of legends and myths in support of their basic values.

Typically these values address the firm's commitment to employees, customers, and society. The value shaping leader is concerned with developing vision and excitement for employees and customers. These values are instilled through scores of daily events; through deeds rather than words.

Amoral firms are reluctant or embarrassed to write about, talk about, or think about value systems. They typically express their objectives in quantified statements of mission such as earnings per share or growth measures. These objectives are effective in motivating management but are seldom effective in motivating employees several layers down to energetically and creatively pursue the firm's objectives.

Implementing information technology in organizations with values that address the employee's need for personal growth or the firm's commitment to excellence should be less difficult than where the firm has not addressed these issues. Employees will feel more comfortable with innovation if they know they are considered something more than factors of production.

## Executive Leadership

EXECUTIVE LEADERSHIP, NOT HARDWARE, SOFTWARE, OR technical expertise, is the key to success with information systems. Many managers with problems in information systems departments could quote Pogo the comic strip character, "We have met the enemy and he is us." Due to a lack of confidence in managing what they regard as essentially a technical activity, many managers have abdicated responsibility for developing and managing information systems to technicians.

Hayes and Abernathy, in a thoughtful article in the *Harvard Business Review* entitled "Managing Our Way to Economic Decline," addressed this same issue. They refer to this problem as the "Gospel of Pseudo-Professionalism." This philosophy is practiced by managers who do not believe that technical expertise or hands on experience counts for very much. Managers with this philosophy are forced to rely on the technical judgments of others. Frequently, they want all decisions to be reduced to a set of numbers.

Hayes and Abernathy suggest that this leads to a conservative management style that is comfortable saying "no" to innovation. Managers who do not understand technology are frequently afraid of the risks associated with investing in technology.[17]

Executive champions of innovative information technology projects are vital to their success. Commitment requires an understanding of the technology. It requires that managers must do their homework.

Information systems are too important to leave them to computer professionals alone. The information systems professionals do not generally have a broad vision of the firm's purposes. Top management's attention is vital in defining the overall objectives of an information system, determining priorities and developing a long term plan. Too often Information Systems departments lacking an overall plan pursue the policy of servicing the squeaking wheel, or the department with the most political clout. The result is a short term focus that is unsatisfactory to end-users, management, and MIS professionals.

What can management do to facilitate information systems success? Several aspects should be considered.

## Develop an Overall Framework

As James Martin says, it would be unthinkable to build a battleship without an overall plan for the entire ship.[18] Yet information systems in most corporations are being built without an overall plan. Frequently, the builders of subsystems find the component parts don't fit together. The result is a lack of integration between subsystems or an expensive conversion problem.

Why is top management involvement necessary to assure a successful organization-wide information systems plan? Most information systems executives recognize they do not have the political clout to introduce an information systems plan and to insist that the organization adheres to it. Secondly, the computer professionals do not understand the organization and its information needs well enough to develop a plan. Finally, top management is more likely than computer professionals to perceive strategic opportunities for information systems.

Information systems plans tend to create political problems that can be solved only when top management has given unmistakable support to an organizational information systems plan. Organization-wide sharing of data and integration of information systems applications is threatening to those who harbor a parochial view of their function or application.

Some new technologies promise significant increases in application development productivity. These will not be realized if the organization persists in the usual uncoordinated application development and excessive maintenance and conversion activities. An overall organization-wide framework for information systems development is needed to avoid this result.

## INFORMATION RESOURCE MANAGEMENT

Information is a resource that can be managed like other assets such as personnel, materials, and capital equipment. Recognition of this fact is reflected in the creation of the position of Chief Information Officer. It is also implied by the application of resource management techniques such as planning, costing, and budgeting to information resources.

Information resource management (IRM) is a set of management approaches that enable an organization to manage information as a corporate resource. At the center of this concept is the determination to establish order in the previously uncoordinated and chaotic use of information technology. The objectives of IRM are to harness information technology for business purposes, increase the accuracy and accessability of information, implement new applications in less time, and reduce information systems maintenance. A diagram of the purposes of IRM is shown in Figure 2.3.

FIGURE 2.3

*Achieving Competitive Advantage with Information Technology*

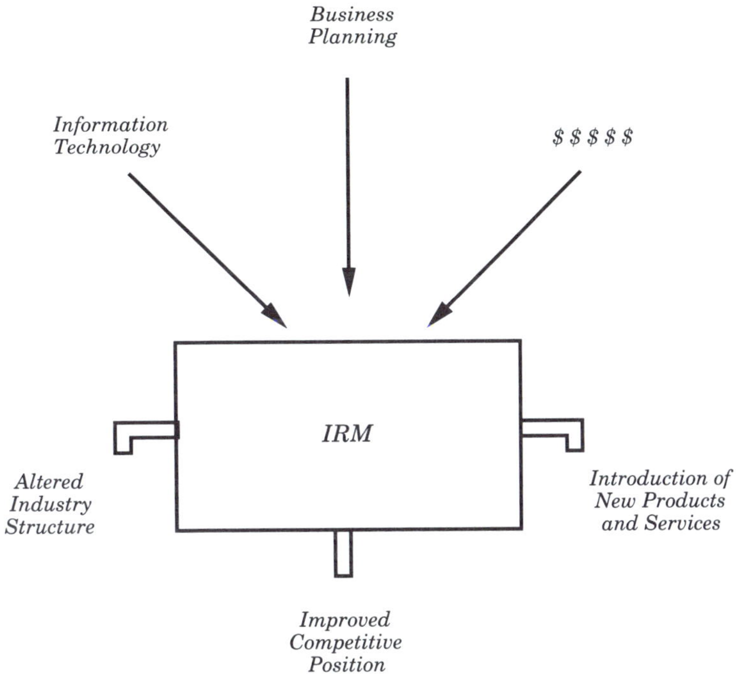


Porter & Millar's 3 objectives for competitive advantage

Information resource management must address the six components of an information system which were described in Chapter 1 as:

1. Hardware
2. Software
3. Data
4. Networks
5. Methodologies
6. Personnel

In the past, data has received little attention in information systems planning. Database technology requires more careful planning of the data architecture of the organization. The goal is to provide data organized by subject category which is shared by multiple applications. This structure also facilitates fast, convenient self service access by the end user.

Integration of information systems requires careful planning to ensure that all of the component parts work together. One of the characteristics of information technology is that it is difficult to integrate. Top management support and involvement is necessary to secure agreement on standards and to prevent the development of multiple incompatible fragments that cause excessive conversion costs and prevent management from obtaining the information they need.

## DEVELOPING AN EXECUTIVE STEERING COMMITTEE

Executive steering committees are mechanisms for development of MIS priorities, strategies, policies and objectives. They are usually composed of non-MIS executives with an MIS executive serving as a resource person. The use of steering committees allows the computer professionals to pursue well-defined long term goals instead of short-term fire fighting. It determines the priorities for developing new systems instead of responding to the most vocal end-user.

In a study of management involvement in MIS development, Doll found that firms with successful MIS development were more than twice as likely to have an executive steering committee as firms with unsuccessful MIS development.[19] The successful firms also had written plans for MIS development almost three times as frequently as unsuccessful firms. Finally, Doll found that firms with successful MIS development were about twice as likely to have criteria to determine which systems to develop first as unsuccessful firms.

## EXPERIMENTING WITH INFORMATION TECHNOLOGY

Lockheed Aircraft is noted for its "skunk works." Clarence "Kelly" Johnson, an imaginative and gifted aeronautical engineer, developed several of Lockheed's most successful products in his "skunk works." The "skunk works" was a small department isolated from the rest of the organization with a specific charge of developing advanced products. Several organizations have set up small groups to investigate advanced information technology. These are discussed in When Things Go Right.

**When things go right**

## Skunk Works for Information Systems Technology

Fidelity Investments, the Boston-based mutual fund, recently asked its advanced technology group to investigate new communications networks that would replace its separate voice and data networks with a single integrated network. The advanced technology group (ATG) researched the literature, talked to several vendors and narrowed their focus to a single vendor.

The proposed vendor's network was brought into the lab for testing. The tests ran 60 days and included simulated full voice and data loads. At the conclusion of the testing process, the vendor was given a contract and began installing the network. During this time, the ATG has not disrupted the MIS department with testing or installation.

Boeing Computer Services is also a believer in ATGs. It has over 100 personnel investigating advanced information technologies.

Equitable Life Insurance Company's seven member ATG group scouts and disseminates information on emerging technologies that can be used in pilot tests. Last year the group published 12 bulletins, five reports and sponsored 25 forums attend by 700 people. From its $4 million dollar project, it underwrote 18 projects in cooperation with other units.

There are some critics of ATGs, and although it is difficult to assess their effectiveness, they seem to be a growing phenomenon. Most of the advocates and critics agree that implementation is more important than innovation. New technologies tend to be used in old ways, or, as Wetherbee sums it up: "Technique lags technology."

Adapted from Richard Layne, Advanced Technology Groups: Can You Afford (Not) to Have One?" Information WEEK (January 19, 1987), pp. 56-62.

The advantage of this type of experimentation is that the risks of failure are contained and manageable. Trial runs and experimental models or prototypes allow the developers of innovative information systems technology projects to get the bugs out before actual implementation. Risks in these types of experiments are not limited to technical risks but include social and market risk as well. Customers may not accept innovative new information services. Citicorp's use of ATMs was slowed by consumer acceptance. Gradually, however, the ATMs won them over.

## Realizing the Productivity Promise of the Computer

PRODUCTIVITY GROWTH AMONG WHITE COLLAR WORKERS, clerical personnel, professionals, and managers has been flat for the past 20 years. There is little evidence that the computer has made much contribution to productivity growth. In fact, computers and other office automation products are frequently cited as contributing to information overload - a condition that creates management paralysis.

This statement is hard to believe.

Back in the 1950s early buyers of the computer invariably asked: "How many clerks will it replace?" They quickly found that, while it did replace some clerical workers, it added data processing professionals. The net productivity gain from installing a computer was zero.

Realizing the productivity promise of the computer requires attention to systems improvement and not just systems automation. This will be particularly true in the new applications of the 90s in office automation and factory automation. Application developers need to address the issue of how the system can be improved to provide lower costs, increased revenue, improved quality, and better service to customers.

The difficulty with computer is that we have been pioneering. Pioneers tend to be ambushed along the way. We now have the benefit of the pioneers who have chartered the way. They have pointed out hazards to avoid and the rewards of breaking new ground.

Airline reservation systems are an outstanding example of productivity enhancement that can result from the application of computers. It is unlikely that the airline industry could exist in its present form without reservation systems, which have displaced hordes of clerks. However, as it has already been pointed out, airline reservation systems took *15 years to develop.*

The systems described in this chapter are complex systems. Complex systems often take a long time to develop and sometimes don't work the way they were envisioned. It may take several iterations to get these systems perfected.

## Guidelines for Managers

INFORMATION IS A MAJOR RESOURCE THAT MUST BE *MANAGED*. Managers must take the initiative and leadership role in information systems planning. New developments require a comprehensive plan and an organization-wide focus to exploit the benefit of information systems.

Some organizations have recognized the power of information as a strategic weapon. These organizations are developing new businesses and new relationships with existing customers using information systems for competitive advantage. Managers knowledgeable about information systems technology are in the best position to exploit its competitive potential.

## Guidelines for MIS Professionals

INFORMATION SYSTEMS PROFESSIONALS MUST RECOGNIZE THAT new technology is changing the role of information systems departments from a supporting role providing essentially a clerical function, to a leading one—vital to organizational success. This new role will require giving greater emphasis to organization-wide information systems planning.

## Key Terms

- Information as a Competitive Weapon
- The Extended Enterprise
- Standards
- Protocols
- Product Codes
- Information Middleman
- Single Point of Contact
- Source Data Automation
- Extended Development Period
- Peter Principle
- Corporate Culture
- Executive Leadership
- Information Resource Management (IRM)
- Executive Steering Committee
- Information Overload
- Prototypes

## Review Questions

1. Does the strategic use of information technology require an external or internal focus? Why?
2. Discuss some of the current problems faced by information systems departments.
3. Define Information Resource Management (IRM).
4. What type of culture is conducive to the implementation of strategic information technology?
5. How does the pre-database approach differ from the database approach?
6. List the three basic objectives for a firm to achieve competitive advantage with information technology.
7. Compare the traditional view of information systems with the new or emerging view of information systems.
8. Name three examples of source data automation.
9. Why is top management involvement necessary to assure a successful organization-wide information systems plan?
10. What are the six components of an information system?

## Case Study

### OWENS-CORNING FIBERGLASS CORP.

Scores of U.S. companies are discovering that they possess valuable information resources that can be used as potent strategic weapons. For instance, Owens-Corning Fiberglass Corp., the home insulation giant, is turning information developed by inhouse research and development into what could prove a lucrative new marketing tool. The Toledo company generated substantial data on the energy efficiency of a wide variety of house designs when it was conducting research to develop new insulation materials several years ago. Now, to boost sales of its home insulation products, Owens-Corning has developed a computer program that uses these data to come up with energy-efficiency ratings for new designs. Owens has begun to offer builders free evaluations of their designs if they agree to buy all of their insulation from the manufacturer and meet a minimum standard of efficiency.

By creating the energy-efficiency ratings and launching an advertising campaign to promote them, Owens is trying to increase its business by persuading consumers to demand more insulation. Don

R. Morgan, the company's market development manager, concedes that the program is a roundabout way to stimulate demand for Owens' products. But "it couldn't be done simply by telling builders to use more insulation," he says. Owens hopes its ratings will become as powerful a sales tool for builders as miles-per-gallon ratings are for carmakers.

1. Was Owens-Corning's development of a computer program for energy-efficiency ratings a move to alter industry structure, improve competitive position or spawn new business?
2. How would you describe the corporate culture of Owens-Corning?
3. Is Owens-Corning an extended enterprise? Why or why not?

## Suggestions for Further Reading

Porter, Michael E. and Victor E. Miller, "How Information Gives You Competitive Advantage," Harvard Business Review, July-August, 1985, pp. 149-160.

*This article identifies the reasons why information technology has achieved strategic significance. The authors discuss how information technology has changed the nature of competition in three specific ways: industry structure, lowering costs and enhancing differentiation, and creating new business. Examples of organizations which perceived the change and have used it to their advantage are provided. Five steps are outlined to assist in assessing information technology opportunities that can create a competitive edge.*

Charles Wiseman, Strategy and Computers (Dow-Jones-Irwin, 1985)

*This book examines the strategic use of information systems. It is rich in case studies of corporations that have used MIS technology for competitive advantage.*

# 3

# Information Resource Management

*"The organizations that will*

*excel in the 1980s will be*

*those that manage information*

*as a major resource."*

*John Diebold*

## Overview and Objectives

INFORMATION RESOURCE MANAGEMENT (IRM) ALIGNS INFORMATION systems objectives with those of the firm. The IRM concept attempts to create information systems that produces meaningful, timely information that is accessible to managers and professionals and assists them in carrying out their responsibilities.

IRM adds to the traditional information systems focus on efficiency a concern for effectiveness. Managing information as a strategic resource requires MIS professionals to determine the information needs of the organization and, more specifically, of managers and professionals.

AFTER READING THIS CHAPTER YOU SHOULD BE ABLE TO:

- Discuss the goals of information resource management (IRM).
- Explain the requirements for success with IRM.
- Identify the support structure for implementing IRM.
- Explain an enterprise model.
- Discuss the subject database approach to database organization.

## Introduction

MANAGEMENT OF TECHNOLOGY IS AN EMERGING INTERDISCIPLINARY field that is separate from, yet integrated with, both management and technology. Some researchers argue that it is the management of technology, rather than the development of technology, that has led to Japanese success in several industries. For example, the integrated circuit was invented in the U.S. but the Japanese have exploited its potential in consumer electronics, whereas America's use of this technology has been mainly limited to computers and defense applications.

There is considerable concern that we are not managing information technology effectively. IRM is an attempt to manage information technology and to insure that it is effectively applied. To manage information technology effectively we must determine the information needs of the firm.

There is a growing recognition that information is a resource that must be managed. Information that is relevant, timely, and accurate does not happen by chance; it is the result of careful planning and development. As managers attempt to use information and information systems for competitive advantage they must be more conscious of the need for information systems planning that relates to business purposes.

Information resource management (IRM) is a recognition of the value of explicitly-managed information. The centralized control and coordination of all information resources is a key feature of IRM. It focuses on the information requirements of the organization rather than hardware or software.

MIS managers have attempted to solve their problems with techniques like structured programming and structured analysis, or tools like fourth generation languages and database management systems. These tools and techniques, when properly used, improve the implementation process, but they are not relevant to the larger issue of addressing the information needs of the organization.

IRM also developed out of a recognition that database technology required a new approach for developing a database that can be shared by two or more applications. Many companies and government organizations have misused this technology and, consequently, have failed to obtain the promised benefits.

## Goals of IRM

INFORMATION RESOURCE MANAGEMENT (IRM) IS A SET OF management methods that enable an organization to manage information as a shared resource. IRM is predisposed towards sharing data, a position that is supportive of database technology. While IRM does not require an organization to use a database management system (DBMS), it facilitates the proper use of a DBMS when an organization uses this technology.

### ALIGN INFORMATION SYSTEMS GOALS WITH BUSINESS STRATEGY

The primary objective of information systems should be to produce meaningful and timely information to users, who can then use it to carry out the organization's purposes and objectives. This shifts the focus from automating clerical systems where the objective is cost reduction, or *efficiency*, to providing information that is useful to increase revenue, or *effectiveness*.

### SUPPORT END-USER COMPUTING

The personal computer introduced the era of do-it-yourself computing. The initial euphoria for PCs has been tempered by a realization of the limitations of a free-standing personal computer. Many end-users need to access transaction data stored on mainframe computers. IRM supports and facilitates the movement towards end-user computing by making data more accessible. This is done by creating a consistent, easy-to-use interface that enables end-users to extract data.

## IMPROVE THE PRODUCTIVITY OF SOFTWARE DEVELOPERS

Software development is a complex task that is by nature labor intensive. Improving the productivity of information systems professionals involved in software development is a high priority of many organizations. Creating a plan for a database that doesn't need restructuring for each new application is a major contribution of IRM to this goal. IRM also facilitates new methods of application development that are aimed at increasing the effectiveness and productivity of the application development process.

## PROVIDE RELEVANT, HIGH QUALITY INFORMATION

Information quality, like the quality of products can be improved if there is a consistent commitment to doing it right the first time. IRM attempts to provide organizational support for maintaining the quality of information by instituting a data administration function, which is given a charge to maintaining information quality and security.

Information relevance is achieved by determining the information needs of managers and professionals. IRM focuses on identifying these information needs, rather than hoping that an automated clerical system provides the required information as a by-product.

## Requirements for IRM Success

MANAGING INFORMATION AS A MAJOR RESOURCE REQUIRES four conditions:

1. An infrastructure
2. Database modeling
3. Standards
4. An Enterprise Model

## INFRASTRUCTURE

An infrastructure is an underlying base or supporting structure. As this concept applies to IRM, it means the support personnel and tools which are given the task of managing information as a major resource. These would be the Chief Information Officer and the functions of data administration, the development center, and the information center. The position of Chief Information Officer is a recognition of the need for top-down integration and effective implementation of information technology. It also signals an awareness, in the executive suite, of the potential role of MIS as a competitive weapon.

CHIEF INFORMATION OFFICER: A Chief Information Officer (CIO) is concerned with the management of information technology. This position has as its primary function the overall responsibility for MIS planning. MIS planning might be accomplished with the assistance of a planning staff within the information systems function, by an ad hoc planning group within the MIS department, or by a planning group drawn from end-user departments.

Some of the specific problems being addressed by CIOs include the proliferation of incompatible computer systems, the need for greater integration of these systems, personnel training, and improving the productivity of application developers.

DATA ADMINISTRATION: The data administration function assists with the responsibility for developing an enterprise model or strategic data plan which relates business purposes to data collected, stored, and distributed. Data administration is responsible for the consistency, accuracy and completeness of data throughout the organization. They are also responsible for developing a database that can be shared by different applications and organizational units. Finally, they are given the responsibility for developing and enforcing standards relating to the access, updating, and naming of data elements.

DEVELOPMENT CENTER: A development center is designed to facilitate new software development tools including fourth generation languages, prototyping, and CASE tools. It is not intended to implement unproven technologies nor experiment with state-of-the-art tools. Rather, it is meant to provide training, consultation, and support to information systems professionals. Development Centers also provide a mechanism for standardizing development tools and methods. They are intended to implement new technology and methodology in a disciplined and ordered way.

INFORMATION CENTER: An information center supports end-user computing. This is accomplished by selecting a limited number of hardware and software products which become standard. An information center's functions include training and consultation for end-users.

Data administration departments support both information centers and development centers. They develop a data resource that is shared by information systems professionals as well as end-users. This shared data resource is created and maintained by the data administration group. Data administration assists both of the other groups by being a source of information about data, and all are coordinated under the direct control of the CIO. The importance of this IRM infrastructure is discussed in Issues and Controversies.

## Issues and Controversies

### IRM Infrastructure

**The information systems industry is moving rapidly toward an infrastructure to support data-driven development and managing information as a corporate resource. The term infrastructure implies a platform for supporting a whole class of activities.**

**A historical analogy might be worthwhile in explaining an IRM infrastructure. Early settlers in the American West built isolated settlements largely cut off from the rest of the world. These settlers were mostly self-sufficient pioneers who neither wanted nor needed extensive traffic and contact with the world they left behind.**

**Gradually as the West became more settled these isolated outposts were linked by a network of railroads, roads, and telegraphs. Within the settlements - now on their way to becoming towns and cities - infrastructures were developed to provide water, gas, and other amenities of civilization. Civilization also brought curbs on what rugged individualists were permitted to do within these communities. These controls were enacted in the interests of the community as a whole.**

**The information systems industry is at a point in time where the isolated outposts of information that they've built (application by application, system by system) must be replaced by an infrastructure which permits further growth and development. The trail blazing pioneers must be replaced by individuals concerned with the flow of vital resources -**

**information - within the business and its impact on the business.**

**What is included in an IRM infrastructure?**

- **Standard naming conventions and formats for data elements.**
- **An organization-wide resource that stores data element names and definitions which is accessible and understandable to end users as well as information systems professionals.**
- **A uniform access method for all data stores which makes this data available to a wide range of users.**

**One might ask why is this infrastructure important to a firm? A firm that lacks an organized information resource will not be competitive with those that do. For example, a country that lacks roads, railroads, navigable rivers, and harbors is not competitive in industry. Its infrastructure can't handle the load regardless of how well trained and tireless its people are.**

**In the next five to ten years organizations that have built an information infrastructure will enjoy a significant competitive advantage. By the end of the century it will be a prerequisite for success in many industries and a barrier to entry.**

Adapted from Richard Hunger, "The Concept of Infrastructure and the Case for IRM," Data Base Newsletter (January-February, 1988), pp. 3-5.

## DATABASE MODELING

Database design has generally been viewed from three different perspectives:

1. A logical view is one that represents the perspective of the end user—a view for each application area. A logical user view is a group of related data elements required for an application. A logical model represents a synthesis of several views, which relate to a particular set of applications.
2. A conceptual model is concerned with the fundamental information requirements of the organization. It identifies the objects and events about which a firm cares enough to store data. It is intended to provide a framework for developing a logical database model. The focus of conceptual modeling is determining which objects and events in the organization are important, and defining their relationship to each other.
3. Physical models are concerned with actual database implementation. Developing a physical model require examining usage patterns and the specific DBMS upon which the model is to be implemented. The implementation of a database may require

some compromises from the logical model. The compromise required at the physical level should be transparent to users and based on performance criteria. A diagram showing the three perspectives to database modeling is shown in Figure 3.1.

FIGURE 3.1 *Database Design Perspectivwes*

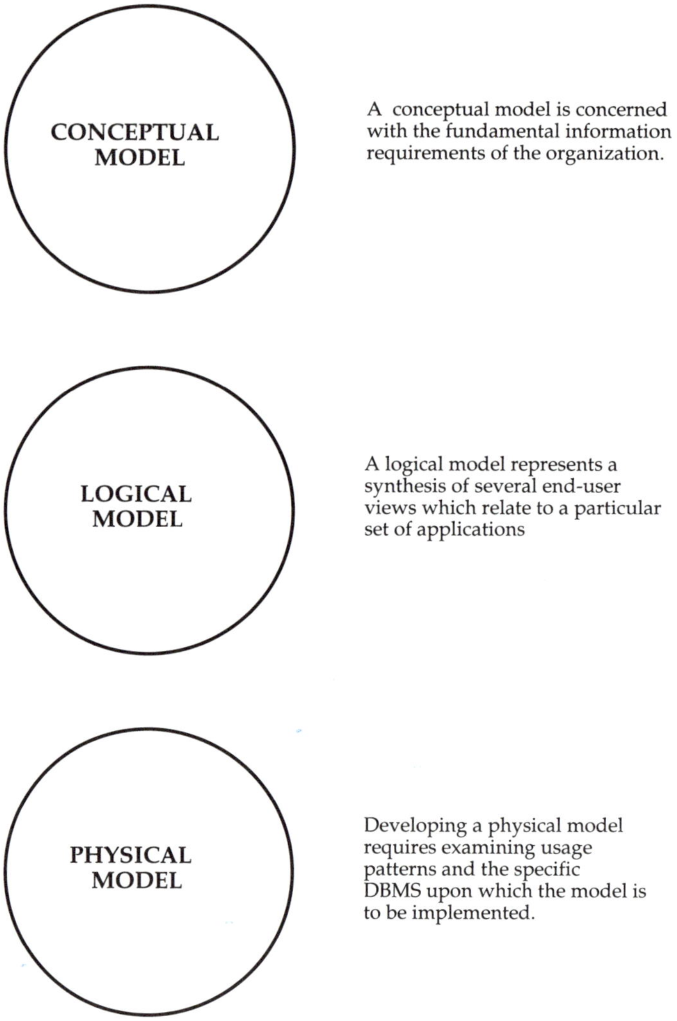


## STANDARDS

Standards are policies that prescribe the accepted patterns of practice and decision making in information systems. Standards may relate to hardware, software, methodologies, networks, and data. Since data is of particular concern we will discuss how standards relate to data.

As they relate to data, standards refer to the order imposed on the process of creating, naming, accessing, and updating data elements so as to make them uniform. This process is the responsibility of a data administrator or data administration group. This function of data administration is addressed in a later chapter.

## AN ENTERPRISE MODEL

An enterprise model is the bridge that links strategic planning of the firm and software development. It provides a set of priorities for software development and a starting point for conceptual data modeling.

An enterprise model provides a framework for sharing data and developing an integrated information system. It ties business direction to information systems development. It identifies the information required for management to plan and control the organization.

# Approaches to Information Systems Development

TRADITIONAL INFORMATION SYSTEMS WERE NOT PLANNED. They were developed application by application with little overall planning. The technology of the 1960s and 1970s did not lend itself to integration. The result was suboptimization—highly developed individual applications, but no overall integration. Most application development was less concerned with management information than clerical automation, as a brief review of historical approaches to information systems development will reveal.

## HISTORICAL APPROACHES TO INFORMATION SYSTEMS DEVELOPMENT

THE BY-PRODUCT APPROACH: This view suggests that management's information needs can be derived from routine reports provided by the organization's transaction processing system. This by-product approach is undoubtedly the predominant view used in the design of information systems. It has considerable value in developing systems in which the objective is to monitor current operations and take corrective action as required. This type of application might be referred to as a management control system.

The by-product approach has several weaknesses that should be noted. Frequently, it leads to a proliferation of reports in which valuable information is lost in excessive detail. Second, it is more applicable for management control than for planning.

Transaction data as presented in periodic reports is essentially a historical summary of past transactions. The value of historical information for planning purposes is often diminished as the planning horizon increases because we are less certain that the past will be repeated. Finally, transaction data is internal data, whereas management planning frequently requires external data. For example, if an organization is considering a new product, sales data on existing products is of less value than data about customers, markets, and competitors.

THE NULL APPROACH: This approach suggests that management is an intuitive process which relies heavily on oral communication with subordinates for decision making. It also suggests that management's activities are continuously changing which makes it difficult to predict the information required for decision making.

Proponents of the null approach point to the inadequacies of reports provided by the by-product approach and the reliance of chief executives on face-to-face communication to suggest that all computer based information systems are essentially useless. The null approach suggests that management information needs are based on judgments of the situation for which no numbers are available. Furthermore, it suggests that management information needs are ad hoc in nature and frequently based on external environments, while conventional information systems provide routine reports of internal data. While there is much truth in this view, it is heavily supported by the observed inadequacies of the by-product approach.

THE KEY-INDICATOR APPROACH: This approach is an enhancement of the by-product view. This view suggests that management should select a set of key indicators which indicate the health of the organization. These key indicators are usually ratios of income statement and balance sheet items or variances from expected performance.[1]

This approach is enriched by the concept of "Management by Exception." Management by exception suggests that a manager's time is limited and should be focused on significant problems. This concept, when applied to management information systems, suggests the option of omitting routine results and spotlighting significant deviations from planned performance. Management by exception is a sound principle should can profitably be applied to any approach of designing management information systems.

Frequently this approach is enhanced by comparisons of actual performance with budgeted expectations and the differences presented as variances. This enhancement of management information systems draw heavily from the discipline of management accounting.

Key indicator systems are really a refined by-product approach and share most of the same shortcomings. They are biased towards financial indicators and internal data.

## More Recent Approaches

More recent approaches have attempted to link the strategic goals of the firm with information systems development. These approaches first examine the firm and its objectives and then focus on the data requirements to achieve these goals.

CRITICAL SUCCESS FACTORS: This approach attempts to define the keys to success in a given industry. Critical success factors are a limited number of areas in which satisfactory results will insure competitive success for the organization. These factors must be favorable for an organization to flourish in an industry.

The current status of critical success factors should be monitored continuously by management to achieve the desired goals. Critical success factors are not an end but a means to an end.

Rockert has suggested four sources of critical success factors. These are:[2]

1. Structure of the industry
2. Competitive strategy, industry position, and geographic location
3. Environmental factors
4. Temporal factors

The structure of a given industry by its very nature determines some critical success factors. For example, the semi-conductor industry requires technological leadership to be successful.

A firm's strategy, market niche, and geographic location may give it unique critical success factors within an industry. Digital Equipment has been successful in the computer industry by concentrating on engineering excellence of mid-sized computers. Its reputation for engineering quality has enabled it to compete with IBM, which has a larger product line and a more sophisticated marketing organization.

Environmental factors constantly change. For example, the collapse of oil prices in the mid-80s has led some organizations to remove energy related items from their list of critical success factors. Other environmental factors include tax laws, interest rates, and international competition.

Temporal factors are temporary factors either internal or external that require organizational adjustment. An example of a temporal factor would be a new product introduction. Successful introduction of a new product could be a critical success factor for an organization.

Once critical success factors are identified, a means of measuring and reporting them should be determined. Clearly some critical success factors will require measures of non-financial factors external to the firm, such as market share, customer satisfaction, or a market growth rate. An example of critical success factors for an emerging electronics firm are found in Table 3.1.

TABLE 3.1
*Critical Success Factors for an Electronics Firm*

| Critical Success Factor | Measure |
|---|---|
| Reputation for state-of-the-art technology | Order/bid ratio on contracts (hard)<br>Opinions solicited during interviews (soft) |
| Market success of products | Change in market share, by product line (hard)<br>Advance reports by sales rep (soft) |
| Performance within cost and time constraints for new product development projects | Job cost and time statistics--planned versus actual (hard) |

BSP: Business system planning (BSP) is an approach developed and marketed by IBM to provide a framework for information systems development. It attempts to develop a business plan which identifies the functions, processes, and activities of an organization. These functions, processes, and activities of an organization are related to their data requirement.

For example, a university typically has three functions: education, research, and service. Each of these functions can be divided into processes. For example, education can be divided into admission, registration, and instruction. Instruction can be divided into activities including lecture, and supporting activities in the laboratory, library, and computer facilities. Once we have divided an organization's functions into processes and activities we are able to identify the information required to support these activities. An example of identification of functions, processes, and activities is shown in Figure 3.2.

FIGURE 3.2
*The Identification of Functions, Processes and Activities*

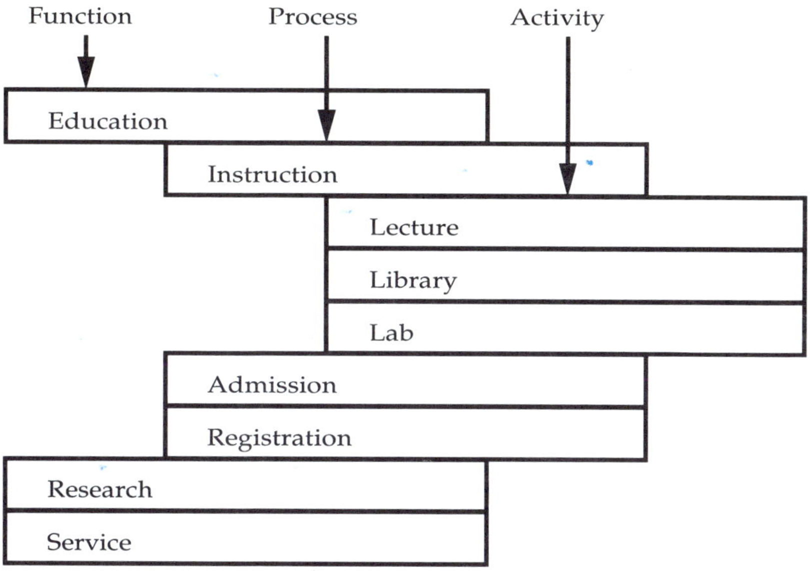


The outcome of BSP is an enterprise model which serves as a framework for information resource planning to provide a clear definition of the business. It describes how the goals and objectives of the firm are achieved by various business functions. The enterprise model is a functional model that describes how information is created, used, updated and deleted by different business functions.

## Developing an Enterprise Model

FROM THE ENTERPRISE MODEL ARE DERIVED THREE DELIVERABLES: an information architecture, an application architecture, and a technical architecture. The term architecture suggests a plan to build in accordance with principles determined by aesthetic and practical consideration. The term also signifies a shared vision of the future.

### INFORMATION ARCHITECTURE

The process of developing the requirements for a database begins with a definition of an information architecture. This step defines an organization's functions, processes, and activities. Each function, process, and activity is mapped against the required entities and/or subject databases.

SUBJECT DATABASE: A subject database is data organized by subject rather than by application. This contrasts with traditional information systems which organize data by application. For example, a payroll system would typically store data in a master payroll file.

From a technical standpoint, a subject database can be defined as a group of closely-related entities. The grouping of entities into subject databases is a key activity in enterprise modeling.

ENTITIES: Entities are persons, objects, or events about which an organization stores data. Examples of entities are customer, employee, order, shipment, and product. Entities can be identified as singular noun.

Entities are categories for classifying data. For example, *employee* is an entity—a person—Michael A. Johnson is an entity occurrence. Entity names should be singular nouns.

Entities are associated with other entities. A named business association is called a relationship. For example, the relationship between customer and order is shown in Figure 3.3.

The arrows represent the relationship between the two entities. A single arrow shows that each order is associated with exactly one customer. A customer may be associated with zero, one, or many orders as shown by the double arrow.

The advantages of the subject database approach are described in Issues and Controversies.

FIGURE 3.3
*Entities*

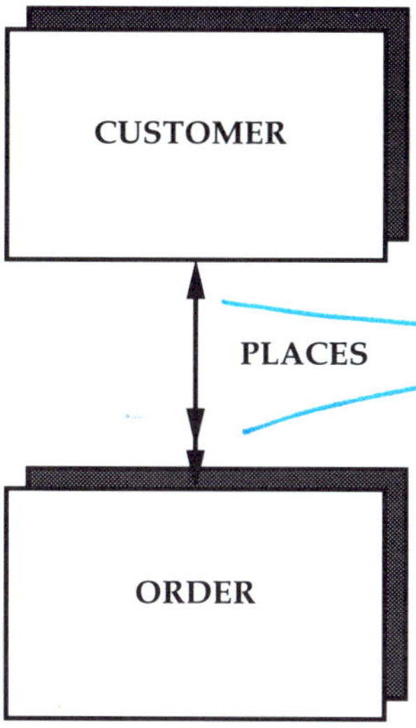


**Issues and Controversies**

## The Objective of IRM: A Supermarket of Data

Information systems might be compared with a supermarket. Let us suppose that a supermarket was organized by recipe. All the ingredients for a given recipe would be stored in one location. If you wanted to make lasagne you would look for one location where the noodles, cheese, meat, spices, and sauce would all be displayed. If you wanted to prepare cookies, you would have to find the location of that recipe. This type of organization would serve some shoppers very well and might be preferred by them to other organizational schemes.

The difficulty with a supermarket organized by recipe is the inconvenience of finding what one needs if the supermarket does not have your recipe. Then expert help is required to locate the necessary ingredients in different areas. The disadvantage from the perspective of the store is that the same ingredients are stored in many locations which makes it difficult to manage the inventory.

Supermarkets have found it advantageous to store items by category. Meat is stored in one location and is subdivided by beef, pork, lamb, chicken, and fish. Each of these are further subdivided into additional categories. Each item is found in one place. In contrast to the supermarket organized by recipe it can serve an infinite number of recipes. Clear labeling and organization by category facilitates self service and leads to fast, convenient, and economical shopping.

An organization that uses a subject database scheme for organizing its data is organized like a supermarket. Each data element is stored in one location. Clear labeling of data facilitates

**self service. A broad variety of purposes can be served by a subject database organization.**

Adapted from William Smith, Database Design Seminar, San Francisco, CA, February 1988.

An information architecture is a blueprint describing the subject databases required for the enterprise. This process groups entities that are commonly shared by two or more business functions into subject databases. This can be accomplished by grouping closely related entities into meaningful classes or clusters.

A subject database matrix shows processes or functions along one axis and subject databases along another. An example of such a matrix prepared at Western Airlines is found in Figure 3.4.

This planning process not only spotlights gaps in the existing information systems; it suggests priorities for future application develop-

FIGURE 3.4 *A Subject Database Matrix*[a]

**Subject Areas**

| **Functions** | Financial Performance | Market | Competition | Regulations | Airports | Tariffs and Fares | Load Forecasts | Flight Schedules | Aircraft | Agents | Facilities | Equipment |
|---|---|---|---|---|---|---|---|---|---|---|---|---|
| Provide Business Direction | | | | | | | | | | | | |
| Assess Market Opportunities | | | | | | | | | | | | |
| Assess Regulatory Requirements | | | | | | | | | | | | |
| Assess Altern-ative Routes | | | | | | | | | | | | |
| Assess Altern-ative Tariffs/Fares | | | | | | | | | | | | |
| Assess Alternative Flight Schedules | | | | | | | | | | | | |
| Provide Route/ Schedule Plan | | | | | | | | | | | | |
| Provide Fleet Plan | | | | | | | | | | | | |
| Provide Marketing/ Sales Plan | | | | | | | | | | | | |
| Provide Logistics Plan | | | | | | | | | | | | |

[a] From Dennis M. Fitzpatrick and Earl F. Hadden, II, "Information Engineering Based Systems Development" Database Newsletter (May/June, 1987), p. 11

ment. It may also lead to reorganization of the firm itself. Western Airlines recognized in their subject database matrix that Airlines Revenue Accounting was closely related to Marketing Information Systems. The matrix provided insight that the major users of data generated by Revenue Accounting functions were not financial but marketing functions. This led to a change in the placement of the Revenue Accounting function.[3]

The information architecture for an organization is based on two types of requirements:

1. Transaction processing data requirements. This is the data required for existing information processing applications.
2. Managerial information requirements. This is data that might be from existing systems or may not currently be captured.

Determining the data requirements for managers is more difficult and may require an approach such as Critical Success Factors. There are other techniques not discussed in this chapter that might be useful as well.

## APPLICATION ARCHITECTURE

An application architecture describes in a preliminary way the business systems and subject databases that are required to support the information architecture. While the details will be determined in later stages the application architecture attempts to predict the subsequent applications to be developed. An application architecture definition also develops a set of priorities for the development of business systems.

## TECHNICAL ARCHITECTURE

The technical architecture describes the hardware and software environment that is required to implement the application architecture. This environment is compared with the current technical environment.

These three architectures define a framework from which an enterprise can build systems to support its long term needs. An enterprise model focuses on using information as a resource and on effectively using this resource to enhance an organization's opportunities for success.

## Enterprise Modeling Implementation Issues

ENTERPRISE MODELING IS PERHAPS BEST ACCOMPLISHED WITH the aid of an external consultant who has been through the process several times. Typically, several weeks' effort is required to define the enterprise information architecture. This process requires management involvement. Obtaining this type of commitment from top management is difficult.

Once in place, the information architecture is a framework around which an integrated database can be built. The advantages of this method are that it provides direction and a set of priorities for future application development.

The principle criticism of this technique is that, in practice, it is difficult to get top management support for enterprise modeling because of the time commitment required. Some practitioners have evolved an evolutionary or iterative approach to building an information architecture. This approach integrates one project at a time into a detailed and logically consistent information architecture.

James Kerr is an advocate of an evolutionary approach, which he refers to as a "bottom up approach." His views are discussed in Issues and Controversies.

## Issues and Controversies

### Corporate Data Models Built from the Bottom Up

**Enterprise data models being built from the bottom up. Isn't that a contradiction in terms? Everyone knows that enterprise data models are built from the top down, defining the data within an organization, right?**

**Several years ago, Pratt and Whitney embraced what was then a revolutionary idea—an integrated data base. The acceptance of database technology inspired an investigation of information engineering techniques and database modeling methodologies.**

**Enterprise data models delineate a firm's business rules by showing a graphical representation of the relationships between an enterprise's entities. The enterprise model serves as a blueprint for later stages of database design. The broad scope of enterprise modeling has traditionally made it a top down effort.**

**Unfortunately, top down modeling requires several months of daily meetings with top management. Getting top management commitment to this kinds of effort is next to impossible given their other responsibilities.**

**Without top management involvement, how can MIS build an enterprise model? No enterprise model means no integrated database. Is there a way of developing an enterprise model without the top down approach, which requires heavy management participation?**

**Pratt and Whitney believes that a bottom-up approach can be used effectively in building an enterprise model. The bottom-up approach is an iterative process which integrates project-level data models into a detailed and logically consistent enterprise model.**

**A bottom-up approach to database modeling becomes a vehicle through which a firm replaces its current application-specific stand-alone databases with an integrated database. As a result , MIS can minimize redundancy, cut maintenance costs, and free up time to attack the application backlog.**

Adapted from James M. Kerr, "Corporate Data Models Flourish from the Bottom Up," Computerworld, May 11, 1987, pp. 71-78.

Regardless of the strategy chosen for database requirements definition, it is desirable to proceed it with some top down planning that defines the basic information architecture of the firm.

EVOLUTIONARY STRATEGY - This strategy defines an information architecture, but all data elements are not defined initially. New data elements are added when there is an identified need either from new applications or other unmet needs. This approach takes more time but has less impact on the organization's current activities. It defers benefits but also spreads implementation expense over a longer period.

REVOLUTIONARY STRATEGY - This approach builds an information architecture not only for existing applications, but anticipated applications as well. It builds a detailed model of entities and their relationships. This approach is time-consuming and may put application development on the back burner until a detailed database model is in place. This disruption of current application development may create political problems and foster efforts to evade the new database standards.[4]

A recent study has shown there is a range of data planning alternatives. This study is discussed in Issues and Controversies.

## Issues and Controversies

# A Range of Data Planning Processes

There is a broad range of data planning methods used in information resource management. These approaches range from global, well defined rigorous methods through narrower scope, frequently less formal approaches to no planning at all.

The global methods are known by such names as strategic data planning, or enterprise modeling. The underlying assumption of these top-down data planning methodologies is that it is impossible to plan an information system if one does not know what the business is or what data it uses. It is difficult to argue with these assumptions.

In a study of five firms that attempted a global, top-down data planning effort none experienced the type of success envisioned by their advocates in the literature. The outcomes varied but none of the plans resulted in the implementation of new systems or subject databases.

There are several reasons why these firms were not more successful in implementing an enterprise model. The bottom line is that it is difficult to gain a commitment to the process, for many times the process is too expensive, the benefits too uncertain, and the results too difficult to implement.

The most common data planning methods observed inn the study were those limited to a function or business area. Data planning was limited to a target area. This method of data planning while limited in scope was found to be effective and feasible.

A third type of data planning observed was termed an 80/20 approach. The aim of this approach is to focus on the outcomes of data planning and minimize the top down planning effort. This approach suggests that 80 percent of the benefits can be achieved with 20 percent of the total top down planning effort.

The difficulty with the targeted approach is that it is likely that inconsistencies will be developed from multiple targeted projects and that in some firms the most important targets may not be evident. An 80/20 approach appears to offer most of the benefits of both the global and targeted approaches without their disadvantages.

There are also information resource management actions that can be taken without any data planning. For example if a firm decides to provide improved access to data without addressing the need for changes in the structure of that data is data planning necessary?

Adapted from Dale L. Goodhue, Judith A. Quillard, and John F. Rockart, "Managing the Data Resource: A Contingency Approach," MIS Quarterly (September 1988), pp. 373-391.

Another study of 80 firms implementing strategic data planning methodologies found that the most important problem common to the four planning methodologies studied was a lack of top management commitment. The study also showed that information systems planners are not particularly satisfied with their methodologies, that planning requires too many resources and further analysis was required before execution of the plan. Consequently, the execution of the plans developed was not very extensive.[5]

## Information Resource Management Deliverables

GOODHUE ET AL. SUGGESTS THERE ARE FIVE INFORMATION RE-source management deliverables. These are (1) subject databases for operational systems, (2) common systems, (3) information databases, (4) data access services, and (5) architectural foundations for the future. A subject database for an operational system contains data that is organized around important business entities or subject areas such as customer and product.

Common systems are applications developed by a single organizational unit to be used by other organizational units. Common systems require resolution of data definition issues since old systems and the old definitions are discontinued.

Information databases are subject databases created to support analysis and decision making. Information databases are secondary databases drawn from operational databases and sometimes external sources. Information databases do not require a rewrite of current systems instead they require "bridges" to current systems to provide the appropriate data.

Data access services are more limited in scope than the first three deliverables. The focus is on improving access to existing data without attempting to improve the quality or structure of that data. This is accomplished by the use of fourth generation languages (4GLs) to extract data from production files. This assumes that existing data is of reasonable quality.

An architectural foundation of the system is developing a structure, policies, and standards that guide future systems development efforts. Clearly there is a danger in developing information resource management function by function, application by application and subject area by subject area. The danger is that the firm may find difficulty if it desires to integrate data across these boundaries. This is the reason many firms have attempted to develop an information architecture.[6]

## The Misuse of Database Technology

DATABASE TECHNOLOGY, WHICH PROMISED TO PROVIDE A common software management tool for sharing data supporting one or more applications, was to be the most revolutionary approach to managing data since the invention of the computer. It promised several benefits to the organization such as:

1. Increased productivity in application development
2. Increased data integrity
3. Increased flexibility
4. Data independence
5. Greater accessibility to data

Many companies and government organizations have not enjoyed these benefits because they have misused the technology. Unfortunately, the technology itself is often blamed for failure to achieve the expected advantages. Most of the failure are actually attributable to the *method* by which this technology was applied in these organizations.[7]

### THE APPLICATION SPECIFIC APPROACH

Prior to the development of data base technology in the 1960s, programmers developed files in support of application programs. These files were designed to serve a specific application. Payroll systems had files to support payroll applications. Data files ordinarily did not serve more than a single application. This approach is illustrated in Figure 3.5.

In using this approach, the programmer has several data handling responsibilities for each application. Each program accessing a file must have software procedures for:

Data descriptions
Data identification
Data access method
Data validation
Data security

Since these requirements were common to all programs, and some programmers were less capable than others in providing these services, many organizations turned to a DBMS as an answer to these problems. If a DBMS is used only as a sophisticated data-access tool, the vision of an integrated data base is lost. Unfortunately, this has occurred far too frequently.

FIGURE 3.5 *Application-Specific Approach*

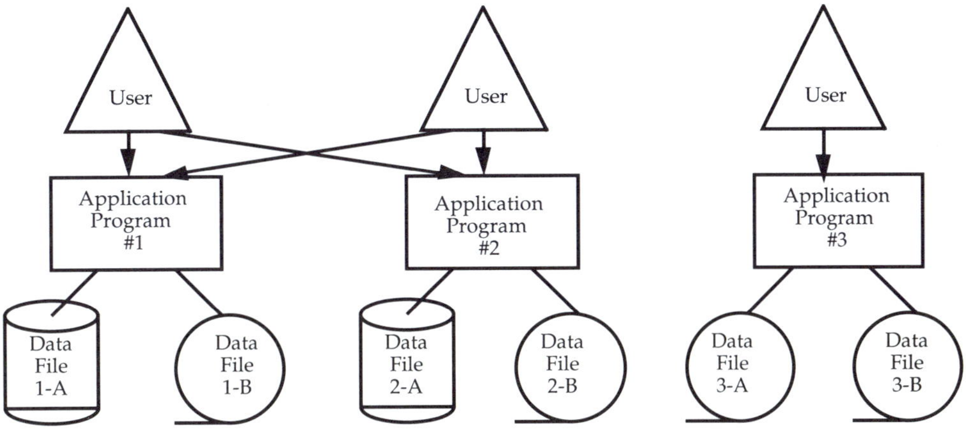


## FAILURE TO ESTABLISH DATA ADMINISTRATION FUNCTION

Another misuse of database technology is allowing uncoordinated application development with a DBMS. This inevitably leads to application-specific database applications. This results in redundancy. Redundancy inevitably leads to inconsistent data from different applications; which we have referred to as a data integrity problem.

Data administration is a centralized coordinating function charged with the management of data. Data administration is responsible for identifying, naming and documenting data and data relationships. Data administration leads to the development of subject databases which are shared by several applications. This concept is illustrated in Figure 3.6.

Database technology, particularly relational database technology is often misused because managers and MIS professionals fail to implement it correctly. The technology has great promise but it must be implemented as a subject database or organized like a supermarket to achieve its full potential.

FIGURE 3.6
*Subject Database Approach*

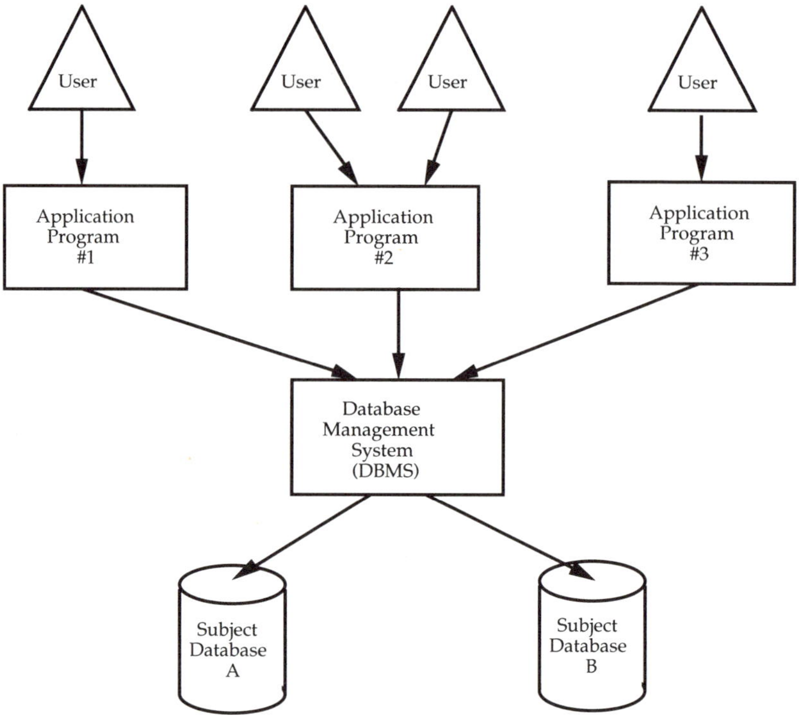


## Guidelines for Managers

IRM REPRESENTS A PROMISING APPROACH TO MANAGING IN-formation technology. It suggests greater emphasis on information planning to avoid incompatible systems. Integration of information systems can be achieved only with careful attention to enterprise modeling and database design.

## Guidelines for MIS Professionals

IRM PROVIDES DIRECTION AND GOALS FOR THE MIS PROFES-sional. Management determines how MIS can be used to contribute to organizational effectiveness. This exciting new role for MIS promises greater visibility for and more emphasis on information technology.

## Key Terms

Business Systems Planning (BSP)
By-Product Approach
Chief Information Officer Management
Critical Success Factors
Data Administration
Database Modeling
Development Center
Enterprise Model Development
Entities
Information Architecture
Information Center
Information Resource
Infrastructure
Key-Indicator Approach
Management of Technology
Null Approach
Productivity of Software
Subject Database

## Review Questions

1. What are the goals of IRM?
2. What is the distinction between a development center and an advanced technology group which was discussed in the previous chapter?
3. How does the supermarket approach differ from the conventional view of organizing data?
4. What are the limitations of the by-product approach?
5. What is an entity?
6. What are some of the difficulties of developing and implementing an enterprise model?
7. What is the distinction between an information database and a subject database?
8. Discuss the underlying conditions which are necessary for the success of IRM.
9. Discuss several reasons why database technology has not lived up to its original expectations.
10. Why is the data administration function critical to the success of information resource management?

## Case Study

### IRM AT WESTERN AIRLINES

Corporate managers and information systems executives are becoming aware of information systems technologies being used as competitive weapons in many industries. A recently developed measure of the importance of information systems to a company is the "intensity factor." Firms with a high intensity factor are described as the information handlers that will dominate the future economy.

In late 1983, Western Airlines Information Systems Division considered how it was going to address the long-term needs of the Corporation. Attempting to emerge from the brink of bankruptcy, the airline was faced with enormous challenges. Western was an airline that competed in an area of the country that was more competitive than most and in an industry that, since deregulation, had become intensely competitive. A handful of larger U.S. airlines had begun to dominate the market, continually increasing their market share.

Not surprisingly, these were air carriers which had heavily invested in information systems technology. These were firms that had a high degree of intensity factors.

Looking to the future, Western noted a number of problem areas that existed in its application development activities. Among these were the following:

- Current application development projects did not emphasize the strategic thrust of the company.
- "Survival mode" approaches needed to be discarded in favor of "planning mode" approaches.
- The division needed to reassess the data capture requirements against the information needs of the company.
- Development practices, including development life cycles, standards, project management and control, had been abandoned.

These factors made Western Airlines an excellent candidate for Information Resource Management (IRM) as a management philosophy. To do this Western retained a consulting firm for assistance in developing and implementing a new development approach.

The first stage of implementing IRM should be a planning stage. Within the context of planning Western accomplished several efforts. Western's Information Systems division developed a Business Systems Planning (BSP) model employing the classical IRM methodologies. This effort defined the basic functions, processes and activities of the firm and the information required for each.

The next step was to identify the necessary resources. Western found that it needed hardware, software and people. To add the necessary people skills, Western initiated an intensive training program to upgrade the skills of its staff. For some personnel such as systems analysts and members of the Data Administration group, a recruitment effort brought in new people.

Western also established data standards. This was viewed as the most difficult step to implement. One of the reasons for this is the reluctance to go back and change the thousands of already existing data elements and attempt to "standardize" them.

The compromise struck at Western was to apply the new standard only to new projects. The standard was relaxed for existing data managed by the DBMS. This will allow Western to phase-in its data administration standards over time.

Western's experience is that while IRM has philosophical and theoretical merit, it is not easy to implement. Considerable planning, expert guidance, and an assessment of where the firm is in implementing data management and related technologies is required before implementing IRM.

Adapted from "Information Engineering Based Systems Development: IRM at Western Airlines," Database Newsletter, May/June 1987, pp. 1, 10-14.

1. What does this case illustrate about the difficulty of implementing an IRM philosophy?
2. What types of changes were required of Western to change from an ad hoc survival mode to a planning mode?
3. What types of difficulties does a firm like Western face in competing with firms which have competitive advantage with information systems?

## Suggestions for Further Reading

Donald A. Marchand and Forest W. Horton, Jr., Infotrends (John Wiley and Sons, 1986)

*This book addresses the need for the firm to manage information as an organizational resource. The approach is managerial not technical. It discusses both information resource management and strategic uses of information and information systems.*

# 4

# Integrated Database Management Systems

*"Relational database management systems are a necessary foundation for several emerging technologies including CASE and cooperative processing."*

*William Arntz*

## Overview and Objectives

THIS CHAPTER EXAMINES THE CONCEPT OF A DATABASE. WE will clearly define the advantages of database processing; explain the functions and components of an integrated database management system; show the ease of accessing information from a relational database; and describe the keys to success in implementing a DBMS.

This chapter also explains how a relational database foundation is vital to several emerging technologies. The strategic value of this foundation is frequently not recognized and as a result the synergism between this technology and emerging technologies not realized.

AFTER READING THIS CHAPTER YOU SHOULD BE ABLE TO:

- Describe the advantages of database processing as opposed to file processing.
- List and describe several components of an integrated database management system.
- Describe why users are essential in data modeling.
- Define several database terms.
- Explain the keys to success for implementing a DBMS.
- Explain the relational database architectural alternatives.
- Describe the relationship between a shared database and end-user computing.

## Introduction

RELATIONAL DATABASE TECHNOLOGY IS A KEY NEW DEVELOPment. While this technology is valuable on its own merits in making application development easier, cheaper, faster and more flexible it is particularly valuable as a foundation for several emerging developments. These developments include CASE tools, local area networks, expert systems, end-user computing and information engineering. Relational database technology has great synergism with several emerging information technologies. This relationship is shown in Figure 4.1.

Relational database technology is particularly valuable in integrating related but different applications. This property of integration is changing relational database technology from a nice thing to have to a required component for moving to advanced technology. An example of this type of integration would be the sharing of common data by a hospital clinical laboratory system and a hospital accounting system.

FIGURE 4.1
*Relational Database Foundation*

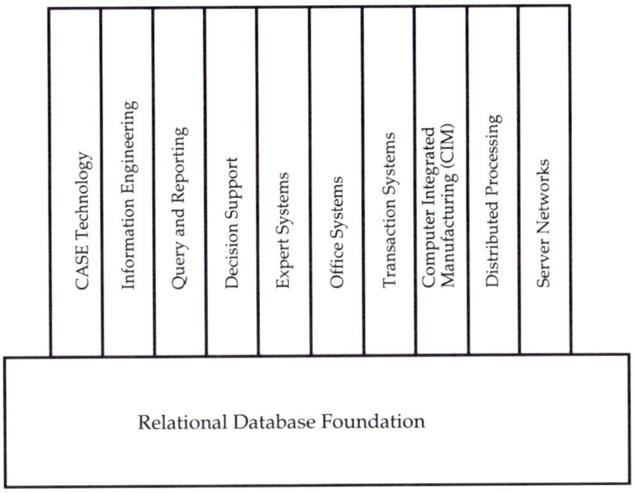


It is difficult to underestimate the impact of this technology on organizations and MIS departments in particular. The effects of relational database technology will change MIS professionals' skills and job titles, change software development methodologies, and make transaction data readily available to end-users.

## A DATABASE VS. DATA FILES

A database is data designed for sharing. It is an integrated collection of data which is organized to be used for multiple purposes.

In contrast, data files are usually designed for a specific application. Application-specific files require redundancy, which means that the same information is contained in different files. For example, an employee's name and address would usually be found in both a payroll and personnel file. This leads inevitably to data integrity problems. Data integrity refers to a situation in which data in one file has different values than the same data item in another file. For example, if an employee moves it is possible that someone will forget that an employee's address is contained in both the payroll master file and the personnel master file and thus not make changes to both which creates a problem of data integrity. The quality of data is not the only reason for adopting the database approach.

New concepts in data-base management software provide substantial productivity improvements for programmers in developing and maintaining applications software compared to conventional file-processing techniques. Improved productivity in software development is an important reason to adopt database technology.

Perhaps the most fundamental idea in database is *data independence*. Most of the advantages of data base are the result of data independence.

## DATA INDEPENDENCE

The fundamental idea behind a database management system is to separate data definitions from the programs that use the definitions. Data definitions are the description of how data is stored. An example of data definitions is shown in the data division of a COBOL program shown in Figure 4.2.

FIGURE 4.2
*Data Division of a COBOL Program*

```
DATA DIVISION
FILE SECTION
FD   DISKFILE
     LABEL RECORDS ARE STANDARD
01   DISKREC.
     05  PART-DESCRIPTION-IN           PIC X(20).
     05  PRICE-IN                      PIC 999.
     05  UNITS-SOLD-IN                 PIC 9(5).
FD   PRINTFILE
     LABEL RECORDS ARE OMITTED.
01   PRINTLINE                         PIC X(120).
```

Data definition includes information about the order, type (numeric vs. character) and size of data items. The separation of data definition from application programs results in data independence. Data definitions in a data-base environment are maintained separately by an integrated data dictionary. The data dictionary becomes a source of definitions about data.

Data independence has been defined as: (1) the separation of data descriptions from application programs,[1] (2) the ability of an end-user to use data without knowing the details of representation and location,[2] and (3) the ability to alter the structure of the data without altering the application programs that access the data.[3] A diagram illustrating the first definition is shown in Figure 4.3.

FIGURE 4.3

*Data Independence - Separating Data Definitions from Programs*

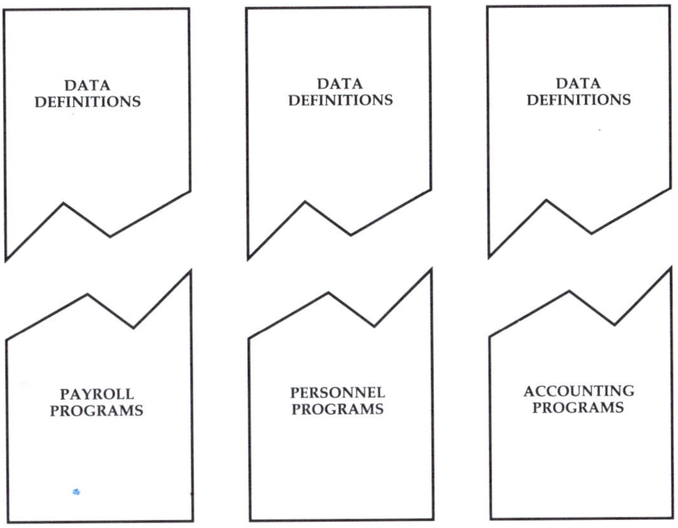


## Advantages of Database Processing

### FLEXIBILITY

Perhaps the most important advantage of database processing is flexibility. In file processing, the description of the data is imbedded in applications programs, whereas in database processing the data definitions are maintained independently of application programs by means of an integrated data dictionary. Maintaining data definitions separately from applications creates more flexibility.

The advantage of data independence is flexibility in accommodating change. This means less maintenance for application programmers. In a file processing environment, if a new application requires some of the same data elements as an existing application, the developer has two options: (1) to add new data elements to the existing file to accommodate the new application or, (2) to develop a new file which duplicates some of the data elements of the existing file. Both of these alternatives have significant disadvantages. Adding data elements to an existing file will require extensive maintenance for other applications using the same data. The second alternative requires the designer to create data redundancy with attendant problems of data integrity. For example, one or more data items may be changed in one file and not changed in the other. Inconsistent data will create credibility problems for information systems professionals.

Data independence allows different applications programs to be modified without affecting the access of other applications to the data. In addition, new data items can be added to the database without disturbing existing applications. Database processing provides greater flexibility to programmers because it maintains independence between data and applications software.

## PRODUCTIVITY

Improvements in productivity in a database environment comes from two sources: (1) data independence makes it possible to change one application without affecting other applications which results in less maintenance, and (2) powerful fourth generation languages (4GLs) and CASE tools associated with database management systems provide significant productivity improvements over conventional high level programming languages such as COBOL. One of the advantages of 4GLs and CASE tools is they eliminate the necessity of describing data previously defined in an integrated data dictionary.

## ACCESSABILITY

The power and simplicity of accessing a database with a query language makes it possible for end-users to obtain access to data required for their ad-hoc decisions. The use of query languages is only one manifestation of a movement towards end-user computing which is made possible by the ease of use and capability of database tools.

For example, suppose that a bank wished to know the names and addresses of all its customers in zip code 68144. The vice-president of marketing calls the information systems department and requests such a list. This is an unusual request, which was not anticipated by the developers of the original system. In a file processing environment, the request would require a new program to be written which would probably take several days.

In contrast, an end-user using a database query language could obtain the required information in a few minutes without professional assistance. Accessability means end users can extract the data they need, when they need it, and without consulting a programmer.

## DATA SECURITY

A database management system has provision for data security. For example a payroll clerk in a bank should have access to payroll information but not customer accounts. A teller should have access to customer accounts but not the salaries of the bank personnel. A database management system has the security mechanisms to enforce these controls whereas most file processing environments do not. This is accomplished by a subsystem known as a data dictionary which maintains a profile of user privileges and controls access to the data.

## Integrated Database Management Systems

DATABASE MANAGEMENT SYSTEMS ARE USUALLY DEFINED AS software systems for managing the storage, access, updating and maintenance of a database. The difficulty with this definition is that there is now hardware (database machines) which performs some of these functions.

An integrated database management system consists of a set of components that provides a complete application development and production environment. An integrated database management system is illustrated in Figure 4.4.

FIGURE 4.4

*An Integrated Database Management System*

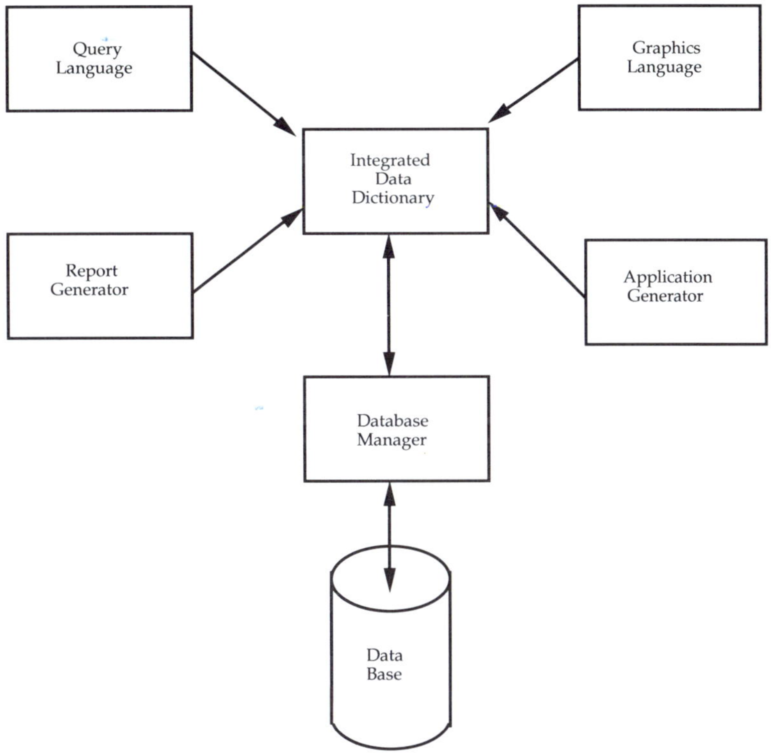

THE COMPONENTS OF THIS INTEGRATED SYSTEM ARE AS FOLLOWS:

## QUERY LANGUAGE

A query language is a fourth generation language designed for end-users to answer questions, such as "How many CD players did we sell in the Midwest district last month?" A query language is easy to learn and easy to use. It is designed for ad hoc information needs. The term "ad-hoc" means as required.

Query languages are very flexible and powerful. They can extract information from a single file or perform more complex searches involving multiple files.

The data independence ideal of allowing end-users to access data without knowing the details of location and representation must be balanced against the risk of their tying up the CPU (central processing unit) with complex searches. A sensible middle ground is to teach the user something about the structure of the data and the types of questions the database can support.

## REPORT GENERATOR

This module has the capability of extracting information from a file or database and formatting it into reports. Well designed report generators will allow some arithmetic and logical operations to be performed on the data. Ideally, report generators are associated with a query language and give additional capabilities for formatting output obtained with a query language.

## APPLICATION GENERATOR

Application generators are sometimes referred to as fourth generation languages. Application generators are designed to be used to develop an entire application. This would include input, editing, arithmetic and logical operations, and output. Most application generators particularly those suitable for computer professionals, are associated with and dependent upon a database management system although some are not.

### GRAPHICS LANGUAGE

A graphics language allows a user to interactively create graphic displays in the form of graphs and charts. These languages allow the user to extract data from the database, perform arithmetic operations and specify how the output should be displayed. When coupled with a graphics terminal and a color plotter these languages give users very impressive capabilities for creating high quality graphics.

### INTEGRATED DATA DICTIONARY

An integrated data dictionary provides an automated tool for maintaining the documentation of an organization's descriptions of its data. An integrated data dictionary also provides a consistent set of data definitions for applications which access the database and provides controls to limit unauthorized users from modifying or accessing data.

Integrated data dictionaries have become the focal point of modern database management systems. Traditionally data dictionaries were passive documentation tools which contained an organized collection of definitions about data. An integrated data dictionary, however, is the heart of a database management system.

### DATABASE MANAGER

The database manager is the workhorse of an integrated database management system. It manages the functions of storage, modification and retrieval of data. It interfaces with the data dictionary to communicate with the other modules.

These modules which have been described comprise a state of the art database management system. Some commercial database management systems (DBMS) are missing several of the components. In some cases, vendors other than the database vendor provide some of these modules.

## Types of Database Management Systems

### HIERARCHICAL

The oldest type of database management system is the hierarchical model. It is embodied in one current product, IMS.

A hierarchical database requires data to be represented as hierarchies known as parent-child relationships. This can be illustrated in Figure 4.5.

FIGURE 4.5
*Hierarchical Database Relationship*

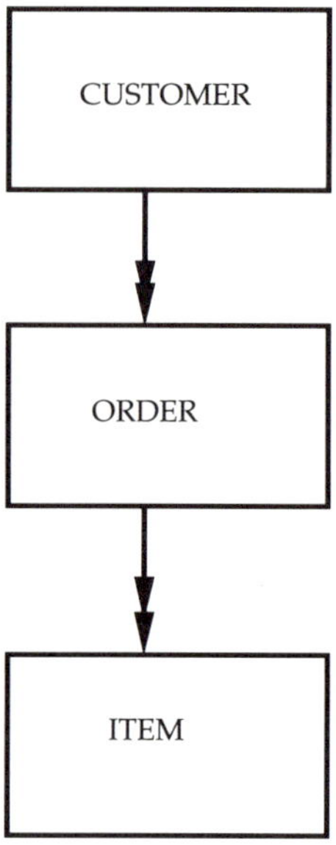


The double arrow shows there can be zero, one, or many orders per customer. The customer file is the "parent" and the order file is the "child." Similarly, there can be zero, one, or many items per order.

The hierarchical structure permits efficient access of related records. The parent record contains a pointer which shows the storage location of the child. If a "parent" record is deleted (customers) the corresponding "child" record or records are deleted as well. The difficult with a hierarchical structure is its inflexibility. A "child" record can be accessed only through the "parent." This does not permit, for example, one to access a "parent" record (customer) by entry to the database at the "child" level (orders).

The hierarchical database does not permit unanticipated searches through the database. It permits access to data only in prespecified structures.

## NETWORK

The network database model is more flexible than the hierarchical model. Where a hierarchical model permits a record to have only a single parent, the network model permits the representation of plex structures such as the one shown in Figure 4.6.

FIGURE 4.6

*Network Database Relationship*

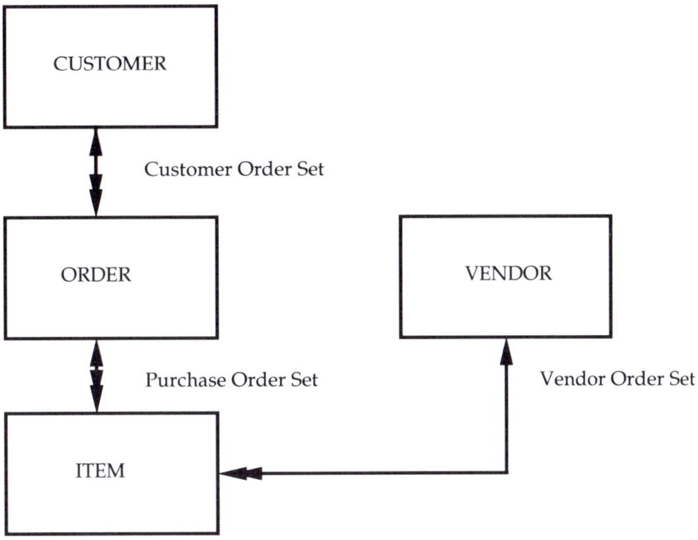


The parent-child terminology is replaced by the terms owner-member. Each owner-member relationship is referred to as a set type. Each set type is named. This feature enables a record to appear in more than one relationship. In the above example, order-item appears in both the purchase-order set and the inventory-order set.

The network database model is more flexible than the hierarchical model, but generally is considered more complex. Like the hierarchical model, it uses pointers to efficiently access member records.

## RELATIONAL

The newest database model today is the relational model. Its primary advantages are flexibility, ease of use and simplicity. All of the major database software vendors have developed new relational products or are in the process of converting their old DBMS products to the relational model. The impact of IBM's introduction of DB2, their relational database product is discussed in Issues and Controversies.

## Issues and Controversies

## Excerpts from an Interview with Paul Hessinger by Database Newsletter

Newsletter: "IBM announced DB2 in June, 1983. What impact has DB2 had on the market place since that time?"

Hessinger: "There have been three major areas of impact. In retrospect, the first of these - the endorsement of the relational model - is rather obvious, although it wasn't nearly so obvious in 1983 or 1984.

The second is a catalytic effect. Sensing that there is something very significant about the new relational technology and DB2 in particular, organizations have been taking a hard new look at data resource management. In the process, the concept of shared or integrated data has been revitalized. Organizations also began to feel more comfortable with multiple data management facilities that suit different purposes.

The third area of impact has been more subtle. From an industry perspective, DB2 is the first outward sign that IBM as a corporation intended to view software as a very strategic element. This reflects relatively sweeping changes in the way that IBM develops and then markets its software products."

Newsletter: "For practical purposes, one might say that the relational model is now essentially a done deal."

Hessinger: ". . . relational isn't really a done deal at this point in time. Although its an accepted concept, I estimate we've only seen the initial 15% of its ultimate impact as a database platform."



The relational database stores data in flat files or two dimensional tables as illustrated in Figure 4.7.

FIGURE 4.7 *Relational Database Model*

CUSTOMER Relation

| Customer-Number | Customer-Name | Customer-Address |
|---|---|---|
| 103 | Frank's Fruit House | 6620 F Street |
| 162 | Corporate Diversified, Inc. | 8805 Indians Hills Dr. |
| 204 | DeCoppia Sporting Goods | 970 South 72nd |
| 096 | Cassem, Tierney & Adams | 800 American Center |

It does not use pointers like the hierarchical and network database models to point to related records; instead it uses a data element to perform the cross reference function. This is illustrated in Figure 4.8.

FIGURE 4.8

*Cross-Reference Function in a Relational Database*

CUSTOMER Relation

| Customer-Number | Customer-Name | Customer-Address |
|---|---|---|
| 103 | Frank's Fruit House | 6620 F Street |
| 162 | Corporate Diversified, Inc. | 8805 Indians Hills Dr. |
| 204 | DeCoppia Sporting Goods | 970 South 72nd |
| 096 | Cassem, Tierney & Adams | 800 American Center |

ORDER Relation

| Order-Number | Order-Date | Order-Total | Customer-Number |
|---|---|---|---|
| 0634 | 10/08/87 | 69.95 | 103 |
| 0972 | 01/19/88 | 2069.50 | 103 |
| 0773 | 11/23/87 | 15.00 | 096 |
| 0692 | 2/04/88 | 565.00 | 204 |

The data element, CUSTOMER-NUMBER, appears in the order record. This answers the question, "Which customer placed this order?" It ties the two related tables together.

A relational database permits a high degree of data independence. This allows a user to access data without knowing the structure of the data. It also permits automatic navigation which allows a user to access data a set of records at a time, as opposed to the customary record at a time access in a file processing environment. This feature will be illustrated with query language commands.

Data stored in relational flat files allows users to utilize powerful commands (relational operators) to combine files, and select specific columns or rows from these files. These operators are known as SELECT, PROJECT, and JOIN.

The relational SELECT operator retrieves selected rows from a table. The selection criteria is a logical statement which is either true or false. If true a record is selected. A SELECT command displays just selected rows but all columns from a table. This is illustrated in Figure 4.9.

FIGURE 4.9

*Example of a Relational Algebra Select*

SELECT ORDER WHERE CUSTOMER-NUMBER = '103'
GIVING RESULT

ORDER Relation

| Order-Number | Order-Date | Order-Total | Customer-Number |
|---|---|---|---|
| 0634 | 10/08/87 | 69.95 | 103 |
| 0972 | 01/19/88 | 2069.50 | 103 |
| 0773 | 11/23/87 | 15.00 | 096 |
| 0692 | 2/04/88 | 565.00 | 204 |

Specified Records (rows 0634 and 0972)

RESULT Relation

| Order-Number | Order-Date | Order-Total | Customer-Number |
|---|---|---|---|
| 0634 | 10/08/87 | 69.95 | 103 |
| 0972 | 01/19/88 | 2069.50 | 103 |

A relational PROJECT operator retrieves all rows but only selected columns from a table. This command is illustrated in Figure 4.10. A PROJECT command can be combined with a SELECT command to give both a horizontal and vertical subset of a table.

The relational JOIN operator is the most powerful of the three commands. It joins two or more tables together. This command conditionally joins two records from two different tables when the join variable from the two tables matches. The result is a new table which contains information common to both of the parent tables. This is illustrated in Figure 4.11.

The relational flat files permits end users to browse and query the database using powerful query languages. Illustrated in Figure 4.12

FIGURE 4.10

*Example of a Relational PROJECT*

Project Order Over (Order-number And Order-total)
Giving Result

ORDER Relation

Specified Attributes

| Order-Number | Order-Date | Order-Total | Customer-Number |
|---|---|---|---|
| 0634 | 10/08/87 | 69.95 | 103 |
| 0972 | 01/19/88 | 2069.50 | 103 |
| 0773 | 11/23/87 | 15.00 | 096 |
| 0692 | 2/04/88 | 565.00 | 204 |

RESULT Relation

| Order-Number | Order-Total |
|---|---|
| 0634 | 69.95 |
| 0972 | 2069.50 |
| 0773 | 15.00 |
| 0692 | 565.00 |

are end user queries using SQL, a language developed by IBM. This implementation of a query language does not use the operators SELECT, PROJECT, and JOIN, but the illustration shows these capabilities. The select command in SQL has a broader meaning than the relational operator SELECT. The select command in SQL means retrieve.

## Database Terminology

DATABASE HAS ITS OWN TERMINOLOGY OR JARGON. SOME OF these terms are as follows:

ENTITY - An entity is an underlying object or event about which an organization stores data. Examples of entities are customer, order, employee, and pay period.

PRIMARY KEY - A data item which identifies an instance of an entity (e.g., CUST-NMBR, ORDER_NMBR, and EMPL-NMBR).

FIGURE 4.11 *Example of a Relational JOIN*

CUSTOMER Relation

| Customer-Number | Customer-Name | Customer-Address |
|---|---|---|
| 103 | Frank's Fruit House | 6620 F Street |
| 162 | Corporate Diversified, Inc. | 8805 Indians Hills Dr. |
| 204 | DeCoppia Sporting Goods | 970 South 72nd |
| 096 | Cassem, Tierney & Adams | 800 American Center |

ORDER Relation

| Order-Number | Order-Date | Order-Total | Customer-Number |
|---|---|---|---|
| 0634 | 10/08/87 | 69.95 | 103 |
| 0972 | 01/19/88 | 2069.50 | 103 |
| 0773 | 11/23/87 | 15.00 | 096 |
| 0692 | 2/04/88 | 565.00 | 204 |

RESULT Relation

| Customer-Number | Customer-Name | Customer-Address | Order-Number | Order-Date | Order-Total |
|---|---|---|---|---|---|
| 103 | Frank's Fruit House | 6620 F Street | 0634 | 10/08/87 | 69.95 |
| 103 | Frank's Fruit House | 6620 F Street | 0972 | 01/19/88 | 2069.50 |
| 204 | DeCoppia Sporting Goods | 970 South 72nd | 0773 | 11/23/87 | 15.00 |
| 096 | Cassem, Tierney & Adams | 800 American Center | 0692 | 2/04/88 | 565.00 |

FIGURE 4.12 *The SELECT Command in SQL*

```
SELECT   SNAME, MAJOR, GPA
FROM     STUDENT

SELECT   SNAME, GPA
FROM     STUDENT
WHERE    MAJOR = 'ACC'
```

ATTRIBUTE - An attribute is a data item which is a characteristic of an entity. For example, customer-name, and customer-address are attributes of customers. A primary key and a set of attributes comprise a data item group. These three terms are illustrated in Figure 4.13.

FIGURE 4.13 *Database Terminology*

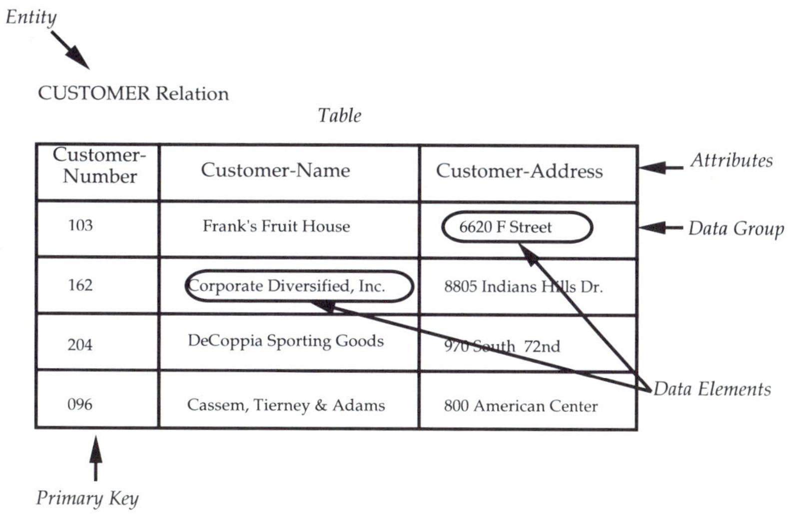


In some cases, there are multiple database terms with essentially the same meaning. For this reason we will present a table of database synonyms. The first column represents a term which is used in this text and the remaining columns are synonyms.

TABLE 4.1 *Database Synonyms*

| TERM | SYNONYMS |
|---|---|
| Table | File, Relation |
| Data Group | Record, Tuple, Segment |
| Data Element | Data Item, Field |
| Logical User View | Subschema, Application View |

## TABLE

A table represents a collection of data concerning an object or event about which an organization stores data. If a table, for example, contained data about orders, then each row would represent an individual order. Each column of the table would represent a characteristic or an attribute of the order such as order date.

### DATA GROUP

A group of logically related data elements which are treated as a group by an application program. Data groups are often referred to as records. A data group consists of a primary key and other data items which are dependent upon the key. Dependency is determined by a relationship in which the value of the key identifies one and only one value of the other data elements. For example, student number is associated with a single value of a student-name.

### DATA ELEMENT

A data element is the smallest unit of data in a database environment. It is synonymous with data item or field.

### LOGICAL USER VIEW

A user's or programmer's perception of a data item group or groups of data items required for a specific application. This term is explained in greater detail in the supplement to Chapter 5.

## Performance Issues in Relational Database Management Systems

RELATIONAL DATABASE MANAGEMENT SYSTEMS HAVE BEEN maligned for performance in on-line transaction processing (OLTP) applications such as airline reservation systems and automatic teller machine (ATM) networks in banking. Recent improvements in RDBMS performance and new technical developments such as database machines have combined to produce more application opportunities for RDBMSs in OLTP applications.

Although most RDBMSs still cannot compete with hierarchical DBMS products in terms of pure speed, many firms have come to realize that transactions per second is less important than transactions per dollar. The RDBMS may not be faster but it will be cheaper.

The savings comes from the flexibility that the relational model offers. The result is that a relational database application is faster and less costly to develop compared with traditional database systems. The maintenance costs of hierarchical systems are so high that an organization can spend more on hardware for a relational system and still save money.[4]

## FILE PROCESSING VERSUS DATABASE

Applications with very high transaction processing volumes may not be candidates for relational database implementation for performance reasons. Relational DBMS applications will execute less efficiently than file based applications as a general rule. The overhead of the DBMS requires more execution time. However, performance of DBMSs have improved dramatically in the past few years and further improvements are expected. One possible solution to high volume OLTP applications is the database machine.

## DATABASE MACHINES

Relational database management systems are very powerful but consume up to 50% of the resources of a host computer. The result may be a performance problem in applications with high transaction volumes. The mainframe becomes bogged down with the overhead of the DBMS software.

Several years ago mainframes were relieved of the complex task of controlling communications. The solution was a front-end processor which was given the task of terminal control. Now a group of firms have developed a similar concept for database functions. This concept is referred to as a database machine.

A database machine is a specialized computer which is designed to perform the DBMS functions normally performed by software. The database machine is the functional equivalent of the database manager. It is sometimes referred to as a back-end processor.

The ability of database machines to handle high transaction volumes is indicated by the positive reviews they have received from users such as Citibank which has peak transaction volumes on its ATM network of 120 to 150 transactions per second.[5] For a relational database management system to function credibly in this environment is impressive.

Another benefit of the database machine approach is that database machine processing power is currently significantly less expensive than equivalent MIPS (millions of instructions/second) purchased for a mainframe.[6] The Teradata database machine is the first commercial implementation of parallel processing using the Intel 80286 Microprocessor. This database machine consists of multiple microprocessors working in parallel, each connected to its own disk storage unit. If additional processing power is desired, additional modules can be added up to 1024 processors.[7]

One of the most impressive advantages of some database machines is their connectivity. Database machines can serve more than one processor. They, in effect, provide a connection between a variety of processors in a heterogeneous computer environment. An example of this is shown in Figure 4.14.

FIGURE 4.14

*Database Machine Configuration*

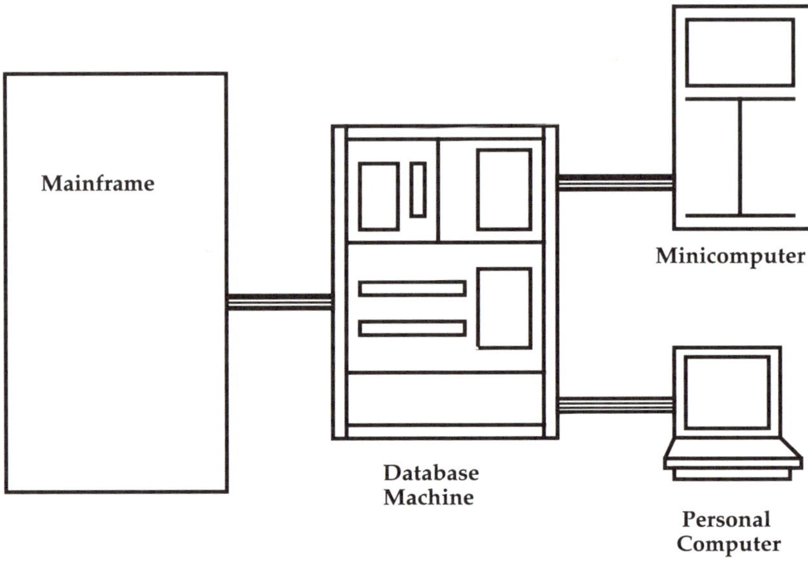


Most of the disadvantages of database machines are related to their immaturity. Currently they lack some of the components of an integrated database management system. Specifically they tend to lack data dictionaries and other application development tools. This should be a temporary condition as software vendors develop packages to interface with database machines.

Another disadvantage of database machines is that they are a specialized processor. They are not suitable for any type of computing other than database processing.

There are in addition several factors that limit the growth of database machines. These are: (1) the performance improvements in conventional systems, (2) the reluctance of mainframe vendors to build database machines which would compete with their established and profitable products,[8] and (3) the reluctance of MIS managers to buy a new technology from a less established vendor.

## Alternative Relational DBMS Architectures

THE WIDESPREAD USE OF RELATIONAL TECHNOLOGY FOR NEW applications has changed the debate in DBMS circles. As the arguments for Network vs. Relational DBMS die down the differences between relational architectures are beginning to surface.

Jeff Tash of Database Decisions, Inc. has identified three relational architectures: process, server, and memory linked. A process architecture is one in which the application and the DBMS both reside on the host computer. IBM's DB2 is a good example of a process architecture.

A server architecture can be identified by the separation of the application and the DBMS each running on separate processors. Separating the application from the DBMS allows typically faster performance for server architectures in transaction processing applications.[9] Some authorities believe the server model will become the dominant architecture in information processing not only for performance reasons but because it offers a clean separation of applications from the DBMS.

A server architecture would typically link computers running applications to a server by means of a local area network (LAN). A server could be a mainframe, mini, microcomputer or a database machine. The microcomputer's cost/performance advantages make it an ideal choice for running applications in a server architecture.

The third alternative for relational DBMS architecture is memory-linked architecture has both the application and the DBMS occupy the same memory space. This saves the operating system from the overhead task of linking an application to a DBMS. This approach has been followed by IDMS/SQL and InterBase.

## Workstation DBMS Directions

PERSONAL COMPUTER DATABASE PRODUCTS HAVE MATURED TO a point where they must choose a specialty area. Three distinct alternatives are emerging.

Many of the products created specifically for personal computers are beginning to concentrate on the user interface. They are called *front-end* products. Those which concentrate on database functions are *back-end* products. These products are designed to function as a database server. A third grouping are those products which try to do it all.

These three categories might be further identified as front-end tools, back-end "engines", and a middle ground which combines tools and engines. The third category is satisfactory for an average video store, with a standalone version of a popular PC database product, but it is not satisfactory for a major bank.

Many vendors have recognized that PCs have grown into workstations and are trying to enlarge the scale of applications for which their product can be used. Existing PC database products lacked the data integrity, security and concurrent access controls that are considered necessary for heavy duty computing.

The result has been the development of database server products designed to work in a network of workstations. These products anticipate that applications will be developed and executed on workstations linked to a server. The applications will be developed using front-end tools.[10]

## Additional Benefits of a Database Environment

### INTERFACE FOR DECISION SUPPORT AND END-USER COMPUTING

One of the hidden benefits of a database environment is how it facilitates decision support systems and end-user computing. With a DBMS in place, end-users can access transaction data without assistance from information systems professionals by using query languages.

Currently many end-users are dependent upon computer professionals or the periodic reports generated by the transaction processing system to obtain the data they need for analysis. Adding to their frustration is the fact that they must re-enter the data into their personal computer.

Ideally, end-users can extract the data they need from a transaction processing database and store the result on their personal computer. Data can be accessed by knowing *what* is desired without having to know the details of *where* and *how* the data is stored. This makes the end-user independent and able to obtain the inputs required for decision support applications.

This ideal may not always be practical because it puts end-users in the position of competing with high priority transaction processing applications. Many information systems managers would cringe at the thought of unsophisticated end-users tying up the mainframe with complex queries. Still it may be possible to provide entirely satisfactory compromises. One alternative is to periodically copy the database onto another machine available to end-users. In other firms with moderate transaction volumes, well trained end-users would pose no threat to transaction processing applications.

A Data Base Management System is a vehicle for integrating transaction processing and decision support applications. It makes data readily accessible in machine readable form to end users. A relational database acquisition is a strategic decision. It provides a framework for supporting end-user computing and information resource management.

## Costs of Database Management Systems

THE COSTS OF DATABASE MANAGEMENT SYSTEM SOFTWARE ARE significant. The costs will range from a few hundred dollars for a personal computer DBMS to approximately one half million dollars for software for large mainframes.

The costs of data modeling are also not insignificant. Database design takes considerable time and the effort of experienced data base professionals. This time and effort will be compounded if the database analysts are forced to start from ground zero. Firms anticipating a switch to database can reduce the conversion time and expense by starting with data administration and a data dictionary prior to the actual change.

Conversion costs are the costs associated with conversion from file processing to database or from one database to another. Conversion costs include not only start up data-modeling costs, but the costs of purchasing or developing software to copy data from one environment to another. Conversion from Hierarchical Data Bases to Relational are more difficult than from a file processing to a Relational database environment.

Training costs include costs for both computer professionals and end-users. Most computer professionals will require training to learn a new technology. End-users need to learn the fundamentals of a query language and how to access the database.

## Keys to Success With Database

### SELECTION OF DBMS SOFTWARE

What should be the criteria for selecting DBMS software?

The primary purpose of moving to a database environment is faster application development, a high degree of flexibility, and low maintenance costs. Consistent with these advantages, improved productivity in application development ought to be the prime criteria for DBMS selection

### DATA MODELING AND DATA ADMINISTRATION

A key to success with database is a recognition that products (hardware and software) do not insure a satisfying outcome; success comes from how these products are used. If an organization implements its old applications in a database environment without bothering with data modeling or data administration, it will probably not realize the benefits of the database approach. There is a human tendency to perpetuate old methodologies with new technologies. New technologies usually require new methodologies.

Many of the causes of failure with new technology cannot be blamed on the products (technology). These problems are political, organizational and managerial in origin. To expect technology to solve these problems is unrealistic.

The difficulty is that changes in technology are often easier to achieve than changes in human behavior. Changes in hardware or software can be accomplished faster than changing the way people perform their jobs. Changing the method in which a human being does his work requires persuasion, communication, and showing a need. These efforts require time and commitment.

The installation of a DBMS and a data dictionary is not an end in and of itself, but rather a means to an end. The objective is to obtain the benefits of the database approach discussed at the beginning of the Chapter. These benefits will not be realized without data modeling and data administration. The objective of data modeling and data administration is to create a database that will allow uniform and consistent access. Consistency and standardization of data is a must in a database environment.

## TOP MANAGEMENT INVOLVEMENT

The changes made as a result of shifting to a database environment are pervasive. James Martin suggests it must also involve a change in management.[11] No longer can managers abdicate responsibility for information systems. The problems experienced in many organizations are not the result of inadequate budgets or outdated technology rather these stem from a lack of consensus on long term objectives, and the limited vision of technical personnel. Managers are responsible for how technology is used to contribute to the goals of the firm. The future information needs of the enterprise should be described in policies that include considerations such as the timeliness, accuracy, accessability, and security of information.

Top management involvement is required to insure that the database approach, which is often slow to get off the ground, is not killed in its early stages. The disadvantages of the status quo are often forgotten in the turmoil of change. Management commitment is required to stay the course.

The requirement that database embodies not only new technology but new methodology is bound to meet with political opposition from those more secure with old technologies and methodologies. Change is threatening to those whose skills and knowledge are rendered obsolete. This requires a firm but sympathetic signal from management that it is committed to database technology.

The failure to recognize the strategic value of relational technology has limited its success. Successful implementation requires a reexamination of MIS roles. A need also exists for training within the organization extending upward through management and downward through the MIS department as well.

## Emerging Computing Environment

THE EMERGING COMPUTING ENVIRONMENT IS DATABASE PROCESSING. Modern database management systems have powerful application generators associated with them that provide much faster applications development than high level languages such as COBOL. DBMS query languages and application generators have caused many firms to rethink their software development methods giving greater emphasis to prototyping and user based computing. A DBMS makes it possible for end users to browse and query a database without professional help. The emerging computing environment is shown in Figure 4.15.

FIGURE 4.15

*Emerging Computing Environment*

| | COMPONENT | CHARACTERISTICS |
|---|---|---|
| Mode of Processing | Database Processing | Flexibility - Adaptive to Change<br>Data Accessibility<br>Data Independence |
| Programming Language | 4th Generation Languages/ CASE Tools | High Level of Programmer/ Application Developer Productivity |
| Dpplication Development Methodology | Prototyping | Fast Application Development |

| OBJECTIVES |
|---|
| Ad Hoc Inquiries by End Users |
| Elimination of Application Backlog |
| Decision Support Applications Receive Greater Emphasis |
| Greater User Involvement and Satisfaction |
| Improved Programmer Productivity |
| Faster Application Development<br>mproved Software Quality |

This computing environment has been described as an information engineering computing environment. It has several dimensions that will be described in the following chapters, including:

1. A relational database management system
2. Data administration
3. Data modeling
4. Prototyping
5. Information engineering
6. Information centers
7. Information resource management (IRM)

This list includes both technology and methodology. These developments give greater emphasis to end users and their concerns. Information systems professionals will find it profitable to facilitate the end-user revolution.

## Guidelines for Managers

DATABASE TECHNOLOGY HAS GREAT PROMISE FOR SOLVING THE problems that have plagued information systems departments. This technology has the potential to improve the productivity of the information systems department staff, is more flexible in accommodating change and makes data more accessible to the end-user.

Database technology, however, represents change. Specifically, it will require new methodologies like prototyping for software development. Getting people to change how they work will require extensive training, and consistent top management support. The political barriers and organizational inertia that must be overcome to implement database technology are formidable.

## Guidelines for MIS Professionals

MIS PROFESSIONALS MUST RECOGNIZE THAT END-USERS AND top management have valid concerns when they complain of application backlogs. It may be that the difficulties that many MIS departments are experiencing are not due to poor management or incompetence but are indicative of "the nature of the beast." Current file processing technology and the related software development methodologies are relatively inflexible and makes software development very slow.

MIS professionals will have to learn new skills and new methodologies if they are to succeed with database. These new skills, coupled with new methodologies and an improved technology, should allow information systems professionals to develop applications more quickly and with less resources than conventional file processing technology or older database models.

## Key Terms

| | |
|---|---|
| Data Integrity | Database Management System (DBMS) |
| Data Independence | Data Security |
| Query Language | Report Generator |
| Application Generator | Graphics Language |
| Intergrated Data Dictionary | Passive Data Dictionary |
| Database Manager | Hierarchical Database Model |
| Network Database Model | Relational Database Model |

| | |
|---|---|
| Automatic Navigation | PROJECT |
| SELECT | JOIN |
| Entity | Primary Key |
| Attribute | Table |
| Data Group | Data Element |
| Logical User View | Sequential File Organization |
| Indexed Sequential File Organization | Direct File Organization |
| Database Machines | |

## Review Questions

1. Explain why data independence is such an important concept in database processing.
2. Name the two sources of productivity improvements in a database environment.
3. Discuss a method of resolving the conflict between the data independence ideal and the risk of tying up the CPU with complex searches.
4. Discuss several reasons for a integrated data dictionary
5. Compare and contrast a hierarchical, network and relational database model.
6. What are the advantages and disadvantages of a database machine?
7. What is the major criteria for selecting DBMS software?
8. Give at least one synonym for the following terms:
   a. Data Element
   b. Data Group
   c. Table
   d. Logical User View
9. Prepare a table showing the major advantages of each of the following file access methods:
   a. Sequential
   b. Indexed Sequential
   c. Direct or Hashed
10. Many commercial data processing products claim to use the relational data model. What criteria would you apply to evaluate such a claim? That is, what characteristics must the product

**Case Study**

## THE CITY OF LINCOLN

The City of Lincoln, Nebraska, is an enthusiastic user of DB2, a relational database, and SQL, a query language. The city, a midwestern city of about 200,000 citizens, is a state capitol and university community.

The selection of DB2 grew out of a decision to employ an outside firm to manage its computer facilities and staff. The facilities management firm, eager to make a favorable impression, pushed the city to adopt DB2.

The original applications built were personnel and financial applications. The original file based applications were converted to database applications. To support end-user queries a number of views and queries were developed to allow end-users to access data directly without assistance from the MIS department. End-users were also given training on QBE and SQL. Query By Example (QBE) is a tabular query system which some end-users find easier to use than SQL.

The finance and personnel departments became enthusiastic advocates of the capabilities of the new system. Several other departments desired to have similar capabilities including the fire, water, public defender, county court, and the area agency on aging.

The fire department has 75-100 pre-specified queries and a graphic display capability which allows it to determine what types of activities it responds to, during what times of day, and at what locations. Answers to these questions and others can be obtained in a manner of minutes.

The MIS department activity encourages end-users to use the query capabilities and assists them in formulating difficult queries. The impact on the performance of the computer has been minimal with no significant performance problems due to queries interfering with production applications.

Randy Ober, the database administrator, indicates that most database applications are written in COBOL with embedded SQL. The staff normalizes each application on a project by project basis but no effort has been made to build an overall data structure.

The programming staff have learned to use SQL and according to Ober use it in testing software. He believes there has been a significant improvement in productivity by the programming staff in developing applications in a relational environment but is unable to say how much.

1. What benefits of database are evident in the City of Lincoln?
2. Is Lincoln using a supermarket or recipe approach to database design?
3. How was the decision to select DB2 different in the city of Lincoln from the typical firm?

*Supplement*

# SQL - Structured Query Language

*"SQL is like playing chess. You can learn all the basic moves in half an hour. But it takes practice for the rest of your life to become any good."*

*George Schussel*

## Introduction

SQL IS AN ACRONYM FOR STRUCTURED QUERY LANGUAGE. Many users refer to it by its former name, Sequel. SQL has emerged as the *de facto* standard for query languages. Now, with its success in the marketplace, it has become a standard adhered to by all the major database vendors and the basis for an American National Standards Institute (ANSI) relational standard called RDL.

## SQL Commands

THERE ARE THREE BASIC SQL COMMANDS. THESE ARE USED AS follows:

| | |
|---|---|
| SELECT | Retrieves data from a table |
| CREATE | Defines a database table |
| INSERT | Enter a data row into a table |

### THE SELECT COMMAND

The SELECT command lets the end-user retrieve data from one or more tables. The SQL SELECT command is used to implement the three relational operators discussed in chapter four — Select, Project, and Join.

There are three basic SQL clauses: SELECT, FROM, and WHERE.

- SELECT - The select clause is used to list the data items to be retrieved.
- FROM - specifies the table, tables, or view from which retrieval is to be done.
- WHERE - specifies the conditions which must be satisfied.

The SQL SELECT command **must** contain a least two parts:

1. A SELECT clause
2. A FROM clause

The following query retrieves specified columns in the student table.

FIGURE S4.1

*Retrieve Specified Columns From Student Table*

```
SELECT SNUMBER, NAME, MAJOR, GPA
FROM STUDENT;
```

| SNUMBER | NAME | MAJOR | GPA |
|---|---|---|---|
| 134514455 | Thomas J. Mixan | Economics | 2.62 |
| 123423465 | Jerry L. Hassett | MIS | 2.44 |
| 213434563 | Susan L. Douglas | Psychology | 3.45 |

| SNUMBER | NAME | MAJOR | GPA |
|---|---|---|---|
| 591298541 | Eden K. Cohn | Biology | 3.89 |
| 543929954 | Chris G. Otwell | Foreign Language | 3.28 |
| 203398521 | Bill T. Zadick | Physical Education | 1.56 |
| 391394941 | William Y. Vala | MIS | 3.52 |
| 593929301 | Gregory D. Suing | EET | 3.59 |
| 490399301 | Tammy C. Pietz | Home Economics | 2.03 |
| 531009384 | Jeff L. Henninger | MIS | 3.61 |
| 111223334 | James F. McGovern | Computer Science | 2.98 |
| 111111111 | Linda D. Schiessler | Computer Science | 3.15 |
| 119444511 | Ron J. Mahoney | Computer Science | 2.80 |
| 112726343 | Greg M. Ostravich | Computer Science | 3.32 |
| 450925445 | Joyce C. Crockett | Sociology | 3.85 |
| 303125668 | Randall J. Mendenhall | Computer Science | 3.97 |
| 512345690 | Bonnie F. Fink | MIS | 3.50 |
| 113497321 | Rae M. Dyer | MIS | 3.94 |
| 213414565 | Maureen L. Pritchard | MIS | 3.62 |
| 212444598 | Mary C. Cupich | MIS | 3.51 |
| 209384890 | Jane M. McLendon | MIS | 3.83 |

21 records selected.

The command specifies that data elements — student number, name, major and grade point average are to be retrieved from a table named student. Note that commas are used to separate data element names.

SQL commands can be in free format — they can be entered on one line or several, but they must be terminated with a semicolon. SQL permits the use of a wild card or asterisk if all columns in a table are to be printed. The following query retrieves all columns from the student table using the asterisk specification.

FIGURE S4.2

*The Asterisk Spe cification*

```
SELECT *
FROM STUDENT;
```

| SNUMBER | NAME | MAJOR | GPA |
|---|---|---|---|
| 134514455 | Thomas J. Mixan | Economics | 2.62 |
| 123423465 | Jerry L. Hassett | MIS | 2.44 |
| 213434563 | Susan L. Douglas | Psychology | 3.45 |
| 591298541 | Eden K. Cohn | Biology | 3.89 |
| 543929954 | Chris G. Otwell | Foreign Language | 3.28 |
| 203398521 | Bill T. Zadick | Physical Education | 1.56 |
| 391394941 | William Y. Vala | MIS | 3.52 |
| 593929301 | Gregory D. Suing | EET | 3.59 |
| 490399301 | Tammy C. Pietz | Home Economics | 2.03 |

| SNUMBER | NAME | MAJOR | GPA |
|---|---|---|---|
| 531009384 | Jeff L. Henninger | MIS | 3.61 |
| 111223334 | James F. McGovern | Computer Science | 2.98 |
| 111111111 | Linda D. Schiessler | Computer Science | 3.15 |
| 119444511 | Ron J. Mahoney | Computer Science | 2.80 |
| 112726343 | Greg M. Ostravich | Computer Science | 3.32 |
| 450925445 | Joyce C. Crockett | Sociology | 3.85 |
| 303125668 | Randall J. Mendenhall | Computer Science | 3.97 |
| 512345690 | Bonnie F. Fink | MIS | 3.50 |
| 113497321 | Rae M. Dyer | MIS | 3.94 |
| 213414565 | Maureen L. Pritchard | MIS | 3.62 |
| 212444598 | Mary C. Cupich | MIS | 3.51 |
| 209384890 | Jane M. McLendon | MIS | 3.83 |

21 records selected.

Specific columns from a table (a relational project) can be retrieved by naming only the data items desired. The following query retrieves only selected columns from the student table.

FIGURE S4.3
*Retrieve Selected Columns from Student Table*

```
SELECT NAME, GPA
FROM STUDENT;
```

| NAME | GPA |
|---|---|
| Thomas J. Mixan | 2.62 |
| Jerry L. Hassett | 2.44 |
| Susan L. Douglas | 3.45 |
| Eden K. Cohn | 3.89 |
| Chris G. Otwell | 3.28 |
| Bill T. Zadick | 1.56 |
| William Y. Vala | 3.52 |
| Gregory D. Suing | 3.59 |
| Tammy C. Pietz | 2.03 |
| Jeff L. Henninger | 3.61 |
| James F. McGovern | 2.98 |
| Linda D. Schiessler | 3.15 |
| Ron J. Mahoney | 2.80 |
| Greg M. Ostravich | 3.32 |
| Joyce C. Crockett | 3.85 |
| Randall J. Mendenhall | 3.97 |
| Bonnie F. Fink | 3.50 |
| Rae M. Dyer | 3.94 |
| Maureen L. Pritchard | 3.62 |
| Mary C. Cupich | 3.51 |
| Jane M. McLendon | 3.83 |

21 records selected.

The order of data items printed can be controlled by listing the data items in the order desired.

CONDITIONAL SELECTION OF ROWS: The WHERE clause allows you to specify a condition which determines if a particular set of row values should be displayed. The condition is specified in the WHERE clause as shown in the following query which retrieves a list of students with a GPA greater than 3.5.

FIGURE S4.4

*The Where Clause*

```
SELECT *
FROM STUDENT
WHERE GPA > 3.5;
```

| SNUMBER | NAME | MAJOR | GPA |
|---|---|---|---|
| 591298541 | Eden K. Cohn | Biology | 3.89 |
| 391394941 | William Y. Vala | MIS | 3.52 |
| 593929301 | Gregory D. Suing | EET | 3.59 |
| 531009384 | Jeff L. Henninger | MIS | 3.61 |
| 450925445 | Joyce C. Crockett | Sociology | 3.85 |
| 303125668 | Randall J. Mendenhall | Computer Science | 3.97 |
| 113497321 | Rae M. Dyer | MIS | 3.94 |
| 213414565 | Maureen L. Pritchard | MIS | 3.62 |
| 212444598 | Mary C. Cupich | MIS | 3.51 |
| 209384890 | Jane M. McLendon | MIS | 3.83 |

10 records selected.

The WHERE clause is a logical expression which is compared to each row in the table. If the expression is true the row is displayed, if false it is not selected. The WHERE clause has the general format as shown below:

| | | | |
|---|---|---|---|
| WHERE | GPA | > | 3.5 |
| WHERE | data element name | logical operator | constant |

The value of the constant can be either numeric or character as shown below in the following query which will retrieve a list of students who are majoring in MIS.

FIGURE S4.5

*Retrieve a List of Studens majoring in MIS*

```
SELECT *
FROM STUDENT
WHERE MAJOR = 'MIS';
```

| SNUMBER | NAME | MAJOR | GPA |
|---|---|---|---|
| 391394941 | William Y. Vala | MIS | 3.52 |
| 531009384 | Jeff L. Henninger | MIS | 3.61 |
| 512345690 | Bonnie F. Fink | MIS | 3.50 |
| 113497321 | Rae M. Dyer | MIS | 3.94 |
| 213414565 | Maureen L. Pritchard | MIS | 3.62 |
| 212444598 | Mary C. Cupich | MIS | 3.51 |
| 209384890 | Jane M. McLendon | MIS | 3.83 |
| 123423465 | Jerry L. Hassett | MIS | 2.44 |

8 records selected.

A character constant must be enclosed in single quotes as shown above.

A list of logical or boolean operators is given as follows:

| | |
|---|---|
| = | equal to |
| != | not equal |
| > | greater than |
| < | less than |
| <= | less than or equal to |
| >= | greater than or equal to |

COMPOUND SELECTION: The WHERE clause can be stated as multiple conditions connected by the words AND or OR. Two logical expressions connected by an AND means both must be true for the row to be displayed. This is illustrated in the following query which retrieves a list of MIS majors with grade point averages greater than 3.5.

FIGURE S4.6

*A Compound Selection*

```
SELECT NAME, MAJOR, GPA
FROM STUDENT
WHERE MAJOR = 'MIS'
AND GPA > 3.5;
```

| NAME | MAJOR | GPA |
|---|---|---|
| William Y. Vala | MIS | 3.52 |
| Jeff L. Henninger | MIS | 3.61 |
| Rae M. Dyer | MIS | 3.94 |
| Maureen L. Pritchard | MIS | 3.62 |
| Mary C. Cupich | MIS | 3.51 |
| Jane M. McLendon | MIS | 3.83 |

6 records selected.

The use of OR in a WHERE clause means that a row is displayed if either condition is satisfied. This is illustrated in the following query which retrieves a list of students with a major in either MIS or Computer Science.

FIGURE S4.7
*The Use of OR in a WHERE Clause*

```
SELECT SNUMBER, NAME, MAJOR, GPA
FROM STUDENT
WHERE MAJOR = 'MIS'
OR    MAJOR = 'COMPUTER SCIENCE';
```

| NAME | MAJOR | GPA |
|---|---|---|
| William Y. Vala | MIS | 3.52 |
| Jeff L. Henninger | MIS | 3.61 |
| James F. McGovern | Computer Science | 2.98 |
| Linda D. Schiessler | Computer Science | 3.15 |
| Ron J. Mahoney | Computer Science | 2.80 |
| Greg M. Ostravich | Computer Science | 3.32 |
| Randall J. Mendenhall | Computer Science | 3.97 |
| Bonnie F. Fink | MIS | 3.50 |
| Rae M. Dyer | MIS | 3.94 |
| Maureen L. Pritchard | MIS | 3.62 |
| Mary C. Cupich | MIS | 3.51 |
| Jane M. McLendon | MIS | 3.83 |
| Jerry L. Hassett | MIS | 2.44 |
| Tim Grotheer | Computer Science | 3.15 |

14 records selected.

Both AND or OR may be used in the same WHERE clause to select rows., This is shown in the following query which retrieves a student if the student is majoring in either Computer Science or MIS and has a GPA > 3.5.

FIGURE S4.8
*The Use of Both AND and OR in the WHERE Clause*

```
SELECT NAME, MAJOR, GPA
FROM STUDENT
WHERE MAJOR = 'MIS' OR MAJOR = 'COMPUTER SCIENCE'
AND GPA > 3.5;
```

| NAME | MAJOR | GPA |
|---|---|---|
| William Y. Vala | MIS | 3.52 |
| Jeff L. Henninger | MIS | 3.61 |
| Randall J. Mendenhall | Computer Science | 3.97 |

| NAME | MAJOR | GPA |
|---|---|---|
| Bonnie F. Fink | MIS | 3.50 |
| Rae M. Dyer | MIS | 3.94 |
| Maureen L. Pritchard | MIS | 3.62 |
| Mary C. Cupich | MIS | 3.51 |
| Jane M. McLendon | MIS | 3.83 |
| Tim Grotheer | Computer Science | 3.15 |

9 records selected.

Parentheses are used to group logical expressions in a desired sequence. In the following query, the use of parentheses changes the meaning of the WHERE clause. This query will retrieve a student if the student is majoring in Computer Science or if the student is majoring in MIS and has a GPA greater than 3.5.

FIGURE S4.9

*The Use of Parentheses in the WHERE Clause*

```
SELECT NAME, MAJOR, GPA
FROM STUDENT
WHERE MAJOR = 'Computer Science' OR (MAJOR = 'MIS' AND
GPA > 3.5);
```

| NAME | MAJOR | GPA |
|---|---|---|
| William Y. Vala | MIS | 3.52 |
| Jeff L. Henninger | MIS | 3.61 |
| James F. McGovern | Computer Science | 2.98 |
| Linda D. Schiessler | Computer Science | 3.15 |
| Ron J. Mahoney | Computer Science | 2.80 |
| Greg M. Ostravich | Computer Science | 3.32 |
| Randall J. Mendenhall | Computer Science | 3.97 |
| Rae M. Dyer | MIS | 3.94 |
| Maureen L. Pritchard | MIS | 3.62 |
| Mary C. Cupich | MIS | 3.51 |
| Jane M. McLendon | MIS | 3.83 |
| Tim Grotheer | Computer Science | 3.15 |

12 records selected.

A comparison of Figure S4.8 and Figure S4.9 will show the difference in outcomes that are the result of the parentheses.

SELECTION OF ITEMS IN A LIST: The IN operator allows you to select all rows that match items in a list. This feature is shown in the following query which will retrieve all students majoring in Biology, Computer Science or Economics.

FIGURE S4.10

*The IN Operator*

```
SELECT NAME, MAJOR, GPA
FROM STUDENT
WHERE MAJOR IN ('Biology', 'Computer Science',
 'Economics');
```

| NAME | MAJOR | GPA |
|---|---|---|
| Eden K. Cohn | Biology | 3.89 |
| James F. McGovern | Computer Science | 2.98 |
| Linda D. Schiessler | Computer Science | 3.15 |
| Ron J. Mahoney | Computer Science | 2.80 |
| Greg M. Ostravich | Computer Science | 3.32 |
| Randall J. Mendenhall | Computer Science | 3.97 |
| Thomas J. Mixan | Economics | 2.62 |
| Tim Grotheer | Computer Science | 3.15 |

8 records selected.

The NOT operator negates the IN operator by selecting only those rows not in the specified list. This is shown in the following query which will retrieve students not majoring in Biology, Computer Science or Economics.

FIGURE S4.11

*The NOT Operator*

```
SELECT NAME, MAJOR, GPA
FROM STUDENT
WHERE MAJOR NOT IN ('Biology', 'Computer Science', 'Eco-
nomics');
```

| NAME | MAJOR | GPA |
|---|---|---|
| Chris G. Otwell | Foreign Language | 3.28 |
| Bill T. Zadick | Physical Education | 1.56 |
| William Y. Vala | MIS | 3.52 |
| Gregory D. Suing | EET | 3.59 |
| Tammy C. Pietz | Home Economics | 2.03 |
| Jeff L. Henninger | MIS | 3.61 |
| Joyce C. Crockett | Sociology | 3.85 |
| Bonnie F. Fink | MIS | 3.50 |
| Rae M. Dyer | MIS | 3.94 |
| Maureen L. Pritchard | MIS | 3.62 |
| Mary C. Cupich | MIS | 3.51 |
| Jane M. McLendon | MIS | 3.83 |
| Jerry L. Hassett | MIS | 2.44 |
| Susan L. Douglas | Psychology | 3.45 |

14 records selected.

PARTIAL MATCHING OF CHARACTER STRINGS: SQL uses the operator LIKE to perform partial matches on character string data. This is illustrated in the following query which will retrieve students with names starting with the letter J.

FIGURE S4.12
*The LIKE Operator*

```
SELECT NAME, MAJOR, GPA
FROM STUDENT
WHERE NAME LIKE 'J%';
```

| NAME | MAJOR | GPA |
|---|---|---|
| Jeff L. Henninger | MIS | 3.61 |
| James F. McGovern | Computer Science | 2.98 |
| Joyce C. Crockett | Sociology | 3.85 |
| Jane M. McLendon | MIS | 3.83 |
| Jerry L. Hassett | MIS | 2.44 |

5 records selected.

SQL supports two special characters for use with the LIKE operator:

% The percent character indicates a string of characters of unspecified length.

_ The underscore specifies a single character position.

The use of the underscore is illustrated in the following query which will retrieve a student with the first name of "James" and a last name beginning with "Mc".

FIGURE S4.13
*The Use of the Underscore*

```
SELECT NAME, MAJOR, GPA
FROM STUDENT
WHERE NAME LIKE 'James _Mc%';
```

| NAME | MAJOR | GPA |
|---|---|---|
| James F. McGovern | Computer Science | 2.98 |

1 record selected.

SORTING A QUERY: A query may be sorted by SQL with use of the ORDER BY clause. The ORDER BY clause **must** be the last clause in a query. An example of the ORDER BY clause is shown in the fol-loiwng query which will select MIS majors and sort them by GPA.

FIGURE S4.14

*The ORDER BY Clause*

```
SELECT NAME, MAJOR, GPA
FROM STUDENT
WHERE MAJOR = 'MIS'
ORDER BY GPA;
```

| NAME | MAJOR | GPA |
|---|---|---|
| Jerry L. Hassett | MIS | 2.44 |
| Bonnie F. Fink | MIS | 3.50 |
| Mary C. Cupich | MIS | 3.51 |
| William Y. Vala | MIS | 3.52 |
| Jeff L. Henninger | MIS | 3.61 |
| Maureen L. Pritchard | MIS | 3.62 |
| Jane M. McLendon | MIS | 3.83 |
| Rae M. Dyer | MIS | 3.94 |

8 records selected.

Default for the ORDER by clause is ascending order. If a sort in descending order is desired, this can be done as shown in the following query which will retrieve all MIS majors and sort them in descending order by GPA.

FIGURE S4.15

*A Sort in Descending Order*

```
SELECT NAME, MAJOR, GPA
FROM STUDENT
WHERE MAJOR = 'MIS'
ORDER BY GPA DESC;
```

| NAME | MAJOR | GPA |
|---|---|---|
| Rae M. Dyer | MIS | 3.94 |
| Jane M. McLendon | MIS | 3.83 |
| Maureen L. Pritchard | MIS | 3.62 |
| Jeff L. Henninger | MIS | 3.61 |
| William Y. Vala | MIS | 3.52 |
| Mary C. Cupich | MIS | 3.51 |
| Bonnie F. Fink | MIS | 3.50 |
| Jerry L. Hassett | MIS | 2.44 |

8 records selected.

MULTIPLE TABLE QUERIES: Thus far, queries have been limited to data in a single table. The means of accessing data in more than one table with a single query is a **JOIN**. JOIN conceptually creates a new table from two or more existing tables. To be joined, tables must have a column with one or more values in common.

Suppose you want to know the grades of a student named Jeff L. Henninger. The STUDENT table does not have grades but does have names. The SEM_COURSE_STU Table does not have names but has grades. What both tables have in common is student number (SNUMBER). By finding rows in both tables with matching student numbers, a JOIN is performed which combines the information in both tables. Sample data from both tables is shown below:

**STUDENT** Table

| SNUMBER | NAME | MAJOR | GPA |
|---|---|---|---|
| 531009384 | Jeff L. Henninger | MIS | 3.61 |
| 512345690 | Bonnie F. Fink | MIS | 3.50 |

**SEM_COURSE_STU** Table

| SNUMBER | COURSE-ID | GRADE |
|---|---|---|
| 531009384 | DSCI 3110 | A |
| 525906184 | DSCI 4300 | C+ |

A JOIN on these two tables is shown in the following query which will retrieve grades for Jeff Henninger.

FIGURE S4.16
*A JOIN*

```
SELECT STUDENT.SNUMBER, NAME, COURSE_ID, GRADE
FROM STUDENT, SEM_COURSE_STU
WHERE STUDENT.SNUMBER = SEM_COURSE_STU.SNUMBER
AND NAME = 'Jeff L. Henninger';
```

| SNUMBER | NAME | COURSE_ID | GR |
|---|---|---|---|
| 531009384 | Jeff L. Henninger | DSCI-3110 | A |
| 531009384 | Jeff L. Henninger | MOB -4480 | B |
| 531009384 | Jeff L. Henninger | CSCI-3450 | B+ |
| 531009384 | Jeff L. Henninger | DSCI-4300 | A |
| 531009384 | Jeff L. Henninger | DSCI-4170 | A |

5 records selected.

Since both of the two tables have columns named SNUMBER (Student Number) the table names are required in the SQL command to avoid ambiguity. The table name is separated from the column name with a period.

Table names can be abbreviated as shown in the following query which retrieves the grades of computer science majors.

FIGURE S4.17
*The Use of Abbreviated Table Names*

```
SELECT NAME, COURSE_ID, GRADE
FROM STUDENT S, SEM_COURSE_STU SCS
WHERE S.SNUMBER = SCS.SNUMBER
AND MAJOR = 'Computer Science';
```

| NAME | COURSE_ID | GR |
|---|---|---|
| James F. McGovern | MATH-1970 | C+ |
| James F. McGovern | CSCI-1620 | A |
| Linda D. Schiessler | CSCI-1620 | B+ |
| Linda D. Schiessler | CSCI-2300 | B |
| Ron J. Mahoney | CSCI-2300 | B |
| Ron J. Mahoney | CSCI-4350 | C+ |
| Greg M. Ostravich | CSCI-4350 | A |
| Greg M. Ostravich | CSCI-2300 | B+ |
| Greg M. Ostravich | MATH-1970 | B |

9 records selected.

SQL permits the use of a temporary abbreviation by defining the abbreviation in the FROM clause immediately after the table name separated by a space.

GROUP FUNCTIONS: So far the examples used have selected individual rows stored in the database. SQL also computes summary information about groups of rows in a table. There are five group functions that can be used for groups of rows:

AVG - Computes the mean value of a group
SUM - Computes the arithmetic sum of a group
MIN - Determines the minimum value
MAX - Determines the maximum value
COUNT - Counts the number in the group

The use of the AVG function is shown in the following query which computes the average GPA for MIS majors.

FIGURE S4.18
*The AVG Function*

```
SELECT AVG(GPA)
FROM STUDENT
WHERE MAJOR = 'MIS';
```

AVG(GPA)

3.49625

SQL computes the average for the column in parentheses for all rows satisfying the WHERE clause. Note that a single value is displayed.

The previous example computed the GPA for a single major. Suppose you desired the average GPA of several majors. The GROUP BY clause permits this in a single query.

This is shown in the following query which will compute the average GPA by major.

FIGURE S4.19
*The GROUP BY Clause*

```
SELECT MAJOR, AVG(GPA)
FROM STUDENT
GROUP BY MAJOR;
```

| MAJOR | AVG(GPA) |
|---|---|
| Biology | 3.89 |
| Computer Science | 3.22833333 |
| EET | 3.59 |
| Economics | 2.62 |
| Foreign Language | 3.28 |
| Home Economics | 2.03 |
| MIS | 3.49625 |
| Physical Education | 1.56 |
| Psychology | 3.45 |
| Sociology | 3.85 |

10 records selected

The COUNT function can count the number of rows satisfying the WHERE clause or the number of rows in a group by use of the function COUNT(*). The use of this function is illustrated in the following query which will count the number of students and compute the average GPA by major.

FIGURE S4.20
*The COUNT Function*

```
SELECT MAJOR, COUNT(*), AVG(GPA)
FROM STUDENT
GROUP BY MAJOR;
```

| MAJOR | COUNT(*) | AVG(GPA) |
|---|---|---|
| Biology | 1 | 3.89 |
| Computer Science | 6 | 3.22833333 |
| EET | 1 | 3.59 |

| MAJOR | COUNT(*) | AVG(GPA) |
|---|---|---|
| Economics | 1 | 2.62 |
| Foreign Language | 1 | 3.28 |
| Home Economics | 1 | 2.03 |
| MIS | 8 | 3.49625 |
| Physical Education | 1 | 1.56 |
| Psychology | 1 | 3.45 |
| Sociology | 1 | 3.85 |

10 records selected.

## THE CREATE COMMAND

The CREATE TABLE command is used to define a table and must be used prior to inserting data into a table or retrieving data with a SELECT command. The command that created the STUDENT table is shown below in Figure S4.21.

FIGURE S4.21

*The CREATE TABLE Command*

```
CREATE TABLE STUDENT
(SNUMBER CHAR (9), NAME CHAR (20),
MAJOR CHAR (18), GPA NUMBER (4,2));
```

The CREATE TABLE command must specify the table name (STUDENT) and the columns in the table (SNUMBER, NAME, MAJOR, AND GPA). The type and maximum length of the data to be stored in a column is also specified. Data is either numeric (NUMBER) or character (CHAR) which can be numbers, alphabetical and special characters. Decimal positions can be designated as shown for GPA - the field width is 4 positions with two positions to the right of the decimal.

## THE INSERT COMMAND

Data can be inserted into an existing table by use of the INSERT command. The following example shows a row being inserted into the STUDENT table in Figure S4.22.

FIGURE S4.22

*The INSERT Command*

```
INSERT INTO STUDENT (SNUMBER, NAME, MAJOR, GPA)
VALUES (213231287, 'John Young', 'Computer Science', 2.89);
```

The INSERT command requires the table name and data values for each column in the table. Data values are separated by commas. Character values are enclosed in a single quotation.

The INSERT command is limited to a single row at a time. To enter multiple rows of data into a table, most database management systems have either utilities to copy files or programs which create a skeleton of the table and allow the user to fill in the blanks.

## Strengths and Limitations of SQL

C. J. DATE BELIEVES SQL IS DEFICIENT IN THREE MAJOR RE-spects. It lacks support for several relational features, lacks orthogonality, and it is quite redundant. He faults SQL support for primary keys, foreign keys, and referential integrity.[1]

Orthogonality refers to independence. It means language constructs are clearly separated. The advantages of orthogonality are a simple, straightforward structure, and a lack of exceptions or special cases. Redundancy means that all but the most trivial of problems can be expressed in a variety of ways. As a result users are forced to spend time and effort to find which version performs best.

Date is by no means opposed to SQL. His attitude is, "...SQL is great. But it could have been so much better."[2]

There is a growing body of opinion that SQL is not suitable as an end-user language. This view is that SQL will become more important as a software interface than a human interface. SQL will become the standard language for data manipulation, definition, and control.

According to this view SQL generators will become important as application development tools. The advantage of SQL generated applications will be their portability to different hardware and software environments.[3]

SQL is an important tool to access data stored on different database systems and on different computer systems. This is an important advantage as more computers are linked together in networks. In this way SQL aids connectivity.[4]

There are some who believe that SQL is a mixed blessing. Stephen Gerrard is one of these individuals.

## Issues and Controversies

# SQL

**There is a tendency in the DP industry to over-emphasize the benefits of a new technology. Some industry observers are promoting SQL and attributing it with capabilities it does not possess. These observers are not the developers of SQL nor the academicians who made important contributions to its evolution.**

**Some of the proponents are promoting SQL as a quick fix. While SQL has many good qualities it has a "dark side" that will come back to haunt the DP manager who believes it is a cure-all.**

**Some important contributions of SQL are as follows:**

A SOLID THEORETICAL FOUNDATION. **SQL is rooted in a firm footing of mathematical principles. It allows complex queries to be represented in a rigorous fashion.**

STANDARDIZATION. **SQL as emerged as the de facto standard for query languages. This would enhance the portability of applications written in SQL between different hardware and software systems.**

SET AT A TIME PROCESSING. **SQL allows set at a time processing as contrasted with the record at a time processing of conventional high level languages. Non-procedural languages are a great advantage since they allow the user to concentrate on what is desired rather than how it is to be accomplished.**

**The "dark side" of SQL is shown as follows:**

NO CONCEPT OF A PROGRAM. **SQL commands do not constitute a program. Tasks that cannot be addressed by SQL can be solved only by embedding SQL in a high level language.**

PORTABILITY. **While it may be possible to have an SQL application that is portable, applications embedded in other languages would rarely be portable.**

ACADEMIC ORIENTATION. **SQL supports esoteric functions not required by the vast majority of end-users. Its academic rigor makes it less easy to use than competitive products.**

Adapted from Stephen Gerrard, "Standard Query Language: It's a Standard, but is it a Language?", Computerworld, September 22, 1986, pp. 71-81.

# 5

# Data Administration

*"Data administration--An island of discipline in an ocean of disorder."*

*William R. Durell*

## Overview and Objectives

SHARING DATA INCREASES THE IMPORTANCE OF COORDINATING the task of defining and naming data elements, as well as maintaining data security, integrity, and quality. This coordinating function is referred to as "data administration." The functions of the data administrator are described in this chapter.

Query languages increase the accessability of data. This development requires that controls be implemented to limit access to data. These controls are required to protect the privacy of individuals and the security of organizational data.

In this chapter we will also examine the impact of database technology on auditing and the auditor's role.

AFTER READING THIS CHAPTER YOU SHOULD BE ABLE TO:

- Define the role of the data administrator
- Distinguish between data administration and database administration
- Be able to describe database access/update controls
- Distinguish between privacy and security
- Describe some primary objectives in auditing a computer system with a DBMS

## Application versus Information Focus

THE SOFTWARE DEVELOPMENT METHODS OF THE PAST WERE application focused. The application approach focuses on getting applications up and running as quickly as possible. It defines data requirements only within the confines of the application being automated. The long term result is that the same data exists either in different files with different names, or the same name may be used for different data.

Application-focused software development is giving way to an information focus. This approach identifies data that is shared by several applications, gives it a standard name, and stores it in a single location accessible to several applications.

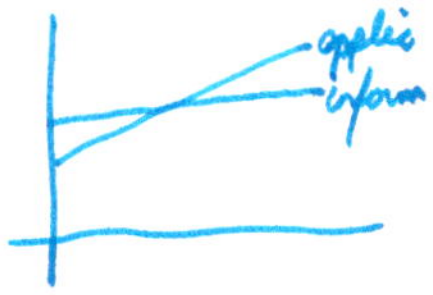

This approach requires more time in the beginning, but applications can be developed more quickly once the foundation is in place. There are several subtle but important differences between an application focus as opposed to an information focus. These differences are summarized in Table 5.1.

**TABLE 5.1**
*Focus of Information Systems*

| | APPLICATION FOCUSED | INFORMATION FOCUSED |
|---|---|---|
| SCOPE | Department or Function | Organization Wide |
| DATA ORGANIZATION | Application Specific | Subject Data Base |
| DATA OWNERSHIP | Data "owned" by application or function | Data is an organization resource |
| TOP MANAGEMENT INVOLVEMENT | Rare | Vital to success |
| STRATEGIC INFORMATION PLANNING | Usually Not Done | Determines Overall Framework and Priorities |
| OBJECTIVE | Efficiency | Effectiveness |

Data in an applications oriented information system is psychologically "owned" by a department or function. Personnel within a department or functional area have a strong sense of ownership of their data. Psychological ownership of data ought to be replaced with concerns of accuracy, security, and access.

In contrast to the application approach, the information approach to developing information systems views data as an organizational resource. It provides a conceptual foundation for future application development. An organizational data model describes the relationship between the entities used in that organization.

An information orientation assumes that data is an organizational resource designed for sharing across departmental and functional boundaries. Data organization is in the form of subject databases. A subject database is data stored about subjects of interest to an organization. Examples would include employees, products, customers, and orders. Data organized in subject databases tends to be more stable than application specific data files. The contrast between application specific files and a shared database is shown in Figure 5.1.

Finally, an information focus requires information strategy planning to provide a framework for the development of specific applications, to identify which subject databases are required and which applications have priority. This planning effort requires top management involvement to identify the strategic information needs of the organization and to link information systems plans to strategic business plans.

FIGURE 5.1 *Application-Specific versus Shared Database*

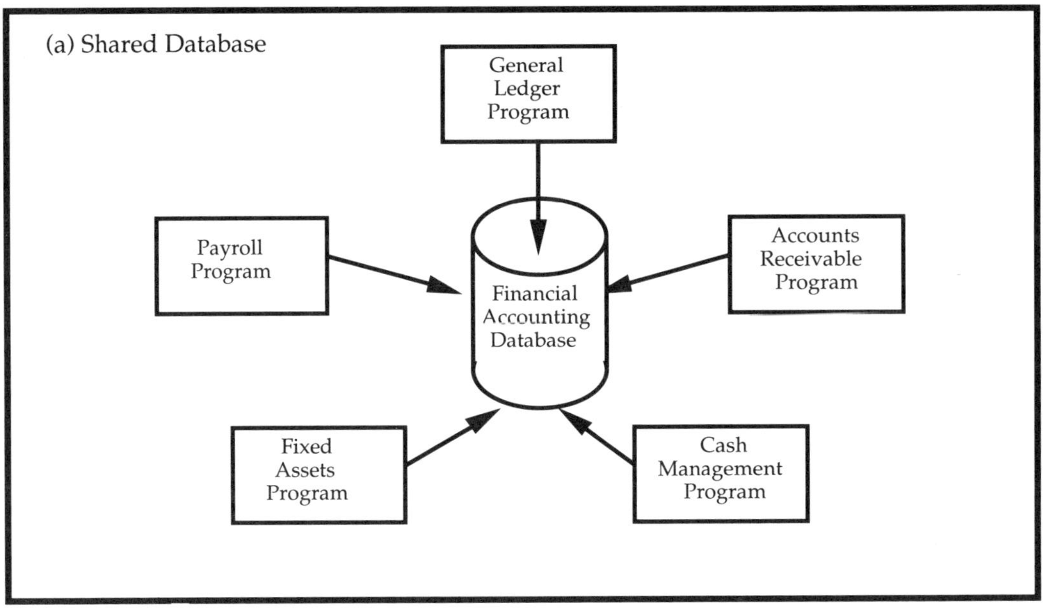


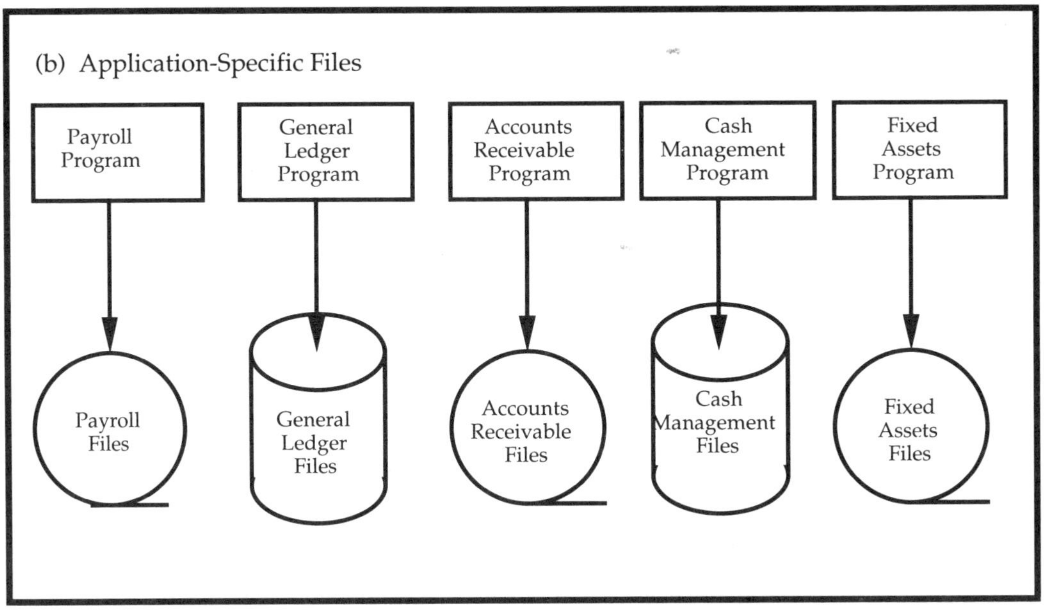

In contrast, an applications focus usually operates on the principle of "the squeaking wheel gets the grease." Rarely does this approach seek to identify the information requirements of top management. While some application focused organizations do have data processing steering committees composed of managers, typically this committee determines the priorities of the MIS department rather than determining the information needs of top management.

A database approach is a necessary but not sufficient condition for an information focus. An information approach is not assured if an organization has a DBMS. Some organizations with a DBMS are applications-focused, using a DBMS to build an application database. An information focus requires strategic data planning, data modeling, data administration, use of an integrated data dictionary and top management involvement. Data administration builds subject databases. The benefits of data administration and Fourth Generation Technology are highlighted in Issues and Controversies.

## Issues and Controversies

## Automobiles and Fourth Generation Technology

In America in the 19th Century people traveled by railroad. The railroad made a big contribution to the economic growth of the country. There were, however, some limitations of traveling by rail: (1) you could travel only where the railroad track went, (2) advanced reservations were required, and (3) as usage increased trains became crowded and passengers began to believe that railroads didn't really care about their welfare.

About this time, along came the automobile. In the beginning it appeared to be a fun thing for a joy ride. As the automobile improved, cars became affordable by the common man. This changed the fortunes of the railroads. The automobile provided freedom, convenience, and flexibility. Unlike the railroad the owner of the automobile could start their journey any time they wanted and go to any location. The owner was in control of their schedule and could drive themselves anywhere at their convenience. Now you know the rest of the story - the demise of the railroad's passenger business.

The history of information systems so far parallel's the railroad. Information systems departments have done all the work for end-users including development, maintenance, and production work. The end-user is at the mercy of the Information Syst ems department. When the end-user need an application the Information Systems department puts the request in a long queue. When the system is developed the end-user is subject to the schedule and constraints of the IS department s to what can be done and when the results can be obtained. The end-user finds themselves in the same position as the railroad passenger.

The arrival of fourth generation technology gave the user the tools required to obtain their own information needs without the assistance of Information Systems professionals. The user thinks it's great. It gives them freedom, flexibility, and convenience. Fourth generation technology puts them in the driver's seat.

The impact of the automobile on the economy and our way of life was pervasive. It led t the development of suburbs, freeway systems, shopping malls and the petroleum industry. In contrast, the railroad industry despite the need for freight traffic has declined.

What will be the fate of Centralized Information Systems departments, do they have the same future as the railroad industry? Does 4th generation technology have the same future as the automobile did? Probable answers to these two questions are yes, but with some qualifications.

The automobile flourished because of several complementary developments. The development of highways made it possible to travel long distances. Maps made it possible to venture into unknown territory.

Automobile manufacturers have standardized on the placement of controls such as steering wheels, accelerator, brake and clutch pedals. State and national regulations have made it possible to obtain the right kind of fuel anywhere in the country.

Perhaps even more important is the regulation and enforcement of mechanisms that ensure that every car and driver are properly licensed. Drivers are qualified by examination before they are allowed to independently drive the vehicle. Every organization needs a function which allows end-user computing to flourish and yet be controlled.

For fourth generation technology to reach its destiny, a mechanism must be in place to provide the discipline necessary to avoid abuses. That is precisely what the Data Administration function is about.

Once an end-user is qualified they need data. Providing fourth generation tools without data is like providing cars without highways. Without a well planned shareable data resource each end-user could create their own fragmented and non-compatible database. To foster data integration, enterprise modeling an information architecture are necessary. This is the first step in developing a shareable data resource.

A data dictionary provides a roadmap of the organization's information resources. It should be easy enough to use to allow the user to traverse through the organization's database.

Data Administration has to provide the following key services:

- Development of an information architecture
- Organization of corporate databases
- Data dictionary facilities
- Data standardization

- **Management of data resource security**
- **Qualifications of end-users**

**Qualification of end-users would most likely be accomplished with the cooperation of the Information Center.**

**Data administration should facilitate fourth generation technology. It provides a framework and discipline which allows end-user computing to blossom.**

Adapted from: Arvin D. Shah, "The Growth of Fourth Generation Technology: A Management Perspective," Database Newsletter (March/Apr8il, 1987) pp. 3-5.

Database technology has the promise of data independence, a reduction in data redundancy, improved productivity in software development and greater accessability to data. Many organizations have purchased a DBMS without giving adequate attention to data modeling, data administration or data dictionaries. These organizations have not caught the vision of database technology and have implemented applications without proper attention to sharing data. They have created a mess which will require considerable time and expense to get straighted up. The most difficult case would be an organization implementing an integrated data dictionary and data administration after having used a DBMS for several years.

Durell, an authority on data administration, has suggested:

> Although the technical challenges of implementing data administration are formidable, they are relatively small in comparison to the political, organizational and emotional issues facing the data administrator. If these issues are not understood or are ignored by an organization prior to instituting a data administration function, the long term success of data administration could be jeopardized.[1]

A data dictionary and data administration require commitment. Purchase of a data dictionary is a necessary but not sufficient condition to have data administration. The individual charged with creating order out of chaos is the data administrator. Management must give unmistakable support to this function for it to be effective. A survey of 210 mainframe database sites during 1985 showed half did not use a data dictionary and only slightly more than half had implemented data administration.[2]

Some of the reasons for failure of data administration are described below in When Things Go Wrong.

## When things go wrong

### Reasons for Data Administration Failure

- Organizational politics, prevailed, partly because of a lack of strong management with a clear perception of what was to be accomplished.
- The human problems of making different accountants or managers agree on the definitions of data items was too great.
- The magnitude of the task was underestimated.
- The data administrator was a low-paid technician.
- Methodologies for the design of stable data structures were not understood.
- The necessary data models were too complex to design and administer by hand, any appropriate computerized tools were not used.
- There was not an overall architect who could use the design methodology.
- Attempts of data modeling took too long and users could not wait.
- Data model design was confused with implementation and physical database design.

From James Martin, An Information Systems Manifesto (Englewood Cliffs, NJ: Prentice Hall, Inc., 1984), p. 84.

## Data Administration

THE ROLE OF DATA ADMINISTRATORS IS RELATIVELY NEW. Most of the organizations which have this job title have created it since 1983 when DB2 was announced. The rise of data administration parallels the growth of database management systems.

The maintenance of the data dictionary is the focal point of the data administrators job. This involves maintaining data definitions and data structures. In addition, data administrators are frequently given tasks that involve data modeling and data security. Typically, they also perform an information and consulting role for those desiring access to the database.

The role of the data administrator is to coordinate the design and definition of a database, to maintain the integrity and security of data stored in the database, and to be a source of information and assistance for those requiring access to data. In the past, the term "database administrator" often included these functions as well as the task of coordinating computer operations which included monitoring and improving system performance. Martin has pointed out there are really two separate sets of skills required in database administration.[3] One set of skills is administrative in nature, requiring the ability to work with people in defining a database, and maintaining database standards and controls. The other set of skills is essentially technical, requiring a systems programming background for monitoring and improving database system performance as well as coordinating computer operations. This suggests two separate functions—one administrative and the other technical.

Some authorities on data administration emphasize a role of enforcing standards. Others see this enforcement role in conflict with a consulting and supporting role. This view is expressed in When Things Go Wrong.

**When things go wrong**

## Why Data Administration Fails

Although the concept shows a good deal of promise the majority of data administration organizations fail to live up to expectations. This is not so much because the concept of data administration is flawed, rather it is because the new administration often falls prey to one of several traps that may lead management to conclude that it doesn't work.

A survey of a number of data administration groups reveals the reasons for failure of these groups include one or more of the following reasons:

- Lack of a clear understanding of the role of data administration
- No organizational identity
- Insufficient management support

The benefits of data administration will be limited for the first project. Major benefits will not accumulate until sometime later. Inevitably data administration faces start up costs and learning curves.

These realities may obscure the long term benefits of data administration and make it appear as a large burden with little immediate benefit. This will generate political pressure to bypass data administration and revert to the previous methodology.

Data administrators are frequently given the responsibility for developing and enforcing corporate information policies. At the same time, data administration departments are responsible for supporting application development and end-user computing. This support can range from answering questions about data dictionary use to assistance in design of data structure diagrams. This role requires the full trust and confidence of the users and developers. This trust and confidence is jeopardized, however, if data administration must also enforce corporate data standards. The two functions are simply incompatible.

**There is no better way to kill an organization than to ignore it. Some managers create an organization and wish it "bon voyage." They create an organization, give it a send off and walk away believing its survival will be determined by some Darwinian principle.**

**"Managing the managers" must continue even after they have accepted and implemented data administration. The most effective way to maintain management support is to present a detailed picture of its use, benefits, costs, and function within the organization. A data administrator should avoid the perception that once they have sold management on data administration no more selling is required.**

**The corporate waters are cold and hazardous for a fledgling data administration group. Careful attention to detail, organizational climate, and corporate philosophy can improve data administration's chances for survival.**

Adapted from "Why Data Administration Fails," George Tillmann, Computerworld, September 7, 1987.

Enforcement of data administration standards might be compared with quality control in production. The old view that quality control is the responsibility of the quality control department is being replaced by a view that quality is everyone's responsibility. This view emphasizes the responsibility that everyone has in doing quality work. It emphasizes internalizing a standard rather than enforcement. Data administration might benefit from a similar philosophy.

In many organizations, data administration would be performed by a data administration group. Some members of the group would be involved with data definition and design, others with maintenance of the data dictionary, and other members charged with the responsibility of maintaining database controls and security. A rapidly growing function for data administration is the function of providing information and education to programmers and end-users about the structure of the database and how data can be accessed. This function should continue to increase with the growth in end-user computing.

## INTRODUCING DATA ADMINISTRATION

The notion of sharing data may initially be unacceptable to some departments. The data administrator should be capable of persuasion, smoothing over differences and ultimately, if necessary, coercion. This suggests that the data administrator must be politically adept and know how to use power and influence.

Data administration is an attempt to change behavior. It can be successfully implemented in an organization if a strategy of change is carefully worked out. Initially, there should be a program to build support for data administration. This should involve training of the affected groups. The benefits and costs of data administration should be clearly understood. Secondly, management should reinforce the need for change. This reinforcement should stress benefits to the organization rather than personal appeals. Third, affected groups should participate in the implementation process.

The initial period after data administration has been introduced is its most vulnerable period. During this period, there are still some doubts about the wisdom of change; when problems arise, data administration is exposed to criticism, and may even appear not to be working. Only after this initial period, when things have settled into a new routine, are the intended benefits likely to make their appearance.

## DATABASE DESIGN AND DEFINITION

Database design and definition is concerned with conceptual and logical database design, which is described in the appendix. It may include enterprise modeling.

Database design is concerned with (1) identification of entities, (2) determining the relationship of these entities, (3) normalization, and (4) creating tables of fully normalized records. Fully normalized records mean that each data element is stored in one location a scheme that was described earlier as being organized like a supermarket. Database design normally would include the responsibility for naming data elements too.

## Data Dictionary

A DATA DICTIONARY IS A CENTRAL SOURCE OF INFORMATION about the data used in an organization. It stores information about the entities, the attributes of these entities, as well as the meanings, uses, and relationships of these entities and attributes. It might be thought of as a *database about data*.

Data dictionaries can be passive or active. A passive data dictionary is a source of information but does not enforce standards embodied in data definitions. Over time a passive data dictionary tends to become inconsistent with the data stored in the database. For this and other reasons, an active data dictionary is preferred.

An active data dictionary plays an active role in enforcing correct data representation. The active dictionary both controls the usage of data and as assists in processing, queries, screen and report generation.

The trend in data dictionaries as they become more active is that they tend to be more tightly integrated with the DBMS. The data dictionary is increasingly viewed as the center of an integrated DBMS and closely tied to all of the modules. The contrast between an active and passive data dictionary is shown in Table 5.2.

TABLE 5.2
*Active Versus a Passive Data Dictionary*

| ACTIVE | PASSIVE |
|---|---|
| One Copy of Definition | Redundant Definitions<br>--Innconsistency Possible<br>--Multiple Maintenance Required<br>--Addition Storage Required |
| Production Systems Depend on Dictionary Availability | Production Systems Unaffected by Dictionary Failures |
| Dictionary Can Become a Bottleneck | One System Does Not Affect Another |

The data dictionary has three basic functions:

1. It provides a source of information about data.
2. It controls access to data.
3. It provides a cross listing which shows which applications will be affected by changes to the database.

Although data dictionaries are designed for a database environment, many data dictionaries will support data files as well as database. This feature is particularly desirable for those organizations anticipating a switch to database.

An organization considering conversion from file processing to data base ought to start with a data dictionary and data administration. Most data elements are used by multiple applications, multiple end-user groups and with the emergence of distributed systems, multiple computers. The use of a data dictionary and data administration is a step towards coordination and control of data representation.

In organizations without data dictionaries and effective data administration there is often great redundancy of data. The same data in a slightly different but incompatible form is represented in several locations. It can be difficult to find where data is located.

With an active data dictionary in place all programmers must use the same names for the data elements in their programs. All requests for access to data flow through the data dictionary.

Although there is a definite trend towards active data dictionaries there is another view that suggests that passive data dictionaries have a role in a firm with multiple DBMS products from different vendors. Multiple DBMS products each closely integrated with a data dictionary may result in fragmentation of organizational data definitions. A passive data dictionary can serve as a single repository for all data definitions. An interface from the passive dictionary to an active dictionary can be built to provide the necessary data definitions for 4GLs and SQL.[4]

## FILE ACCESS METHODS IN A DATABASE ENVIRONMENT

File access methods refers to the technique for accessing the records of a file on a secondary storage device. Three alternatives are in common usage: (1) sequential access, (2) indexed sequential, and (3) direct access.

SEQUENTIAL: A sequential file organization physically stores records in the same sequence they were written in the file. Usually this would be in ascending order of the primary key. For example, credit card accounts would be stored by credit card number. When charges are processed these charges are sorted in the same order as the accounts. Account records can then be updated efficiently without a random search for the appropriate account.

The difficulty with sequential file organization is that if one desired to access a particular record to find a customer balance then all of the records that precede it must be read first. This is analogous to having to listen to all of the preceding songs on a tape or record before listening to the desired one.

INDEXED SEQUENTIAL: An indexed sequential file is also stored in sequential order according to the primary key. The file management system or access method builds an index. The index contains key values with an address of the corresponding records. This allows records to be accessed directly without accessing the previous records. This would support a random request to access a customer's account to determine the balance. This method of file organization also supports sequential access for batch processing applications such as a credit card billing. Sequential file organization would facilitate this type of application in which all accounts would be billed at the end of the month.

DIRECT: The most popular direct file organization is hash organization. Hash organization requires that a computation be performed on the primary key value. The result of this computation is an address for the disc storage location of the relevant data. This type of file organization is particularly valuable for applications which require an exact match. An example in the field of law enforcement is automobile license plate identification systems. When an officer enters a license plate number the automobile owner's name, address and telephone number are displayed almost immediately.

In a database environment, hashing routines, overflow management, and record management are built into the DBMS. The application programmer is relieved of the necessity of writing these routines and can simply request a record by its primary key value. The ease of using direct-hash addressed file organization is one of the major advantages of a database system. The relational model in particular removes the details of file organization and access method from the user interface.

## DESIRABLE DATA DICTIONARY FEATURES

A data dictionary should ideally represent data in three different models: conceptual, logical, and physical. The conceptual model represents the entities and their relationships. The logical model represents data as views. This representation ties these views to screens and reports. A physical model represents information about how data is stored, for example, length (bytes), mode (character, numeric), picture (for display), edit rules (range, constant), and derivation formula (for derived items).

A data dictionary should provide reports that list the following:

- Data elements in desired sequence

- Cross reference listings
- Logical views of data models

It should be an easy to use tool accessible to programmers, analysts, end users, and managers. It should have a help function to assist beginners.

A data dictionary should provide access control. These controls should specify who may have access to what part of the database and under what conditions. Changes to the data dictionary itself must be subject to access control since unrestricted access to make changes would defeat access controls.

A data dictionary should function in test mode as well as production mode. This allows test versions of applications to be run without being subject to all of the standards of production model.

Some other desirable data dictionary features include the following:

1. Insertion of labels for data elements or columns into queries generated by users.
2. Generation of data definitions for applications written in COBOL, PL/1 or assembler.
3. Support for aliases so end-users can access data using familiar names.
4. Automatic measurement and reporting of accesses to data.
5. Providing data definitions for query languages, screen report, and application generators.

## MAINTAINING A DATA DICTIONARY

Maintaining a data dictionary includes the definition of the following:

1. data elements, their names, type, and range of values
2. logical user views
3. tables
4. output reports
5. data entry screens
6. application programs
7. authorized users
8. edit controls

## TRENDS IN DATA DICTIONARIES

There is a definite trend for the functions of the data dictionary to be broadened. The data dictionary is being used to define not only data, tables, and logical user views, but also screens, report formats, and menus. When these new functions are added, the term "data dictionary" becomes less appropriate. Some of the new terms used for data dictionaries with these broader functions are repository and data encyclopedia.

## Data Element Naming Conventions

THE OBJECT OF DATA ADMINISTRATION IS TO CREATE ORDER, discipline, and structure in the database. A well-structured database allows the user to access data without the assistance of data processing professionals. The data independence ideal would allow a manager or professional to use the computer to access data in his own language, not the jargon of the information systems professional. For example, a client should be able to obtain answers to questions such as:

*What were last months' sales in New York summarized by product?*

There are several disciplines in computing which are attempting to solve this problem. Among these are artificial intelligence, voice recognition, relational database technology, and query languages. This objective will not be solved however, unless we structure the data from which this information is extracted.

Unless our database is built with clear, unambiguous, and standardized data elements, no assimilation, summarization, or synthesis of information is possible. The component parts must be compatible to provide accurate and reliable information. Data element naming standards are essential to achieving this objective.

### DATA ELEMENT NAMING STANDARD

Data elements should be given names that are clear, and convey the gist of the meaning. Data elements which are the same (synonymous) but have different names are confusing. Data element naming conventions are an important component of the standards and controls required in data administration.

A common data element naming standard is illustrated in Figure 5.2.

This standard shows that data element names can consist of three key words which are separated by a period. The first key word

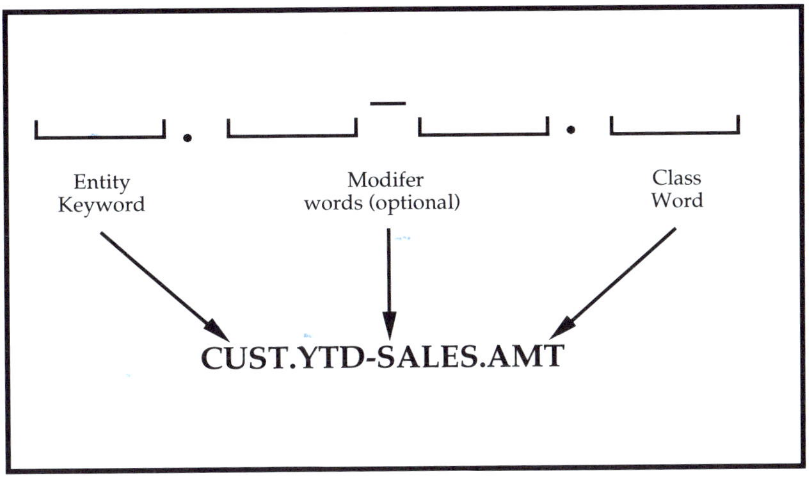


FIGURE 5.2 *Data Element Naming Standard*

identifies the entity which the data element or attribute describes. The entity name is abbreviated. Since the number of entities in an organization are finite, it is suggested that a glossary of entity key words and their abbreviations be maintained. If more than one entity abbreviation is required, these can be separated by a dash. The second part of a data element name is the minor-key word. This portion of the data element name is optional and is used only if necessary. If more than one minor-key word is required, these can be separated by a dash.

The last past of the data element name is the type-of-class abbreviation. These words are nouns used to describe the function of a data element. An example of a naming glossary is shown in Figure 5.3.

THE PRIMARY BENEFITS OF DATA ADMINISTRATION RELATE TO systems development. Data dictionaries provide a framework to

FIGURE 5.3 *Data Element Naming Glossaries*

| Entity Keyword | | Modifer Words (optional) | | Class Word | |
|---|---|---|---|---|---|
| Keyword | Abbreviation | Keyword | Abbreviation | Keyword | Abbreviation |
| Account | ACCT | Account | ACCT | Address | ADDR |
| Contract | CNTRCT | Accountable | ACCTBL | Amount | AMT |
| Customer | CUST | Accounting | ACCTG | Code | CODE |
| Employee | EMPL | Actual | ACTL | Count | CNT |
| Equipment-Item | EQUIP | | | Date | DATE |
| Equipment-Type | EQUIIPTP | | | Flag | FLG |
| | | | | Name | NM |
| | | | | Number | NMBR |
| | | | | Percent | PCT |
| | | | | Quantity | QTY |

## Benefits of Data Administration

applications which facilitates communications between application developers and leads to fewer aborted development efforts.

It also leads to lower development costs by improving the productivity of programmers developing new applications or modifying old applications. This improvement in productivity is the result of data independence; application developers will find that the data they need for new applications is already available.

Some intangible benefits to data administration are the controls it provides to avoid unauthorized access to sensitive organizational data. The control aspects of data administration are discussed later in the chapter.

A data dictionary can be an excellent information resource to end-users as well as information systems professionals. One of the criteria used in selecting a data dictionary should be the human interface. It should be user-friendly.

A data dictionary is an excellent tool for analysis of the effects of change. Most data dictionaries have the capability of showing which applications use a given data element. In addition, most data dictionaries permit operation in either test status or production status. This allows a proposed change to be tested before it is implemented.

## Costs of Data Administration

THE BENEFITS OF DATA ADMINISTRATION ARE NOT WITHOUT cost. Some of these costs are one-time expenditures associated with software acquisition, installation, and training.

The minimum software requirement for data administration is a data dictionary. An integrated data dictionary will cost several thousand dollars. The trend of data dictionaries is toward greater integration, which means that a vendor's data dictionary is usually associated with its own database management system. Selection of a data dictionary, then, is virtually a commitment to a database management system vendor.

Initially, the data dictionary must be populated with information about data used in the organization. Ideally, this effort to build the meta-data base is associated with a data modeling effort. These projects are major commitments by an organization.

Introducing data administration in an organization will require that

Introducing data administration in an organization will require that existing personnel be retrained and, frequently, that an experienced data administrator be hired. The startup costs may also include the costs of consulting help to assist the data administration staff in initially developing standards, policies, and procedures.

The ongoing costs of data administration would be those costs associated with maintenance of the data dictionary and the salaries of the data administration staff.

Data dictionaries and data administration may require additional hardware resources. Data dictionaries may require additional memory and mass storage. Indeed, a data dictionary has been referred to by one group of experts as a "bottleneck." this point of view is discussed in Issues and Controversies.

## Issues and Controversies

### Data Dictionaries: A Bottleneck?

Data dictionaries are complex software systems; it is obvious that repeated executions of data dictionary functions may use up significant computer resources. The first concern must be with the effect a data dictionary system has on the overall throughput of the computer system of which it is a part.

The problem becomes even worse when we consider the effect of an active data dictionary. An active data dictionary does not permit a program to proceed until the dictionary has *done its thing*. It is obvious that the time required for the data dictionary to perform its functions must be added to the execution time required by the program. Given enough such occasions that the services of the data dictionary must be involved, and we have a perfect definition of a bottleneck.

An active data dictionary really means that should the contents of the dictionary not agree with the program the program is not allowed to proceed until a change is made either in the program or the dictionary. An interesting speculation is how many organizations are really willing to live with an active data dictionary or whether they would opt for some means of overriding the data dictionary. If, however, a data dictionary system allows an override the active interface has been defeated.

An answer to the last problem probably can be answered with status facilities. Status facilities would allow a program to interface with an active dictionary in a test mode as opposed to production mode.

The "bottleneck" problem is probably more difficult to solve. A possible solution is to make the data dictionary more efficient, but there are limits to this approach. A more fundamental solution would be to develop a new type

**of architecture for data dictionary systems.**

Adapted from Henry C. Lefkovits, Edgar H. Sibley, and Sondra L. Leftkovits, Information Resource/Data Dictionary Systems (Wellesley, MA: QUE Information Sources, Inc., 1983), pp. 1-42, 1-43.

## Data Base Controls

THE BASIC PRINCIPLES OF CONTROL DO NOT CHANGE IN A database environment. The unique capabilities of database technology however suggest some differences from controls employed in a file processing environment. These differences are the result of the increased accessability of data in a database environment.

At the outset, it might be useful to distinguish between privacy and security. Privacy is an individual right. Individuals have a right, protected by law, against unauthorized disclosure of information about them. Organizations are the custodians and stewards of much of this information, which is maintained in personnel records, medical records, academic records, and legal records.

Security is an organizational concern. It refers to the protection of data against accidents, and unauthorized access or modification. To safeguard the data of an organization, some recognition of the perils it is exposed to is necessary. Data should be protected from criminals, incompetents, and natural disasters, as well as hardware and software failures.

Some of the controls used to protect data include:

1. Physical controls — This would include locked doors, alarms and protection of back-up data.
2. Administrative controls — This level of control represents policies and procedural controls to insure that information systems professionals follow prescribed procedures in testing new systems, that appropriate backup data is maintained, and that the information systems staff do not misuse the system.
3. System Controls — This level of control is found in operating systems and data dictionary access controls. It includes passwords, access privileges, and audit control logs or journals.

Most operating systems require passwords to gain access to the computer system. In addition, many database management systems have their own password protection.

Access/update controls in a data dictionary define the privileges of a given user. This may include controls at the table, row, column, or data element level. It might also include controls which allow these privileges during specified days of the week, certain times of the day, and from a specified terminal.

Users should be identified, their actions authorized and monitored. Users should be given access privileges which allow them to access only those data items that are required for their job functions. A bank teller needs access to customer accounts but not to payroll data.

Updating privileges allow a user to update those data items that are authorized for that user. This includes the right to add, change, or delete the data item. An example of database access controls is shown in Figure 5.4.

FIGURE 5.4

*Implementing Access Privileges*

(a) Access Privileges for Entities

| | Customer Records | Vendor Records | Order Records |
|---|---|---|---|
| Read | Y | Y | Y |
| Insert | Y | N | Y |
| Modify | Y | N | Y |
| Delete | N | N | Y |

(b) Access Privileges for Records

| | Sales-persons | Order Entry | Ware-house |
|---|---|---|---|
| Read | Y | Y | Y |
| Insert | N | Y | N |
| Modify | N | Y | N |
| Delete | N | N | N |

The actions of users can be monitored with an audit trail log or journal maintained by the data dictionary. This feature is also of great benefit in the event of database failure to aid recovery. A log or journal can be used to update a backup copy of the database with the transactions that have ensued since backup occurred.

Transmission of sensitive data can be protected by data encryption. Encryption algorithms are available commercially in the form of mass produced LSI chips. Cryptography refers to a coding process which scrambles data so thoroughly that an unauthorized person gaining access to the transmission is very unlikely to be able to decode it.

Concurrent access controls are controls built into a database management system to protect the integrity of data in a situation where two applications attempt to update the same data item simultaneously. Determination of whether this capability exists in a database management system should be an important criterion in selecting DBMS software.

Data structure representations should be maintained and changed by the data administration staff. They should not be available in update mode to users outside the data administration department. Access to authorization records, passwords, and other security features should be strictly controlled. If an unauthorized intruder gains access to the data administrator's security files, he/she can overcome the system controls.

## The Impact of Data Administration on Information Quality

QUALITY HAS BEEN DEFINED AS FITNESS FOR USE. THIS SUGGESTS that data must possess the necessary attributes of accuracy, relevance, timeliness, and level of aggregation required for an application.

Data administration contributes to accuracy by reducing data redundancy. By sharing data, applications use the same data elements stored in one location and only one change is required to update the data for all applications.

Most integrated data dictionaries have the capability of editing input. These editing features check to see if numeric data is within an appropriate range and to see if data is of the proper type either numeric or character. These editing features relieve the programmer of writing editing routines.

Data administration should insure that cutoffs are coordinated so that accounting reports at the end of a period are consistent across organizational units. Different processing cycles and time sensitive data should be handled in a manner to ensure an accurate historical position as necessary.

## Auditing Considerations in Data Administration

AN EFFECTIVE DATA ADMINISTRATION FUNCTION FACILITATES the work of an auditor. However, some database systems are unauditable. The spread of end-user fourth generation languages without data dictionaries increases the danger of creating unauditable systems.

James Martin has described unauditable systems as follows in Table 5.3.

TABLE 5.3

*Unauditable Systems Characteristics*[a]

- Higher-level languages giving end users access to databases without adequate controls or journals.
- Lack of audit trails. It is not possible to tell who di what.
- Poor authorization control. Unauthorized persons can gain acces to the system.
- Controls that can be bypassed by ingenious techniques.
- Confusion over data definitions and data representations. No data dictionary. Lack of control of homonyms, synonms, and data representations.
- Excessive complexity so that the auditor cannot tell what happened.
- Data volumes that can be removed and tampered with elsewhere.
- Unauthorized access to a system via a network.
- Distributed database operations gathering or associating data from multiple nodes without adequate controls.
- Integrity problems caused by poor software or inadequate restart-recovery control.
- Unpredicatble or uncertain actions taken by programs of excessive complexity. A monolithic program of 50,000 instructions in unauditable.
- Complex and unpredicatble patterns of communication between the nodes.

[a]James Martin, Managing the Database Environment, ©1983, p. 611. Reprinted by permission of Prentice-Hall, Inc., Englewood Cliffs, N.J.

Database technology does not represent a threat to the auditor if an integrated data dictionary is maintained by an effective data administration staff. Indeed data administrators will learn to use the auditor as a political ally in implementing and maintaining the standards and controls required in data administration.

Auditors will find that the data dictionary is a rich source of information. It contains information about data elements which includes the following:

1. name
2. size
3. type
4. edit criteria
5. relationships between components of the database
6. cross reference data which shows which applications use a given data element.

Auditors will find that data dictionaries have assumed functions that were commonly included in application programs. These functions would include edit and validation controls, and access method algorithms. This migration of controls facilitates the work of the author, but also means that auditors should spend more time with the data administration staff.

Auditors should review the security profile of database users and determine if the level of privileges is appropriate. For example, in a payroll application, a payroll clerk should be able to read employee pay rates but not to modify a pay rate. The security profile should be tested to determine if the security mechanism is operative.

## Guidelines for Managers

DATA ADMINISTRATION REQUIRES TOP MANAGEMENT SUPPORT, since it represents a change in the way information systems departments operate. The technical challenges of implementing data administration are relatively modest compared with the political and organizational barriers. The long term success of data administration is in jeopardy if these issues are not understood.

## Guidelines for MIS Professionals

COMPUTER PROFESSIONALS MUST RECOGNIZE THE NECESSITY OF data administration. Data administration is a discipline that will clean up much of the confusion and redundancy that is prevalent in information systems departments.

Data administration is a fast-growing profession that will appeal to many information systems professionals. It requires both technical and human skills: the ability to work with a broad variety of people. These human skills are the key to success for a data administrator.

## Key Terms

Data Administration

Data Redundancy

Data Integrity Planning

Information Strategy

Data Independence

Data Administrator

Database Designer

Database Design

Passive Data Dictionary

Active Data Dictionary

Repository

Data Encyclopedia

Data Element Naming Standard

Data Base Controls

Privacy

Security

Concurrent Access Controls

## Review Questions

1. How do data redundancy problems lead to data integrity problems?
2. Does a DBMS assure an information approach to software development? Why or why not?
3. List the focal point of the data administrator's job?
4. What are the three steps or "strategies for change" that can be taken by an organization to ensure successful implementation of data administration?
5. What are some of the intangible benefits of a data dictionary?
6. Given the existence of an EMPLOYEE entity, use the previous name standards to name data elements to represent the following attributes:

   Identifying Number
   Name
   Age
   Address
   Sex
   Dependents' Names
   Monthly Salary
   Hourly Salary
   Yearly Salary
   Salary Earned
   Department
   Annual Performance Rating

7. What is the difference between privacy and security?
8. What factors result in end-users doing their own computing? What is good about end-user computing? Is there anything bad? Explain.
9. Discuss data redundancy with respect to:
   a. Updating of records
   b. Error detection
10. What single factor is contributing the most towards unauditable systems?

**Case Study**

## DAYTON HUDSON

Dayton Hudson, the Minneapolis based retailing firm, recently established a data administration function. According to Dave Bruns, Directory of MIS Planning and Data Administration, the catalyst for the formation of the data administration organization was the merger of the Dayton and Hudson department store companies four years earlier.

One of the major challenges facing the MIS department after the merger was integrating the two companies' systems. Dayton Hudson encountered numerous problems:

- Redundant files.
- Lack of a global data perspective.
- Fragmented and sometimes unclear ownership of data.
- Inadequate data design methods.
- Data security determined on an application-by-application basis.
- Poor use of data dictionary

The creation of Dayton Hudson's data administration organization was part of a larger reoganization that included the formation of a strategic MIS planning function and a development center.

Selling data administration to top management was accomplished in two steps. The Vice-President of MIS was shown the data related problems encountered in integrating the two companies' systems and was persuaded that data administration could help solve these problems.

The Chief Administrative Officer was further removed from the integration problems. One of his key MIS objectives was the development of a systems architecture. Knowing that a systems architecture could not succeed without the data architecture component, Bruns convinced him that a data administration was critical to the successful development of a systems architecture.

Bruns notes that a breakthrough in gaining management support came about through seizing opportunities that arose in the corporate environment. When two of Dayton Hudson's MIS directors resigned, Bruns presented a reorganization plan that proposed the establishment of a data administration function without a significant increase in headcount.

Because of the difficulties of presenting the detailed and sometimes technical issues involved in data administraiton to senior management, Bruns recommends a different approach. He recommends that high-level symbols and abstractions be used in communicating issues and progress to top management--in essence, emphasizing the "sizzle" instead of the steak.

Bruns considers the marketing of data administration to be a continual necessity, particularly since the costs of data administration are readily identified but the benefits of expense reduction and revenue increases are difficult to quantify.

Adapted from: Carolyn Green, "Management Commitment to Data Administration: A Report From the Front Lines, Database Newsletter (March/April 1989), pp. 3-4.

1. What can the data administration function contribute to an organization that has experienced a merger?
2. Why are the benefits of data administration difficult to quantify?
3. Dayton Hudson experienced success in convincing management of the need for data administration, but would programmers and analysts have to be persuaded also?

## Suggestions for Further Reading

Durrell, William, "The Politics of Data," Computerworld, September 9, 1985, pp. ID/25-ID/36.

*Discusses the role of data administration in implementing data oriented information systems. Emphasizes the need to consider the nontechnical aspects of information management in order to create high quality data and to increase the involvement of end users. Compares the traditional DP role with the role of data administration. Considers trends in information management emphasizing programmer productivity and an increased need for data administration.*

# 6

# Systems Analysis and Design

*"When the traditional systems analyst and potential end users first come face to face, they come from widely different cultures. It is rather like a Victorian missionary first entering an African village."*

*James Martin*

## Overview and Objectives

THE SYSTEMS ANALYST PERFORMS A FUNCTION QUITE SIMILAR to that of an architect. Both are involved with defining a problem, developing specifications, preparing design documents and interfacing with the builders of a system to see that the design is carried out to the satisfaction of the end-users.

This chapter discusses the activities, tools and changing role of the systems analyst.

AFTER READING THIS CHAPTER YOU SHOULD BE ABLE TO:

- Explain the systems life cycle.
- Explain the primary structures of programming logic.
- Describe the weaknesses of early systems analysis tools.
- Have a fundamental understanding of structured analysis tools.
- Explain the function of a data dictionary.
- Describe three conventions for representing process logic.

## The Process of Systems Analysis

THE PROCESS OF SYSTEMS ANALYSIS IS DIRECTED TOWARDS THE goal of understanding existing data processing systems, and with this understanding, designing improved solutions. One might ask why it is necessary to use an outsider, a systems analyst, in the process. What advantages does the analyst possess over end users? Why not have the people most familiar with the problem get together and come up with a solution?

A systems analyst has several advantages over end users in defining the problems with an existing system and designing a new solution. A systems analyst has been through the process several times and has a broad perspective based on that experience. A systems analyst is an impartial outsider with no fixed commitment to the current system and thus is free to create new solutions. A final advantage is expertise in the analysis and design of systems. Typically, a systems analyst is skilled in using diagramming techniques which document an existing or proposed system. These tools provide a blueprint for modifications of an existing system or the development of a new one.

While each systems analysis project is unique, there are some common threads in the process that can be identified.[1]

1. Iteration
2. Decomposition
3. Use of Diagramming Techniques
4. Modeling
5. Synthesis

Iteration refers to a process of successive refinements. Systems analysis is an imperfect art. An analyst usually will not have a perfect first-time understanding of a system. This will be refined in contacts with end users. This process of refinement and feedback continues until the systems analyst is satisfied.

Decomposition refers to breaking things down into modules. Systems are broken down into subsystems and subsystems into functions. The objective is to deal with complexity by breaking complex systems into manageable parts or divide and conquer.

Diagramming techniques are used to help understand an existing system and to document what a future system will be. They are used much like blueprints prepared by an architect as a guide to builders of a system. Furthermore, like blueprints they are useful in the maintenance and modification of a system.

Modeling involves building representations of an existing or proposed system. Models can be (1) iconic, (2) symbolic, or (3) analogic. Iconic models are graphic or diagrammatic representations. Symbolic models use words or mathematical symbols to represent systems. Analogic models represent the dynamic function of a system or how it works.

Systems analysis models have made heavy use of iconic and symbolic models of systems. The difficulty with these types of models is they are often misunderstood by end users.

A new type of analogic modeling has been referred to as prototyping. It is rapidly gaining acceptance and has real potential as a modeling tool; it should gain in popularity over the next few years.

The object of modeling is to test a proposed system before building it. A model allows us to simulate a proposed system before committing ourselves to the real thing.

Synthesis is the process of putting pieces together so they function as an integrated whole. Synthesis requires planning to insure that subsystems interface properly.

## Traditional Systems Development Life Cycle

THE SYSTEMS DEVELOPMENT LIFE CYCLE IS CONCERNED WITH the activities that are required for developing application software. The nature of these activities hasn't changed very much during the first thirty years of commercial computing. What has changed are the tools used by the systems analyst and the time required for the early stages of the systems life cycle. The increased attention given to analysis of existing systems reflects three factors: 1)the increased complexity of integrated computer systems, 2) the conviction that poor definition of the problem has frequently been the cause of failure in developing new systems, and 3) the high cost of correcting errors made early in the systems life cycle. The activities that make up the systems life cycle are:

ANALYSIS - Analysis is the study and documentation of an existing data processing system. The purpose of analysis is to understand how an existing system functions and to identify its strengths and weaknesses. A systems analyst gathers reports produced by a system, interviews end users and documents the existing system by preparing charts and graphs.

DESIGN- The process of design involves determining a solution to the problems defined in the analysis stage. Design activities also include the preparation of documents, which guide the programmers through the coding phase. Specifications prepared include the format of reports and data files.

CODING - Coding refers to the programming task. It involves implementing the design document in a computer language.

TESTING - Testing is concerned with determining if the completed program is free of *bugs* or errors. It typically involves executing the program with test data to determine if the correct output is obtained. Testing is also concerned with determining whether software interfaces properly with existing programs and if procedures for a new system are appropriate and complete.

IMPLEMENTATION - Implementation involves training end users managing the conversion process and file building. File building is necessary to initially capture information that will be maintained automatically once the system is in operation.

## SEQUENTIAL VS. SPIRAL APPROACH

There is a tendency to view the system life cycle as a set of sequential activities. The sequential approach is shown as Figure 6.1.

FIGURE 6.1 *Systems Life Cycle Viewed as Sequential Activities*

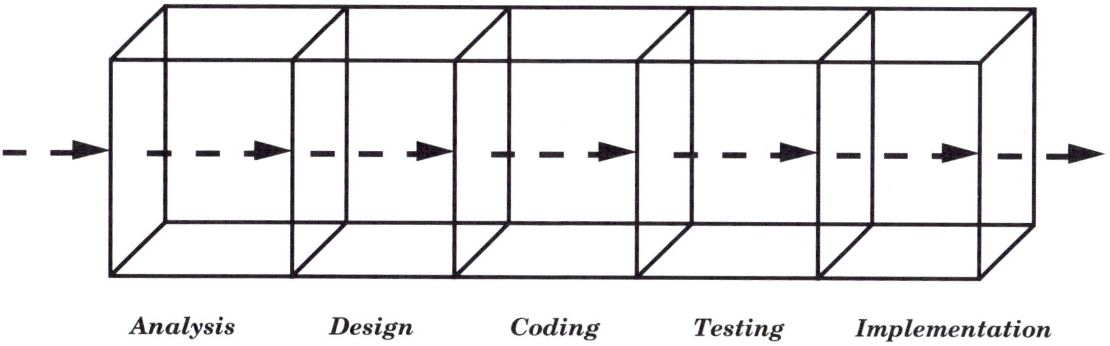


As clean and manageable as the sequential approach may appear, it does not seem to correspond with actual experience in well-managed software development projects.

Actual experience in software development projects suggest that projects tend to be iterative by nature. Analysis is followed by design which reveals some flaws in analysis and thus requires additional analysis.[2] This concept of the systems life cycle is revealed in Figure 6.2.

FIGURE 6.2 *Systems Life CycleViewed as a Spiral Approach*

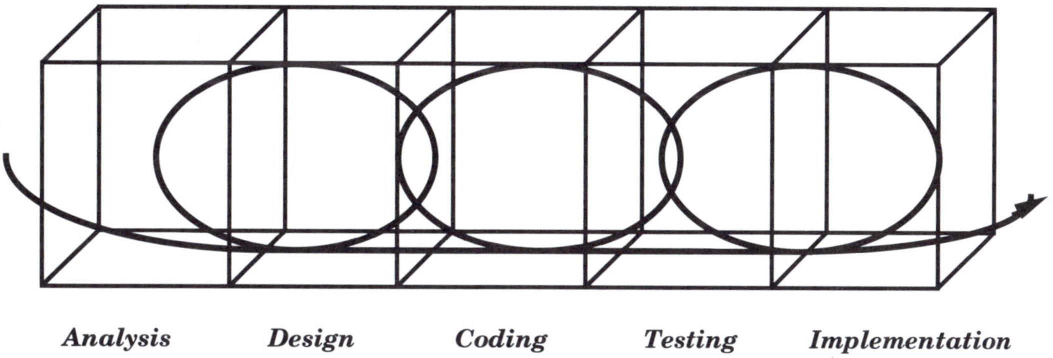

## Four Generations of Systems Analysis Tools

IT IS MUCH EASIER TO DESCRIBE A COMPLEX SYSTEM WITH A diagram than with text. A picture is worth a thousand words because it is concise, precise, and unambiguous. Narrative descriptions tend to be imprecise, subject to interpretation, and unmanageable.

Systems analysts need diagramming techniques that communicate the details of system design to the individual or team that puts it together. This allows a team to work on different modules of a system simultaneously with assurance that the result will fit together in a precise way.

Systems analysis is a relatively new discipline; consequently, there is a lack of consensus on which tools to use. Whereas architecture and engineering have formalized a set of diagramming tools that have been used for several years and are widely understood, systems analysis tools are still being refined.

The tools of the systems analyst have developed in four distinct generations.[3] These are described in Table 6.1.

TABLE 6.1

*Development of Systems Analysis Tools*

| | TOOLS | CHARACTERISTICS |
|---|---|---|
| 1ST GENERATION | Program Flowchart<br>Systems Flowchart<br>File Descriptors<br>Input/Output Descriptors | Focus on computer logic, document flow input/output and file format |
| 2ND GENERATION | Decision Table<br>Grid Charts<br>ADS (Accurately Defined Systems)<br>SOP (Study Organization Plan) | Detailed logic and relationships between data and reports, files and functions |
| 3RD GENERATION | Data Flow Diagrams<br>Data Dictionary<br>Structured English<br>Structure Charts | Modularization<br>Top down design |
| 4TH GENERATION | Action Diagrams<br>Data Structure Diagrams<br>Entity-Relationship Diagrams | Data Base Techniques<br>Comprehensive and Integrated |

## PROGRAM FLOWCHARTS

Program flowcharts were the first design and documentation tool. Although program flowcharts are rarely used by systems analysts today they provide an excellent vehicle for describing the fundamentals of programming logic. They are often used in an educational environment to illustrate the logic of programming without having to refer to a specific language syntax.

The logic of programming is described with the symbols found in Figure 6.3.

FIGURE 6.3
*Flow Chart Symbols*

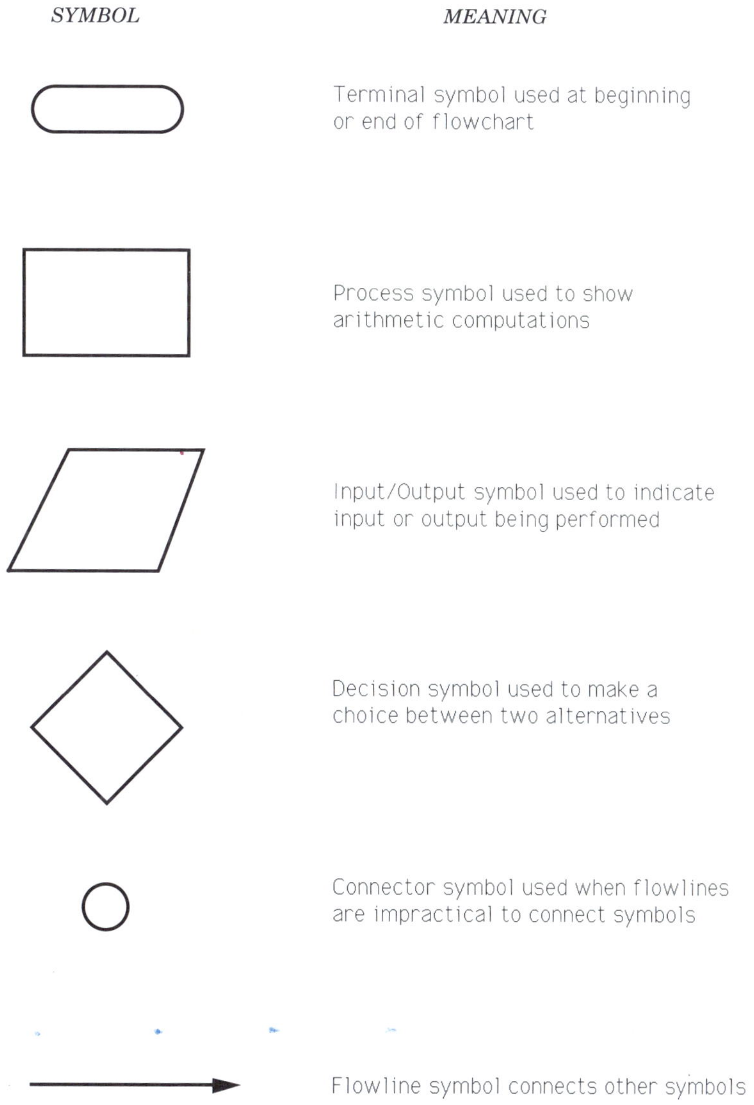

Flowlines are used to connect the other symbols and show the logical flow. The terminal and connector symbols do not represent computer functions, but are conventions that assist with the clarity of flowcharts.

For example, Midwest Industries, Inc. wants to develop a program to calculate its payroll. Employees may work over 40 hours, which requires an overtime computation. No deductions other than income tax and social security are taken. Inputs are employee identification number, hours worked, and hourly rate. A flowchart solution is shown below in Figure 6.4.

FIGURE 6.4

*Flowchart of Payroll Program*

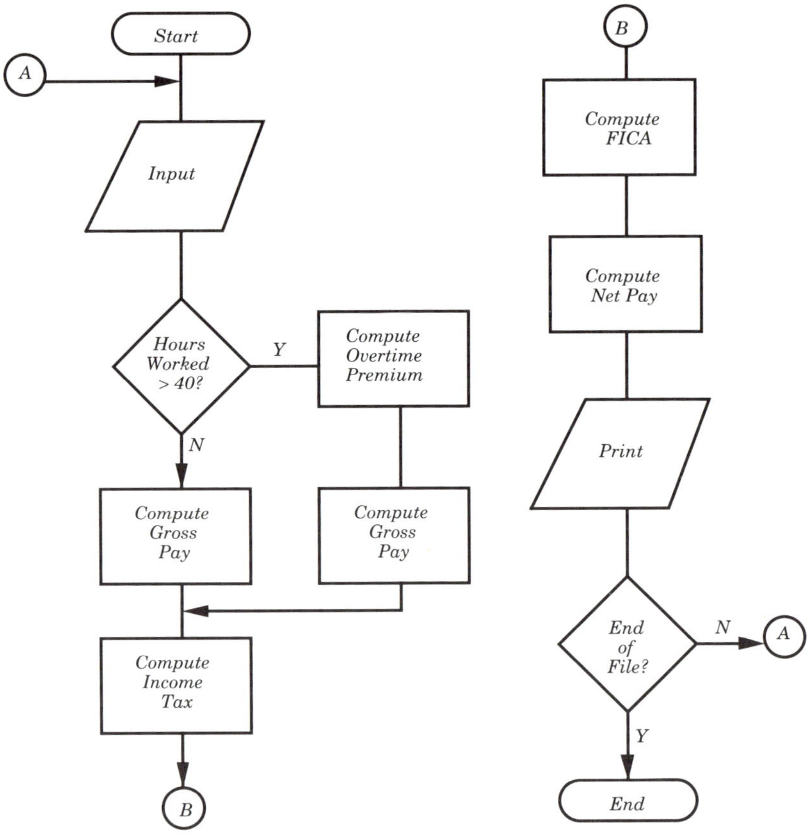


This flowchart illustrates the three primary structures of programming logic: sequence, branch, and loop. These are illustrated in Figure 6.5.

FIGURE 6.5

*The Primary Structures of Programming Logic*

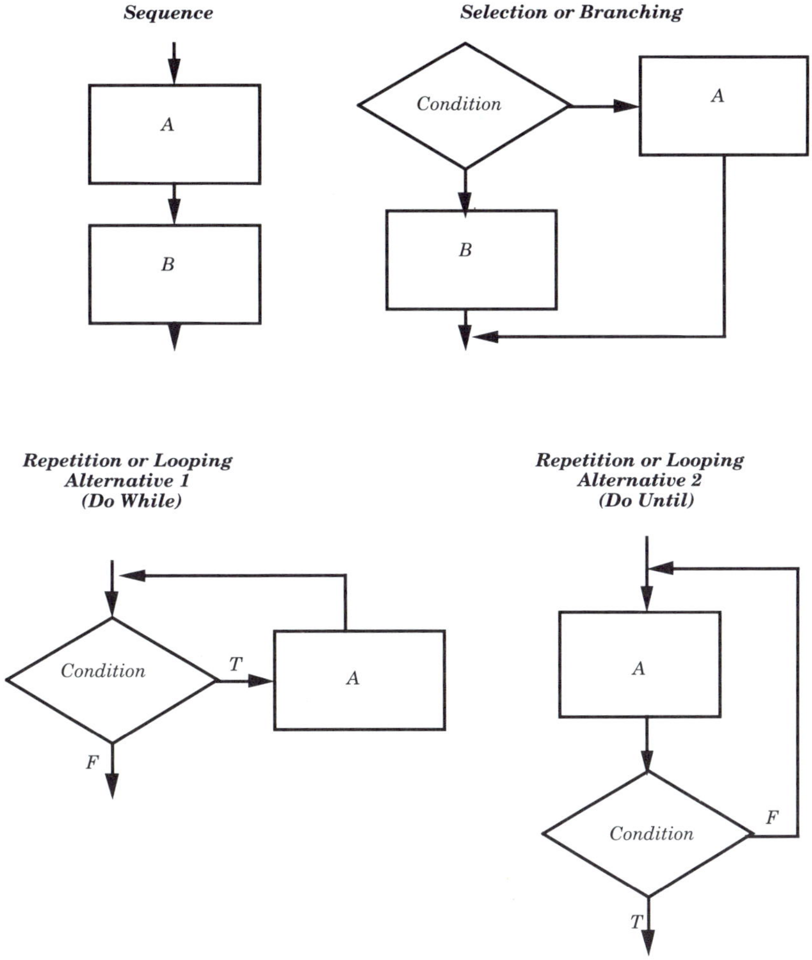


The difficulty with program flowcharts is that they are too time consuming to prepare and maintain. They fail as design and documentation tools in the following ways:

1. A program flowchart may be larger than the program it documents. Documentation should be concise.
2. They do not work well on large or complex systems. Program flowcharts become difficult to work with if they require several pages.
3. Useful documentation tools should be at a higher level of generality than the program code.
4. They do not show the hierarchical relationships between related systems.
5. Documentation tools should be problem oriented, not program (solution) oriented.

## System Flowcharts

System flowcharts were designed to complement program flowcharts. They show an overview or a macro view of an application, in contrast to the detail of a program flowchart.

System flowcharts were originally used to show data flows and processing components for a system or program. Systems flowcharts represent the logic of a program in a single process rectangle. Some of the symbols used in systems flowcharts and their meaning are shown in Figure 6.6.

Figure 6.6 *Systems Flowchart Symbols*

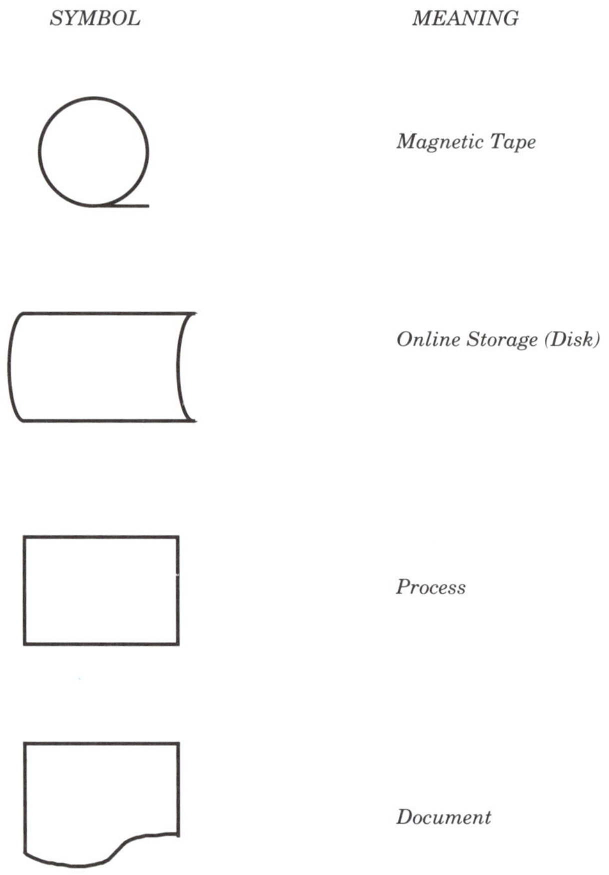


A sample systems flowchart for a payroll program is shown below. Input consists of a weekly transaction file, which contains the number of hours worked per employee. The payroll master file contains the permanent payroll records, which show year-to-date payroll information, as well as information unique to the employee:

name, social security number, pay rate, and weekly deductions, etc. The master file is updated at the conclusion of processing each employee's weekly pay. Two different types of output are shown in Figure 6.7-- a payroll register, which shows the detail for each employee, and a payroll check.

FIGURE 6.7
*Systems Flowchart for a Payroll System*

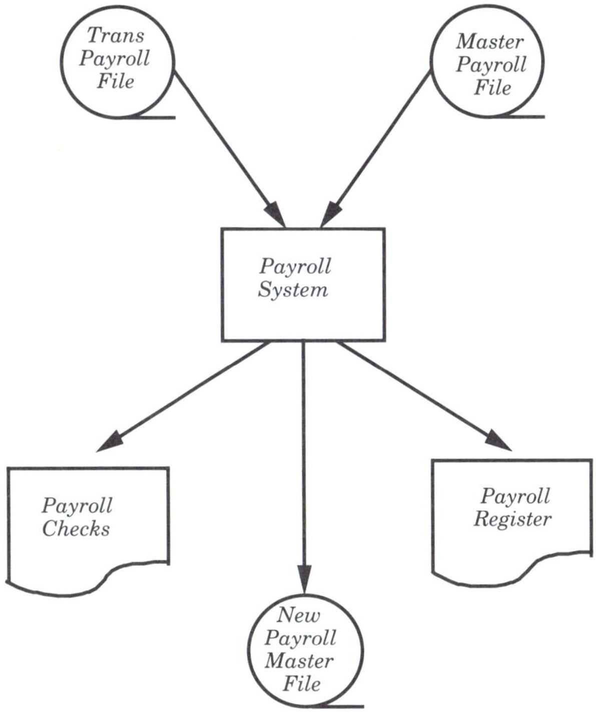


First generation systems analysis tools tended to be useful only as documentation tools and were not viewed as useful design tools. Typically, systems were documented after-the-fact. As Weinberg wryly observed, "Documentation is the caster oil of programming - managers think it is good for programmers, and programmers hate it!..."

## DECISION TABLES

Decision tables provided a much more concise alternative than program flowcharts for design and documentation of complex logic. A decision table is ideal for presenting complex decisions, which are dependent on a variety of conditions that can occur in any combination.

Consider the following hypothetical problem:

> Farmington Water Department bills residents of the city for water usage. The minimum bill is $3.00. Users with usage greater than 300 gal. but less than 1000 gal. are charged .01/gal. If usage exceeds 1000 galls in a month, gallons used in excess of 1000 gallons are billed at a rate of .005/gal.
>
> Customers with bills 30 days past due receive a reminder that the previous month's bill is overdue. Customers with bill over 60 days past due receive a warning that water will be disconnected if the bill is not paid promptly.

For purposes of simplifying the problem we will categorize the billing rates and account status as follows:

| CONDITION | ACTION |
|---|---|
| Less than 300 Gallons | Bill<br>Minimum rate |
| Greater than 300 Less than 100 Gallons | Bill<br>Usual rate (.01 per gal.) |
| Greater than 100 Gallons | High Volume Usage Rate ($10 + .005 per gal. for gal. in excess of 1000) |

| ACCOUNT STATUS | ACTION |
|---|---|
| Current | Current (No reminder) |
| 30+Days Overdue, Less than 60 Days Overdue | Print Reminder<br>Reminder |
| 60+Days Overdue | Print Warning |

A decision table is divided into four parts. The general form of a decision table is shown in Table 6.2..

TABLE 6.2
*General Format of Decision Table*

| | |
|---|---|
| List of Conditions | Columns representing different combinations of conditions |
| List of Actions | X's indicating action to be taken for a given set of conditions |

For the water billing problem the logic would be represented as follows:

TABLE 6.3
*Water Billing Decision Table*

| | | | | | | | | | | |
|---|---|---|---|---|---|---|---|---|---|---|
| CONDITIONS | Usage < 300 Gal. | Y | Y | Y | N | N | N | N | N | N |
| | Usage > 300 Gal. 1000 | - | - | - | Y | Y | Y | N | N | N |
| | Bill Current | Y | N | N | Y | N | N | Y | N | N |
| | Bill 60 + Overdue | - | N | Y | - | N | Y | - | N | Y |
| ACTIONS | Bill Minimum Rate | X | X | X | | | | | | |
| | Bill Usual Rate | | | | X | X | X | | | |
| | Bill High Usage Rate | | | | | | | X | X | X |
| | Print Reminder | | X | | | X | | | X | |
| | Print Warning | | | X | | | X | | | X |

Decision tables were not widely adopted, although they are clearly superior to program flowcharts in representing the logic of large and complex systems.[4] Decision tables are compatible with 3rd generation systems analysis techniques or structured methods which are discussed in the next section.

## THE DEVELOPMENT OF STRUCTURED METHODS

Early software developers had no accepted methods to follow and few role models. As a result, programming was more of an art than a science. The lack of programming standards within organizations and generally in the industry produced numerous problems. The most serious of these problems was poor quality software which had hidden errors (bugs). Some of the other problems included the low productivity of programmers and high maintenance costs.

During the 1970s, several software experts developed a set of standards for programming and a set of tools for documenting computer applications. The two fundamental ideas of this group were: 1) top-down design; and 2) modularity. Top down design refers to working from the general to the specific. For example, in architecture, it would involve developing the overall configuration of a building before designing the detailed layout. Modularity is an attempt to deal with complexity by breaking large problems down into workable pieces. The standards and design tools, which were derived from top down design and modularity, are frequently referred to as structured methods.

Structured methods, or, as they are sometimes referred to, software engineering, represent a complete change of emphasis from the early focus on computer hardware. These structured methods responded to the problems of poor software quality, difficult-to-maintain software, and low programmer productivity that existed prior to their development.

## Structured Systems Analysis Tools

THIRD-GENERATION SYSTEMS ANALYSIS TOOLS WERE BY PRODucts of the structured programming revolution. They were designed to implement structured methods in analysis and design. Following is a discussion of third-generation systems analysis tools.

### DATA FLOW DIAGRAMS

Data flow diagrams are a means of documenting an existing or a proposed system. Data flow diagrams are a device for building a model of an existing data processing system. The existing system may be either manual or computerized. Data flow diagrams work equally well in either case. The symbols used in data flow diagrams and their meaning are shown in Figure 6.8.

FIGURE 6.8 *Data Flow Diagram Symbols*

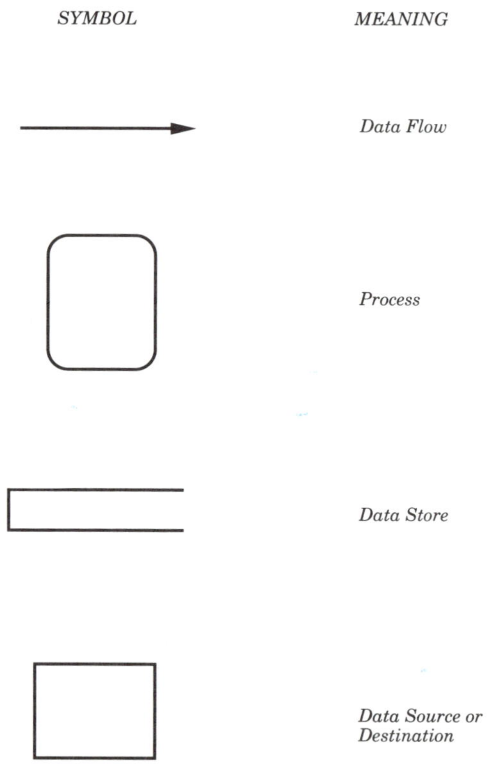

- Data Flow—A data flow is represented by an arrow with an arrowhead showing the direction of a flow. A data flow may be thought of as a pipeline through which data packets of known composition flow.
- Process—A process is represented by a rectangle with rounded corners. The function of a process is to transform or change incoming data flows to outgoing data flows.
- Data Store—Data stores are shown as a rectangle with one end left open. A data store serves as a temporary storage place for a data flow. Processes can add or retrieve data from a data store.
- Data Source or Destination—These are represented as a square. Data sources or destinations lie outside the boundaries of the system being investigated. Individuals, organizations, or other systems can be represented as data sources or destinations.

## AN EXAMPLE OF A DATA FLOW DIAGRAM

Illustrated in Figure 6.9 is an example of a simplified checking system. Two data sources or destinations are shown in the diagram, but Customer is repeated twice to avoid crossing data flow lines. The slash in the lower right-hand corner shows that customer has been repeated. Data stores may be repeated in a similar way, with the slash in the lower left hand corner.

A customer makes deposits to the bank. He writes checks to creditors, who send them to the customer's bank. The bank keeps customer accounts up-to-date by adding deposits and subtracting withdrawals. The up-to-date account balances are stored in Cust-Accts. The checks and deposit slips that reflect these changes in account balances are stored in a data store Cust-Trans.

Periodically, a statement of the customer's account is printed by reproducing the running account balance for the period. The statement is placed in an envelope with cancelled checks and deposit slips and mailed to the customer.

## NAMING DATA FLOW DIAGRAM COMPONENTS

For data flow diagrams to be an effective analysis and documentation tool, the names of data flow diagram components must be chosen carefully. Names should communicate what is occurring in the application being modeled. Data flows and data stores should be given names that describe the content of the data flowing through the system. Processes should be given a name with a strong verb which clearly describes what data transformation is occurring.

FIGURE 6.9

*Data Flow Diagram for Simplified Check Processing*

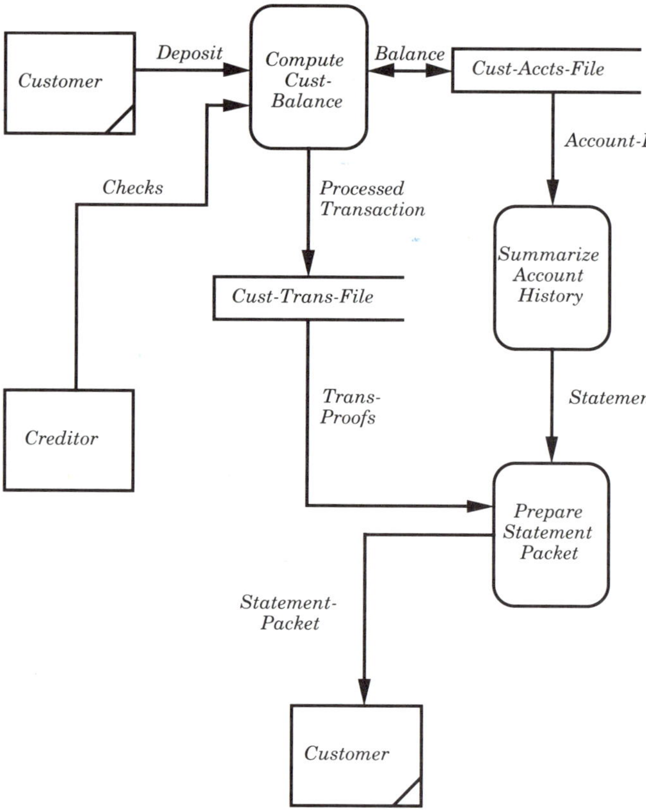


## GUIDELINES IN USING DATA FLOW DIAGRAMS

Data flow diagrams typically require several iterations before one has a satisfactory result. Some other observations that may be helpful in drawing data-flow diagrams include:

1. Processes transform input data flows. If data flows are not transformed, there is no need for a process.
2. All data flows originate or terminate with a process.
3. Processes should have both incoming and outgoing data flows.
4. Data stores should also have incoming and outgoing data flows.
5. Data flow diagramming should begin with a data flow diagram that represents an overview of the system being modeled.
6. Complex processes with multiple data flows can be resolved by breaking them down into two or more simple processes.

There are two alternative data flow diagramming conventions. These conventions are illustrated in Figure 6.10.

FIGURE 6.10
*Alternative Data Flow Diagramming Conventions*

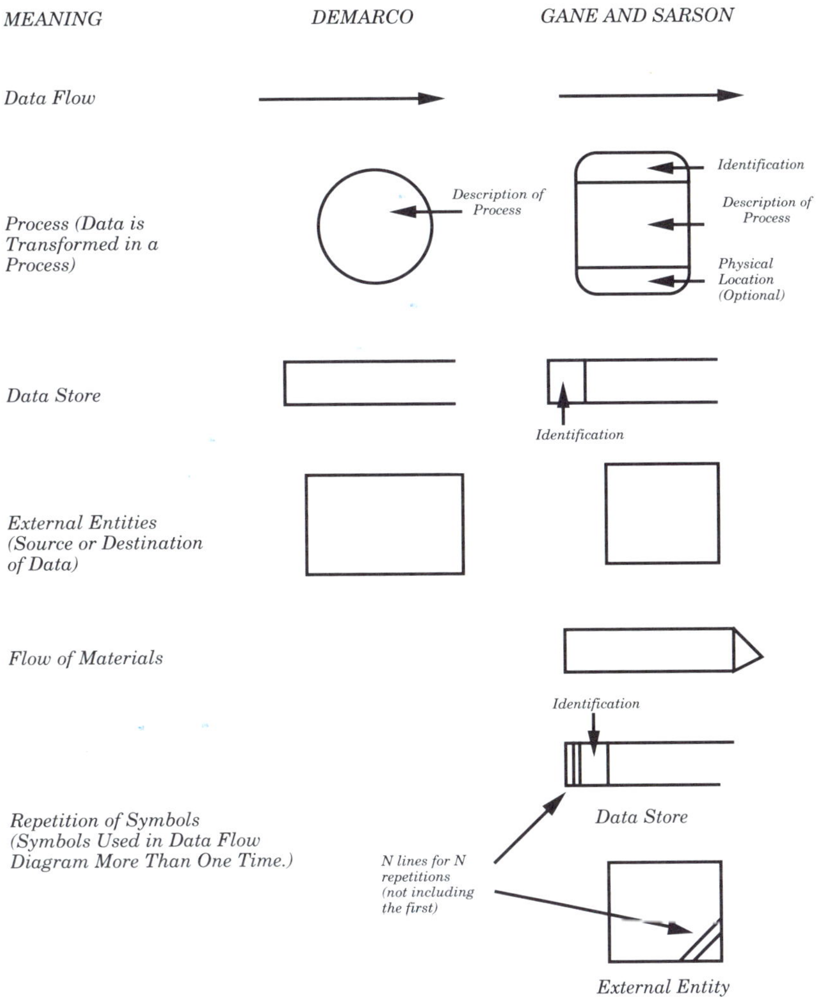


We believe the Gane and Sarson conventions are preferable to the DeMarco symbols for two reasons: (1) The rounded rectangle is better suited than the circle for computer drawn diagrams; and (2) the distinction between data flow and materials flow resolves some of the ambiguity of the DeMarco conventions.

## DATA DICTIONARY

Data flows and data stores are defined in a data dictionary. The purpose of a data dictionary is to clearly define each data element or collection of data elements which are also known as data structures.

The term *data dictionary* as used in system analysis is somewhat different from the same term used in database processing. The systems analyst refers to the data dictionary as a collection of definitions about data. A database specialist uses the term *data dictionary* in a broader context. A data dictionary is a program which not only maintains definitions about data, but which may control access to that same data. In this textbook, we refer to this usage as an *integrated data dictionary*.

The purpose of the data dictionary is to standardize data names to avoid confusion and duplication. It represents the second tool in structured systems analysis. The third tool illustrates the logical steps involved with the transformation of data in a process. The options for illustrating process logic are discussed in the next section.

## REPRESENTING PROCESS LOGIC

Several options are available for representing the transformation of data that takes place in a process. One of these is the program flow chart which was discussed earlier. This option is not recommended because of the amount of effort that is required to prepare a flow chart and to keep it up to date as changes occur in a system. More plausible alternatives are decision tables, structured English or decision trees.

A decision tree for the Farmington Water Department problem, shown earlier as a decision table, is shown in Figure 6.11.

Decision trees are especially applicable when the number of actions is small and not every combination of conditions is possible. If there are a large number of actions based on many possible combinations of conditions, the decision table is preferable. Users generally find decision trees easier to understand than decision tables.

Structured English is the third possibility for describing the logic that occurs in a process. It is particularly useful for logic with both loops and branches. Again, the logic for the water billing problem might be represented as shown in Figure 6.12.

FIGURE 6.11

*Decision Tree for Water Billing Problem*

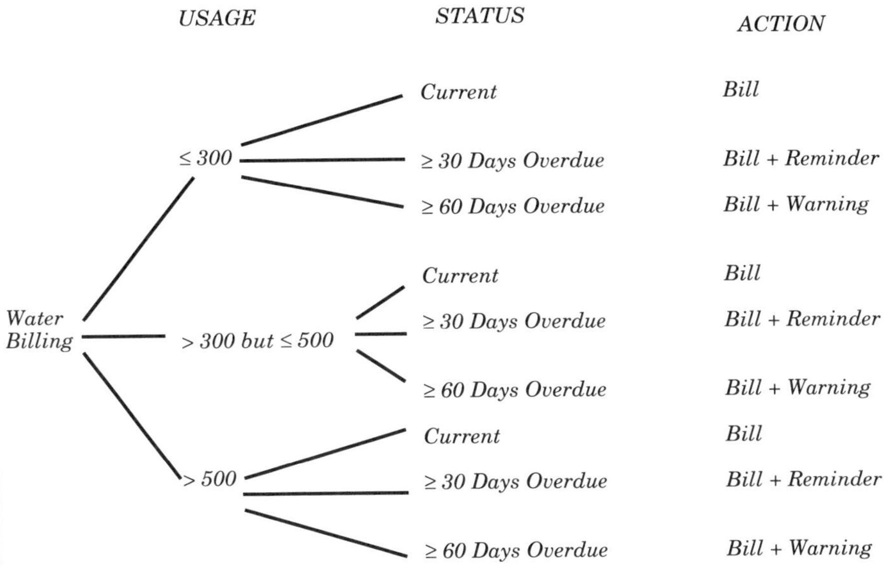


FIGURE 6.12

*Structure d English Version of Water Billing Problem*

```
COMPUTE WATER BILL
  IF USAGE IS LE 300 GAL
    THEN IF BILL IS CURRENT
      THEN BILL MINIMUM RATE
    ELSE IF BILL ≥ 60 DAYS OVERDUE
      THEN BILL MINIMUM RATE
        PRINT WARNING
      ELSE BILL MINIMUM RATE
        PRINT REMINDER

  ELSE IF USAGE IS GT 300 AND LE 500 GA
    THEN IF BILL IS CURRENT
      THEN BILL USUAL RATE
    ELSE IF BILL ≥ 60 DAYS OVERDUE
      THEN BILL USUAL RATE
        PRINT WARNING
      ELSE BILL USUAL RATE
        PRINT REMINDER

  ELSE
    THEN IF BILL IS CURRENT
      THEN BILL HIGH RATE
    ELSE IF BILL ≥ 60 DAYS OVERDUE
      THEN BILL HIGH RATE
        PRINT WARNING
      ELSE BILL HIGH RATE
        PRINT REMINDER
```

Structured English conforms to the standards of structured programming. It does provide an excellent guide for a programmer to implement a process in a programming language. The main criticisms of structured English is that it requires too much effort, may not be understandable to end users and is not standardized.

## AN OVERVIEW OF STRUCTURED SYSTEMS ANALYSIS METHODS

Structured systems analysis techniques represented a major step forward in improving the quality of software. Unfortunately, these methods largely ignored the emergence of database technology and are most applicable in a file-processing environment.

Jones has examined the impact of structured analysis, design, and programming methods on software development productivity, which includes the entire systems development life cycle. His conclusions are as follows:[5]

> The structured methods by themselves have not solved all of the problems of development of programming systems, nor are they able to turn amateurs into top flight professionals. But their records of improvement are solid when rigorously applied, and they do much to lower the risks of massive overruns and perhaps outright project failures that historically were associated with the unstructured programming methods.

Jones shows that structured methods required 52 months and $260,000 to complete a project compared with 92 months and $460,000 for a comparable unstructured project.[6] This represents a significant improvement in productivity.

## COMPUTER ASSISTED SOFTWARE ENGINEERING

Computer assisted software engineering (CASE) is a concept which attempts to automate the systems development life cycle. Some of these products have focused on systems analysis and design. Examples of these products include Excelerator, Case 2000 and Prokit* Workbench.

These case tools attempt to automate structured analysis methodologies such as De Marco and Gane-Sarson. These tools support an analyst working at a workstation equipped with a graphics monitor and a mouse. This environment integrates the diagrams with a data dictionary. An example of a data flow diagram drawn with Excelerator is shown in Figure 6.12.

FIGURE 6.12

*A Data Flow Diagram Drawn With Excelerator*

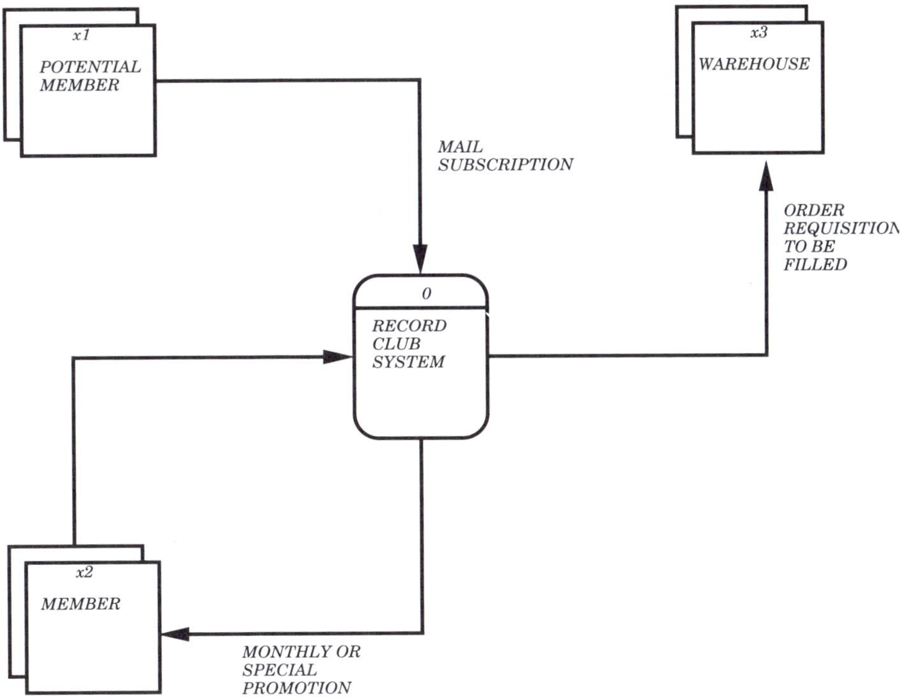


Many of the vendors of these tools are attempting to link them to application generators. If linked to an application generator the CASE tool becomes a vehicle for software automation. The front-end analysis and design component, e.g., Excelerator, is a mechanism for capturing and storing specifications for an application.

## Guidelines for Managers

MANAGERS SHOULD INSIST THAT THE SOFTWARE DEVELOPMENT methodologies used in a firm reflect current leading edge practices. Good methodologies produce higher quality software in less time and at less cost than trailing edge methods. Personnel should be thoroughly and continuously trained to keep them abreast of new developments.

Software development methodologies are constantly being improved. This suggests that an organization should research and experiment with new developments.

## Guidelines for MIS Professionals

INFORMATION SYSTEMS PROFESSIONALS SHOULD SEEK CONTINUOUSLY to enhance the quality of software and the productivity of the software development process. This strategy will keep them up to date and their skills in demand.

## Key Terms

| | |
|---|---|
| Systems Analyst | End-Users |
| Iteration | Decomposition |
| Diagramming Techniques | Iconic Models |
| Symbolic Models | Analogic Models |
| Prototyping | Synthesis |
| Analysis | Design |
| Coding | Testing |
| Implementation | Program Flowcharts |
| System Flowcharts | Decision Tables |
| Structured Methods | Software Engineering |
| Top-Down Design | Modularity |
| Data Flow Diagram | Decision Trees |

## Review Questions

1. What are the advantages of a systems analyst over an end-user in designing data processing systems?
2. What is the difference between iteration and decomposition?
3. List the five activities that make up the systems life cycle. Do the activities tend to occur sequentially or iteratively?
4. How are program flowcharts used today? Draw one for a process you go through every day such as taking a test, answering the phone, making coffee or checking a program out of the library.
5. Draw at least four common symbols used in a data flow diagram and briefly explain what each means.

6. What is the strength of a decision table in documenting processes?
7. What problems existed with software development prior to the structured programming revolution?
8. Discuss the two fundamental ideas behind structured methods.
9. Discuss why the Gane and Sarson conventions to data flow diagramming are preferable to the DeMarco symbols.
10. What is the difference between the term data dictionary as used in system analysis versus the same term used in database processing?

**Case Study**

## RIVER CITY MEATS, INC.

The EDP department of River City Meats, Inc. was recently reorganized and now consists of 7 people in two sections: A development manager and a systems analyst in the new development section and a maintenance/operations section consisting of an operations manager, 2 programmers, a computer operator, and a PC technical suport person.

The operations manager and the two programmers are all alumni of a two year technical college with no previous educational exposure to structured analysis and design techniques

When the EDP department was recently divided into these two groups, the new development staff instituted plans to adopt a structured design methodology. This new methodology, it was hoped, would redress some of the problems that had been building as the company grew larger and more complex.

Before the introduction of a structured design methodology at River City Meats, Inc., projects were handed to each of the programmers, relying upon each of them to analyze the needs of the user as well as design, code, and test the solution. This approach worked well for one of the programmers. She went to the user departments requesting information and clarification before coding. The other programmer, however, designed, coded, tested and implemented solution systems without leaving his desk. User involvement was not considered necessary.

Both programmers were guilty of supplying little or no documentation for the programs they wrote. And without individual module documentation, system documentation was impossible to construct.

The operations manager created flowcharts when giving assignments to the other programmers, but the standard flowcharting symbols were used interchangeably for each other, reducing their overall clarity.

In addition, the operating mode of the department before the restructuring was largely reactive rather than anticipatory. Very little time could be devoted to developing sound and effective systems because so much time was spent in maintenance and *fire fighting*. Many runtime errors were not investigated because finding the reason for the ABEND would take too long. The usual solution would be to restart the program from where it had left off.

The staff, realizing they had entered a cycle of deteriorating effectiveness, recognized a fundamental restructuring of procedures and resources was necessary in order to break the cycle.

The Gane and Sarson technique of data flow diagramming was selected. It was felt that these diagrams would be extremely useful in providing the system overviews that were so desperately needed. The utility of these diagrams could be seen in both new development and maintenance applications. Oftentimes, in the old operating environment, analysis of a modification's impact was incomplete because certain segments of a system had been overlooked.

1. Which phases of the systems life cycle will be aided by the introduction of data flow diagrams?
2. Do you think the introduction of structured methods will alleviate most of the problems in the EDP Department at River City Meats, Inc.? Explain your reasoning.
3. How would you proceed with implementing this new design methodology within the EDP Department?

## Suggestions for Further Reading

Colter, Mel A., "A Comparative Examination of Systems Analysis Techniques," MIS Quarterly, March 1984, pp. 51-66.

*This article gives an excellent overview of many systems analysis techniques. Included in the article are charts evaluating each technique in eight key analytical dimensions. The author briefly follows the development of systems analysis from traditional techniques to the more current structured techniques. In summary, the author suggests that a combination of techniques will dominate the next generation of system analysis.*

# 7

# Software Development Issues

*"Oil and software are the two principle obstacles to economic progress."*

*The Wall Street Journal*

## Overview and Objectives

THIS CHAPTER EXAMINES THE PROBLEMS WITH CURRENT software Development methods. The primary problems are that these methods lack flexibility; they are slow; and perhaps most important, they are inefficient.

Solving these problems requires a broad based attack that includes new tools for programmers and end users, new methods for systems analysts and a new relationship between computer professionals and end-users.

In this chapter, we will examine several new methodologies for software development and discuss the environment most suitable for each. Finally, we will analyze the environmental factors that impact the development method selection.

AFTER READING THIS CHAPTER YOU SHOULD BE ABLE TO:

- Describe the maintenance trap;
- List several promising alternatives for increasing the productivity of programmers;
- Discuss the advantages and disadvantages of developing versus buying software;
- Illustrate the benefits of user involvement in software development;
- Explain the concept of prototyping;
- Discuss why application backlogs are common to most organizations involved with data processing;
- Explain the problems associated with software development and some general approaches to a solution.

## Software Development Methodology

### PURPOSE OF SOFTWARE DEVELOPMENT METHODOLOGIES

A *methodology* refers to a set of practices and procedures. A software development methodology is a conceptual approach which includes a set of techniques that are used in application development. Many organizations have attempted to standardize using a software development methodology which implements the software-development life cycle. Typically, this involves training data-processing professionals to use the forms, diagramming techniques and procedures prescribed in a software development methodology. Several commercial methodologies are available, and purchasing them entitles the buyer to training and documentation.

The intent of organizations to enforce more discipline in application development is understandable, even if it is sometimes misguided. The classical systems-development life cycle is suitable for applications in which the user's requirement can be specified in great detail before programming begins. There are, however, a large number of applications which do not fit the classical systems-development life cycle, and consequently are inappropriate for applying a related software-development methodology. Furthermore, there are some new software development technologies that require new approaches to software development.

## Methodology Lags Technology

A new technology calls for new methodologies. People tend to accept new technologies, but use them with tried-and-true but inappropriate methodologies. Wetherbe illustrates this point with an historical example showing how the technology of the rifle was slow to be exploited in the tactics of war because of a lag in methodology. During the Revolutionary War, the British came to America with rifles but used a methodology of warfare that was designed for swords, shields, and long bows.

The British tactics consisted of massing their soldiers shoulder-to-shoulder in ranks and marching them directly at the enemy. The British troops wore red jackets with white webbing across the chest. The colonials, untutored in modern warfare, did what came naturally. They hid behind the rocks and trees in their drab clothing, took aim at the white cross on a red background, and inflicted great damage on the British.

Why did the British use a methodology that was so unsuitable for their technology? Their tactics had been effective in an earlier era with a different technology, but their failure to recognize that a new technology required a different methodology was their undoing and they suffered great losses as a result.

Later, in the Civil War, both the North and the South had become converted to "modern" theories of warfare. They massed their troops and marched them directly at the enemy. The result was a greater loss of life in the Civil War than that of World War I and World War II combined. It wasn't until the 20th century that camouflage clothing and digging foxholes became accepted methodologies.[1]

The lag in methodology is a major problem with fourth generation and database technologies. There is great difficulty in changing the way people work.

In the next section we examine the current software development technologies and methodologies. The term "current" implies the most widely used methodologies as opposed to state of the art.

## Problems Related to Current Methodologies

THE CURRENT COMPUTING ENVIRONMENT IS CHARACTERIZED by problems of inflexibility, low productivity of the programming staff, and applications backlog. Figure 7.1 describes the components of this environment and their characteristics. The outcomes illustrated in Figure 7.1 are the result of interaction of all of these factors.

FIGURE 7.1 *Problems With the Current Computing Environment*

| | Component | Characteristic | Outcomes |
|---|---|---|---|
| Mode of Processing | File Processing | Data dependence, inflexibility and inaccessible data | Application backlogs |
| Programming Language | COBOL | Low programmer productivity | Maintenance trap |
| Application Development Methodology | Systems Life Cycle | Slow application development | Low priority for decision support |

### INFLEXIBILITY

Inflexibility in the current computing environment is the result of several factors including data dependence and complexity. Not only is the technology complex but the applications being developed are complex. The combination of complex technology and complex problems leads to the adoption of software development methodologies that are inherently inflexible. One source of inflexibility is data dependence.

Data dependence is the result of file formats being imbedded in application software. Several application programs typically access the same file. In each program, the file format is a part of the program. Changes in a file require changes in the formats of each program accessing the file. The inevitable result is that minor changes in one program trigger a whole series of changes in other programs.

The disadvantage of data dependence are two-fold: first, it requires the programmer to define the format of the data in each application program and, second, if the format of a data file is changed, then the data definition in each application program accessing that file must be changed. The first disadvantage is especially dramatic in COBOL, where a typical program would be almost 50% Data Division, which comprises the data definition. The second disadvantage is of greater importance, however, because of the inflexibility it creates when making changes. Inflexibility leads to what we have referred to as the "maintenance trap."

Inflexibility creates maintenance problems. Minor changes in one application triggers a cascading set of changes in other programs.

## THE MAINTENANCE TRAP

As a result of the increased complexity of software maintenance, the proportion of programming resources devoted to new applications falls over time, and the proportion of programming effort devoted to maintenance rises. In some organizations maintenance, is estimated to require 80% of the programming budget. This result is illustrated in Figure 7.2 below.

FIGURE 7.2

*The Maintenance Trap*

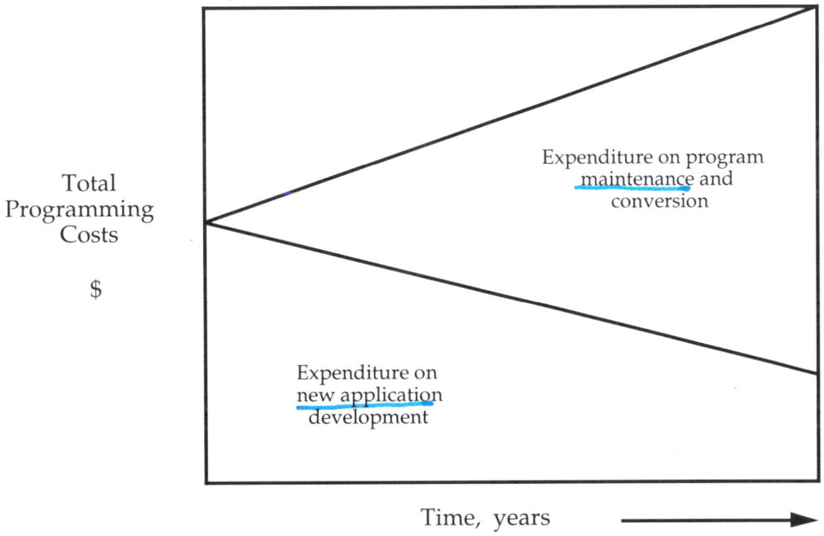

The dilemma illustrated in Figure 7.2 explains the backlogs of new applications, which in some organizations have reached 5 years. An IBM survey of its major customers revealed that only 14% of the human data-processing resources were used for writing and testing new applications.[2] The remaining 86% was used for systems analysis, writing specifications, documentation existing applications, and maintenance.

The emphasis on maintenance of transaction processing applications has had two effects: (1) the development of application backlogs, and (2) the neglect of decision support applications. Automation of clerical systems or transaction processing has been the first priority of MIS managers since the beginning of computer applications in organizations. The preoccupation of the MIS professionals with development and maintaining transaction processing systems and the consequent neglect of decision support applications has been a source of frustration and annoyance for middle and top management.

## APPLICATION BACKLOG

Application backlogs in most organizations are increasing because the demand for new applications is growing faster than the Information Systems staff resources. The visible backlog actually understates the problem. Discouraged end-users, in many cases, are aware of this backlog and have not requested new applications. Application backlogs are especially frustrating to managers requesting applications to provide information for management planning and decision making. These applications, which have been referred to as decision support applications, are essential to provide management with information for planning and control uses.

Many organizations have turned to personal computers to solve their information needs. This is only a partial solution. Much of the data which is required for decision making is a by-product of the transaction processing system and remains relatively inaccessible to free-standing personal computers. The difficulty of accessing data in a file-processing environment makes access to transaction data almost impossible for end-users. More accessible data storage is required.

## EXCESSIVE SPECIALIZATION IN SOFTWARE DEVELOPMENT

Some critics of the degree of specialization used in the data-processing industry have suggested that the industry is creating software assembly lines. The result is narrow jobs which reduce the motivation and satisfaction of the application developer and lead to excessive documentation and red tape.

There are several advantages to the high degree of specialization used in software development: (1) It allows an organization to use programmers and analysts with limited education; (2) It permits an organization to divide the software development task into independent modules which permits parallel development; and (3) It facilitates the development of experts in the more technical aspects of software development.

However, there are also some hidden costs to the high degree of specialization of labor in software development. The use of programmers with narrow backgrounds requires greater supervision and coordination. Furthermore, this degree of specialization insulates the programmer from the end-user. The effect of little-or-no feedback from end-users is two-fold: (1) the programmer is forced to rely on formal specifications or supervisory instructions to understand what is desired; and (2) the motivational impact of feedback from users is lost.

An extensive division of labor for software development requires more extensive and formal specifications for a proposed application. These requirements require considerable time and resources to develop. In addition, the potential for communications problems and misunderstanding of the user's requirements is multiplied as the number of interpretations increases.

## The User's Role in Software Development

THE END USER IN THE TRADITIONAL SYSTEMS LIFE CYCLE HAS occupied a passive role. Some observers have suggested that some of the difficulties associated with the traditional life cycle are at least partly due to the frustrations of end-users.

The development of computer software within an organization is a sensitive process, involving both end-users and computer professionals. The need for end-user involvement in software development is often given lip service by technical personnel whose objective is to minimize their involvement in the process itself. Some computer professionals feel that users "muddy the waters." While most technical people recognize the importance of selling the user on the merits of a software project, they frequently do not feel that the user has much to contribute in its development.

Users' satisfaction and acceptance of a project is frequently critical to the success of the installation and subsequent operation of new computer systems. Alter found that in 15 software development projects with significant implementation problems, 11 involved no user involvement in implementation or project initiation. In contrast, in 31 systems initiated by users, or in which users had an active role in implementation, only 4 had significant implementation problems.[3]

Texas Instruments has used a concept called Joint Application Design. This is a simple idea which is just what its name implies. Managers, end users, systems analysts, and programmers come together at the beginning of a project to systematically define the needs and basic design of a new project. The Texas Instruments program is discussed in more detail in When Things Go Right.[4]

**When things go right**

## Texas Instruments' Use of Joint Application Design

Industry surveys show that 85% of the bugs in computer programs are the result of errors in analysis and design. A better understanding of users' requirements should improve the quality of systems delivered to the end user.

Joint Application Design (JAD) is a concept that is implemented in a 2-4 day workshop. It brings together managers, end users, a systems analyst responsible for developing a system, and a JAD moderator who conducts the session. The outcome is a user requirements specification.

The pilot JAD session of Texas Instruments concerned a purchased material inventory system in the semiconductor division. The initial session required three and a half days. It resulted in twenty-six screen designs and the systems manager estimated that it shortened development time by three months.

The pilot program was highly successful in over 70 projects at TI. The concept has been found to have particular applicability in situations where the application development staff and the end users are not at the same location. The JAD session reduces the amount of travel required to complete the design effort.

Reaction of end users to JAD has been highly favorable. Following JAD sessions a questionnaire is

**distributed to participants. Eighty-five percent of participants have rated the system design as good or better than conventional design outcomes.**

**Texas Instruments has been moving towards a new concept in application development which is called Information Engineering. They find JAD interfaces well with Information Engineering. Computer based tools which are a part of Information Engineering may be used in a JAD session in the following ways: (1) to document the results of a JAD session, (2) to develop screen diagrams during a session, and (3) to project and document results of a JAD session.**

Adapted from Joint Application Design at Texas Instruments by Linda Speckmann, Technology Transfer News, Winter 1986/1987, pp. 12-13.

There are actually several group design methodologies. In all of these methods the facilitators play a crucial role. They must be good at group dynamics and be able to listen.[5]

These methods claim to speed up the application development process by compressing the analysis and design phases of the system life cycle. A bonus benefit is the ease and speed with which applications can be introduced into the organization.[6]

The involvement of end users recognizes the problem that has plagued the data processing industry from its inception; the development of technically correct, but functionally ineffective, software. Users have a perspective that is frequently unrecognized by MIS professionals—they understand the problem. While users lack technical skills, an informed user typically has a conceptual understanding of the problem that exceeds that of the designers. The subtle aspects of a problem that are not picked up by a software analyst are well known to the experienced user.

## Assumptions of Traditional Systems Analysis

SYSTEMS ANALYSIS AS CURRENTLY PRACTICED ASSUMES THAT:

1. End-users need a middleman to communicate effectively with computer professionals.
2. The requirements for a project must be thoroughly documented and signed off by end users to avoid future misunderstandings.
3. System specifications must be frozen and subsequent change minimized before programming begins to implement a system successfully.
4. End users can anticipate what is required in a proposed application.

Systems analysts occupy an intermediary role between end users and computer professionals. Organizations have found this role necessary to bridge the gap between programmers with little understanding of business applications and end users with a cursory understanding of the computer. Obviously, as end users learn more about computing and programmers learn more about business applications, this intermediary role of the system analyst becomes less important.

The specifications of a proposed computer system are prepared by the systems analyst and written up as a requirements document. Requirements documents, which consist of text, diagrams, and tables describing a proposed computer system may run hundreds of pages for complex computer systems. Typically, end users are asked to review this document and sign-off on the proposed system.

Several questions could be asked about this procedure. How well do end-users understand a complex technical document? What is the purpose of end-user sign-off? Is it to avoid blame if a system fails to meet end-user expectations? There is no argument with careful planning, but frequently end-user sign-off appears to be a device to avoid responsibility in the event of failure.

The complexity of most traditional computer systems makes changes unwelcome once a project has reached the implementation stage. This reflects the inflexibility of file processing and the interdependence of data and application programs. This problem of inflexibility is inherent in file processing and third generation languages. The sign-off also represents a specification freeze to avoid the problem of attempting to hit a moving target.

Finally, the assumption that end users can describe exactly what they want depends a good deal on the sophistication of the user and their ability to visualize a solution.

## Problems with Traditional Systems Analysis

SEVERAL CRITICISMS HAVE BEEN DIRECTED AT THE TRADITIONAL methods of systems analysis. The most devastating criticism is that it takes too long and frequently gets poor results.

The criticisms of the role and methodology of systems analysis are expressed in the slogan "paralysis by analysis." Sheil has stated that "the implementation disasters of the 1960s are slowly being succeeded by the design disasters of the 1980s." He suggests that the methods of systems analysis and design can't cope with the complexity and rapid change encountered in modern organizations.[7]

Communication problems are the rule rather than the exception in developing new systems using conventional methods. English is not a precise language for specifying computer applications. Furthermore, computer professionals have their own set of jargon which they use without recognizing that the uninitiated frequently do not understand. To try to bridge this communications gap, systems analysts have developed a set of symbolic tools which define computer systems. This requires users to learn a technique such as data-flow diagrams. While appearing to be simple, they are often misunderstood by end users.

Systems analysts using the traditional systems life cycle ask users to sign off a detailed set of specifications. There is a very high probability that something will be missed. Because of the inflexibility of conventional development tools, changes suggested by the user after sign off are resisted. Furthermore, users are sometimes hesitant to suggest changes that require extensive effort. Systems analysts attempt to freeze specifications early in software development projects. Conflict and missed deadlines are the usual result of changes.

## What Do We Need in Software Development Methodologies?

THE PRIMARY NEED IN SOFTWARE DEVELOPMENT IS FOR TOOLS that improve the productivity of the developers. Current methods are too time consuming, require too much effort by skilled computer professionals, and are too complex. The problem is too broad to solve with a single solution. A comprehensive but integrated solution is required to solve the problems of software development.

Automation of as much of the programmers' and systems analysts' job as is possible is a starting point. The computer has frequently been used to automate the work of other professions; why can't it be applied to the work of computer professionals?

Computer professionals should avoid hand drawn diagramming techniques and hand programming as much as possible. These can frequently be replaced with computer drawn diagrams and code generators. This development is discussed in the next chapter.

Encouragement of end-user computing relieves the programming staff of many routine demands which compete for their time and attention. End-user computing requires that users be able to use query languages, report generators, financial-planning languages, and other decision support tools. Careful attention must be made to the selection of the tools, the training of the users, and to their continued support.

A tool that allows applications to be developed more quickly is fourth-generation data-base languages used for prototyping. Some of these languages are suitable for developing heavy-duty applications, whereas others are suitable for prototyping and low volume applications.

The need for greater flexibility indicates the need for relational database products which eliminate the difficulties of data dependence associated with typical file-processing systems. These products must be used correctly to obtain the benefit of data independence. Databases must be designed correctly to be stable and accommodate new applications.

Improved methodologies must also communicate more effectively with end-users. Prototyping is an approach that attempts to build on users' understanding of the subtleties of their own application. End-user development also effectively addresses this issue.

End-user computing contributes to faster application development because it involves more people in the process. The extreme frustration with MIS departments that many users feel is relieved by their ability to obtain the applications they want.

A contemporary approach to software development also suggests a different approach to software development than the software factories of the past. It proposes that instead of using MIS professionals with narrow skills, using individuals with broad backgrounds who understand the application, as well as having the required development skills. In many cases, using high productivity 4th-generation language tools or CASE tools, a single individual can complete the entire task. Martin shows the comparison of 4th generation approach to traditional software development in Figure 7.3.

This diagram shows that a fourth generation approach completes the software development task in less time, using less resources. The quality of the finished product is a bonus benefit. The integrity of the original design is maintained because the designer is also the application developer.

FIGURE 7.3

*Fourth Generation Application Development Compared With Traditional Application Development*

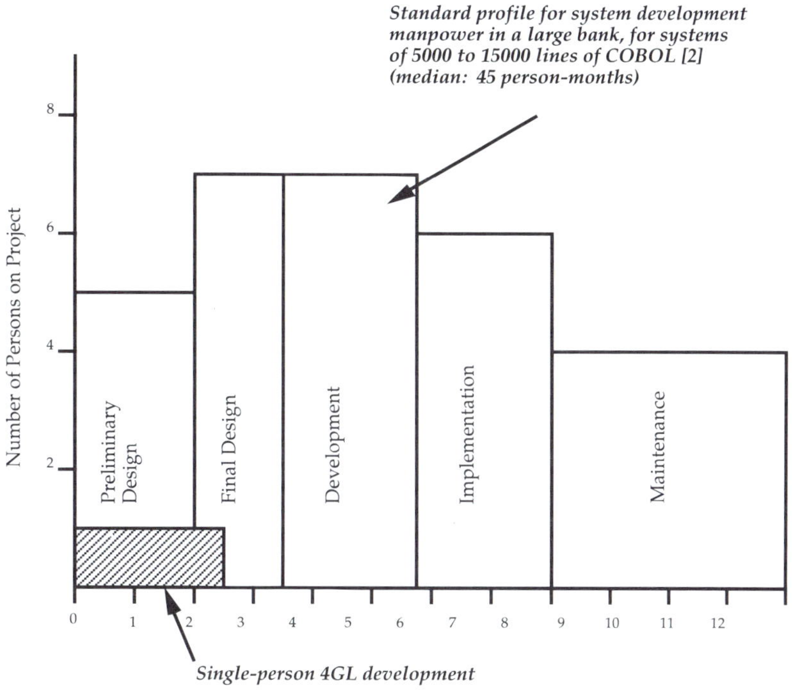


## Alternatives to Conventional Software Development

### PURCHASING A SOFTWARE PACKAGE

If a satisfactory commercial product is available, it is usually advantageous to purchase applications software instead of developing it. This is particularly true for the unsophisticated first-time user who cannot afford the staff necessary to develop and maintain software.

The primary advantage to purchasing software, as opposed to developing it internally, is cost. It has been estimated that internal-development costs using conventional methods are approximately 10 times greater than the same package purchased on the open market. For most small businesses making their first computer purchase, the advantages of purchasing software, as opposed to developing it themselves, are usually quite substantial. The primary reasons for purchasing software would be: 1) lower cost; 2) time savings: 3) the difficulty of obtaining the services of a skilled programmer; and 4) the observable quality of an existing product compared with the unknown quality of a internally developed system.

Most small business organizations need basic accounting software packages which are readily available. To duplicate these packages would usually cost several times their purchase price and several man-months of design and programming. Furthermore, a reputable product which has evolved through the experience of several users is frequently of higher quality than can be developed by a small organization with limited resources.

The president of a firm involved in selling small business computer systems confided that he felt that most of his customers would be better off using a standard off-the-shelf software package for an initial period, rather than trying to customize it to fit their particular business. Frequently, small businesspeople experience difficulty in defining their needs, and use of software product that closely approximates their needs can assist them in clarifying the desired end result.

In spite of the overwhelming advantages for a small business to purchase software, many have purchased hardware and tried to develop software themselves or with the assistance of a programmer. Many small businesses do not seem aware that something beyond programming skill is required to develop business systems. Design and implementation are two different tasks: for example, an architect specializes in design and a carpenter in implementation. The assumption that an inexperienced programmer is qualified to design software is comparable to the assumption that an apprentice carpenter is a qualified home designer.

One of the limitations of purchased software is that frequently a purchased package requires modifications. Depending on how extensive these modifications are, the apparent savings for purchasing may disappear. A second limitation is the difficulty of integrating a purchased package with existing software or another application package. Integration of two packages may be difficult and time-consuming. Finally, some purchased packages are difficult to modify as the needs of the business change. Many commercial packages were designed with 2nd generation technology and are inherently inflexible and difficult to modify.

Packages developed with fourth generation or CASE technology are relatively easy to modify and integrate with other applications. The ease of tailoring fourth-generation software makes it possible to adapt software to the organization rather than the organization to the software. Furthermore, with a core of functional applications in place, custom software can be developed to extend the functional capabilities of purchased software.

The need to modify software that is purchased is illustrated by a wholesaler's experience in purchasing a complete distributor's software package. The original software package was developed in California for wholesalers and distributors who sold their products almost exclusively within the state of California. Consequently, in applying a sales tax to a purchase, it had provision for a single rate only. The distributor did business in several states and cities in the Midwest with different sales tax rates, and was required by law to keep records of total sales and sales tax collections for each city or state. The distributor engaged a programmer to modify the software he purchased to provide this feature. The modifications turned out to be far more extensive than either the distributor or the programmer originally anticipated.

Evaluation of a software product alternative requires that it be thoroughly investigated to determine: 1) the adequacy of documentation; 2) the difficulty of software modifications required to tailor it to fit the organization; 3) the degree of difficulty to interface the software product with existing software; 4) the compatibility of the product with existing hardware and its operating system; 5) the quality and reliability of the product; and 6) the ease of modifying the package as the needs of the business change. Typically, an evaluation would require an organization to talk to other users and to conduct demonstrations or testing of a proposed package.

One of the primary disadvantages of purchasing software is that it generally does not provide a competitive advantage. Software that is developed by firms which gives them a strategic advantage is generally not sold to their competitors. Purchased software packages which dominate the banking industry have left regional banks vulnerable to competition from top-tier banks that have developed their own banking systems.

## PROTOTYPING

Application prototyping is an exciting new development made possible by the use of fourth-generation languages and CASE tools. A prototype is a working model of a proposed system. Prototypes enable users to visualize computer systems in a familiar role, that of a consumer. Consumers walk through model homes, test-drive cars and try personal computer software before they buy it. In application prototyping, the computer professional occupies the role of developer, and the user, the role of customer.

It is often said that a picture is worth a thousand words. A working model is worth a thousand diagrams and graphs in assisting users to visualize computer systems. It is easy for users to make suggestions for improvement when confronted with a working model.

The need to visualize working models should be emphasized. Users should be encouraged to change their minds. People need an atmosphere which encourages experimentation in order to maximize their contribution.[8]

Prototyping advocates make several assumptions about the development of computer systems:[9]

1. It is difficult to do something right the first time.
2. It is easier to modify or improve something than to start from scratch.
3. Learning is gradual, iterative, and accomplished by example.
4. Users cannot visualize systems accurately until they see working models.
5. The experience and insight of people are the most important factor in creating new systems—not a prescribed methodology.

The prototyping process can be described in diagram form. This is shown in Figure 7.4.

The benefits of prototyping are: (1) the user gets immediate feedback from the application developer; (2) problems are solved and ambiguities are clarified early in the project; (3) the user can see and experiment with a model of the proposed system; (4) the ease of modification makes the user less likely to accept a flawed solution.

Prototyping requires an integrated set of software tools which are described below:

1. Integrated data dictionary—stores definitions of data, programs, screen panels, and reports. It serves as a central repository of definitions for all other software tools.
2. Fourth generation language—an interactive high-productivity programming language which permits programs to be written in a fraction of the time compared with languages such as COBOL.

3. Report generator—a report generator is a software tool for structuring output in report formats quickly and easily.
4. Screen painting—a tool to produce CRT input screen formats. Input screen formats or panels in prototyping should have both the appearance and function of a desired system.
5. Query language—an easy to use tool for extracting ad hoc information requirements. This may be coupled with the report generator.
6. DBMS—a data base management system capable of interfacing with other software components and facilitating access to data.

FIGURE 7.4

*The Prototyping Process*

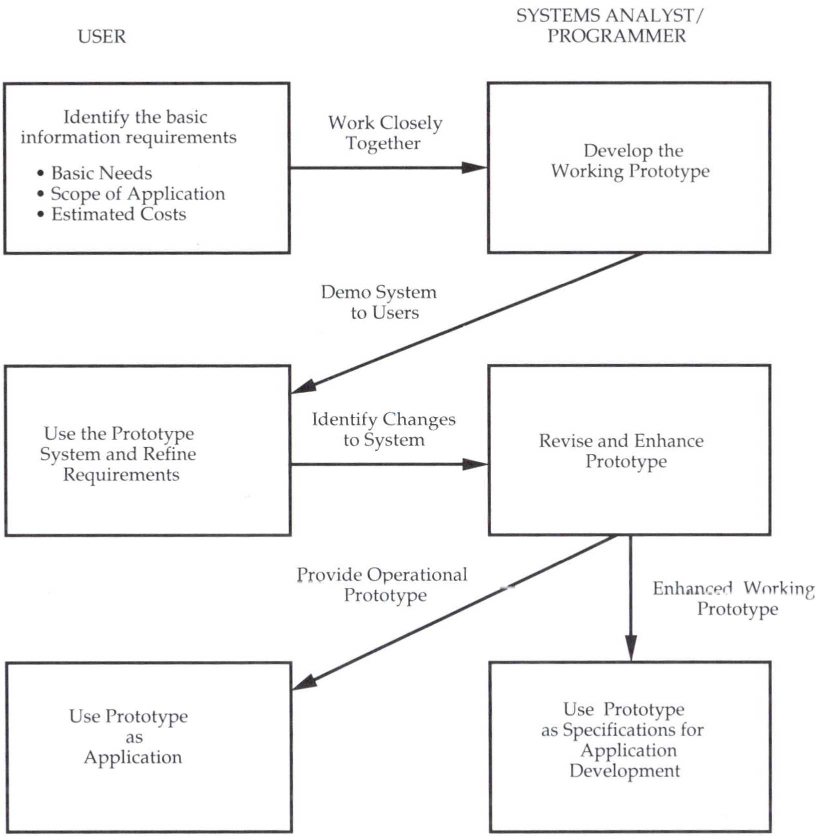


## USER DEVELOPMENT

The software tools described in this chapter make it possible for end users to create applications software without using COBOL and the traditional approach. These new languages include FOCUS, NOMAD2, RAMIS II, and DBASE IV.

These languages are easy to learn and all of them provide productivity improvements, compared with COBOL, of at least 200%. All of them are associated with data-base technology which allows the user to access an existing data base or a specially created one.

NOMAD2, RAMIS II, and FOCUS, while often referred to as fourth-generation languages, combine a database management system with a very high level programming language. dBASE IV is a similar product in the personal computer environment. These languages excel at getting results quickly. For this reason, they are often used for prototyping.

## Selection of a Software Development Method

ALL SOFTWARE DEVELOPMENT METHODS, EVEN THE MOST TRAditional, have their place in a well-managed information systems facility. Management of the software development process requires awareness of the alternatives and matching the method of development with the problem. The alternatives are as follows:

1. Traditional systems life cycle—this process includes systems analysis, design, coding, testing, and implementation.
2. Purchased package—purchase of software from a software vendor.
3. Prototyping—prototyping involves experimentation and iterative improvements.
4. User-based development—users can frequently develop their own software for some applications.

Gremillian and Pyburn have said that the key factors in determining which of these methods to use are: (1) commonality, (2) impact, and (3) structure.[10]

### COMMONALITY

The commonality factor refers to the degree to which the problem is common to other organizations. The extent to which other organizations have similar applications or problems is a measure of commonality. The opposite of commonality is uniqueness.

An application with a high degree of commonality usually allows the organization to purchase a standard package to solve the problem. If a high degree of uniqueness is present in the problem, some sort of in-house development is suggested.

## Impact

Impact is the degree to which the proposed software will affect the organization. Software professionals should be involved with projects with a high level of impact. Professional involvement is desirable to develop software that exhibits a high degree of execution efficiency, maintainability, integrates effectively with other software, and is adequately documented.

Low impact applications can often be developed by end users. Involvement of data-processing professionals may not be justified for systems confined to one or two persons, or for which the consequences of failure are small.

### STRUCTURE

Structure is the extent to which we understand the problem. Problems with a low degree of structure lend themselves to prototyping. The strength of prototyping is the intimate involvement of the end user in the development process.

A project with a high degree of structure exhibits inputs and outputs that are well understood. High-structure problems are candidates for either traditional development methods or purchased software.

Table 7.1 summarizes the relationship between these three factors and the method of software development used.

TABLE 7.1 *Selecting a Software Development Methodology*

| PROPERTIES | | | |
|---|---|---|---|
| COMMONALITY | IMPACT | STRUCTURE | SUGGESTED METHOD |
| High | Broad | High | Package |
| Low | Broad | High | Traditional |
| Low | Broad | Low | Prototype |
| High | Limited | High | Package |
| Low | Limited | High | User-developed |
| Low | Limited | Low | User-developed |

Several observations could be made about the relationships shown in Table 7.1.

1. When confronted with problems with a high degree of commonality, an organization should consider a purchased package. In most cases, it should be possible to find a suitable high quality product with excellent documentation.
2. When a high degree of uniqueness exists, a custom-development project should be considered. The factors of impact and structure should determine if it should be developed using the traditional life cycle, prototyping, or user-development. Limited impact indicates a user-developed solution.
3. Situations with a low degree of structure are candidates for prototyping. The systems analyst is still responsible for creating the system, but the user is responsible for the design.

Alternatives to the traditional life cycle can frequently provide higher-quality solutions and/ora less expensive solutions. The factors of commonality, impact and structure provide a contingency decision rule for selecting the appropriate development method.

## A Comparison of Alternative Approaches to Software Development

AT LEAST FOUR TYPES OF APPLICATION DEVELOPMENT ARE NOW possible.

1. Traditional development using the systems life cycle. The problems with conventional development have been discussed earlier, including application backlogs, excessive maintenance, and neglect of decision-support applications.
2. Prototypes developed using a 4th-generation language by application developers and end users are modified until it is suitable for development in a high level language. The prototype serves as a blueprint for implementation in a high level language.
3. Development of a prototype using a 4th-generation language. This may be a joint effort between an end user and an application developer or it may be an end-user project. The 4th-generation language code becomes the production application.
4. Use of an integrated computer-assisted software engineering (CASE) tool. This development harnesses the computer to assist in the development of computer systems. It is described in more detail in the next chapter.

Application development in the 1990s is addressed in Issues and Controversies.

## Issues and Controversies

## Application Development in the 5th Generation

The framework for building applications in the 1990's is being formed by movement toward three-tiered computing architectures, SQL-based database management systems, computer aided software engineering (CASE) application generators, and expert system techniques. Using the capabilities of these technologies, most applications in the 1990s will be built on the descendants of today's microcomputers. Application development in the future will also be made easier by the development of software packages that can be readily customized.

There is enormous economic incentive for distributing the computering workload over several machines and away from the mainframe. The cost of a million instructions per second (MIPS) for microprocessors is $4000 versus $160,000 for mainframes. In addition the microprocessors can hold their own in speed comparisons. A COBOL compiler on an IBM PC-AT is comparable in speed to an IBM 3083.

Given these benefits, one might predict a massive migration toward distributed processing. This has not occurred yet due to immature application development tools for microcomputers. These tools have not yet hit their stride. Distributed database technology, networks, user interfaces, and database access tools will be in place in the next five years.

The idea behind a distributed database is to have a single logical database implemented on diverse machines. Early versions of distributed database management systems have been introduced by Relational Technology, Oracle Corp., and Applied Data Research.

Relational and distributed are the two key terms for database systems in the fifth generation. Relational technology is expected to dominate database systems through the next decade.

One of the weaknesses of relational technology is handling applications that generate 20 to 200 transactions per second. One important solution to high volume transaction processing is database machines. Two such machines are currently available, Britton Lee and Teradata. The Teradata machine has demonstrated a tenfold price/performance advantage over software-only DB2 implementations.

CASE technology is to programmers what CAD/CAM is to engineers. By the 1990s many firms will be building applications without programmers using business analysts.

Much of the power and potential of CASE tools comes from their data dictionaries/repositories.

**The repository stores not only data but information on data entry screens, report formats and processing steps. The repository is an active rather than passive tool which provides control.**

**The new applications built in this environment will be revolutionary because they take advantage of advances in microcomputer technology, as well as distributed relational database systems, SQL, CASE, and expert systems. They will be revolutionary in another way because small firms will be able to develop systems that are leading-edge applications. The new software tools will enable firms to develop systems for strategic advantage that would have cost hundreds of millions of dollars in the 1970s.**

Adapted from George Schussel, "Application Development in the 5th Generation," Datamation (November 15, 1987, pp. 94-107.

## Guidelines for Managers

THERE ARE SEVERAL ALTERNATIVES TO CONVENTIONAL SOFTware development. These methods promise greater productivity and better quality software. The environment for each of these alternatives varies, so care must be exercised in choosing the software development method.

## Guidelines for MIS Professionals

NEW TECHNOLOGY MAKES IT POSSIBLE TO IMPROVE THE PROductivity of the software development process. This new technology requires new methodologies which are tailored for the new technology. The new methodologies dramatically change the role of systems analysts and end-users in the software development process.

## Key Terms

Software Development Methodology
Data Dependence
Maintenance Trap
Applications Backlog
Joint Application Design
User Primacy
Applications Prototyping
Traditional Systems Life Cycle
User-Based Development
Commonality
Impact
Structure
Error-Free Code

## Review Questions

1. What problems characterize the current computing environment?
2. Why is the use of personal computers only a partial solution to an organization's information needs?
3. Discuss some of the advantages and disadvantages of narrow job scope or task design in software development.
4. Under the concept of "User Primacy," what is the role of the computer professional?
5. Name the four primary reasons for purchasing "off-the-shelf" software packages. What are some of the drawbacks associated with such a purchase?
6. Define prototyping as it relates the applications development and list its benefits.
7. What are the common elements of FOCUS, NOMAD, RAMIS II, and IDEAL?
8. Identify the Software Development Method we have studied that would be most appropriate for each of the following applications, and give the reasons for your choice. Chose from:

   Traditional Systems Life Cycle
   Purchased Package
   Prototyping
   User-Based Development

   a. A report listing all employees in an employee database who work in the Distribution Center who live within a particular zip code area.
   b. An integrated accounting system for international divisions of a soda pop/fruit drink company.
   c. A report listing sales, by product line, and by geographic area, planned versus actual on a monthly basis.
   d. A mailing list of all customers listed in a customer database.
   e. A production scheduling system for all the plans of a manufacturing company.
9. Explain the value of data independence.
10. Why is end-user participation in system development commonly advocated? Why is it difficult?

**Case Study**

## INFORMATION TECHNOLOGY IN BANKING

The banking industry is in a period of rapid change. For years bankers lived by the three, four, three rule. This meant to borrow funds at 3%, loan at 4%, and go home by three o'clock. Today banking is being redefined and the rule is no longer valid.

Deregulation has altered bankers hours—today it means 24 hours following the sun as it shines on the world's financial markets. The key to competing in this new environment is information technology. Right now with few exceptions banks are missing the technology boat.

The transition from a regulated environment to a deregulated environment has shown that the information systems put in place before deregulation are unable to handle the change. Although the top-tier banks have spent millions of dollars on leading edge banking systems, experts are in agreement that the vast majority of banks are not technically prepared for today's marketplace.

Major concerns include the following:

- Banks have invested heavily in back office automation but are unable to access these automated accounting systems to provide management information that will provide a competitive advantage.
- Integrated software packages purchased from external software vendors have not fulfilled their early promise and have left MIS executives wary of this solution.
- Electronic transaction systems such as direct deposit are seeing limited use. Banks content with inexpensive checking systems are not aggressively implementing this technology.
- As barriers to regional and national banking come down banks need to develop better methods of data communication. Networks must move beyond automatic teller machines (ATMs) and platform teller applications to full-blown branch banking.
- Global banking competition is now challenging U.S. banks for markets long held by domestic banks. The banking industry is faced with problems similar to those that have struck manufacturing.
- Senior management in banks must be continuously pushed by MIS executives to make them aware of the strategic potential of information technology.

- The combined forces of information technology and deregulation are widening the gap between the big banks and the second tier of banks who struggle to survive in a newly competitive marketplace.

Banks invested heavily in back office automation 10 to 15 years ago. The automated accounting systems were put in place before database management systems existed and transition to newer technology will be difficult. The top-tier banks have made the transition to newer technology but second-tier banks are mostly still tied to older technology.

One of the difficulties in implementing new information technology is the view that it is a cost cutter rather than a revenue generator. Many senior managers have not caught the vision of using information technology for competitive advantage.

While integrated software packages have generally been disappointing, a new set of vendors are entering the market. The market, however, is skeptical.

Adapted from Glenn Rifkin, "Technology in Banking: Who Is Cashing In?" Computerworld (March 9, 1987), pp. 65-79.

1. Why are regional banks not able to use information technology for competitive advantage?
2. Why have purchased banking software packages not fulfilled their promise?
3. Is there any reason to believe that small and medium sized organizations can develop software that will give them competitive advantage?

## Suggestions for Further Reading

Gremillion, Lee L. and Philip Pyburn. "Breaking the Systems Development Bottleneck," Harvard Business Review (March-April 1983), pp. 130-137.

*The article assesses available methods for decreasing the amount of time necessary for systems development. Application software packages, prototype development and user-developed systems are cited by the authors as the most promising solutions. The authors encourage the evaluation of projects on the basis of three criteria: commonality, impact, and structure. Using these criteria, the manager can determine the most expeditious method of system development.*

Naumann, Justus D. and A. Milton Jenkins. "Prototyping: The New Paradigm for Systems Development," MIS Quarterly (September 1982), pp. 29-44.

*Naumann and Jenkins review the current literature on prototyping and related concepts. The authors develop a prototyping model addressing the interaction of users and builders in developing an information system. Discussed in this article are the new technologies: interactive systems, DBMS, generalized I/O software and high level languages which have diminished the need for traditional control. The economics of prototyping are examined, illustrating prototyping's ability to reduce the costs of developing information systems.*

Jones, Capers, Programming Productivity, McGraw-Hill, 1986.

*This book examines the problems of measuring software and the related measurement of software productivity. The author proposes a method for overcoming this historical measurement problem. The last part of the book examines the effects of several variables on software productivity. Several variables are shown to have a significant impact on productivity.*

*Supplement*

# Programming Languages: Four Generations

*"Intense demand for simplified access to computers and for increased development productivity has resulted in dozens of new and improved fourth-generation language tools. The ensuing competition has led to a striking improvement in the way computers are used."*

*Pieter Mimno*

## Overview and Objectives

PROGRAMMING LANGUAGES, LIKE COMPUTER HARDWARE, have evolved through four distinct generations. Each generation of programming languages has increased the productivity of programmers at a cost of greater computer usage.

Fourth-generation languages (4GLs) have recently emerged as tools for substantially improving the productivity of programming. These tools have been estimated to provide productivity improvements as great as 10 to 1 compared with COBOL.

The productivity improvements of fourth generation languages are but one component of the changes these languages are expected to make in the traditional computing environment. These tools are expected to impact the process of software development, provide greater end-user involvement in computing, and foster a movement towards automation of manual application development processes.

AFTER READING THIS SUPPLEMENT YOU SHOULD BE ABLE TO:

- Identify the primary categories of fourth generation languages.
- Explain some of the trends that are predicted as a result of the adoption of fourth generation languages.
- Understand the impact of this new technology on computer professionals and on students aspiring to become computer professionals.
- Explain the benefits of fourth generation languages.
- Describe the components of fourth generation languages.

## Four Generations of Programming Languages

FOR THE MOST PART, SOFTWARE DEVELOPMENT HASN'T changed very much for the past 20 years. Now that situation is changing, due to new programming languages that harness the power of the computer itself to improve the productivity of programmers.

Programming languages, like computer hardware, have evolved through four generations. With each generation fewer instructions are required to instruct the computer to perform a given task. Thus, a fourth generation program may require significantly fewer instructions than a machine language program.

The evolution of computer languages has increased the productivity of programmers. This increase in productivity has come about as a result of reducing the detail required to instruct the computer *how* to perform a given task. Typically, this increase in programmer's productivity required some corresponding increase in the amount of computer resource used. This tradeoff has typically been quite profitable, since the cost of hardware is decreasing and the cost of skilled computer professionals is increasing. Most organizations have found that the additional cost of the computer resources required by third- and fourth-generation languages is substantially less than the savings resulting from the increased productivity of programmers.

## First Generation: Machine Language

A GIVEN COMPUTER HAS ONLY ONE PROGRAMMING LANGUAGE that can be executed — its machine language. Instructions written in COBOL, FORTRAN or BASIC must be translated to machine language. Machine languages are hardware dependent. That is, a program written in a machine language for one computer will not execute on another computer of different design.

Prior to the development of computer languages the only means of programming available was machine language. Machine language programs are written in binary numbers. Binary numbers are combinations of 0 and 1's. Machine language instructions are of two types — an operations code and an operand. An *operations code* specifies what operation is to be performed, e.g., add, subtract, or move a value from one storage location to another. An *operand* specifies where the value to be used in the operation is stored. The two types of machine code instructions are illustrated in Figure S7.1.

FIGURE S7.1 *The Parts of a Typical Computer Instruction*

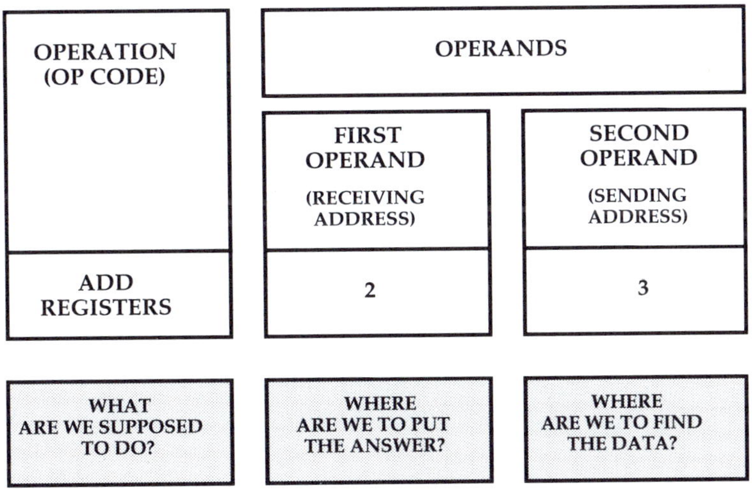

The extreme detail required in machine language programming results in very tedious and time-consuming effort required to develop even simple machine language applications.

For example the computation:

A = B X C + D

The equivalent machine language commands are shown below in Figure S7.2.

FIGURE S7.2

*Machine Language Commands for the Statement A=B*C+D*

| Operation | Operand 1 | Operand 2 | Comments |
|---|---|---|---|
| 100010 | 000 000 000 000 011 | 010 110 100 000 000 | Load register with B |
| 001100 | 000 000 000 000 011 | 011 010 000 000 000 | Multiply by C |
| 011100 | 000 000 000 000 011 | 010 101 011 000 000 | Add D |
| 010111 | 000 000 000 000 011 | 100 001 000 000 000 | Store as A |

## Second Generation: Assembly Language

ASSEMBLY LANGUAGES WERE THE SECOND LEVEL OF COMPUTER languages. Assembly language instructions and machine language use the same basic structure. The difference is that assembly languages use symbols to represent operations codes and operands. For example, the symbolic code "LR" is used to represent the instruction to load the register instead of the binary operations code "100010." An assembly programmer also uses the name of the variable stored in a given storage location instead of the binary number representing a storage location. A variable name becomes the address of a storage location instead of a binary number address. An example of an assembly program is shown in Figure S7.3.

While assembly programming improved the productivity of programmers, it still represented a very detailed set of instructions to the computer of how to do it. Even simple programs might take a hundred or more instructions.

The advantage of assembly programs is that they execute with great efficiency. Although third- and fourth-generation languages require less programming effort, the machine efficiency of assembly languages may make it the preferred language for some applications such as system software. The difference in efficiency between assembly programs and high level languages, however, has narrowed in recent years due to improvements in third generation languages.

FIGURE S7.3

*An Assembly-Language Program for the Statement X=(A+B)*(C-D)/E*

| Program | Comment |
|---|---|
| LDA A | Load A into A register |
| ADD B | Add B to A register |
| STA T | Store the sum in a temporary location |
| LDA C | Load C into the A register |
| SUB D | Subtract D from the A register |
| DIV E | Divide the results by E |
| MLT T | Multiply the results by T |
| STA X | Store the final result in X |

## Third Generation: High Level Languages

THE DEVELOPMENT OF HIGH LEVEL LANGUAGES LED TO INcreases in programmer productivity by an order of magnitude. These languages have dominated computing for the past 30 years. In Table S7.1 is a list of high-level languages, the year they appeared, and the types of applications these languages serve.

TABLE S7.1

*The Development of High Level Languages*

| LANGUAGE | YEAR INTRODUCED | TYPE |
|---|---|---|
| FORTRAN | 1954 | Scientific |
| COBOL | 1959 | Business |
| PL/1 | 1964 | General Purpose |
| RPG | 1962 | Business |
| BASIC | 1964 | General Purpose |
| PASCAL | 1971 | General Purpose |
| APL | 1962 | Scientific |
| ADA | 1979 | General Purpose |
| C | 1975 | General Purpose |

### SCIENTIFIC LANGUAGES

FORTRAN - Fortran was the first high level language. It was designed to solve problems that require extensive computations, such as solutions to mathematical equations, matrix manipulations, simulation, and iterative processing.

During the 1960s and 1970s, FORTRAN was the most widely known computer language. More recently its popularity has waned with the widespread teaching of BASIC and PASCAL.

APL - introduced by IBM, is an interactive language which requires a keyboard with symbols which are unique to APL. It is most popular with scientists, mathematicians, and engineers, who feel comfortable with its rich symbolic instructions. For some types of mathematical problems such as matrix manipulation, it is unexcelled in the time required for programming.

## BUSINESS LANGUAGES

COBOL - was developed for business applications. Business applications differ from scientific applications in two respects; they usually have high input-output requirements, and computations are modest by comparison with scientific applications.

COBOL is perhaps the most widely used computer language. Although it is considered to be a powerful language, many computer experts consider it to be excessively wordy. It was designed to make its instructions as close as possible to English. For example, an instruction to compute gross pay for hourly workers might appear as follows:

```
IF HOURS-WKD IS GREATER THAN 40 PER-
FORM OVERTIME-ROUTINE ELSE MULTI-
PLY HOURS-WKD BY HOURLY-RATE
GIVING GROSS PAY.
```

COBOL, like most third-generation languages, has evolved and changed adding new features from newer languages. The American National Standards Institute (ANSI) has established standards for several languages, including COBOL. The purpose of the standard is to make software machine independent. That is, a COBOL program should be able to run on a variety of machines developed by different manufacturers. Unfortunately, this is an ideal, and computer manufacturers usually have some non-standard features in their compilers which will not allow programs to be portable without some modifications.

COBOL programs consist of four divisions as shown in Figure S7.4.

FIGURE S7.4 *Simple But Complete COBOL Program to Compute Gross Pay*

COBOL Program

```
IDENTIFICATION DIVISION.
PROGRAM-ID. PAY.
AUTHOR. SUSAN HANSEN.
REMARKS. PROGRAM TO READ HOURS-WORKED AND RATE-OF-PAY AND
   COMPUTE GROSS-PAY.
ENVIRONMENT DIVISION
CONFIGURATION SECTION.
SOURCE-COMPUTER. IBM-360
OBJECT-COMPUTER. IBM-360.
INPUT-OUTPUT SECTION.
FILE-CONTROL.
  SELECT PAYROLL-CARD-FILE ASSIGN TO SYS011-UR-25440R-S.
  SELECT PRINT-FILE ASSIGN TO SYS013-UR-1403-S.
DATA DIVISION.
FILE SECTION.
FD  PAYROLL-CARD-FILE LABEL RECORD IS OMITTED
     DATA RECORD IS PAYROLL-CARD.
01  PAYROLL-CARD.
     02  HOURS-WORKED PICTURE IS 99.
     02  RATE-OF-PAY PICTURE IS 9V999.
     02  FILLER PICTURE X(74).
FD  PRINT-FILE LABEL RECORD IS OMITTED DATA RECORD IS PRINT-LINE.
01  PRINT-LINE.
     02 HOURS-PRINT PICTURE IS ZZ99.
     02 RATE-PRINT PICTURE IS ZZ9.999.
     02 GROSS-PRINT PICTURE IS $$$$$$9.99.
     02 FILLER PICTURE IS X(111).
WORKING-STORAGE SECTION.
     77 GROSS-PAY PICTURE IS 999V99.
     77 EXCESS PICTURE IS 99V9.
PROCEDURE DIVISION.
     OPEN INPUT PAYROLL-CARD-FILE OUTPUT PRINT-FILE.
PROCESS-IT. READ PAYROLL-CARD-FILE RECORD AT END GO TO FINISH.
     IF HOURS-WORKED IS GREATER THAN 40 GO TO OVERTIME. MULTIPLY
     RATE-OF-PAY BY HOURS-WORKED GIVING GROSS-PAY ROUNDED. GO TO
     PRINT-OUT.
OVERTIME. COMPUTE EXCESS = (HOURS-WORKED - 40) * 1.5. ADD 40 TO
     EXCESS. MULTIPLY RATE-OF-PAY BY EXCESS GIVING GROSS-PAY
     ROUNDED.
PRINT-OUT. MOVE SPACES TO PRINT-LINE. MOVE HOURS-WORKED TO
     HOURS-PRINT. MOVE RATE-OF-PAY TO RATE-PRINT MOVE GROSS-PAY
     GROSS-PRINT. WRITE PRINT-LINE. GO TO PROCESS-IT.
FINISH. CLOSE PAYROLL-CARD-FILE, PRINT-FILE. STOP RUN.
```

## GENERAL PURPOSE LANGUAGES

PL/1 - (Programming Language 1) was developed by IBM in conjunction with the instruction of System 360 in 1964. It was designed to bridge the gap between scientific and business languages.

The meager acceptance of PL/1 has been disappointing to IBM but may reflect the investment many firms have made in FORTRAN and COBOL software. It may also reflect the inherent resistance to change which is typical of human behavior.

PASCAL - was named for Blaise Pascal, a French mathematician, who developed the first mechanical adding machine. PASCAL, introduced in 1971, is widely used in universities by computer science programs for introductory programming courses. Its popularity is due to its implementation of structured programming concepts.

PASCAL has limited acceptance in the business community. Some of its features have been copied by other languages, however, including FORTRAN, COBOL, and BASIC.

BASIC - was developed as an interactive tutorial language. Its principle strength is the ease of learning and the ease of use. BASIC, unlike most languages, provides a complete software development environment, which includes a set of commands to enter, edit, and execute a BASIC program.

While BASIC is very popular as an introductory language in universities and on personal computers, extended versions have enjoyed some commercial success. The Digital Equipment PDP-11 and VAX Computer systems have extended versions of BASIC that rival the power and flexibility of other high-level languages.

ADA - was developed for use by the Department of Defense. It was named for Augusta Ada Byron, Countess of Lovelace and the daughter of the poet, Lord Byron. The Countess worked for Charles Babbage programming his difference engine. She is considered to be the first programmer in history.

ADA was an attempt to standardize the software used by the Department of Defense. ADA is a derivative of PASCAL, but has several extensions. Critics charge that it is complex and inefficient. Its supporters believe it will eventually replace COBOL as the most-commonly-used-language. The verdict on ADA isn't in yet; and it is too early to tell which view will prevail.

C - was developed at the Bell Laboratories of AT&T and was used to develop the UNIX operating system. It is a favorite of systems programmers and is widely used for development of systems software, especially for microcomputers. Programmers written in C rival assembly languages for machine efficiency. It also contains some of the constructs of high-level languages.

The major advantages of C are its machine independence and the presence of high level language constructs in a language used for system software. An application written in C will run in any hardware environment for which there is a C compiler.

## Productivity Gains with Third Generation Languages

Third-generation languages broke away from the one-to-one relationship between machine language and assembly languages. A single statement in a third-generation language may represent up to 100 machine instructions. This dramatically improved the productivity of programmers. During the decade from 1955 to 1964 programmer, productivity increased dramatically. Schussel estimates a 50 fold increase in productivity from using third-generation languages.[1] Now a new generation of computer languages promises significant gains in productivity.

## A Taxonomy of Fourth Generation Software

Tool vs. language

AT THE OUTSET, IT MIGHT BE USEFUL TO DISTINGUISH BETWEEN computer tools and computer languages. A *tool* is designed for a specific task, whereas a *language* generally is applicable to a broader class of problem. We might visualize a continuum. To determine whether fourth-generation software fits on this continuum one must inquire how broad a set of applications it may serve.

## Query Languages

Query languages are used for ad-hoc information needs. The languages are designed for extracting data from a DBMS by end-users without the necessity of preparing a complete program. Query languages are very powerful and easy to use, but limited in scope. One could not develop a typical payroll application in a query language.

The principle advantage of query languages is that they make it possible for ordinary end-users to extract data from the computer without professional assistance. Typically, one can learn to use a query language with one to two hours of instruction.

Some common query languages include SQL, QBE, DATAQUERY, and ONLINE QUERY. An example of a query and the resulting computer output is shown below in Figure S7.5.

FIGURE S7.5

*An SQL Query and Computer Output*

```
SELECT FIRSTNAME, LASTNAME, AGE, SEX, SALARY
FROM EMPLOYEE
WHERE LASTNAME = "SMITH" OR LASTNAME = "JONES"
AND AGE BETWEEN 30 AND 45
ORDER BY LASTNAME;
```

| FIRST-NAME | LAST-NAME | AGE | SEX | SALARY |
|---|---|---|---|---|
| HENRY | SMITH | 30 | M | $22,500 |
| HOLLY | SMITH | 40 | F | $36,000 |
| CHARLY | SMITH | 33 | M | $20,000 |
| HELEN | SMITH | 42 | F | $25,000 |
| ANN | JONES | 38 | F | $19,200 |
| GRETA | JONES | 42 | F | $13,125 |

6 records selected

## INTEGRATED DEVELOPMENT SOFTWARE

This is the software used by large MIS departments. It consists of a DBMS, an integrated data dictionary, query language, report generator, and an application generator. The data dictionary is the key module which stores data definitions, and controls access to the data. It interfaces with all other modules.

Examples of products that fit this category are Cincom's SUPRA with MANTIS (a 4th generation language), CA's IDMS/R with ADS-ON-LINE, CA's DATACOM/DB with IDEAL, and SOFTWARE AG's ADABAS with NATURAL. These products all run in the mainframe IBM environment, but some now run in a DEC VAX/VMS environment as well.

There are some products that run on other non-IBM mainframes. The most important would be MAPPER, and LINC II which are UNISYS products.

These integrated development packages are expensive, typically selling for over $300,000. They also require a technical staff skilled in data administration, and database design. The time required to learn how to use these products and develop the necessary data administration staff can easily require a year or more.

In spite of the cost of these packages, the productivity gains in using these 4GLS has made them very popular. They are generally viewed as a suitable replacement for COBOL for most applications.

While there are some exceptions, these 4GLs tend to have three components: (1) a screen painting module, (2) a report writer, and (3) a very high level procedural language.

"Screen painting" refers to the process of formatting data entry screens. Fourth generation languages typically use a screen-painting module to define screen layouts, menus, and interactive dialogs. These modules tend to have built-in data editing features which eliminates the programmer having to develop code for editing input.

Report writers aid application generators in formatting output to produce reports. Many of these have features which provide centered headings, pagination, sort sequencing, totals, and column labels.

A very high level procedural language includes input-output statements, arithmetic statements, and statements to implement detailed procedural logic. The use of procedural logic extends the breadth of applications that can be handled by a 4GL.

## MAINFRAME FOURTH GENERATION LANGUAGES

These packages will function without a DBMS and a data dictionary. They provide many of the productivity advantages of the integrated development software without the expense and software overhead of a DBMS and data dictionary. Usually these packages sell for $60,000-$100,000.

Examples of these packages are as follows:

| PRODUCT | VENDOR |
|---|---|
| MANTIS | Cincom |
| NATURAL | Software AG |
| MILLENNIUM | McCormick and Dodge |
| INFORMATION EXPERT | MSA |

These products should not be confused with information center packages such as FOCUS and RAMIS II. Mainframe 4GLs are designed for programmers. According to Schussel, the computer performance of an application developed with one of these languages will be no worse than 100% greater than COBOL. While this may sound high, the productivity for programmers writing the code is enhanced by at least 500%.[2]

These packages excel in screen oriented transaction processing applications. While these languages differ somewhat in their approach they have in common a screen painting productivity tool.

## COBOL SYSTEM GENERATORS

COBOL system generators have much in common with the previous category. The difference is that they generate COBOL source code rather than object code for output. Most of these packages have a data dictionary, automatic documentation, screen painting, DBMS call generation facilities, and project control.

These products take three to eight times longer to compile than COBOL, but may execute faster than the programs produced by all but 5% of the typical information systems department.

COBOL systems generators typically improve the productivity of the programming staff by approximately 100% which is significantly less than the 400% improvements reported by mainframe 4GLs.[3]

## INFORMATION CENTER SOFTWARE

These are 4GLs suitable for application development by end-users. While these languages are not suitable for high-volume, heavy-duty computing applications, they are suitable for low-to-medium volume transaction processing applications. These languages differ from the previous three categories in several ways: (1) these are stand-alone products that have their own DBMS; (2) these languages tend to have some decision-support capabilities such as spreadsheets and graphics; and (3) they tend to have a passive as opposed to an active data dictionary.

Information-center languages are generally quite easy to learn and easy to use compared with the previous categories. Some examples of products in this category are as follows:

| PRODUCT | VENDOR |
|---|---|
| FOCUS | Information Builders |
| RAMIS II | Martin Marietta |
| NOMAD 2 | D&B Computing |

## DECISION SUPPORT SYSTEMS

These software tools are normally used for financial planning. These packages may include data modeling, DBMS, query facility, and simulation language.

PC based spreadsheets like LOTUS 1-2-3 can be thought of as a decision-support tool. Mainframe packages, however, can be substantially more powerful. *Systems W*, for example, provides a multidimensional analytical capability that provides substantially more capability than personal computer spreadsheets. *Express* provides both multi-dimensional modeling and a true DBMS. Some products in this category are now available in PC versions, an example of which is IFPS-Personal.

These products are normally sold to end-users doing financial analysis, market projections, and production planning. They are easier to use than any of the previous categories and normally do not require any programming.

Compared with Information Center Software, which also may have financial-planning modules, these products are superior for modeling difficult and complex problems. Information Center tools can be used to build transaction processing applications. These tools have more limited scope but are superior for the tasks they perform.

## DESIGN AUTOMATION TOOLS/CASE PRODUCTS

These are tools designed to automate the design process. Two types of tools seem to be evolving. One set of tools follows the approach advocated by James Martin. These are design tools which are suitable for automation. An application developer working at a workstation develops diagrams, and specification for an application. The object of this type of tool is to link specification to an application generator. One such tool is described in Chapter 11. Examples of this type of software are:

| PRODUCT | VENDOR |
|---|---|
| Information Engineering Workbench | KnowledgeWare Inc. |
| Information Engineering Facility | Texas Instruments |
| CorVision | Cortex |

The second approach has developed design tools that assist in systems analysis or database modeling. These tools are not linked to application generators. Excelerator is an example of this type of product.

## SUPER-MINI DBMS AND 4GL

Super-Mini computers as exemplified by the popular Digital Equipment Corporation *VAX* have become a big market for fourth-generation software. The products developed for these computers are similar to mainframe integrated development software. Some of these packages have, in fact, been converted to the super-mini environment from the mainframe environment. These products are frequently used to provide a link between PCs and a mainframe DBMS.

In contrast to the mainframe environment, where there is still a large number of firms using hierarchical databases, this is an environment dominated by relational technology. These products have matured to the point that they are suitable for transaction processing. They have excellent application development facilities that are equal to or superior to many mainframe tools. Many of these firms have migrated to mainframes. Here are some examples of Super-mini DBMS and 4GLs:

| PRODUCT | VENDOR |
|---|---|
| ADABAS/NATURAL | Software AG |
| ULTRA/MANTIS | Cincom |
| INGRES | Relational Technology |
| ORACLE | Oracle |

## SUPER-MINI 4GL

Super-Mini 4GLs are products that provide fourth-generation language for building applications in a file management—as opposed to a DBMS—environment. These are high productivity tools that match and sometimes exceed their mainframe counterparts.

| PRODUCT | VENDOR |
|---|---|
| ALLY | Foundation Computer Systems |
| APPLICATION FACTORY | Cortex |
| POWERHOUSE | Cognos |

## PERSONAL COMPUTER DBMS

Personal Computer DBMS are designed for a single-user environment. They are typified by dBASE IV which is a DBMS/programming language combination. These products are differentiated from file management software by their ability to search for and report on a field value without reading complete records or searching complete files. They also have the ability to join two or more tables.

Since these products were designed for a single-user environment, their capabilities are a subset of a mainframe DBMS. There are many such products now available. For example:

| PRODUCT | VENDOR |
|---|---|
| dBASE IV | Ashton-Tate |
| R-BASE | Microrim |
| PROGRESS | Progress |

## MICRO-COMPUTER DBMS—MULTI-USER SYSTEMS

These products were developed for multi-user operating systems running on micro-computers either UNIX or OS/2. Compared with PC DBMS products, they are more sophisticated in their security controls, concurrency controls, and database utilities. This category is very dynamic with several new products under development. It is expected to be a big software market for the 90's.

## Procedural vs. Non-Procedural

THE TERMS **PROCEDURAL** VERSUS **NON-PROCEDURAL** ARE closely related to the words *how* and *what*. A procedural language requires explicit instructions as to *how* a task is to be performed. A non-procedural language, in contrast, only requires the user to specify *what* information is required.

Fourth generation languages are frequently referred to as non-procedural languages. To refer to fourth generation languages as non-procedural languages, however, is misleading since most fourth generation languages have some procedural elements. Procedurality may be recognized in a language by the presence of von Neumann constructs. John von Neumann introduced three fundamental structures to programming (1) sequence, (2) branch, and (3) loop.

These logical constructs are recognizable in the first three generations of computer languages. These structures provide the logical framework for a computer language. Third-generation languages have quite different syntaxes but are generally similar in their logical constructs. Third-generation languages process information a record at a time. They navigate through a data base record-by-record. An illustration of the non-procedural progression of language from 2nd to 4th generation is shown in Figure S7.6.

FIGURE S7.6
*Procedural vs. Non-Procedural Computer Languages*

Assembler

```
215    LA     R2,@IDTW0(,R9)
216    LA     R1,@PTENDL+@PTNEXT(,R1)
217    B      PTM1
::::   ::     :::::::::::::::::::::::
```

COBOL

```
330820 IF PRIORBAL NOT NUMERIC MOVE 'Y' TO YES-NON
MOVE
330822 'PRIORBAL  ' TO MVLAB PERFORM NONNUM-1 THRU
            NONNUM-1-EX
330824 MOVE ZEROES TO PRIORBAL.
:::::  :::::::::::::::::::::::::::::::::::::::::::::
```

SQL Query language

```
SELECT ACCOUNT-NUMBER, NAME,
CURRENT-BALANCE,
  PRIOR BALANCE
FROM CUSTOMER
WHERE BUSINESS TYPE=17
ORDER BY BRANCH;
```

Shown above are portions of three programs--one in Assembler, one in COBOL, and one in a query language. Each is designed to generate the same report showing the account balances for a list of customers. But to do the job, the Assembler program takes more than 3,000 lines. The COBOL program runs more than 600 lines. But the five sentences in SQL query language is all that is needed.

The term *automatic navigation* is often used in place of the term *non-procedural*. Automatic navigation allows one to describe a set of records to be processed in a single statement. This is especially characteristic of query languages, perhaps the most non-procedural of fourth-generation languages. In IDEAL, a fourth-generation language developed for computer professionals, an application developer can specify a set of records using a FOR EACH command.

The most powerful fourth-generation languages can operate in two modes: 1) a record at a time, and 2) a set of records at a time. The record-at-a-time processing is facilitated by von Neumann constructs similar to those found in third generation languages. Set-at-a-time processing can be recognized by the use of commands that relate to a set or more than one set of records. Here are some examples:[4]

SEARCH
SORT
SELECT
PROJECT
JOIN
DUPLICATE
FOR EACH

Set-at-a-time processing is facilitated by the use of logical or compound logical selection. An example of this is shown in a query in SQL illustrated in Figure S7.7.

FIGURE S7.7

*A Compound Logical Selection in SQL*

```
> SELECT FIRM, MODEL, RIG, LENGTH, BEAM, PRICE
  FROM YACHT
  WHERE PRICE > 50000 AND RIG = "KETCH"
```

| FIRM | MODEL | RIG | LENGTH | BEAM | PRICE |
|---|---|---|---|---|---|
| CHALLENGER | SPIRIT | KETCH | 41 | 13 | 51228 |
| ISLANDER | FREEPORT | KETCH | 41 | 13 | 54970 |
| OLYMPIC | ADVENTURE | KETCH | 42 | 13 | 80500 |

The logical statements are often referred to as *Boolean*. This type of statement can be identified by the use of an expression which is either true or false. If true, the record is selected, and if false, it is discarded.

The procedural components of a fourth-generation language extend the breadth of applications that can be addressed with the language. Procedural components usually add complexity and require more programming when compared with non-procedural alternatives. Procedural instructions usually relate to a single record. This may require branching and looping logic. An example is shown in Figure S7.8. This example is illustrated by Natural, a fourth Generation language. Note the If statement.

FIGURE S7.8

*Procedural Logic in NATURAL*

```
0010  SET GLOBALSTR=ON
0020  INPUT 'SAMPLE DATA ENTRY APPLICATION TO ADD NEW YORK CITY RESIDENTS'/
0030  'ENTER A NAME: '#NAME(A20)
0040  'ENTER A FIRST INITIAL:'#INITIAL(A1)//
0050  'ENTER A CITY: '#CITY(A20)42T'ENTER STATE:'#STATE(A2)/
0060  'ENTER A SEX CODE:'#SEX-CODE(A1)5X
0070  'ENTER AN AGE:'#AGE(N3)
0080  IF #NAME EQ ' ' REINPUT WITH 'NAME MUST BE NON-BLANK' MARK 1
0090  IF #CITY NE 'NEW YORK' REINPUT WITH 'CITY MUST BE NEW YORK' MARK 3
0100  IF #STATE NE 'NY' REINPUT WITH 'STATE MUST BE NY' MARK 4
0110  STORE PERSONNEL NAME=#NAME INITIAL=#INITIAL
0120  CITY=#CITY  STATE=#STATE
0130  SEX=#SEX-CODE  AGE=#AGE
0140  END OF TRANSACTION
0150  END
```

```
SAMPLE DATA ENTRY APPLICATION TO ADD NEW YORK CITY RESIDENTS

ENTER A NAME:                     ENTER A FIRST INITIAL:

ENTER A CITY:                     ENTER STATE:

ENTER A SEX CODE:                 ENTER AN AGE:
```

Fourth-generation languages have significantly less procedural content than third-generation languages. This is particularly true of query languages, the report generator, and screen-painting components of application generators.

## Compilers vs. An Interpreter

AS WAS INDICATED EARLIER, ALL COMPUTER LANGUAGES MUST be translated to machine language. Two alternatives are available - a compiler or an interpreter.

Compilation is not done until a program is completed. A compiler translates an entire program at a time. The input to the compiler is referred to as source code. Source code is a program written in a third- or fourth-generation language. The output from a compiler is known as *object code* which is executable on the computer for which the compiler was designed. A compiler may scan the source code several times before producing an object code program.

If syntax errors are detected during compilation, no object code version of the program is produced. Instead, the user receives one or more error messages. Syntax errors are errors that violate the rules of the language and are detected by the compiler. A program may have no syntax errors but still have logical errors which give incorrect results. Errors in a program are often referred to as *bugs*, and the process of eliminating these errors is called *debugging* a program. An illustration of a compiler is shown in Figure S7.9.

FIGURE S7.9

*The Translation of Symbolic Programs*

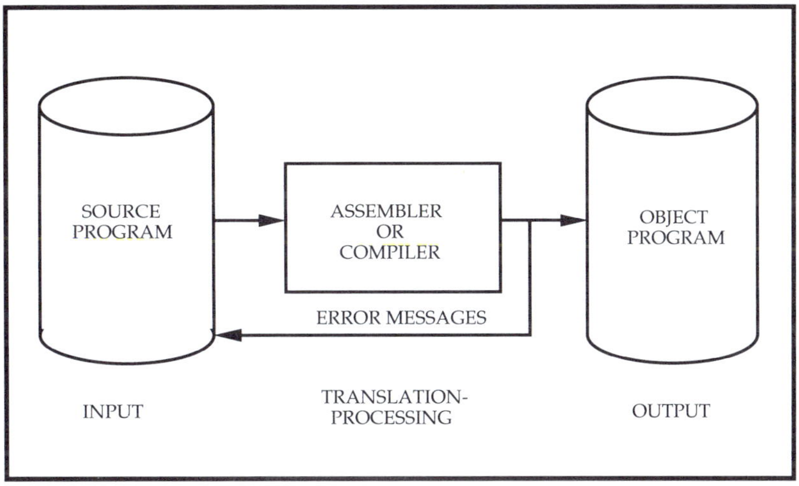


An interpreter works quite differently from a compiler. It translates and executes each line of source code as it is entered. No object code version of the program is produced. Whereas a compiler produces an object code version of the original program (which can then be executed to produce the desired results), an interpreter produces just the result.

The advantage of interpreters is that they give immediate feedback if syntax errors are detected. The programmer must fix these errors before proceeding. The immediate feedback facilitates learning the syntax of a language and immediate error correction.

The disadvantage of an interpreter is that it must translate the source program each time it is executed. An object code version of a program produced by a compiler can be saved and executed without repeating the compilation processes. A combination of a compiler and an interpreter might be ideal. This would allow a program to be developed in interpreter mode and, when tested, it could be compiled and the object code saved for future execution.

## The Impact of Fourth Generation Languages

### SOFTWARE DEVELOPMENT

The impact of fourth generation languages on software development is in its early stages but some of the effects seem to be:

1. Greater involvement and interest by end-users in application development.
2. Organized support for end-user computing in Information Centers. Information Centers typically provide consulting and training to end-users.
3. Newly-evolving methods of application development. The systems analysis life cycle is being changed to take advantage of high productivity tools.
4. Movement towards automation of programming and systems analysis. Information engineering technology which is closely related to fourth generation languages, is now making great strides.
5. Development of new systems analysis and design tools suitable for fourth generation languages. New diagramming techniques suitable for fourth generation languages are emerging.
6. Different backgrounds for programmers. Technical expertise is less important and broad understanding of applications becomes more important.
7. Small Software development teams working with 4GLs, often a single individual.

## APPLICATIONS SOFTWARE INDUSTRY

Software vendors have recognized the potential of 4GLs and are beginning to offer mainframe application packages written in 4GLs. Packages that are available include human resources, accounting, and manufacturing.

Two patterns of 4GL application development by software vendors are emerging. The first pattern is the DBMS vendor developing application software using their own products. The second pattern emerging is the DBMS vendor selling their products to another software vendor, who develops applications for specific vertical markets. Vertical markets have emerged in accounting, banking, distribution, education, and manufacturing.

The advantages of 4GL applications packages are that they are easily customized, easy to extend, functionally integrated and that the data is more readily accessible to end users. At first impression many organizations may appear to operate in a common fashion, yet beneath the surface each is unique. Thus, it is important to tailor or customize software to fit an organization's way of doing business rather than have the organization adapt to fit the software. Fourth-generation applications are relatively easy to adapt to the unique requirements of the business.

As an organization grows or changes, it needs to add functional extensions to existing software applications. Using 4GLs, MIS departments can quickly develop new reports or new applications which share common data. The ease of extending 4GL application software is an important advantage in purchasing this software.

Organizational information needs usually require applications broader than a single function. What is required to meet this need is the capability to integrate information across functions and share data from different applications. This capability recognizes the interdependence of organizations. Applications written in 4GLs should meet this requirement.

Many of the application software vendors are building semi-custom software. Semi-custom software is designed to meet 80-90% of users' requirements. The software is deliberately designed to be customized or extended either by the customer or by the application-software vendor. The results are usually quite good, resulting in a better fit of the users' needs.

## PROGRAMMER PRODUCTIVITY

There has been surprisingly little research to test the 4GLs vendors' claims of up to 1000% increase in programmers' productivity. Most of the evidence is anecdotal.

At the outset, we should point out that programming represents only a small portion of the total manhours required to develop new applications. One authority has estimated programming represents only 10% to 15% of the time spent in software development.[5] A ten fold increase in programming productivity without any changes in the other elements of the system's life cycle would have relatively small impact on the time and effort required to develop new systems.

Harel and McLean, in a study which compared development times in COBOL compared with Focus found significant differences in cases involving simple programs, complex programs, and beginning programmers. The differences related to expert programmers were not statistically significant although the ratio of development time favored Focus nearly 2 to 1. Below are the ratios of development time for the cases shown.[6]

| CASE | RATIO OF DEVELOPMENT TIME COBOL/FOCUS |
|---|---|
| Beginning programmers | 4.95 |
| Expert programmers | 1.86 |
| Simple programs | 3.85 |
| Complex programs | 2.66 |
| All Cases | 3.01 |

The actual programming time ratios were more dramatic, ranging from 100/1 for one of the simple programs to approximately 2/1 for a complex program.

Capers Jones shows that a COBOL application required 3.3 months of effort and cost $16,500, whereas the same application took .4 of a month and cost $2000 when developed in a fourth-generation language. Again ,the gain in productivity in programming exceeded the gain in other activities involved in the development process. However, Jones points out that fourth-generation languages dramatically reduce the design time as well as programming time.[7]

Professor Eberhard Ruduloph which compares the productivity of programmers using COBOL and PL/1 with LINC a 4GL which was developed for Burroughs computers. This study showed programming productivity increases using LINC that ranged from 17/1 for small applications, to 45/1 for large applications. This study, in contrast to the Harel and McLean study, shows that the advantage increases as the application becomes larger.[8]

Productivity in application development has traditionally been significantly lower in large projects as compared with small projects. Martin suggests that the increasing advantage of 4GLs in large applications is the result of being able to divide a project into several autonomous modules which can be completed by a single programmer. This, he believes, leads to less coordination between programmers and simplifies the interface problems.[9]

The experience of DuPont with a 4GL is highlighted in When Things Go Right.

**When things go right**

## New Products Speed Tedious Task of Programmers

Automation which has arrived in the typing pool, the accounting department and the factory floor is advancing another labor intensive activity—programming. Some programmers may soon be replaced by a computer.

It's none too soon. The information systems departments of big companies are backlogged with requests to develop new programs. The departments, however, are preoccupied with keeping their existing programs running. In many organizations they spend up to 75% of their time, talent and budget keeping existing programs up-to-date.

"Like the shoemaker whose children are without shoes, computer programmers have spent their time making life easier and more productive for everyone but themselves," says Jack Crawford of Hartford Insurance Group.

A group of new small software firms is trying to change that, developing software that assists programmers. In addition, some larger firms including Callinet and Texas Instruments have indicated they are developing similar products.

DuPont estimated it would take a team of three programmers about nine months, using conventional methods, to develop software to track the packaging and shipment of nylon at a South Carolina plant. Using a product called Application Factory two people completed the job in two months. The project which was expected to cost about $168,000 was finished for $30,000.

Application Factory, which was developed by Cortex Corporation of Waltham, MA, automatically generates programs from specifications developed by information systems

**professionals. Schott Schultz, manager of information engineering at DuPont estimates the software wrote 70% of the program which left 30% of the two programmers.**

**While management is pleased with these results the systems analysts and programmers who develop software aren't so enthusiastic. According to Shultz, "You don't have to be a technical genius to build systems anymore." It's very threatening to people who make their living and have built their reputations doing that.**

Adapted from Wall Street Journal, September 24, 1986, p. 6.

The evidence to date suggests that 4GLs have made a significant impact on programmers' productivity. They also impact some other elements of the system's life cycle, systems design in particular. It is now recognized that further improvements in software development productivity depend on automation of systems analysis and design.

New CASE products have been developed to bring to systems analysts the capabilities that workstations have brought to design engineers. This new technology referred to as computer aided software engineering (CASE). These CASE products, based on powerful PCs equipped with sophisticated graphics-based design tools, help analysts create diagrams to design new systems. This new technology is discussed in Chapter 8.

## Disadvantages of 4GLs

THE BIGGEST DISADVANTAGE OF 4GLS HAS BEEN THEIR PERFORMance problems. These languages require the computer to do more so the programmer does less. This performance problem is highlighted in a well known disaster as discussed in "When Things Go Wrong.

## When things go wrong

### A Fourth Generation Language Disaster

**The New Jersey Department of Motor Vehicles (DMV) contracted with Price Waterhouse and Company, a Big Eight accounting firm, to develop a database application for registration and titles of vehicles and licensing of drivers. The developers who were quite inexperienced in the development of large systems became enamored with the promise of Ideal, a 4th generation language. Specifically, they believed they could develop the system with Ideal with less cost and less time than COBOL.**

**What the developers failed to account for was the volume of transactions, more than 1000 terminals generating tens of**

**thousands of transactions per day, and the immaturity and untested nature of a new software product which had been released only a few months before.**

**The development project was plagued with technical problems with Ideal and test results which indicated that performance and response times were unsatisfactory. In spite of these problems the new system was implemented. The result was a backlog which left thousands of the state's 7 million motorists to drive with invalid registrations or licenses through no fault of their own. The resulting complaints from citizens led to a legislative investigation which embarrassed the Kean administration.**

**Price Waterhouse contracted for developing the system for $6.5 million and penalties of $10,000 for the first two months and $50,000 thereafter for over runs. Price Waterhouse agreed to "remedy the system...at our expense." Initially, the state insisted on a complete conversion to COBOL. As it turned out total conversion was unnecessary.**

**The original system contained about 800 modules written in Ideal. According to ADR, the developers of Ideal, only eight batch modules had to be written to eliminate the backlog. However, state officials state an additional 50 online programs which handle about 85 percent of the systems transactions were rewritten.**

**Some of the participants in the DMV project worry that Price Waterhouse's failure with Ideal may be viewed as an Indictment of the product or fourth generation languages in general. There have been noticeable successes with fourth generation languages including Ideal. Washington Metro, the public transit agency in Washington, D.C., developed a bus maintenance application in Ideal at a cost of $320,000 including $200,000 to purchase the software. A comparable project for railroad car maintenance in COBOL cost $500,000 and required two years as opposed to six months for the bus maintenance application.**

Adapted from David Kull, "Anatomy of a 4GL Disaster," Computer Decisions, (February 11, 1986), pp. 58-65.

Performance problems should be expected of complex software early in its life cycle. The vendors of these products have made some significant improvements in performance as these products have matured.

What can a firm do to minimize the machine performance problems and still benefit from the productivity gains associated with 4GLs? Several alternatives could be considered.

Some of the performance problems associated with 4GLs are the result of the database overhead associated with these languages.

One alternative is to minimize their use for high volume transaction processing applications or to write critical high volume modules in third generation languages. This is the New Jersey Department of Vehicles solution. Database machines are a second alternative to the 4GL performance problem. This is a solution that several database experts believe has real merit.

A 4GL will use much less machine resources for medium- to high-volume applications if it is a compiler language as opposed to an interpretative language. Interpretative languages are suitable for end users but not for production applications.

Another risk associated with 4GLs is the danger that a vendor may not survive. If an organization purchased a 4GL from a vendor that went out of business, it would probably not be able to get technical support and updates to the language. Thus, one should be careful in selecting a 4GL developed by a vendor with a high probability of survival.

Fourth-generation languages are proprietary, which means there is no standardization and very little hardware independence. Many of these languages are machine- and DBMS-dependent. Some 4GL experts despair of the lack of standards, but others feel it is healthy to explore different approaches and let the market decide which language will become the *defacto* standard.

Fourth-generation languages are quite expensive. Many of these languages are integrated with a DBMS; the buyer must purchase not only the language but also the associated DBMS and data dictionary.

Database management systems represent a new technology to many information system professionals, who will require additional training and experience to use them effectively. One critic has suggested that 4GLs are frequently purchased as a panacea to solve an organization's data processing problems.

## Issues and Controversies

## Fourth Generation Languages: Not a Panacea

**The appeal of fourth generation languages is seductive. Improving programmer productivity is an attractive goal. The advocates of fourth generation languages have suggested that they are the key to reducing the application backlog. These languages are appropriate for decision support applications, prototyping and situations with limited data and/**

or processing. However, for operational systems there is evidence that fourth generation languages don't deliver the productivity gains their advocates claim.

A study of eighteen information systems departments in t he U.S., Canada, and Europe showed no correlation between productivity and the use of fourth generation languages. Productivity was measured by comparing output in terms of numbers of transactions, reports produced and the number and size of systems. The measure of input was the number of data processing personnel excluding computer operators and data entry personnel.

The most productive departments were achieving the same amount of productive work with one-third the personnel. While fourth generation languages were fairly common in the nonproductive departments not one productive department had a fourth generation language.

Six differences were noted between the productive and non-productive departments.

1. Quality of Systems - Productive departments produced high quality systems that required few rewrites or modifications. Nonproductive departments tended to try to solve problems with technicians, technology, warm bodies, and a big budget.

2. Parochialism - Nonproductive departments pursued personal goals with little regard for the needs and goals of the organization. In productive departments there was a strong team spirit which was able to subjugate egos and personal goals to the achievement of departmental objectives. Productive departments had a clear sense of direction.

3. Minimal Bureaucracy - Nonproductive departments were characterized by extensive specialization, committees and a laborious approval process.

4. Proper Use of Technology - Nonproductive departments tended to have amazing array of hardware and software. They were anxious to find technical solutions for everything. Mangers in these departments tended to have technical backgrounds.

5. Blending Long-term and Short-term Goals - Nonproductive departments tended to be divided into two groups, 1) those on a crisis treadmill, and 2) those who employed many "blue-skiers."

6. Management Awareness - The final factor was management's understanding of the issues facing the information systems department and how resources were made available to address those issues. Resource allocation in nonproductive departments was usually made on political grounds - the department that was most vocal.

There was one common thread throughout. Productive departments were consistently run with a tight budget. It is apparent that an open checkbook and a purely technical approach are destructive to productivity.

Adapted from Bill Inman, "Rethinking Productivity," Datamation, June 15, 1984, pp. 185-188.

To use these languages effectively, a firm must make the commitment to training and reexamine its software development methods to insure that they are consistent with this new technology.

## The Future of 4GLs

FOURTH GENERATION LANGUAGES HAVE NEVER BEEN PARTICULARLY easy to define. Their identity crisis is probably going to get worse. Unlike most computer technologies which have sought standards, the 4GL standard is one defined in the market place. One school of thought suggests that 4GLs, at least those intended for heavy duty computing, will become components of integrated CASE products. These products have a major advantage over 4GLs in their ability to address the need for improved productivity in the entire systems development life cycle not just programming.

On the other hand, CASE products are not designed for end users. Fourth generation languages will continue to be used by end users to develop applications.[10]

## Guidelines for Managers

ENTREPRENEURS HAVE RECENTLY DEVELOPED NEW COMPUTER languages which dramatically improve the productivity of programmers. Effective use of these languages requires organizations to use new methods of developing software. New wine requires new bottles.

## Guidelines for MIS Professionals

MIS PROFESSIONALS MUST RECOGNIZE THAT A PROFESSION OR craft is evaluated on how it meets the needs of its constituency. Current methods of software development require too much programming effort and are too inflexible. Fourth generation languages represent a promising technology to improve the productivity of software development.

## Key Terms

| | |
|---|---|
| Machinge Language | COBOL |
| FORTRAN | BASIC |
| Operations Code | Operand |
| Assembler | APL |
| PL/1 | PASCAL |

| | |
|---|---|
| BASIC | ADA |
| C | Query Language |
| DBMS | Integrated Data Dictionary |
| Report Generator | Procedural Language |
| Non-Procedural Language | Screen Painter |
| Sequence | Branch |
| Loop | Automatic Navigation |
| Boolean | Compilers |
| Interpreter | Object Code |
| Systems Analysts Workbench Products | Computer-Aided Software Engineering (CASE) |

## Review Questions

1. Why has programming traditionally been such a time-consuming task?
2. How do business applications and scientific applications differ?
3. Name at least two major characteristics of each of the following levels of programming language.
   a. First-generation
   b. Second-generation
   c. Third-generation
   d. Fourth-generation
4. Compare and contrast automatic navigation and non-procedural languages.
5. Why has it been suggested that the ideal situation would be to have both an intrepetor and a compiler for a 4GL?
6. Why are fourth generation languages well-suited to a changing business environment?
7. What can firms do to minimize the machine performance problems and still benefit from the productivity gains associated with 4GLs?
8. Why is language compatibility between different types of computers important to a data processing center?
9. What do you feel were some of the underlying factors in creating a standardized language like COBOL? Why was it important that a standardized language be developed?

10. Fourth-generation languages have made it possible for users to obtain access to data in existing databases and to generate reports using these data on demand, rather than waiting for a programmer to program these applications. What do you feel will be the impact of these fourth-generation languages on a traditional business-application programming language like COBOL?

# 8

# Computer Aided Software Engineering (CASE)

*"There will always be a need for software Picassos who can create totally novel solutions. But, right now the greater need is for house painters."*

*Yachiam Yemini*

## Overview and Objectives

THERE IS A WIDENING GAP BETWEEN HARDWARE AND software performance: the microprocessor has led to increases in computer performance by leaps and bounds; but so far there is no software counterpart to microprocessor technology.

Computer aided software engineering (CASE) is a new software technology that attempts to harness the power of the computer itself in automating the tedious task of writing computer programs. This emerging technology may be the answer for improved software development productivity.

This chapter examines the characteristics of CASE and how this technology will interface with systems analysis, programming, database, data dictionaries, and software maintenance.

AFTER READING THIS CHAPTER YOU SHOULD BE ABLE TO:

- Distinguish between front-end CASE and back-end CASE.
- Describe the difference between an information repository and a data dictionary.
- Explain the advantages of CASE vs. 4GLs in supporting the full software development life cycle.
- Discuss the pros and cons of software reverse engineering.

## Introduction

DEVELOPERS OF INFORMATION SYSTEMS HAVE BEEN SLOW TO apply computer-based tools to the task of improving the quality, reliability, and productivity of their own work—a phenomenon which has been called the "shoemakers children" from the story of the shoemaker whose own children were last to get shoes. This tradition is changing with the adoption of CASE technology.[1]

Programming is a tedious labor-intensive task that is ill-suited to accommodate the growing demand for new applications. Advances in software development have not kept pace with hardware performance and the demand for new software.

Programming is time consuming and costly enough even when it is done correctly. Many programmers under pressure of application backlogs, have skipped analysis and design in favor of getting the job done. The attitude seems to be: "It can be fixed later." Unfortunately, undisciplined software development eventually leads to higher maintenance costs and poor solutions, not to mention slower application development.

Structured analysis and design methods were proposed in the 1970s to solve the quality and reliability problems associated with programming. Despite the obvious advantages of these methodologies, it is estimated that less than 10 percent of the 750,000 programmers in this country use structured analysis and design.[2]

Although structured analysis and design methods increase programmer productivity by reducing maintenance, they increase software development lead times. Programmers oriented towards short-term results as opposed to long-term productivity have resisted these methods because they believed their productivity would be impaired.

A second factor in programmers' resistance to analysis and design is their perception of their task as largely creative; programmers resist methods that treat software development as a disciplined engineering process. Programmers think of themselves as more like artists than engineers.[3]

The acronym CASE stands for computer aided software engineering. The software industry has developed a set of products to automate software development. These products vary in scope: some focusing on analysis and design; others focusing on programming; and still others focusing on the entire software development life cycle.

> The one technology that will truly define fifth generation application development is CASE....During the next few years, many companies will already be building applications without programmers. And by the middle of the decade, business analysts will be using CASE techniques routinely to build their applications.[4]

Most students are familiar with CAD/CAM, computer-aided design/computer-aided manufacturing. This technology allows an engineer working on a computer screen to create an image of a machine part on a screen, and to alter or adjust the configuration, when the design is complete, to pass the specification of the part to a machine tool which in turn manufactures it automatically. Now several tools which similarly automate the application development process are available to software developers. Thus, it may be useful to think of CASE as CAD/CAM for programmers and analysts.

CASE tools, like CAD/CAM, are an attempt to harness the power of the computer to improve the quality and productivity of human effort. CASE, like CAD/CAM, is an attempt to introduce engineering discipline to what had essentially been a craft.

## Variations of CASE

THE FUNDAMENTAL IDEA BEHIND CASE TECHNOLOGY IS TAPping the power of the computer in enhancing the productivity, reliability, and quality of the software development process. This concept encompasses automated support for all phases of software development. In practice, however, most software products that are sold as CASE tools are much narrower in scope. CASE products can be divided into three categories, front-end CASE, back-end CASE, and integrated CASE.

### Front-End CASE

Front-end CASE products are intended to automate systems analysis and design. Running typically on a microcomputer based workstation equipped with a mouse, these tools often incorporate a structured methodology that guides the analyst step by step through the specification process. The output from front-end products are diagrams, data dictionary input, and screen formats. The screen formatting capabilities allow many of these products to be used for prototyping data entry screens (this mode of prototyping has been referred to as *conceptual prototyping*).

The front-end process is usually accomplished on a software development workstation used to automate the design and specification phase of software development. The application developer manipulates symbols and creates structured diagrams. While design and specification are a relatively small portion of the software-development life cycle, they are considered to be the most important part because it provides a conceptual framework for application development.

### Back-End CASE

Back-end CASE products are code generators, i.e. they generate computer code. The code may be a standard 3rd generation language such as COBOL or ADA or it may be a proprietary 4GL code. Most code generators lack the flexibility to generate 100% of the code automatically, so custom code is written by a programmer to interface with the generated code providing unique or special features.

Application generators automate the labor-intensive component (programming) of the software development life cycle. Most application generators have been designed for mainframe computers.

## INTEGRATED CASE

Integrated CASE combines front-end CASE with back-end CASE. There are many ways in which this can be accomplished: one is to take independent products and attempt to interface them. A second way is to develop an *open architecture* such that a front-end or back-end tool can be interfaced with several alternatives. Finally, one can develop front-end tools that are designed to integrate with a back-end tool in a seamless interface that is transparent to the user. The integrating mechanism for CASE tools is an extended data dictionary which is called a repository. Paul Winsberg identifies integration as a sign of growing maturity in CASE technology in Issues and Controversies.

**Issues and Controversies**

## Excerpts from an Interview with Paul Winsberg in Database Newsletter

NEWSLETTER: "CASE technology is often described as having direct forebears and parallels in CAD technology. Do you find this to be true?"

WINSBERG: "CAD technology—that is, computer-aided design of buildings, highways, automobiles, and so forth—developed slowly over a period of ten to fifteen years. By the time the PC became widely available, the technology had been carefully elaborated on larger systems. The underlying methodologies and project management techniques of traditional CAD technology were well developed and understood. In contrast, CASE technology is developing suddenly, in a period of only several years. It comes at a time when PCs are in widespread use. As a consequence, the technology is becoming available before it has had a chance to fully mature. Furthermore, with CASE there is not just a single methodology, but many, which are neither standardized nor, for the most part, widely understood. As a result we find ourselves in a period of rapid flux and evolution—virtual chaos— for which there was no direct parallel in CAD."

NEWSLETTER: "Are the underlying objectives of the respective technologies similar?"

**WINSBERG: "Yes, very much so. Both technologies address the automation of an engineering discipline—in one case, of physical structures, and in the other, of software. Both must deal with a life cycle, from specification through schematics, detailed design, implementation and maintenance. Both must effectively integrate a variety of engineering disciplines throughout to leverage the early analysis stage to maximize productivity."**

**NEWSLETTER: "What would you look for as a sign of maturing CASE technology?"**

**WINSBERG: "One key characteristic is thorough integration of the life cycle phases and all software engineering disciplines in a single tool. What we see today, in contrast, is a sharp division between those tools that focus on the early stages—that is, requirements specification, analysis and conceptual design—and those tools that focus on the later stages, especially application building and code generation. Support for database design should also be integrated with the production of application code. Some tools are making progress towards integrating these areas, but I feel that most have a long way to go.**

**A second key indicator of a maturing CASE technology would be a reduction in the number of available diagramming techniques. This would indicate emerging consensus in the industry on which of the current variations work best.**

**A third indicator would be integration of all data pertaining to any given software project within a single computer-based dictionary or repository. This would provide a single database for managing all change and supporting additional functions such as code generation. Unfortunately, not all vendors are merging different functional components of their CASE offerings."**

**NEWSLETTER: "How would you rate the data modeling support that most CASE tools currently offer?"**

**WINSBERG: "This is one of the several areas where the immaturity of CASE technology and the associated methodologies is apparent. Most CASE tools do support some type of entity-relationship modeling, but there are still many variations. This is because the industry itself has not settled on a standardized or widely accepted approach."**

**NEWSLETTER: "On what points do these variations differ?"**

**WINSBERG: "They take different positions, for example, on whether relationships may have attributes, or on whether relationships may relate only two or more than two entities, or on whether relationships should be represented by diamonds or by lines, and so on."**

Currently, there are three levels of integration of front-end and back-end processes. These are (1) stand-alone (no integration), (2) upload-linked, and (3) transparently-coupled.[5]

The first level is exemplified by products that concentrate on the planning and analysis phase of the software-development life cycle. These products produce systems-analysis documentation but are not linked to an application generator. Examples are Excelerator, Design Aid, and Prokit Analyst.

The second level of integration is an upload link in batch mode. This is accomplished by creating a data file as output for the front-end process which is input for the back-end process. The difficulty with this solution is that the design specifications developed independently on a PC may contain errors which would not be detected until an application generation was attempted. In interfaces of this type, both the front-end and the back-end tend to have their own dictionary and distinct architectures. Each side creates a file and the files are passed back and forth.[6]

The third level of integration, transparently-coupled processes, link a PC workstation with a computer on which resides a repository. The repository is a shared resource which can be used by several application developers. Thus the repository links not only the front-end and back-end processes but it also integrates the work of professionals working on the same project. This level of integration is shown in Figure 8.1.

Using the PC connected to a central repository as a CASE workstation has several advantages: (1) It offloads the design and specification stage to the most economical computer; (2) It provides a common interface for the application developer in a mixed hardware platform environment; (3) The central repository (data dictionary) continues to reside on a shared computer.

Integrated CASE will require a tightly-coupled environment between an intelligent workstation and a computer on which resides a shared central repository. The workstation tools consist of an easy-to-use interface with interactive color graphics, pop-up windows and on-line help.

FIGURE 8.1

*Third Level of Integration of Automated Application Development*

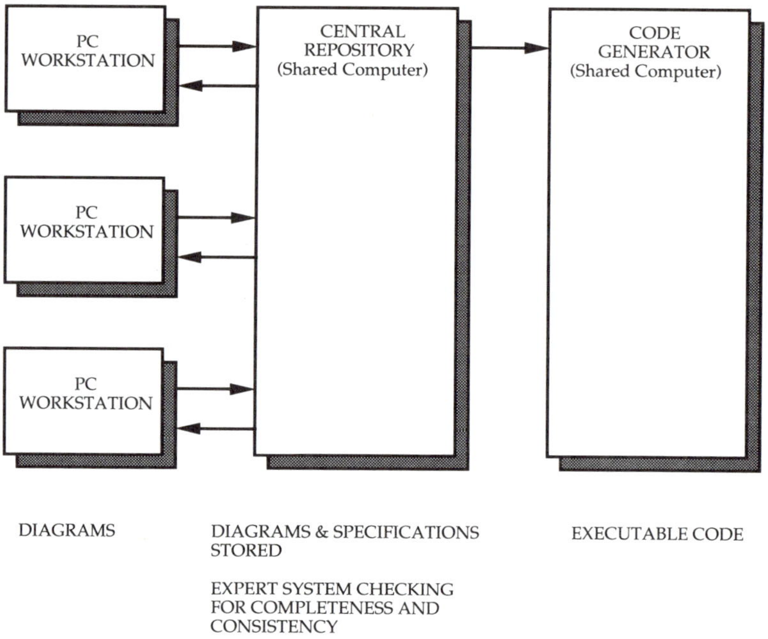


## Components of CASE

THE INTEGRATED CASE TOOL SET SUPPORTS A WIDE VARIETY of software development and maintenance tasks. Some examples of CASE tools include:[7]

- Diagramming tools - Tools for creating computer assisted structured diagrams and drawing pictorial specifications.
- Screen and Report Painters - Tools for creating input/output specifications and prototyping the user interface.
- Repository - A tool for storing, sharing and reporting system information.
- Checking and Analysis - Tools to check the consistency, completeness and accuracy of system specification.
- Code Generator - A tool to generate executable code from the specifications.
- Maintenance - Tools to redocument, restructure, and reverse-engineer existing systems.

### THE REPOSITORY

The repository is perhaps the single most important concept of CASE. The repository stores and manages information allowing it to be shared and reused. The distinction between a repository and a data dictionary is that it stores not only data about data but contains information on screens, reports, and processing. Storing information about these components in a repository enhances reusability and therefore productivity.

The use of a central repository on a shared computer system allows subsets of a model to be used by multiple system developers simultaneously. It also allows for changes and corrections to be automatically reflected across diagrams and applications.

A repository provides a linkage between CASE tools and a DBMS. This linkage is likely to change the role of the Data Administrator at least that component that is responsible for maintaining the data dictionary. The CASE repository is likely to replace the standard mainframe data dictionaries.

Some vendors prefer the term encyclopedia to repository. They distinguish an encyclopedia from a repository in its ability to use artificial intelligence techniques for establishing the correctness of information and to correlate the different types of knowledge found in the encyclopedia. For example, an encyclopedia stores both diagrams and data specifications in one location. This allows for a high degree of integration of all types of specifications and makes the CASE tool more powerful.

The functionality of the repository or encyclopedia is a limiting factor in the development of CASE tools. As repositories broaden their function, the effect will be seen in more powerful CASE tools. The use of expert systems technology is enhancing the capabilities of the repository by automatically checking for consistency and completeness.

## AUTOMATED DIAGRAMMING

One of the characteristics of front-end CASE products is automated diagramming capability. These tools have the capability to automate the requirements, specification, and early design phases of software development. Some CASE tools support a specific software development methodology, whereas others take an eclectic approach which allows an analyst to choose which diagramming techniques will be used. While several different methodologies are supported, there are two primary methodologies supported by CASE graphics tools.

These are *structured analysis tools* as exemplified by Gane and Sarson's methodology and *information engineering*. Information engineering as a software development methodology and the CASE tools that support this methodology are discussed in Chapter 9.

Initially CASE products allowed analysts to create dataflow diagrams on a PC screen. More recently the diagrams have been linked to a repository, which allows the CASE product to perform error checking and to detect missing specifications.

### AUTOMATIC CODE GENERATORS

Automatic code generation is characteristic of back-end CASE products, typically requiring a specification phase and a code generation phase. CASE products may generate code in high level languages such as COBOL or ADA or they may generate 4GL code. Automatic code generators usually have a screen formatting module, a report formatting module, and a data dictionary or repository.

Code generators have been around for some time but only recently, with the advent of front-end CASE, have they received much attention. Some authorities believe that the lack of interest in code generators was due to the fact that they were solving the wrong problem: coding or programming is a small percentage of the effort in software development; therefore, an increase in efficiency in coding has limited value. The value of code generators is enhanced when linked with other life-cycle development products.[8]

## Emerging Directions of CASE

### FULL LIFE-CYCLE COVERAGE

CASE products have been primarily of two types: those that support analysis and design; and those that support coding, testing, and implementation. While CASE tools have historically been either front-end or back-end products there is a clear trend towards full-systems-development life-cycle products. These would incorporate analysis, design, coding, testing, implementation, and maintenance in one integrated tool. Maintenance is a special concern, since many information systems departments spend a preponderance of their time on maintenance as opposed to developing new applications. The basic argument for CASE products that support maintenance is that it is easier to change specifications than to change code.

## SOFTWARE REVERSE ENGINEERING

Some CASE products support software reverse engineering. This allows existing applications developed by conventional software development methods to be reverse-engineered by CASE products.

Software reverse engineering means taking existing programs, and their related file and database descriptions and transforming them into specification level objects. Examples of specification level objects would be entities, data stores, attributes, processes and messages.[9] Once an application has been reverse-engineered to the specification level, it can be regenerated by CASE tools. Furthermore, once the specifications have been captured, the old system design can be updated to reflect changing business needs. Software reverse engineering enables information systems professionals to extract business rules from old applications and use them as the basis of reverse engineering those applications.

There are two schools of thought about software reverse-engineering. One school of thought is that much of existing software is flawed and software reverse-engineering will not be able to restore software to an acceptable level of quality. This view suggests bulldozing existing applications and getting a fresh start. The negative view of software reverse-engineering emphasizes that the productivity of the application development process using CASE technology offsets any advantages of rehabilitating old software.

The second view suggests that the investment in existing applications is too great to be ignored. Using CASE software reverse engineering tools existing software can be renewed. Unstructured code, often referred to as *spaghetti code*, can be transformed into structured code. Undocumented code becomes documented. Massive old programs can be "understood" even though the author is no longer present and the application is not documented.

The original source code is not sufficient for old programs to be reverse-engineered. Application developers will have to identify and fill in the missing pieces by talking to others with specific knowledge of the application. It would be impractical for a single individual to identify the missing pieces; an expert system incorporated in the CASE tool can provide this function.

A software reverse engineering product incorporating an expert system can work interactively with an information systems professional to identify missing information, propose alternatives, and fill in the user's choice when required to complete the process.

The advantage of software reverse engineering is that it captures the essence of the business function in aging but critical applications. This allows the organization to salvage its time, money, and skill invested in old systems.[10]

### SOFTWARE ENGINEERING VS. SYSTEMS ENGINEERING

Some advocates of CASE have argued that CASE should represent *computer-aided systems* engineering, not *computer- assisted software* engineering. Their arguments suggest that the goal of CASE should go beyond automating the software development process. Systems engineering means the improvement of business procedures, not just automation. Furthermore, CASE should include responsibility for training and documentation as well as project management.

Project management is concerned with planning and monitoring software development projects. Managing software development projects is facilitated by several software tools:

- Word Processing
- Electronic Mail
- Spreadsheets
- Calendar and Scheduling Tools
- Access and Version Control
- Project Planning Tools

The systems engineering vision of CASE borrows heavily from the aerospace industry and the defense department's project management requirements. This has been less obvious in commercial information systems departments.

## Software Development Methodologies and CASE Tools

### METHODOLOGIES, TECHNOLOGIES, AND TOOLS

- A *methodology* is a conceptual approach, a strategy or philosophy for solving a problem. It embodies a set of methods, rules, and postulates that are used in solving a problem. For example, structured systems analysis is a methodology.
- A *technique* is a systematic procedure by which a complex task is accomplished. Individuals who are accomplished practitioners of

a technique are said to be skilled or to have good technique For example, one of the techniques for implementing structured systems analysis is a data flow diagrams.

- A *tool* is an object that makes a technique easier to apply. Use of a tool requires knowledge about the tool. Excelerator, for example, is a tool which supports data flow diagrams.

There are significant differences in the degree of coupling between CASE tools and methodologies. There are several CASE products which support only techniques consistent with the methodology ascribed to by the CASE vendor, such as Arthur Andersen's Foundation, which supports Method 1. Other CASE tools take an eclectic approach which allows the user to select the techniques they prefer.

One of the advantages of CASE tools is that they can be used to standardize on a common application development methodology. This methodology will include a common set of design and documentation tools.

Most of these products have a software development methodology embedded in the product. Some CASE products reflect a process approach to software development such as the structured approach to analysis and design advocated by Gane and Sarson, or DeMarco. The data-driven CASE products reflect the view that is consistent with information engineering.

## RAPID ITERATIVE PROTOTYPING

CASE enables user involvement at a higher conceptual level; it enables users to make business oriented contributions without being enmeshed in technical details. Getting a design right the first time becomes less important when the tools that capture the design are flexible and easy to change. The concept of *evolutionary design* is becoming a reality with CASE. Its effect is to move prototyping further back into the life cycle.

Prototyping is developing a working model of a proposed system and using it to refine the design. It can be a rough approximation of a system which is refined by interaction with end users. The advantages of prototyping are quicker systems development and good solutions; this method builds upon the user's intimate knowledge of the application and it bypasses much of the bureaucratic documentation in the analysis and design phase.

Prototyping addresses two problems that have plagued systems analysis: (1) Users are uncertain about the exact nature of a proposed system and (2) systems analysts are not always adept at determining user requirements.[11]

Application developers can user a working model or prototype with the input of end-users to repeat the model modification phase until it is entirely satisfactory. This new relationship between application developers and end users promises greater satisfaction of end users, and better systems which build upon the end-users' experience.

The end-user's role is two-fold: (1) to furnish the initial requirements and (2) to examine the resulting model and suggest modifications. Since most CASE tools are quite flexible, the process allows several iterations until complete satisfaction is obtained. This process has been referred to as Rapid Iterative Prototyping. A comparison of rapid iterative and the traditional systems life cycle is illustrated in Figures 8.2 and 8.3, respectively.

FIGURE 8.2

*Traditional Application Development Life-Cycle*

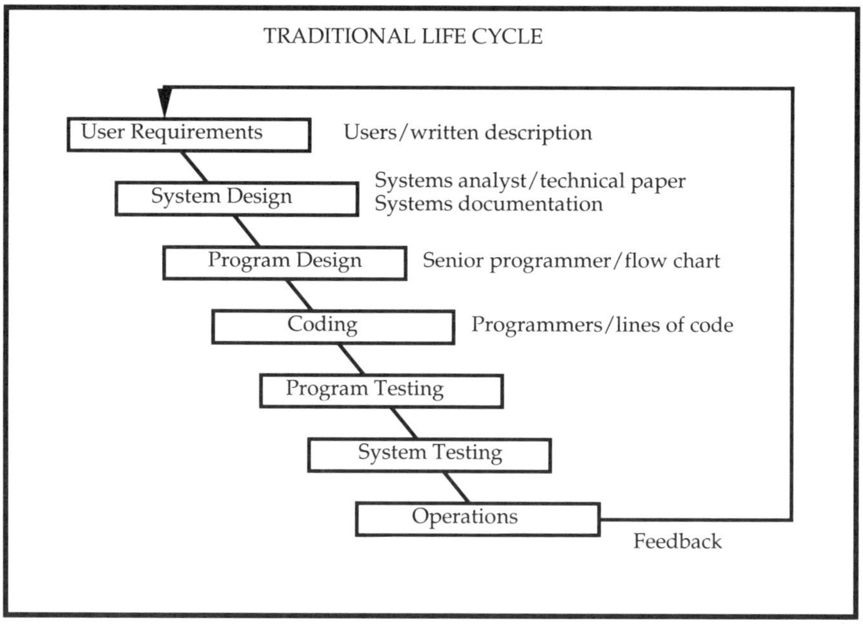

FIGURE 8.3
*Rapid Iterative Prototyping*

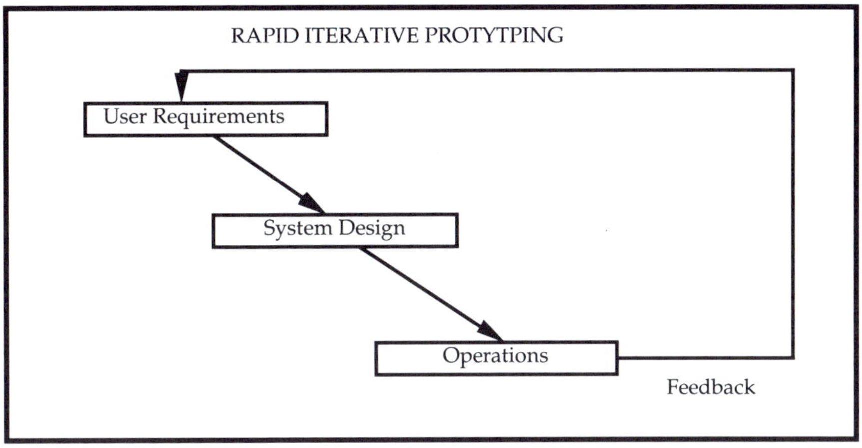


Some purists may suggest that the process described above is crude and undocumented. Two points could be made: (1) It is often easier to develop a working model with CASE tools than to develop a set of written specifications for an application; (2) Most of the CASE tools generate documentation as a by-product of the code generation process.

## Advantages and Limitations of CASE

CASE TECHNOLOGY CHANGES AND IMPROVES THE SOFTWARE development life cycle in many ways. Table 8.1 outlines the benefits of software automation (CASE) versus traditional development.

TABLE 8.1
*Benefits of CASE as Contrasted to Traditional Development*[a]

| TRADITIONAL DEVELOPMENT | SOFTWARE AUTOMATION |
|---|---|
| Emphasis on coding and testing | Emphasis on analysis and design |
| Paper based specifications | Rapid iterative prototyping |
| Manual coding | Automatic code generation |
| Manual documenting | Automatic documentation generation |
| Software testing | Automated design checking |
| Maintain code | Maintain design specification. |

[a]Carma McClure, CASE IS SOFTWARE AUTOMATION, ©1989, P.189. Reprinted by permission of Prentice-Hall, Inc., Englewood Cliffs, N.J.

CASE technology dramatically reduces the time required for coding and testing. Automatic code generation can reduce the time required for programming from 80-100%. The automatic analysis and checking of design specifications greatly reduces the errors that might originate in incomplete or inconsistent specifications. Automatic code generation eliminates the syntax errors which are common in traditional programming.

Analysis and design is changed in CASE technology from the paper specifications that capture user requirements to prototypes that serve as a "live" specification. Lengthy narrative specification documents are eliminated.

Software maintenance is also simplified. Maintenance is performed at the design level. When an application requires modifications, the design specifications are changed and the program regenerated.[12]

One of the advantages of CASE technology is that it incorporates a methodology which enforces a discipline on application development. Absent this discipline, the systems analyst, designer, and programmer will continue to cling to their old ways of developing systems. CASE not only enforces consistent technique usage, it is an excellent tool for training new analysts and application developers in advanced techniques.

CASE tools shift the emphasis of application development from program and programmer towards requirements specification. CASE tools provide single entry specification; they capture specifications in a repository which makes it unnecessary to enter duplicate information in diagrams and other CASE components.

Another advantage of CASE tools is their ability to check all specifications for consistency and completeness. Superior CASE tools guide the user to the next step in specification and inform the user of which steps are missing.

Perhaps the most important advantage of CASE technology is that it enables small and medium-sized firms to develop leading-edge systems that would have cost hundreds of millions of dollars in the 60s, 70s, and 80s. What micros did for the processing power of smaller companies in the 80s, CASE technology will do for application power in the 90s.[13]

One of CASE's major drawbacks is that it has automated yesterday's computing environment. CASE technology has concentrated on mainframe IBM and terminal architectures running software such as CICS, MVS, and IMS. This environment is changing toward micro-processor-based work stations, DB2, SQL, OS/2, and UNIX. CASE tools have not kept pace with these changes. Workstation delivery of CASE-generated applications has been neglected by CASE vendors.

One of the major limitations of CASE is that it requires significant cultural change in MIS departments. The reasons for this change are discussed in an interview with Vaughn Merlyn in Issues and Controversies.

## Issues and controversies

### Excerpts from an Interview with Vaughn Merlyn, Chairman, CASE Research Corporation

NEWSLETTER: "Considerable confusion currently exists about how the CASE market place is defined. What conflicting points of view do you identify?"

MERLYN: "There are currently three major market segments, each based on the systems development efforts supported: analysis and design, program construction, and project planning and support."

NEWSLETTER: "CASE was introduced over five years ago. What are the implications of its having achieved only 20% market penetration?"

MERLYN: "The level of penetration seems to be about on target. The statistic that is more revealing is the number of potential CASE users, i.e., programmers/analysts actually using it. According to the results of our annual CASE survey conducted in 1987, only 4% of all potential users were actually using CASE at the time of the survey."

NEWSLETTER: "What has caused such slow acceptance?"

MERLYN: "A major reason has to do with culture. For example, CASE assumes that MIS personnel already practice structured analysis, structured design, and strategic planning, whereas in reality, such practices are not all widely followed.

...although MIS staff exhibits a significant desire to build correct systems, it seems to have the impression that rigor and creativity are somehow incompatible."

NEWSLETTER: "Dataflow diagramming is the principle technique that most CASE tools support for process analysis. Are you suggesting there is really any rigor to dataflow diagramming?"

MERLYN: "Yes, if you compare dataflow diagramming to

**traditional methods based on textual documentation or flowcharts."**

**NEWSLETTER: "One could argue that rigor consists of the ability to generate executable code from design specifications. Do you know of any CASE tools that will generate code from dataflow diagrams?"**

**MERLYN: "No. It is, however, important to note that there are different levels of rigor in system development. Generation of code from specifications represents an extremely high level of rigor that has yet to be attained."**

**NEWSLETTER: "In the first generation of CASE products, the most commonly offered technique was dataflow diagramming. Do you see future CASE products continuing this emphasis?"**

**MERLYN: "No."**

**NEWSLETTER: "What can an organization do to address the broad issues involved in the acceptance of CASE?"**

**MERLYN: "Organizational changes must be made - for example, implementing the development center concept. A need also exists for enlightenment and education within the organization, extending not only upward through management, but downward through MIS as well."**



Some other limitations of CASE tools are methodology constraints, administration difficulties, documentation inadequacies and the requirement that users be graphic artists. Methodology constraints suggest that some methodologies supported by CASE tools are flawed or that the implementation of the methodologies in CASE tools may be limited in scope.

CASE tools need to be managed. Management of CASE tools will include developing standards and conventions for diagrams, tables, and text. Some CASE experts have advocated the need for a CASE administrator to insure that these tools are implemented and used in a disciplined, consistent way.

CASE tools are designed for interactive development of screen diagrams. Some of the key questions regarding interactive diagramming with CASE tools is found in Issues and Controversies.

## Issues and Controversies

### CASE Interactive Diagramming Capabilities Questions

- What types of diagrams can be drawn?
- Are there limitations on diagram size?
- Can diagrams be saved and retrieved for later use?
- Can the user manipulate the diagrams (connect objects, move, delete, enlarge, label objects)?
- Is a mouse used to create and manipulate diagrams.
- Can an object in a diagram be linked to another diagram which explains it in more detail?
- Can objects in a diagram be customized?
- Are diagrams linked to the repository?
- Can changes to a diagram be automatically reflected in related diagrams.
- Are windows and pop-down menus provided?
- How easily can textual information be added to diagrams?
- How quickly can a diagram be changed and redrawn?

Interactive diagramming with many CASE tools is such a tedious task that analysts avoid it by preparing hand sketches which are passed to a graphic specialist familiar with the tool. These tools also frequently require the user to make numerous decisions about a page's symbol and text layout, decisions that are normally made by graphic artists rather than systems analysts.[14]

It is expected that second-generation CASE tools will be able to automatically draw diagrams based on the underlying data. This will simplify the task of the analyst dramatically.

## CASE Versus 4GLS

INTEGRATED CASE TOOLS HAVE A MAJOR ADVANTAGE COMpared with 4GLs—they address the need for automation in the entire systems development life cycle. An application programmed in a 4GL which required modification would still require that the original 4GL code be altered. Thus, maintenance to a 4GL application is not significantly different from maintenance in COBOL, except that 4GLs are easier to maintain and the maintenance programmer would be more productive.

The maintenance process becomes even more difficult if there is a lack of documentation to explain how the original application was developed. Even with 4GLs, undocumented programs will present a difficult problem for a maintenance programmer.

Integrated CASE tools, on the other hand approach modification to existing applications differently. While the benefits of automation in application development are obvious, automation is perhaps more beneficial to maintenance. The concept, again, is quite simple: It is easier to change specifications than to change computer code. Once the specifications are changed, the modified application can be re-generated.

Documentation for existing applications can be generated automatically with integrated CASE tools. Lack of documentation or the absence of the original developer do not pose a serious problem for maintenance.

Another advantage for integrated CASE tools is the discipline they enforce in application development methodology. A CASE-generated application will be consistent from one application to the next. And, lastly CASE tools offer a repository, which promotes information sharing, reduces the need to re-enter information and promotes information integrity.

CASE tools, it can be argued, generate more efficient code than 4GLs. Furthermore, the code is less likely to be tied to a specific DBMS and hardware platform and therefore is more portable. Since CASE tools usually generate code in COBOL or other third generation languages, the resulting systems are more likely to be compatible with existing systems than 4GLs.

The capabilities that made 4GLs superior to third generation languages have been incorporated into CASE workbenches. These capabilities include screen and report painting, prototyping, and report and database generation.

McClure argues that CASE tools are easier to learn and easier to use than 4GLs.[15] However, this argument is questionable. Fourth-generation languages address only the programming function in the systems development life cycle, whereas CASE tools address the entire spectrum of application development. A CASE user must also be knowledgeable in systems analysis diagramming techniques, data diagramming techniques, and structured programming. Clearly CASE tools are designed for the professional software developer.[16]

Fourth-generation languages, because they are easier to learn and are much less expensive, will continue to dominate as end-user application-development tools.

## The CASE Database Connection

THE RELATIONSHIP BETWEEN CASE AND RELATIONAL DATABASE technology is complementary and synergistic. Most CASE products are designed to develop software for a database environment. Many firms will undoubtedly acquire a relational DBMS because it is closely associated with a CASE tool.

The CASE repository concept represents an extension of the DBMS data dictionary. It is expected that DBMS vendors will develop repositories compatible with their DBMS products which support a variety of CASE tools. IBM has, in fact, announced a repository for DB2.

The merger of the data dictionary and the repository has interesting implications for data administrators and systems analysts. Data administrators have traditionally maintained the data dictionary. Repositories for CASE tools have been maintained by systems analysts/application developers. Combining the responsibilities for maintaining data specifications with process specifications seems to be a logical step.

## Guidelines for Managers

COMPUTER AIDED SOFTWARE ENGINEERING (CASE) REPRESENTS a promising development for shortening the software development lifecycle and improving both the quality and productivity of the process. CASE is not just another software tool, rather it represents a new paradigm for software development.

## Guidelines for MIS Professionals

CASE BRINGS ENGINEERING DISCIPLINE TO SOFTWARE DEVELOPMENT. As a result many MIS professionals will resist it thinking it limits their creativity. The discipline imposed by CASE tools brings significant benefits, which will enable MIS professionals to build strategic systems in less time than using conventional methods.

## Key Terms

Computer Aided Software Engineering (CASE)

| | |
|---|---|
| Front-End CASE | Back-End CASE |
| Integrated CASE | Repository |
| Automatic Code Generation | Full Life-Cycle Coverage |
| Software Reverse Engineering | Systems Engineering |
| Methodology | Rapid Iterative Prototyping |

## Review Questions

1. How do CASE tools resemble CAD/CAM?
2. What CASE component is essential to integrating front-end functions to code generation?
3. How does a repository differ from a data dictionary?
4. What is the objective of software reverse engineering?
5. How does CASE technology affect the users role in software development?
6. What are the limitations of CASE?
7. How does CASE compare with 4GLs?
8. What is the CASE DBMS connection?

## Case Study

### DUPONT'S CASE EXPERIENCE

Most new computer programs are designed and written the same tedious and time-consuming way they were 25 years ago. Basically, it all begins when a computer whiz, called a systems analyst, sits down with someone from accounting or marketing to develop a new program. Once the two agree on what the system is supposed to do the analyst draws a flow chart full of circles, squares and diamonds that serves as a road map. All this is done on paper.

The analyst then says, 'Sign off on this document and I'll come back to you in five months.' Hopefully, your business hasn't changed in five months. And hopefully, I've understood what you wanted." The analyst then writes detailed specifications for the software and gives them to a programmer. The programmer sits at a keyboard and laboriously writes the code that will tell the computer what to do and when.

Like the shoemaker whose children run around without shoes, computer programmers have spent their time making life easier and more productive for everyone but themselves. A group of small, young software companies is out to change that, offering software that, they say, will speed the process of writing software, reduce the number of errors and make updating programs a cinch. Some big companies such as DuPont Co., Georgia-Pacific Corp., Hughes Aircraft Co., and Pacific Bell Telephone Company are trying these products and like what they see.

Besides saving time, the products make it far easier for computer professionals to show users how a program will work even before it is written. They also make altering programs easier just as word-processing and spreadsheet software allow users to make a change in one place and automatically propel the change through a document. And they automatically compile the documentation that explains the programs' inner workings to future programmers.

Du Pont Co. figured it would take a team of three people using conventional techniques about nine months to design and write software to keep tabs on the packaging and shipping of nylon and other products at a plant in Camden, S.C.

Using a product sold by Cortex Corp., Waltham, Mass., that automatically generates software from specifications set by systems analysts, two people did the job in two months, says Scott Schultz, Du Pont's manager of information engineering. He estimates that the software, called Application Factory, wrote about 70% of the program, leaving 30% to be done by humans. A project that was expected to cost about $168,000 was completed for $30,000.

That, of course, pleases Du Pont's cost-conscious top management. However, the systems analysts who design computer software and the programmers who write it aren't quite so enthusiastic. "It's a very difficult sell to the people who have a vested interest in seeing the old ways survive—the supertekkies,'" says Mr. Schultz. "You don't have to be a technical genius to build systems anymore," he says. "It's very threatening to people who make their living and have built their reputations doing that."

Nevertheless, the growing demand for new programs and pressure to cut overhead costs is leading big companies to try these new tools.

1. What are the advantages of diagrams as opposed to text for describing data and processes?
2. Do products such as Application Factory represent a real threat to systems analysts and programers? How can their quality of worklife be positively impacted by the adoption of these tools?
3. What is the benefit of CASE tools in making changes to applications.

## Suggestions for Further Reading

Carma McClure, CASE is Software Automation (Prentice-Hall, 1979)

*This book is perhaps the best description of CASE technology. McClure also analyzes the methodologies embedded in CASE. Several leading CASE products are described and three case studies of firms using CASE technology are included.*

# 9

# Information Engineering

*"Much of the future of computing is a battle with complexity. To push the frontiers forward, we have to learn how to build more complex systems. We cannot do this without harnessing the power of the computer itself."*

*James Martin and Carma McClure*

## Overview and Objectives

THIS CHAPTER DISCUSSES THE INFORMATION ENGINEERING APPROACH to software development. Information engineering is a concept made possible by new developments in information technology and innovation in software development methodologies. It requires automation of both systems design and programming comparable to the level of computer assistance in CAD/CAM. Information Engineering embodies both automation and a methodology for building information systems.

This concept is a data-driven methodology as opposed to a process driven methodology. It is consistent with the goals of information resource management and data administration.

Information engineering requires a new set of diagramming techniques suitable for this technology, which attempts to eliminate hand methods. It also impacts the role of the programmer and system analyst.

There are several software products that embody most of the required elements of information engineering. We will examine one of these products.

AFTER READING THIS CHAPTER, YOU SHOULD BE ABLE TO:

- Describe the elements of information engineering.
- Explain the term *data driven methodology*.
- Explain some diagramming techniques suitable for automation.
- Explain how these new concepts are changing the role of the systems analyst.

## Introduction

INFORMATION ENGINEERING IS A CONCEPT AND PHILOSOPHY born of the necessity to dramatically improve the productivity of software developers. It is now possible to achieve this objective if several complementary developments and organizational practices are in place.[1]

Integrated CASE tools
Information centers
Data administration
Data modeling
Information resource management (IRM)
Business modeling
Rapid iterative production prototyping

> Top management involvement in determination of priorities and information requirements.

Many of these developments and organizational practices have been discussed in previous chapters. In this chapter, we attempt to show how these concepts come together in a coherent philosophy and methodology of software development.

## Stages of Information Engineering

THERE ARE FOUR DISTINCT STAGES IN BUILDING SYSTEMS USING the Information Engineering methodology. These four stages are: (1) Information Strategy Planning, (2) Business Area Analysis, (3) Systems Design, and (4) Construction. Information engineering uses diagrams at each stage of information systems development.[2]

### INFORMATION STRATEGY PLANNING

Information strategy planning is an enterprise-wide examination of strategic opportunities, goals, critical success factors and information needs. It also is concerned with determining how new technologies might be exploited for competitive advantage.

The outcome of information strategy planning is an overview model of the enterprise (enterprise model) and how this model can be subdivided into areas for business area analysis. Some of the diagrams prepared in this phase are an overview entity-relationship model and a matrix which maps entity types to the functions of the enterprise.

### BUSINESS AREA ANALYSIS

The objective of business area analysis is to understand what processes and data are necessary to the enterprise and to determine how they interrelate. Business area analysis should be independent of current systems. The old systems of an enterprise are often inefficient. Business area analysis is concerned with the fundamental data requirements and the fundamental processes that the enterprise must carry out. It should avoid the mistake of paving the cow path without first straightening it.

This stage of information engineering develops a fully normalized data model for the business area. Earlier attempts to develop normalized data models of the enterprise often failed because of the magnitude of the task. Developing a normalized data model is described in the Appendix.

A process dependency or a closely related diagram is also developed in business area analysis. This diagram shows how the processes interrelate. A matrix is also built to show which entities are used, created, and updated by which process.

## SYSTEM DESIGN

System design can be accomplished relatively quickly once business area analysis is complete. Systems design in the information engineering methodology incorporates intensive involvement of end-users using concepts such as prototyping and joint application design (JAD).

The use of CASE tools and 4GLS make systems design more flexible and iterative than it has been in the conventional systems design life cycle. The design work is accelerated because it can be created and changed on a computer screen instead of a drawing board with pencils and plastic templates.

The main type of diagrams created in this stage are screen layouts, report layouts, action diagrams, and data structure diagrams. Action diagrams are discussed later in this chapter.

The diagrams developed in systems design, as well as those developed in earlier stages, are stored in a repository. The repository using expert systems technology checks the diagrams for consistency and completeness. This automated quality control check is an essential element of information engineering.

## CONSTRUCTION

Information engineering emphasizes the development of specifications in the first three stages. In contrast to traditional development methods which focus on programming, information engineering is heavily skewed towards planning and design.

The object of information engineering is to develop specifications with sufficient rigor that programming can be automated. This is accomplished by a code generator using specifications stored in a repository.

Code generation, at least at this point in time, is not completely automated. The information engineering approach is to edit an action diagram and convert it into computer code. Some modules of a system including screen formats, report formats, and data structure are automatically generated.

## A Data Driven Methodology

AN INFORMATION-ENGINEERING APPROACH TO SOFTWARE DEvelopment starts with the design of data, and then designs the activities or processes supported by the data model. This reverses the sequence used by conventional systems analysis. This is shown below.

| | DESIGN SEQUENCE |
|---|---|
| INFORMATION ENGINEERING | Data ⟶ Activities |
| CONVENTIONAL SYSTEMS ANALYSIS | Activities ⟶ Data |

A data driven methodology may be recognized by the design sequence. If data is designed before applications that use the data—the methodology is data driven. If on the other hand, applications are designed before the data stores that support that application—the methodology is process driven.

The advantage of the reversed sequence is that it anticipates data sharing between applications. The conventional approach designs application specific data stores. Information engineering follows the IRM approach to developing subject databases.

Systems development activities have traditionally been a *bottom up* activity in which various functions have to be automated on an application by application basis. Little or no thought was given to integration and optimization at the enterprise level. Firms have discovered that information systems built in this way were increasingly interdependent, incompatible, redundant, and incomprehensible.[3] This point of view is discussed in Issues and Controversies.

## Issues and Controversies

### CASE and the Balkanization of Systems Development

**CASE when improperly introduced can contribute to the Balkanization of systems development. (Balkanization refers to breaking larger structures into smaller often hostile groups.) To realize the full potential of CASE technology an organization must put its data house in order.**

**The long term survival, effectiveness, and competitive strength of a firm depends on the development of an information**

system that supports its mission, purpose, and strategies. This does not refer to accounting, payroll, or inventory systems, but to those that support the doers of the company—the people that design, make, sell, or service.

Few CASE tools being marketed today will assist in building an integrated subject database. They only contribute to the balkanization of the system's development center.

Since few organizations have their data house in order they continue to use the same old process-oriented methodologies of the past. These methods focus on business processes which are constantly changing. In contrast, the data requirements for running the business remain stable unless the firm changes strategic direction.

The old methods of application development require a systems analyst to become an expert to design a system for an organization. This is accomplished through a series of interviews with functional experts.

The specifications go through several iterations of review and change until they are ready for user sign off. By the time the system is ready for implementation it is obsolete. The metabolism of business is increasing every day and the old methodologies cannot keep up with this increased metabolism.

Information systems today must focus on what is strategic to the company. These are goals such as improving quality, increasing productivity, lowering costs, and differentiating services from those of competitors. To effect this change all corporate data must be a shareable resource.

The decision to affect this transformation to an integrated enterprise must come from top management. This leads to the development of a company-wide strategic information plan and data architecture. Once this stable data model has been developed it provides a framework for developing specific systems and design.

At this point in time CASE tools can be used effectively. In summary, investigate, use, accept, and embrace CASE but only after you have put your data house in order with a strategic information plan and corporate data architecture. This can be accomplished with a data oriented *information engineering* methodology.

Adapted from Dean F. Mohlstrom, "CASE and the Balkanization of Systems Development," Mainframe Journal (June 1989), pp. 12-14.

## INFORMATION ENGINEERING AND IRM

Developing a shared database will require cultural, organizational and methodological changes in corporations. CASE tools, especially data driven CASE tools, along with SQL, are partners in forcing corporations to make these changes. The result will be greater emphasis on information resource management (IRM).[4]

The information engineering approach to systems analysis builds applications upon a foundation of existing data models. The linkage between the design of applications and data design is discussed in this chapter. It is vital, however, that the student recognizes that the information engineering approach builds applications only after this foundation of a properly designed data base is in place.

Data driven development emphasizes the need to implement support for enterprise-wide data needs rather than individual applications. It broadens the scope of analyzing business requirements. It identifies and defines the underlying business entities to create a structure that will support the development of future systems. A data driven approach is easier than a process approach in the long run because there are less entities than processes in an organization and entities are more stable.

The use of a process driven methodology by an organization seeking to develop a shared data resource will not work. Information engineering and process driven methodologies are incompatible.[5] This is not to say that process modeling is of no value rather that it should be performed within the framework of a data driven methodology.

## INFORMATION ENGINEERING VS. SOFTWARE ENGINEERING

Information engineering should not be confused with software engineering. The term software engineering refers to the set of disciplines used by analysis, specification, design and programming computer software. Whereas software engineering begins with the requirements for a specific application, information engineering begins by defining the information requirements of the organization. Software engineering emphasizes the logic of applications and thus is a process approach to development. Information engineering represents a data centered approach to software development fully compatible with IRM.[6]

## THE BASIC PREMISES OF INFORMATION ENGINEERING

The basic premises of information engineering are:

- An overall plan that links strategic planning and business goals with information systems development is required to develop systems that better meet the needs of the firm.

- Integration of information systems can be accomplished if data that are shared are controlled centrally and by constructing a logical data model designed for sharing.
- Data models are relatively stable, whereas the processes that use the data change frequently. Therefore the logical data model should be the foundation for systems development.[7]

## Information Engineering Diagramming Tools

AN APPLICATION DEVELOPER NEEDS A VARIETY OF DIAGRAMming tools at their disposal. Some tools are useful for describing data and others for describing activities. Some tools are useful for viewing a system as a whole, others for a close look at details. Martin and McClure have suggested that diagramming tools are required for the eight areas illustrated in Figure 9.1.[8]

FIGURE 9.1 *The Systems Development Pyramid*

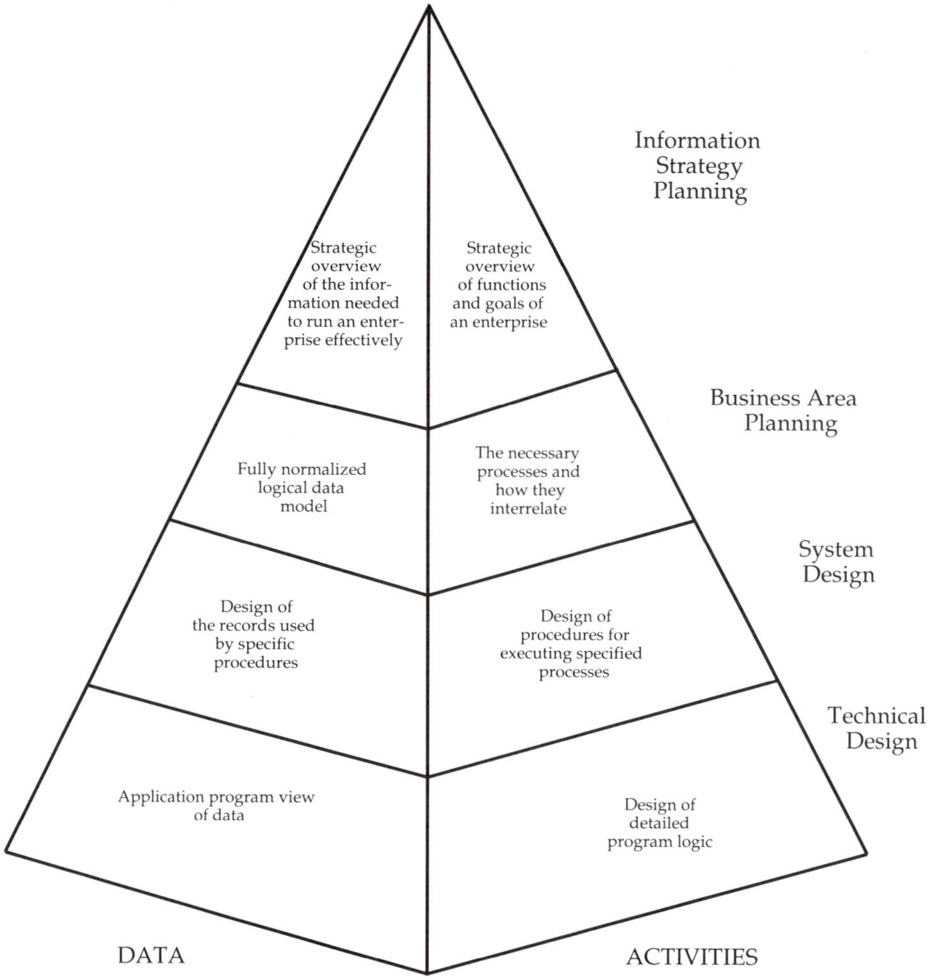

Historically, systems analysis tools have concentrated on the right half of Figure 9.1. Program flow charts, systems flow charts, decision tables, data-flow diagrams, and structured English all relate to the right half of the diagram. The tools that have attempted to deal with data were suitable only for data files and not database, including Warnier-Orr Diagrams and Michael Jackson Diagrams.

The most popular tools for describing data are: Input/Output Descriptors, File Descriptors, and a passive Data Dictionary. These tools are essentially text descriptions of data as opposed to diagrams. Diagrams assist us in describing and understanding complex systems. Good diagrams are an aid to clear thinking and communication. Furthermore, they are typically more concise than text descriptions of data.

Currently the techniques that are used are incomplete and require integration with a variety of tools to provide a coherent result. Martin and McClure have suggested the following criteria for the selection of diagramming techniques for analysts and programmers.[9]

1. User Friendly
2. Designed for Automation
3. Code Generation
4. One Tool Top to Bottom (Macro to Micro)
5. Rigorous
6. Data Base Oriented
7. Oriented to Fourth Generation Languages
8. Speed

User-friendly may have two dimensions for the application developer: (1) easy to use and (2) easy to learn. A technique may be easy to use but difficult to learn. Ideally, diagramming techniques should have both dimensions. For the end user, user-friendly suggests that a diagramming technique should be easily understood. This criterion reflects the growing tendency for end-user involvement in all aspects of computing.

Information engineering represents the automation of systems analysis and programming. To be suitable for automation, a diagramming tool should be designed for ease of sketching and editing at a terminal. It should also be able to interface with other 4th generation tools, including an integrated data dictionary and an application generator.

Conventional systems analysis tools have failed to provide a coherent approach to automation.[10] For this reason new diagramming conventions have been developed to support automation of systems analysis and design.

Code generation represents the ability of an application generator to automatically generate executable program code. This is accomplished with an information engineering work bench, a development which is analogous to CAD/CAM for manufacturing engineers.

It is desirable to use a single diagramming tool from overview to details. To accomplish this, a diagramming tool would have to give a macro as well as a micro viewpoint. Traditional systems analysis diagramming tools required a designer to use different tools to reach different levels of detail.

A rigorous technique assists in the detection of errors and omissions. Omissions and errors in design could exist without being detected by earlier diagramming tools. Computer-based techniques have some obvious advantages in detection of errors and omissions.

The requirement that tools be suitable for both file processing and database reflects the trend towards database processing. Database is the future of computing; therefore, the information engineering diagramming tools must relate to this environment. Data modeling tools are essential for a database environment. These tools related to the left side of Figure 9.1 and are discussed in some detail in the Appendix.

The 4th-generation programming languages associated with database management systems require different systems analysis techniques than traditional programming languages. Whereas traditional languages give instructions for processing one record at a time, 4th-generation languages allow instructions that deal with a set of records at a time. Compound actions such as these must be accommodated by the diagramming techniques.

Ideally, diagramming techniques are easy to draw and easy to modify. Furthermore, since analysts will want to do preliminary work with pencil and paper, they should lend themselves to that environment as well.

## Action Diagrams

ACTION DIAGRAMS ARE A DIAGRAMMING TOOL THAT IS SUITable for an overview, as well as representing the detail of program logic. An analyst using this tools will find it natural to move from an overview diagram to filling in the details of program design.

Action diagrams are also suitable for automation. They are oriented to fourth-generation languages and CASE tools, but can be used with high level languages such as COBOL. They were designed to interface with data-modeling tools used in a database environment but can be used equally well with data files.

Action diagrams are consistent with the philosophy of the structured revolution. They incorporate the concept of modules as basic building blocks. The top down design philosophy is also supported by action diagrams. One of the fundamental constructs of action diagrams is the bracket.

### BRACKETS

The basic structure of an action diagram is a bracket which represents a program module. The bracket can be any height to accommodate as much detail as required. A bracket is entered at the top. Operations within the bracket are executed in sequential order, and exit is at the bottom. An action diagram is illustrated in Figure 9.2.

### REPETITION

Brackets can show the repetition of a process. The items within a bracket with double lines at the top are executed multiple times. An action diagram representation of a repetitive process is shown in Figure 9.2.

### CASE SELECTION

Case selection can also be shown with a bracket with multiple divisions. This is used in a situation with an either/or selection of a process (mutually exclusive). This means that the selection of one case excludes the selection of another case. Case selection is also shown in Figure 9.2.

FIGURE 9.2
*Action Diagramming*

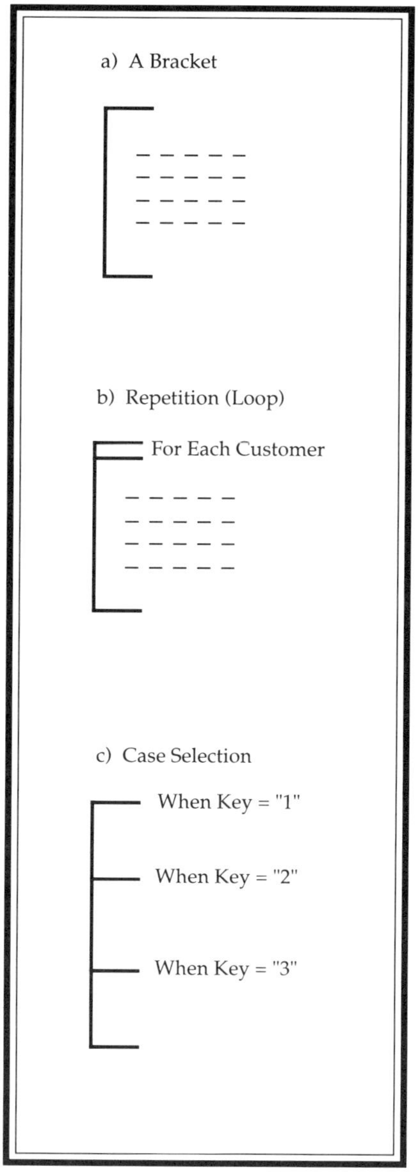


## FUNDAMENTAL PROGRAMMING STRUCTURES

Action diagrams can represent all of the fundamental structures of programming discussed earlier. Illustrated in Figure 9.3 is the fundamental programming structure: on the left with program-flowchart conventions; on the right with a action diagram.

A test or condition for loop termination can be placed before an action or after the action, depending on the requirement. A test before an action is shown as a repeat-while-condition-1-is-true, and a test after is shown as repeat-until-condition-1-is-true.

FIGURE 9.3 *Fundamental Programming Structures*

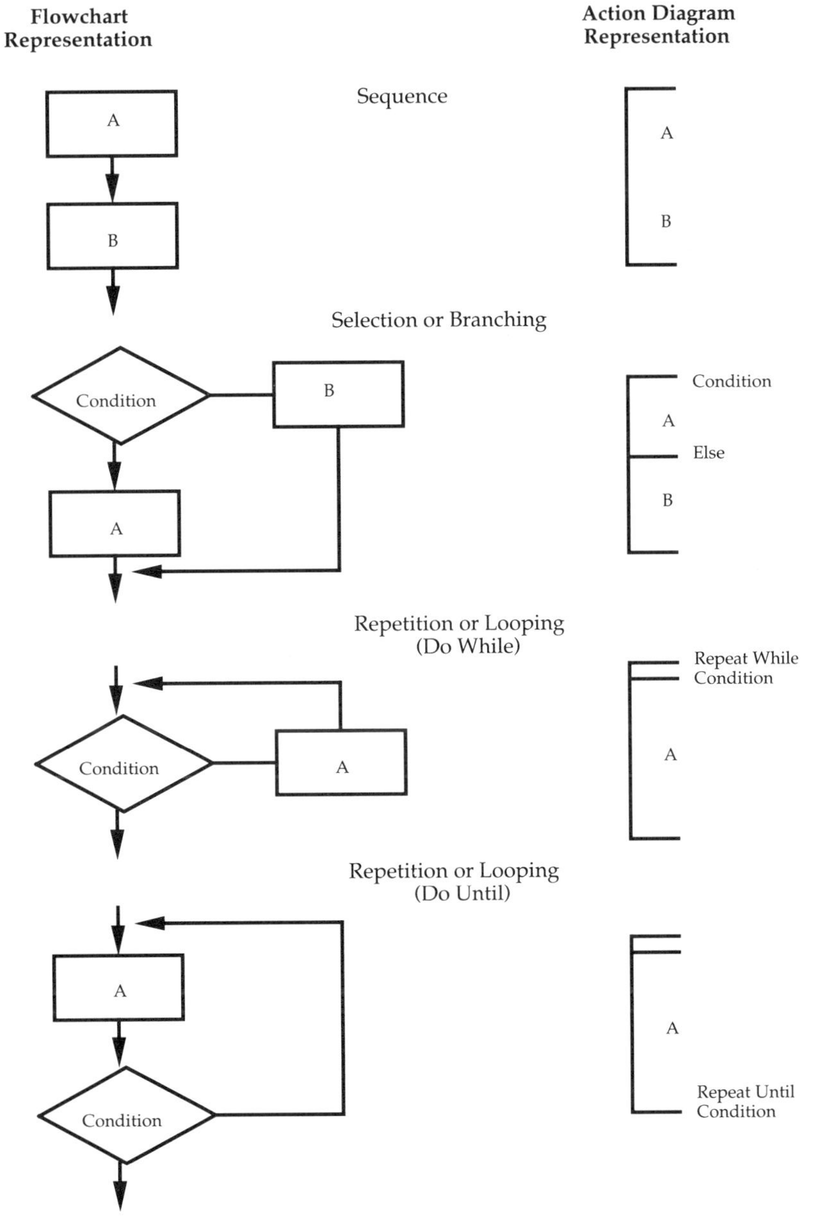

## HIERARCHICAL STRUCTURE

Not only can action diagrams show the logic of programming, they can also shown the hierarchical structure relationships of several modules. Usually this type of structure has been shown as a HIPO chart, a structure chart, or a decomposition diagram. A hierarchical structure is shown in Figure 9.4.

The action diagram equivalent of Figure 9.4 is shown in Figure 9.5. This figure illustrates the ability of an action diagram to show a macro view of a system.

FIGURE 9.4

*Conventional Representation of a Hierarchical Program Structure*

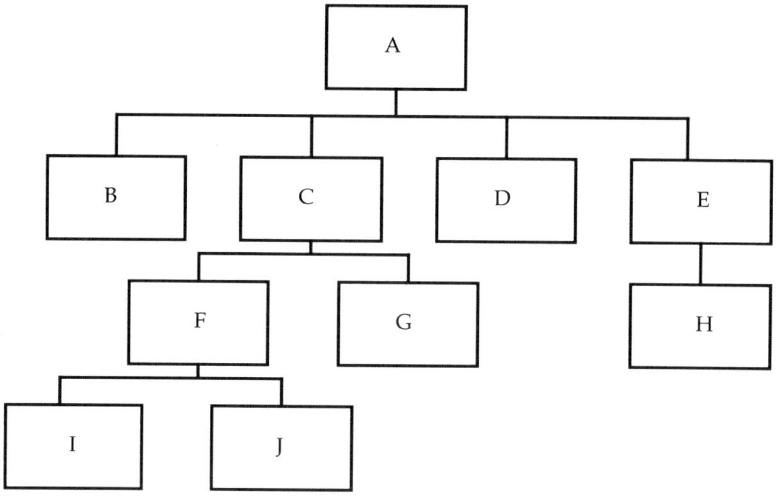


## CONDITIONS

Conditions are used in action diagrams to specify under what circumstances a module will be executed. The condition is written at the top of the action diagram. Conditions can be used to select mutually exclusive choices.

Where multiple conditions are used, we have a situation identical to the case selection shown earlier in Figure 9.2.

FIGURE 9.5

*Action Diagram Representation of a Hierarchical Program Structure*

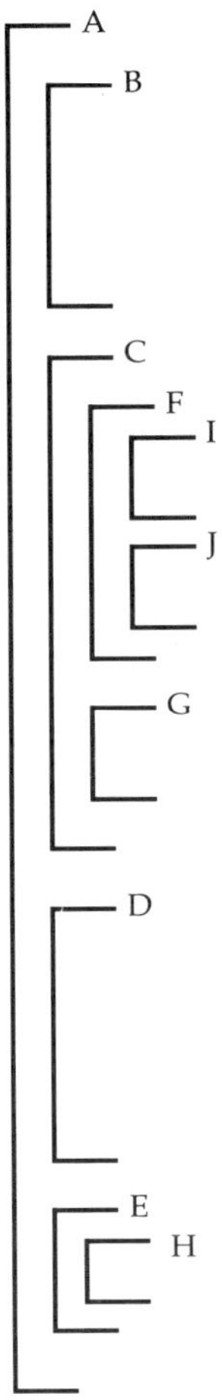


## TERMINATIONS

The termination of a procedure is shown by an arrow which crosses one or more brackets. The condition which terminates the procedure is shown by the arrow. This is shown in Figure 9.6.

Action diagrams fit several of the criterion for selection of a diagramming technique. First this tool is database oriented and interfaces with tools to represent data structure.

Second, action diagrams were explicitly designed for automation. They are easy to sketch and edit on the screen. In addition, the tool, when used in automated mode, can use the computer to check for errors. Rigorous tools require computer checking to detect errors.

FIGURE 9.6
*A Termination*

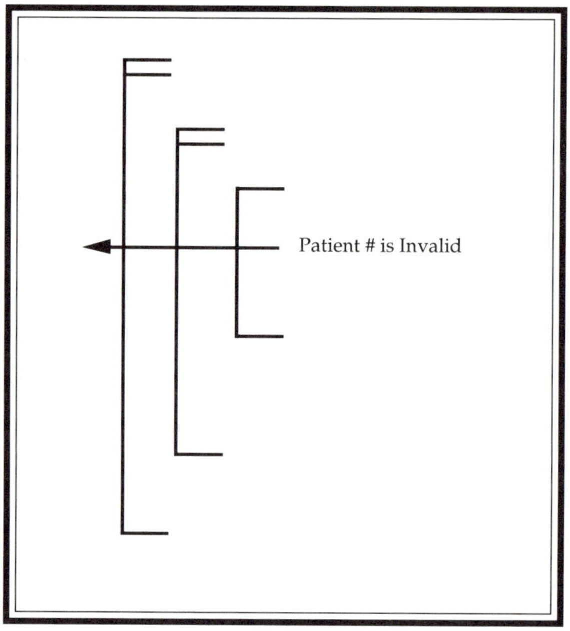


Finally, action diagrams are appropriate for showing both a high level overview of a system and low-level detail. This allows decomposition of an overview diagram to diagrams showing fine detail.

## Linking Data Base Design to Activity Diagramming

THE STRUCTURED-ANALYSIS TECHNIQUES EITHER IGNORED database design altogether or they confused the design of the data with the design of activities or processes. Both data and activities have a structure of their own. The information-engineering approach to applications developing begins with the design of the data and builds applications upon this foundation. This approach is illustrated in Figure 9.7.

The information-engineering approach to application development requires that the database model be linked to the logical structure of an application. This can be done with an action diagram.

An action diagram provides a bridge between the data model and the design of a procedure. It is the logical point of departure in the design of a database program.

FIGURE 9.7
*The Data Model Foundation*

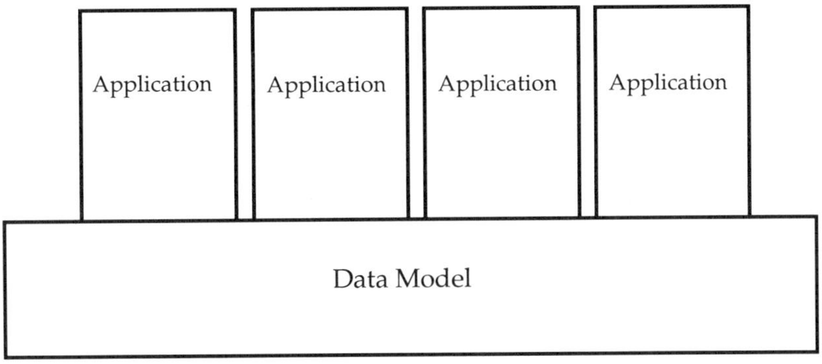


An action diagram shows the access sequence of the entity types to be employed in an application. The nature of the access of each record should also be determined. The designer designates whether a CREATE, READ, UPDATE, OR DELETE will occur. This is shown in Figure 9.8.

FIGURE 9.8
*Action Diagram for Orders*

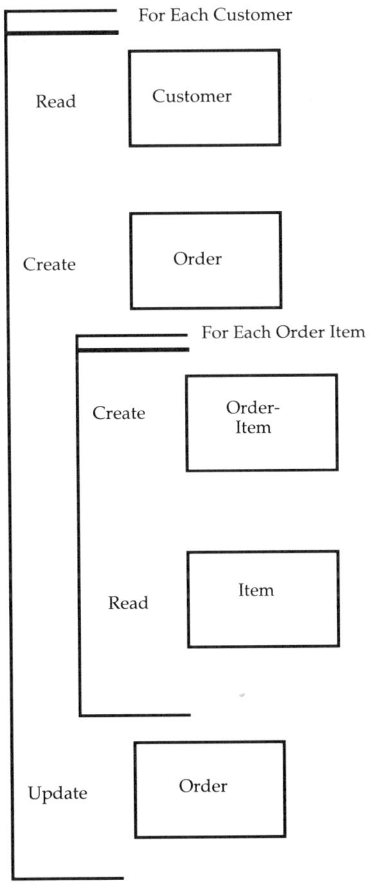

## Information Engineering Facility

INFORMATION ENGINEERING FACILITY (IEF) IS AN INTEGRATED set of software development tools which automates the entire system's development life cycle. This product marketed by Texas Instruments is an implementation of the Information Engineering methodology.

IEF is a tightly integrated set of software development tools. The planning, analysis, and design toolsets reside on a microcomputer based workstation whereas the central repository and code generator operate on a mainframe. The product will function in both a database and file processing environment.

### PLANNING TOOLSET

The Planning Toolset supports the enterprise modeling effort that defines how information is created, used, updated, and deleted by various business functions. One of the components of the Planning Toolset is the Business Function/Entity Type Usage Matrix shown in Figure 9.9.

FIGURE 9.9 *Business Function/ Entity Type Usage Matrix*[a]

Key: (Enter highest classification only)

C=CREATE
D=DELETE
U=UPDATE
R=READ ONLY

| ENTITY TYPES / BUSINESS FUNCTIONS | GOVERNMENT_CONTRACTS | PURCHASING | RECEIVING | WAREHOUSING | LEGAL_SERVICES | GENERAL_ACCOUNTING | COST_ACCOUNTING | ORDER_PROCESSING | SHIPPING | PACKING | MATERIAL_REQUIREMENTS | RELEASE_PLANNING | FINITE_CAPACITY_SCHEDULE | FACTORY-MONITORING | METHODS_ENGINEERING | FACILITIES_MAINTENANCE | BASIC_RESEARCH | PRODUCT_DESIGN | SCRAP_DISPOSAL | EMPLOYEE_RECORDS_MAIN | PAYROLL_AND_BENEFITS | EMPLOYEE_TRAINING | SECURITY | TRANSPORTATION_PLANNING | FLEET-MANAGEMENT | FLEET_MAINTENANCE | VEHICLE_DISPOSAL | |
|---|---|---|---|---|---|---|---|---|---|---|---|---|---|---|---|---|---|---|---|---|---|---|---|---|---|---|---|---|
| SALES_ORDER | | | | | | R | R | C | U | U | R | R | R | | | | R | | | | | | R | R | | | | |
| CUSTOMER | | | | | | | | U | R | R | | | | | | | R | | | | | | | R | | | | |
| CONTRACT | C | | | | | | | | | | | | | | | | R | | | | | | | | | | | |
| SHIPMENT | | | C | | | | | | | | | | | | | | | | | | | | | R | | | | |
| SUPPLIER | R | R | U | | R | R | | | | | | | | | | | R | | | | | | | R | | | | |
| PURCHASE_ORDER | | | | | R | R | | | | | R | R | R | | | | R | | | | | | R | | | | | |
| PRODUCT | | R | R | | | R | | R | R | R | R | R | R | | | | R | C | R | | | | R | | | | | |
| RAW_MATERIAL | | U | U | | | | | | | | U | | | | | | R | | | | | | | | | | | |
| CEMICAL | | U | U | | | | | | | | U | | | | | | R | | | | | | | | | | | |
| SHOP_SUPPLY | | C | | | | | | | | | | R | R | | | | | | | | | | | | | | | |
| WORK_ORDER | | | | | | | | | | | R | C | U | R | | | | | | | | | | | | | | |
| WAREHOUSE | | | R | C | | | | | | | | | | | | U | | | | | | | | | | | | |
| BIN | | | U | C | | | | | | R | | | | | | U | | | | | | | | | | | | |
| SUPPLIER_INVOICE | U | C | | | R | U | | | | | | | | | | | | | | | | | | | | | | |
| LEDGER_ENTRY | | | | | | C | C | | | | | | | | | | | | | | | | | | | | | |
| PRODUCT_INVENTORY | | R | U | R | | | | U | | U | | | | | | | | | U | | | | | | | | | |

This set of tools is designed to tie information systems strategy to business strategy. Unlike the other toolsets the perspective of the planning toolset is enterprise wide. The planning toolset provides support for developing an information architecture consistent with the objectives of IRM.

## ANALYSIS TOOLSET

The Analysis Toolset supports the analysis of a business area. It is designed to produce graphic representations of a business area's data and activities and to show their interactions. Some of the specific tools are Entity Relationship and Process Action diagrams. An example of the Entity Relationship diagram is found in Figure 9.10.

FIGURE 9.10 *Entity Relationship Diagram*[b]

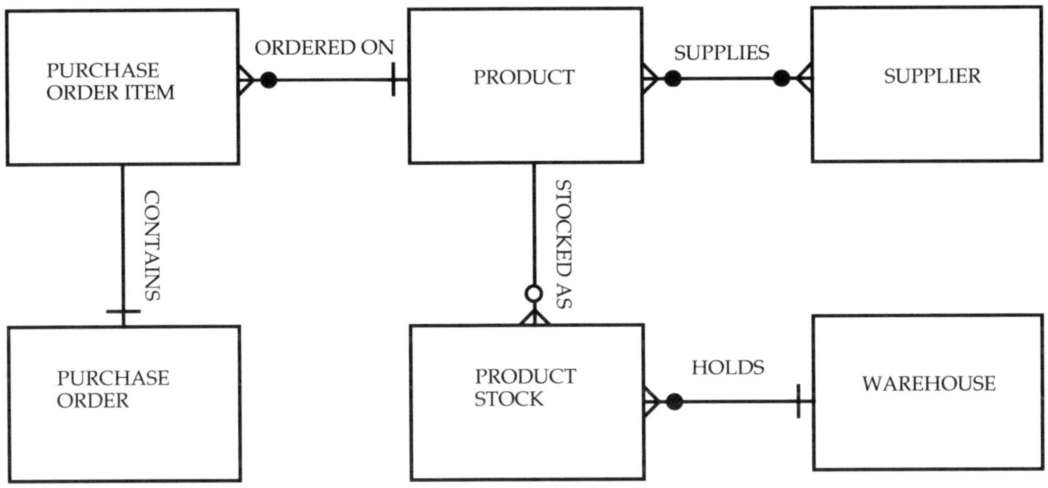




A Process Action diagram shows the detailed logic of a process. It enables an analyst to record the actions which are taken and the conditions under which they are taken. An example of this diagram is shown in Figure 9.11.

The Analysis Toolset contains several tools not discussed here which enable the analyst to fully document the data and processes of a business area. This toolset supports the analysis of both data and processes in an integrated way.

FIGURE 9.11
*Process Action Diagram*[c]

```
RECEIVE_GOODS
  IMPORTS: Entity View receiving warehouse
                Entity View received product
  EXPORTS: Entity View updated product_inventory
  ENTITY ACTIONS: Entity View required warehouse
            Entity View required product
            Entity View required product_inventory
    READ required product
      WITH number EQUAL TO received product number

    READ required warehouse
      WITH location EQUAL TO receiving warehouse location

    READ required product_inventory
      WHICH is_held_in required warehouse
        AND is_stock_for required product

    UPDATE required product_inventory
    SET quantity USING update_inventory_calcs
```



## DESIGN TOOLSET

The Design Toolset supports the system design stage of Information Engineering. During this stage detailed system definition is accomplished with the Design Toolset. This toolset includes a Screen Design tool for implementing data entry screens. It includes a Dialog Flow Diagram which defines the sequence of procedures and the data views passed between them.

A Data Structure Diagram defines how the Entity Relationship Diagram is translated into a table with rows and columns. It identifies primary keys and shows how attributes should be implemented as fields. An example of the Data Structure Diagram is shown in Figure 9.12.

This diagram shows entities, primary keys, and a relationship. The relationship *Supplies* links the entities *Product* and the entity *Supplier.*

## CENTRAL ENCYCLOPEDIA

The Central Encyclopedia acts as a shared repository for storing information developed by the workstation toolsets. The Central Encyclopedia automatically verifies diagrams and other specifica-

FIGURE 9.12 *Data Structure Diagram*[d]

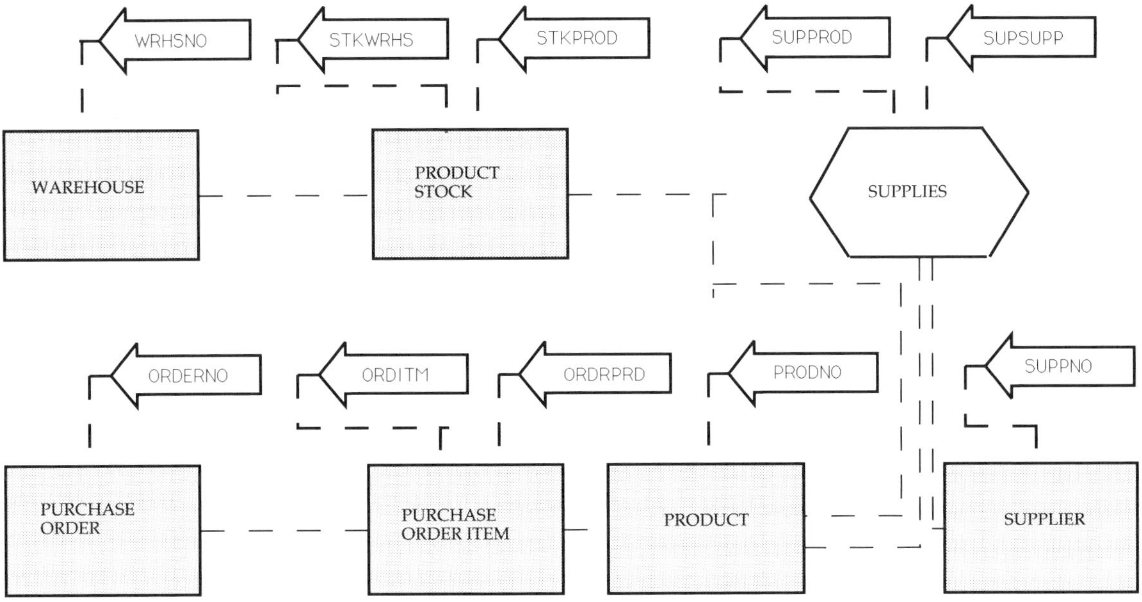




tions using expert systems rules that govern the consistency and completeness of information stored in the encyclopedia.

The encyclopedia differs from a traditional data dictionary not only in its embedded intelligence but also in scope. The encyclopedia stores specifications not only about physical implementation but information about the analysis and planning levels as well.

The Central Encyclopedia defines user access to models and performs the functions of copying, deleting, renaming, and merging models. It also provides a model history tracking record which documents activities that change model contents.

The Central Encyclopedia allows large projects to be broken down into subsets which allows multiple developers to work on the same analysis and design project simultaneously. Model subsets can be defined in the Central Encyclopedia and downloaded to workstations which facilitates parallel development.

## CODE GENERATION

The code generation stage occurs on the mainframe. Code is generated in COBOL in file processing and in COBOL with embedded SQL for access to a database.

## EXPECTED BENEFITS OF INFORMATION ENGINEERING FACILITY

Although IEF is a new product it has great promise. Some of the expected benefits are: (1) It focuses on business need rather than on automation of clerical systems (data processing); (2) IEF should provide higher quality business systems; and (3) Systems can be developed and maintained in less time and with less human resources with IEF.

FOCUS ON BUSINESS: The focus of software development is broadened to include the enterprise perspective with IEF. This should assist firms in developing systems that emphasize business requirements or effectiveness rather than efficiency.

QUALITY ENHANCEMENTS: IEF has implemented the philosophy of Information Engineering which emphasizes the active involvement of end users to ensure that the end result meets the business need. It also emphasizes an iterative approach which encourages more precise communication and understanding of system requirements. Successive refinement using flexible tools is advantageous. Earlier less flexible software development tools were denied this advantage.

Information Engineering Facility replaces craft with engineering discipline. It replaces hand drawn diagrams with computer diagrams that are checked for consistency and completeness. Hand coding is replaced with automatic code generation.

Documentation and specifications for applications reside on a central repository which is shared. This documentation remains current because it is used to generate applications. Maintenance becomes a disciplined process of revising specifications and regenerating the code of the target application.

PRODUCTIVITY: While the evidence to date is limited there seem to be definite productivity benefits in tools like IEF. While the productivity benefits of automatic code generation are obvious potentially more dramatic productivity gains are likely in analysis, design, and maintenance. Greater gains in analysis, design, and maintenance are probable because they use considerably more resources in the traditional system's life cycle than coding.

### LIMITATIONS OF INFORMATION ENGINEERING FACILITY

Information Engineering Facility is currently limited to an IBM mainframe environment. New versions which target powerful microcomputer based workstations are expected.

Perhaps the biggest limitation of IEF is the cultural change it imposes on software development. This type of product requires massive change in the philosophy and mechanics of how software is developed. Some organizations will undoubtedly not be successful in making these changes.

## The Changing Role of the ·stems Analyst

THE SYSTEMS ANALYST'S ROLE IS BEING MODIFIED BY TECHnological developments. The development of the relational database, fourth generation languages, and information-engineering tools to automate the design and documentation of systems will dramatically change the role of the systems analyst. Traditionally, systems analysts have assumed the role of specification writers, designers, and an intermediary with end-users. The preparation of requirements documents is frequently viewed as an unpleasant task synonymous with drudgery and bureaucracy. Rubenstein suggests that the systems analyst role will change from middleman and requirements-writer to that of analyst-builder.[11] In the user driven computing environment, the systems analyst adopts a new role which involves experimentation, iteration, and prototyping. The user is intimately involved, and in some cases may be the developer of new systems.

The concept of information engineering suggests the development of a new role of the systems analyst—that of application developer. Working at an information engineering workbench, the system analyst can do the complete job of application development. This new role of application developer promises greater satisfaction of the systems analyst and avoids the grind of specification development.

## Managing Information Engineering Systems Development

MANAGING AN INFORMATION ENGINEERING APPROACH TO systems development requires obtaining the correct set of tools and the right people. Martin suggests the following characteristics for information engineering systems development.[12]

1. An application generator that enforces fully structured code with the maximum use of defaults and non-procedural functions.
2. Graphics tools for design automation.
3. An action diagram editor for specifications and procedural code.
4. An on-line dictionary.
5. A fully normalized data model.
6. Fast prototyping.
7. An interactive development cycle.
8. Computer-aided conversion of prototypes into final code, if necessary.
9. Automated documentation.
10. A library of reusable modules.
11. One-person projects where possible.
12. Thorough training and practice with the tools.
13. Division of large programs into smaller autonomous modules linked via a data model.
14. Use of preprogrammed functions or packages where possible.
15. Management techniques adapted to the above.

### Management Style in Information-Engineering Systems Development

In their book *In Search of Excellence,* Peters and Waterman describe a management style compatible with an information-engineering approach to software development. They advocate a management style which is experimental as opposed to analytic. They term this style *a bias for action*. This style is not anti-analytical; rather, it recognizes the limits of analysis. It is compatible with prototyping and end-user involvement in developing and improving prototypes.

Information-engineering is effectiveness oriented. It is less concerned about following the correct methodology than getting the system right. This might be expressed as a management style that is results oriented as opposed to appearance-oriented overemphasizing such things as methodology and documentation.

Information-engineering is compatible with a philosophy that Peters and Waterman refer to as *Close to the Customer.* The satisfaction of end users is a source of motivation to application developers, as well as a measure of how well they have accomplished their jobs.

## SMALL GROUP SYSTEMS DEVELOPMENT

The potential for greater satisfaction of application developers in information-engineering ought not to go unnoticed. Software development is fundamentally a people business. Surveys of computer professionals have emphasized the importance of the work itself in factors related to job satisfaction. Stimulating work should assist in attracting and holding skilled employees.

Software development in an information engineering environment can usually be accomplished by a single individual or a small group who work with knowledgeable end users. This approach saves analysis and design time because it does not require preparation of a specification document that is passed on to someone doing the actual development. The designer and developer are the same individual(s). Documentation in information engineering is a by-product of the specification process. It is produced automatically.

Finally, since information engineering systems development methods rely more on the individuals (application developers) with a broad range of skills, a commitment to people is essential. This implies a management commitment to recruiting, motivating, and rewarding outstanding performers.

## Guidelines for Managers

INFORMATION ENGINEERING REPRESENTS A PROMISING NEW approach that is designed to improve the quality of software and the productivity of the software development process. This concept automates programming in a manner analogous to CAD/CAM for engineers. This concept requires a different management approach from traditional software development including smaller development groups and greater attention to recruitment and retention of broadly trained application developers.

## Guidelines for MIS Professionals

Information engineering technology requires new methodologies of software development. These methodologies include a data driven as opposed to a process driven methodology. Information engineering also requires a new set of diagramming techniques that integrate with database design. MIS professionals who learn these new skills will remain productive in the Information Engineering era.

## Key Terms

Information Engineering
Computer-Aided Design/Computer-Aided Manufacturing (CAD/CAM)
Information Centers
Transparently-Coupled
Information Strategy Planning
Computer Aided System Design
Data-Driven Methodology
Program Flow Charts
Data Flow Diagrams
Passive Data Dictonary
Repetition
Hierarchical Structure
Terminations
Stand-Alone
Application Generators
Fourth Generation Languages
Data Administration
Data Modeling
Business Modeling
Prototyping
Software Engineering
Systems Flow Charts
Input/Output Descriptors
Brackets
Case Selection
Conditions
Upload-Linked

## Review Questions

1. Contrast the information engineering approach to software development conventional systems analysis
2. Discuss the differences between information engineering and software engineering.
3. How is an information engineering workbench similar analagous to CAD/CAM for manufacturing engineers?
4. How do Action Diagrams fit the 8 criteria identified by Martin and McClure for selection of diagramming techniques?

5. What is the purpose of a data navigation diagram?
6. Name the three advantages of using the PC as an information-engineering workstation.
7. How is the role of the system's analyst changing?
8. What important systems design component is a by-product of the specification process in information engineering?
9. How does the management approach in information engineering compare to the traditional software development?
10. What are the benefits of a prototyping approach to system development? When is it appropriate?

**Case Study**

## HUNTINGTON NATIONAL BANK

When a regional bank is switching mainframe vendors, building a new data center, and converting existing software applications, the last thing the MIS manager wants to do is to break ground on a CASE project.

In the mid-80's Huntington—which had been using mainframes from Burroughs for nearly a generation—decided to switch to IBM mainframes. The decision was based on the greater availability of software for the IBM environment.

John Voss, vice-president of systems integration, and his team carefully planned a conversion strategy consisting of off-the-shelf conversion packages and specially licensed conversion software products. They were not considering CASE tools.

With an eye towards enhanced customer service the bank decided to create in-house software tailored to its customer needs. The goal was a comprehensive customer account profile which included client demographic information integrated with data on multiple accounts, to be produced on a single screen.

Early in 1988, Arthur Young, was hired as a technology and methodology consultant. Arthur Young suggested Knowledgeware's Information Engineering Workbench for the project's initial data analysis and data modeling platform.

As the analysis proceeded, Voss indicated we asked ourselves,

"What comes after analysis?" "We wondered if it was possible to do automated code generation out of analysis." The bank looked at Knowledgeware's Gamma back end generator and realized it was not integrated with the IEW front-end tools.

Voss remembered hearing about a CASE tool offered by Texas Instruments, the Information Engineering Facility (IEF). Voss contacted Texas Instruments and requested a presentation half hoping the CASE issue would die. The presentation went well and the bank requested a demonstration.

In March 1988, the bank's MIS staff built a prototype of their Customer Information System (CIS). Pleased with the outcome, Huntington committed to the project. Texas Instruments remained on-site until October of 1988 to provide training and support.

The bank is currently running the CIS under IBM's relational database DB2. The system runs 24 hours per day and makes data accessible in both online and batch modes.

The bank considers the CIS to be the hub of their information system. The system has been very reliable. Voss indicates that, "Our transaction productivity has increased. When changes have been necessary, which is seldom, we simply revise the IEF diagrams and automatically regenerate the code."

1. Why did the bank develop software instead of purchasing a package?
2. What type of development methodology was used in this case?
3. What advantages did the bank realize from this approach?
4. Does the bank have a competitive advantage with its Computer Information System (CIS)?

## Suggestions for Further Reading

James Martin, Information Engineering: Introduction, (Prentice-Hall, 1989)

*This book is the first volume of a three volume set. It introduces the Information Engineering methodology which Martin claims is the only software development methodology designed for automation. Information Engineering is not only a methodology it is a mindset that includes a bias for strategic information systems, data driven system design, end user involvement, and productivity improvement.*

# 10

# Distributed Processing

*"The changing information economics that will put 10 MIPS on a desktop will mean there will no longer be a need for a central computing facility."*

*Don Tapscott*

## Overview and Objectives

DISTRIBUTED PROCESSING IS A CONCEPT MADE POSSIBLE BY widespread, inexpensive data communications and relatively inexpensive small and medium-sized computers. It is consistent with the management concept of decentralization. This chapter examines the advantages and disadvantages of distributed processing, and the alternative types of distributed processing available.

The term *connectivity* will be defined and different degrees of connectivity clearly explained. We will further examine the problems in obtaining higher levels of connectivity.

We also explain the concept of a distributed database and define various distributed database alternatives. Lastly, we will discuss the immature nature of this technology and the risks of implementing cutting-edge dbms technology.

AFTER READING THIS CHAPTER YOU SHOULD BE ABLE TO:

- Explain the social, political, and economic factors that are behind the growth in distributed processing.
- Define different levels of connectivity.
- Explain the objectives of a distributed database.
- Define a partioned, replicated, and clustered distributed database.

## Introduction

DISTRIBUTED PROCESSING MIGHT BE CONSIDERED AS A natural evolution from centralized computer facilities. This concept, which emerged in the 70's, represents a dramatic departure from large centralized batch processing systems. Distributed processing involves decentralization of computer processing, bringing processing power in the form of mini-computers, and micro-computers, closer to the user.

Some organizations, notably IBM, prefer the term *cooperative processing* when describing networks of computers in which each category of computer has a specialized role. This view emphasizes the hierarchy of processing roles.

## Distributed Processing Network Alternatives

SEVERAL DISTRIBUTED PROCESSING NETWORKS HAVE BEEN used by various organizations. Perhaps the most common configurations are the peer to peer, two tiered, and three tiered networks.

As illustrated in Figure 10.1, the peer to peer network is an organization of equals. Processors have equal status. One processor may be designated as a file server or a database server. The term file server describes a computer which stores files used by other computers. A database server provides the functions of data storage, and extraction for other processors.

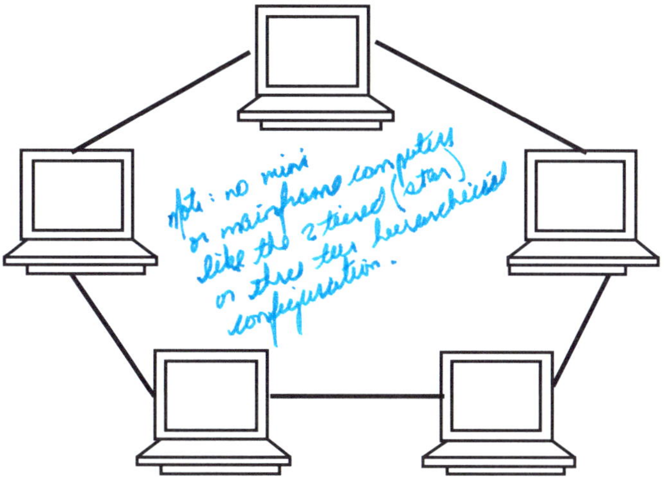

FIGURE 10.1

*A Peer-Coupled Distributed Processing Network*

A two tiered network is a hierarchical network controlled by the host computer. A typical configuration consisting of a host, either a mainframe or a mini, and microcomputers which are networked to the host is shown in Figure 10.2.

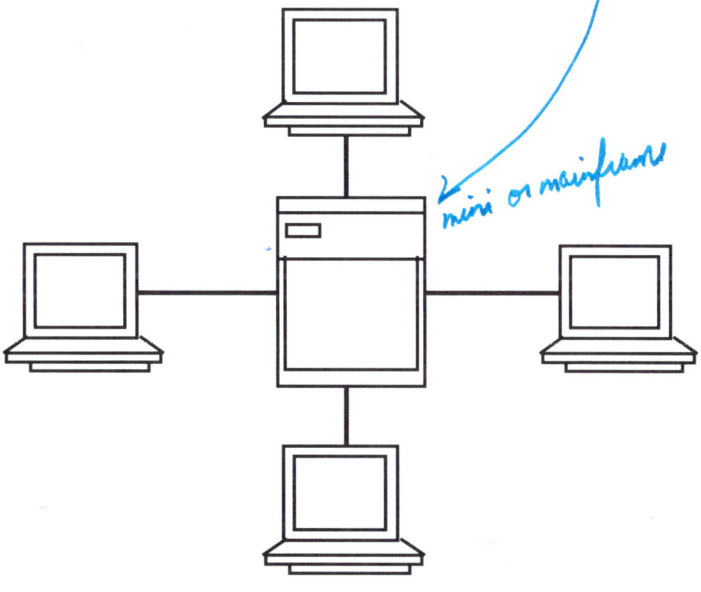

FIGURE 10.2

*A Two-Tiered Distributed Processing Network*

The three tiered network utilizes a hierarchy of processors. It is sometimes referred to as a tree network. An example of a tree network is shown in Figure 10.3.

FIGURE 10.3
*A Three-Tiered Distributed Processing Network*

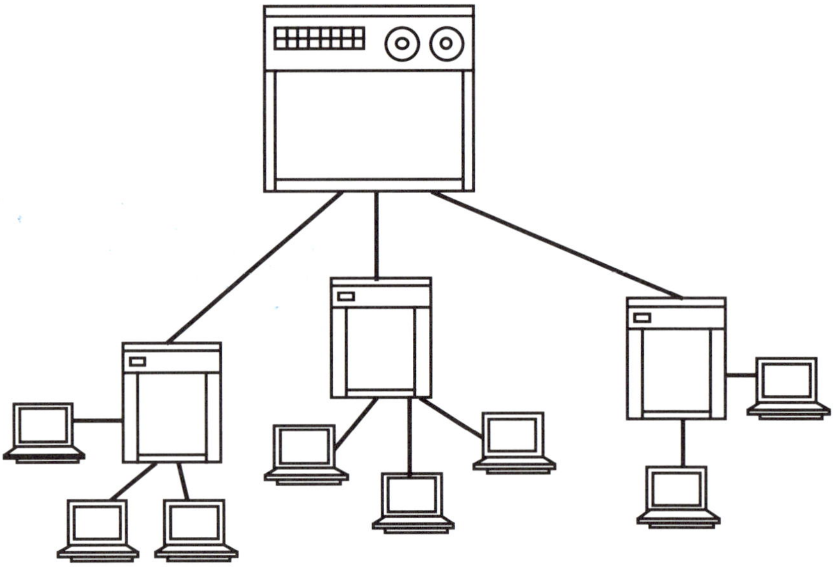

The three tiered network may combine mainframe computer, minicomputers and microcomputer-based workstations in the same network. This is an organization of processors that are not equal and may be referred to as a hierarchical network.

The increasingly favorable price/performance ratios of microcomputers has encouraged a trend towards peer coupled networks. However, although due to rapid advances in network technology all three network alternatives are expected to show considerable growth.

For obvious reasons, mainframe manufacturers have encouraged hierarchical networks. The IBM extensions to OS/2, the operating system designed for multiuser microcomputer networks, are also designed to facilitate PS/2 machine communications with their mainframes.

## Forces Behind Distributed Processing

DISTRIBUTED PROCESSING OF DATA HAS BEEN ENCOURAGED BY several trends in technology, organizations, and changes in society at large.

## TECHNOLOGY

The microprocessor has revolutionized computing. A 32 bit microcomputer workstation has more processing power and memory than a second generation mainframe computer, and some models sell for less than the cost of a terminal. The ability of the semiconductor manufacturers to mass produce microprocessors inexpensively has changed the economics of computing.

During the 1960s and 1970s, most computer experts believed in Grosch's Law, which said that the cost per machine instruction was inversely proportional to the square of the size of the machine. Economies of scale led to the centralization of computing. Many organizations purchased large main frames in excess of their needs to obtain lower unit-computing costs. Excess capacity was sold to other organizations.

Microprocessors have repealed Grosch's Law. Microprocessors now have much lower unit computing costs than mainframes and future developments are expected to widen the difference.[1] The new economics of computing suggest greater use of microcomputers. This development favors more distributed processing.

Current information technology favors distributed processing. The availability of widespread and inexpensive data communications and networking alternatives is complimentary to the development of microcomputers and is a condition favorable for the growth of distributed processing. A controversial view of the future directions of microcomputers and distributed processing is found in Issues and Controversies.

## Issues and Controversies

### Mainframe Dinosaurs

**Are mainframe computers obsolete? Is the current period of slow growth in sales a temporary phenomenon or does it represent the beginning of an era of decline? The fate of an entire industry hangs on the answer to these questions.**

**Until recently, even raising such questions would have been considered crazy. Now, however, there is growing uneasiness and uncertainty about the future of mainframe computing.**

**And for good reason. Mainframes are facing the same fate as the horse and buggy and steam locomotives. These machines are finding their environment increasingly inhospitable, much like the dinosaurs were 65 million years ago when a large meteorite slammed into the earth and altered the climate.**

**The emerging second generation of information systems will not be dominated by proprietary mainframe and minicomputer architectures. Rather, it will be dominated by standardized microprocessor architectures, operating systems, and networks.**

**Traditional mainframe and terminal architectures will be replaced by distributed peer networks of workstations and servers linked by high-speed peer channels. The control that vendors have enjoyed over their installed base will be replaced by a highly-competitive market for standardized hardware and software components.**

**The impending obsolescence of mainframes does not mean that large systems will disappear. Applications requiring large databases or a high volume of transactions will not vanish. However, large mainframes will be replaced by systems such as large high-capacity database machines using parallel processing. The majority of these units will be based on standard microprocessor components and will all but replace mainframes by the turn of the century.**

**Mainframes will not decline simply because of microprocessor and network technology; rather, the primary factor will be economics. One million instructions per second (MIPS) for a 32 bit mainframe costs in excess of $100,000 today. A nearly comparable MIPS capability on a microprocessor can be purchased for $1,000. The 100 to 1 difference in price for equivalent performance will persuade industry to discard mainframes.**

Adapted from "Mainframe Dinosaurs," William Zachmann, Computerworld Focus, November 4, 1987, p. 6.

Current technology and economics favor not only distributed processing but in particular peer-to-peer distributed processing. The trend will be to replace traditional mainframe-and-terminal networks with networks of microprocessor-based workstations and database servers. A database server is a machine dedicated to database functions; either a general purpose computer, a microcomputer, or a specialized database server. There are some advantages in using the mainframe as a database server. This view is discussed in Issues and Controversies.

## Issues and Controversies

## Mainframes Aren't Dead Yet

**Mark Twain once said that, "Reports of my death have been greatly exaggerated." Like Mark Twain reports of the mainframes death have been overstated. The mainframe isn't dead and isn't even dying. It has simply reached maturity.**

**Mainframes have never penetrated small and medium sized businesses and with the advent of PCs are unlikely to do so. Information intensive firms, however, like airlines, insurance companies, banks and brokerage**

**firms will have a continuing need for mainframes to handle their high volume applications.**

**The future of mainframes is closely linked to the trend towards distributed processing. If distributed processing becomes the new mode of computing the mainframe will serve as a database and network server.**

**Mainframes have an advantage in security, backup and data sharing. As one observer says, "mainframes have the features, micros have the efficiency."**

Adapted from Paul E. Shindler, Jr., Phillip J. Gill and Lisa Stapleton, "Mainframes: Here Today and Tomorrow," Information Week, February 1, 1988), pp. 30-34.

## POLITICAL

End users in many organizations are dissatisfied with the level of computing service provided by centralized systems. Requests for new programs or information are frequently ignored or delayed until they are no longer useful. End users are pressing their case for purchasing small computers for transaction-processing and decision-support applications.

## SOCIAL

There is a movement away from large centralized corporate facilities to smaller plants and offices scattered about the country. In manufacturing, small, focused factories are in vogue. Rural areas are increasingly the choice for small and middle-sized production facilities.

This movement toward smaller plants scattered throughout the country, as well as abroad, strengthens the arguments for distributed processing.

# Connectivity

CONNECTIVITY REFERS TO THE DEGREE TO WHICH COMPUTERS can communicate with each other. It is facilitated by the compatibility between two computers. The more things computers have in common, generally, the easier it is for them to communicate.

Connectivity problems are compounded by the proliferation of incompatible computer systems. The three tiered hierarchy of computer systems described earlier in this chapter is very common in the business world. It consists of a mainframe; a second tier of minicomputers or supermini-computers often dedicated to a single function and at a lowest level; microcomputer-based managerial work station. Connecting this hierarchy of systems into a coherent network is an extremely challenging task made more difficult by differences in computer systems. Some of these differences are different operating systems, different computer architectures, and different application software.

Connectivity involves more than the ability to link systems electronically. An analogy to the telephone explains this point: it is easy to pick up the telephone and call someone in Mexico but unless you speak Spanish or your contact speaks English, you're not going to have a conversation.[2]

For computers to communicate, either a common protocol must be used or the data must be converted by a protocol converter. Microcomputers transmit data using an asynchronous transmission protocol. This means that a character is transmitted preceded by an identifying start bit and followed by a stop bit. IBM mainframes transmit data in a synchronous mode, which results in a high-speed stream of continuous data. Data is transmitted in blocks, with the starting and stopping of data controlled at the beginning and end of each block. A timing signal is generated by both the sending and receiving station to synchronize characters.[3] The representation of characters in binary for personal computers is ASCII, whereas IBM mainframes use Extended Binary Coded Decimal Interchange Code (EBCDIC) for representing characters.

These protocol problems have been addressed by a variety of hardware and software products. The protocol conversion problem might be compared to the transmission of messages between a Japanese business person and a French business person as illustrated in Figure 10.4. The message is translated to English which is the standard used by both the sender and receiver. When received the message is translated from English to the local language.

Each layer in this communication system has a corresponding layer in the parallel organization. This provides a standardized interface with clearly designed functions of each layer so new senders and receivers know what is required to join the system.

FIGURE 10.4
*Multilayer Protocol Conversion*

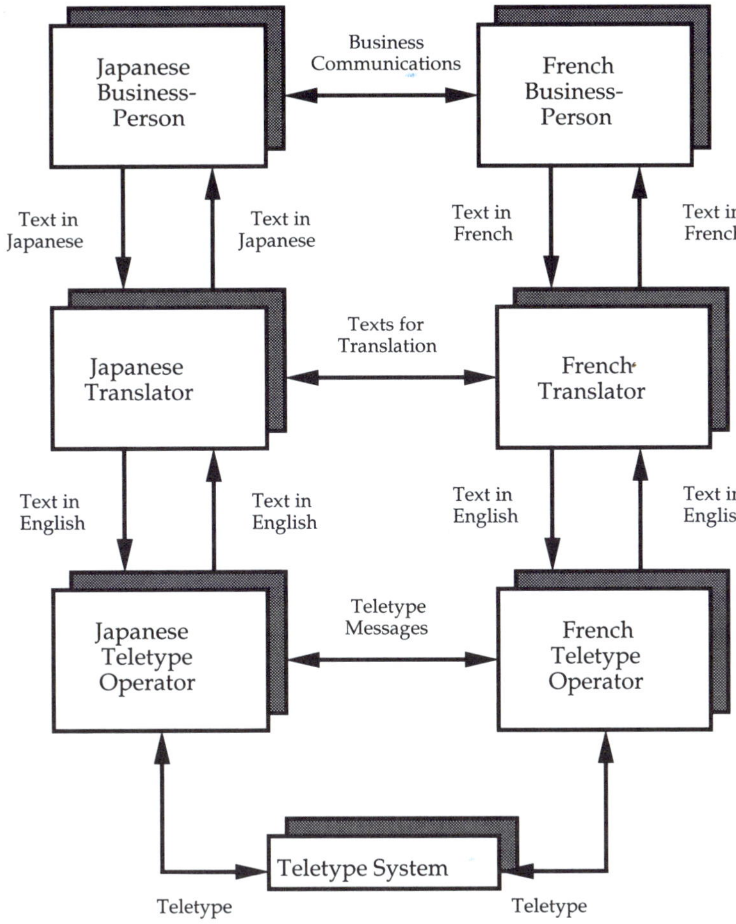


The degree of connectivity between two computers might be described as follows:

1. Terminal emulation
2. File transfer
3. Data extraction
4. Software upload

The first level of connectivity is a terminal emulation mode. This allows a personal computer to function as a terminal. Generally, this level of communication is quite unsatisfactory, since it does not allow the PC to upload files to the host computer or download files from the host. In this mode the PC does not save anything that scrolls across the screen.[4]

File transfer allows the personal computer to transfer a complete file from the host. The difficulty with this compatibility is the size of some host files, the speed of the data communications link, and the limited storage capability of personal computers.

File transfer systems have generally been less than a satisfactory solution to the micro to mainframe connection. The files were often much too big. Files with a few thousand records could tie up the micro for hours. The files themselves contained too many fields, and several times too many records. The end-user was still faced with the task of extracting the necessary information from the plethora of data.

While a file transfer system is preferable to the alternative of entering the data from a report, and certainly less prone to error, it may be a cumbersome solution. A user finds the task of *massaging* the data extensively irksome.

File transfer systems are quite common in peer to peer networks of PCs where they are used to store software on a file server. This eliminates duplication of software.

The next level of connectivity requires the ability to extract data from mainframe files and reformat the data into personal-computer formats. Data extraction will be aided immeasurably by the standardization of SQL as the query language for database-management systems. SQL enables the user to extract only those records specified by the SQL specification. Furthermore, it extracts records in sets rather than a record at a time.

With a query language like SQL, PC users would have the ability to scan various relational databases residing on either remote or local database servers. The combination of LANs and SQL will result in powerful connectivity tools to integrate PCs into networks that allow end users access to transaction data.

The last level of connectivity is the ability to develop and test software on the microcomputer-based workstation and upload the software to the mainframe or other computers for production applications. This allows the economical microcomputer to be used as a software-development workstation.

Connectivity at the highest level is easy to accomplish if the machines have the same architecture and the same operating system.

The difficulties arise when computers at the opposite end of the communications link are different.

## CONCERNS WITH SECURITY

One of the major concerns of MIS managers about increased access to mainframe data is the issue of security. Information systems managers worry that users may gain inappropriate access to sensitive data. A closely related concern is the lack of security of mainframe data once downloaded to a portable floppy disk.[5]

This is an issue that might be partially addressed with database technology, specifically the security functions of an integrated data dictionary. The security features of an integrated data dictionary would allow users to access only data that they were authorized to access. As implemented in relational database systems it would typically involve security of two levels:

1. Table - A user may be permitted or denied access to a table.
2. View - A user may be permitted or denied access to data within a view.

A user may have several different forms of authorization on parts of the database. These would include:

- Create - Allows user to insert new data but not to modify existing data.
- Read - Allows user to read but not to modify data.
- Update - Allows user to modify but not to delete data.
- Delete - Allows user to delete data.

Most data dictionary systems allow users' access to be limited to specified hours of the day and days of the week.

## TRENDS IN CONNECTIVITY

There are a number of trends in linking computers in general, and microcomputers in particular, into distributed processing networks. First, it is obvious that terminal emulation solutions will be replaced by peer-to-peer communications. This allows the user to use intelligence at both ends in both extracting data and performing analysis on it at the other end.[6]

Lee Doyle, the communications analyst at the International Data Corp., said.:

> Over time I expect to see the mainframe become more of a file server and a large database server for a number of intelligent devices linked by a network, as well as controlling access to host data.[7]

## Distributed Networks with File Servers

A FILE SERVER ARCHITECTURE ALLOWS A NETWORK TO SHARE software and expensive peripheral devices. A local area network links microcomputers to a file server. It allows data and software to be stored on a central file server. Files can be accessed from the file server as from one's own workstation.

File server networks have been particularly useful to link PCs together to share software, data and peripherals such as laser printers. This architecture while useful for end-user computing, does not provide a satisfactory solution for transaction processing. File server networks can generate heavy network traffic. Facilities for updating files include a locking mechanism for temporarily locking other users out of a file, making large amounts of information temporarily unavailable to other users.

Database server architectures have more sophisticated locking mechanisms which allows more concurrent users to access data. A number of users can share data without hampering the response time of the system.[8]

## Distributed Networks with Database Servers

THERE ARE THREE EMERGING TECHNOLOGIES THAT WILL BE THE basis of distributed networks of the future. These are (1) microprocessor technology which provides powerful yet inexpensive processing power; (2) relational database technology which provides ease of data access and flexibility; (3) LANs which provide a mechanism for linking together computers, peripherals and database servers. These three technologies will be linked together to form the distributed networks of the future.

Using these three technologies organizations will be able to create *logical mainframes*. This concept refers to a system of many devices integrated to perform the traditional mainframe role. Large mainframes may decline in importance, but the need still exists for high volume, heavy duty computing.

The relational database model is generally accepted to be the most powerful form of DBMS software. The simplicity of this model, which allows the user to manipulate data within a table or tables without programming knowledge is its primary advantage.

On the negative side, the simplicity and flexibility of relational DBMS software generates heavy CPU demand and storage requirements. These demands can severely hamper general-purpose mainframe performance. One solution is to develop networks of computers with one machine dedicated to database functions. This concept has been referred to as a database server architecture.

Database servers are dedicated computers which provide database storage and retrieval of data for other computers in a network running application programs. The server machine stores and manipulates the data and provides facilities for security, locking, transaction logging, and recovery. The application program resides on a microcomputer based workstation. Data requests in the form of SQL commands are transmitted from the workstation to the server and only the records matching the request are sent back.

The microcomputer based workstation constructs a query using SQL or a 3rd generation language such as C or COBOL with embedded SQL commands. Fourth generation languages, in which data requirements are translated to SQL commands, could also be used to access the database server.

Only SQL queries and commands travel across the network to the server. The server processes the request by selecting the data that matches the selection criteria and transmits back across the network only the appropriate data. The server doesn't need to know what type of machine it is connected to. This makes the database server a powerful connectivity tool.

Once processing is complete, the results are transmitted back to the microcomputer via the network. The results are returned in standard relational format - two dimensional tables. The workstation can then present the results in any format desired. This process is illustrated in Figure 10.5.

FIGURE 10.5 *Database Server Access in a Distributed Environment*

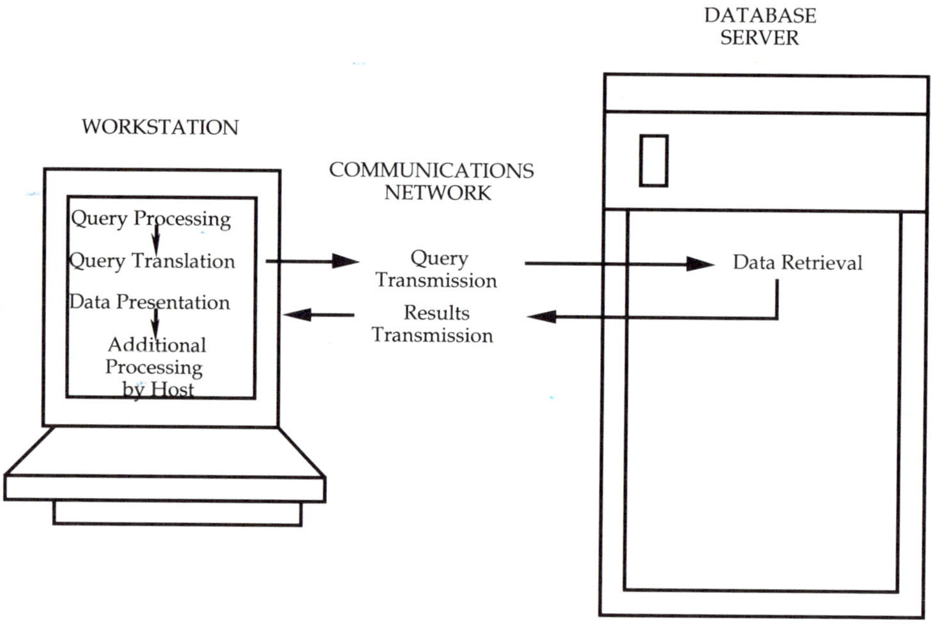


The advantage of a database server architecture compared with a file server architecture is that whereas complete files are transferred in a file server network, only the information that fulfills the request is sent in a database server architecture. This minimizes network traffic and is more suitable for transaction processing by allowing a number of users to share data without hampering system performance.

A database server could be a general purpose computer such as a mainframe, minicomputer or a microcomputer or it could be a specialized computer called a database server. Database machines which have been modified to function as a server are an important approach to high volume transaction processing in a relational environment.[9]

Database machines are a new concept of a specialized combination of hardware and software which is dedicated to relational database processing. The majority of database machines will be based on standard microprocessors working in parallel. Database machines will undoubtedly be the first widescale use of parallel processing. These machines are completely modular and can be sized to fit the task. The database machine provides mainframe power for high-volume transactions processing and large mass-storage capability for applications requiring great amounts of storage.

Database servers, powerful microprocessor based workstations, and local area networks provide a less expensive alternative to large mainframe and terminal architectures. While the mainframe might be used as a network and database server, its price/performance ratio doesn't currently compare with the microprocessor based alternatives.

A microprocessor based workstation can serve the function of a database server. This alternative might be the low cost alternative for small to medium sized organizations in preference to a mainframe or a specialized database server. Furthermore the power of microcomputers is growing rapidly making this alternative feasible for even larger organizations.

Networks of microcomputers have been primarily file server networks for end-user computing. Database server networks are focused on transaction processing applications. Those networks show great synergy between microcomputers, LANs, and relational database management systems. The similarities and differences of distributed processing alternatives are shown in Table 10.1.

TABLE 10.1 *Distributed Processing Alternatvies*

| | TRADITIONAL | FILE SERVER | DATABASE SERVER |
|---|---|---|---|
| HARDWARE COMPONENTS | Mainframe<br>Terminals | File Server<br>Workstations<br>LAN<br>Peripherals | Database Server<br>Workstations<br>LAN<br>Peripherals |
| APPLICATION | General Purpose | Decision support and office automation | Transaction processing |
| ADVANTAGES | Versatility | Shared software and peripherals | Low cost transaction processing |

Centralized computing was fostered by economies of scale in mainframes. Now that the economics favor microcomputers, an era of widescale distributed processing is predicted.

## Distributed Data Base

THE BASIC IDEA BEHIND A DISTRIBUTED DATABASE IS TO HAVE a single logical database implemented on several computers. This allows data access without being aware of its location. Where data is stored is transparent to the user.

A key advantage of distributed database technology is that it allows access to data that is located on a number of physically separate servers. The result is a global view of the data. For example, a regional office could update and view its own local records whereas the corporate office could access data from all of the regions to monitor their performance.[10]

There are four alternatives in database placement. The first method utilizes a centralized database which stores a single copy of the database at a centralized site; users at other sites retrieve data from the centralized database. This alternative, while it is the most common solution to placement of a database, does not represent a distributed solution.

The second method called a partioned database allows each database site to have a unique subset of the organization's database. Partioning may involve rows (horizontal) or columns (vertical) of a database table. This solution is appropriate when storage space is limited at some sites and access to a local database can significantly improve response time and reduce communications costs.

An example of a horizontal partioned database would be a banking system with branches in different cities. Each branch has its own computer and maintains a database for all the accounts at that branch. This concept is illustrated in Figure 10.6. A distributed data dictionary maintains data definitions about all the branches. Transactions in such a system can be local or global. A local transaction is one that accesses accounts only at the site where the transaction was initiated. A global transaction would allow a customer of one site to access an account at another site.[11]

This configuration is described as a distributed database because: (1) each site can execute both local and global transactions and (2) the sites are aware of each other's existence. This capability requires a communication link between sites. Without this linkage, global transactions would require access to a central database, and, in effect, negate distribution.

FIGURE 10.6 *An Example of Horizontal Partitioning in a Distributed Database*

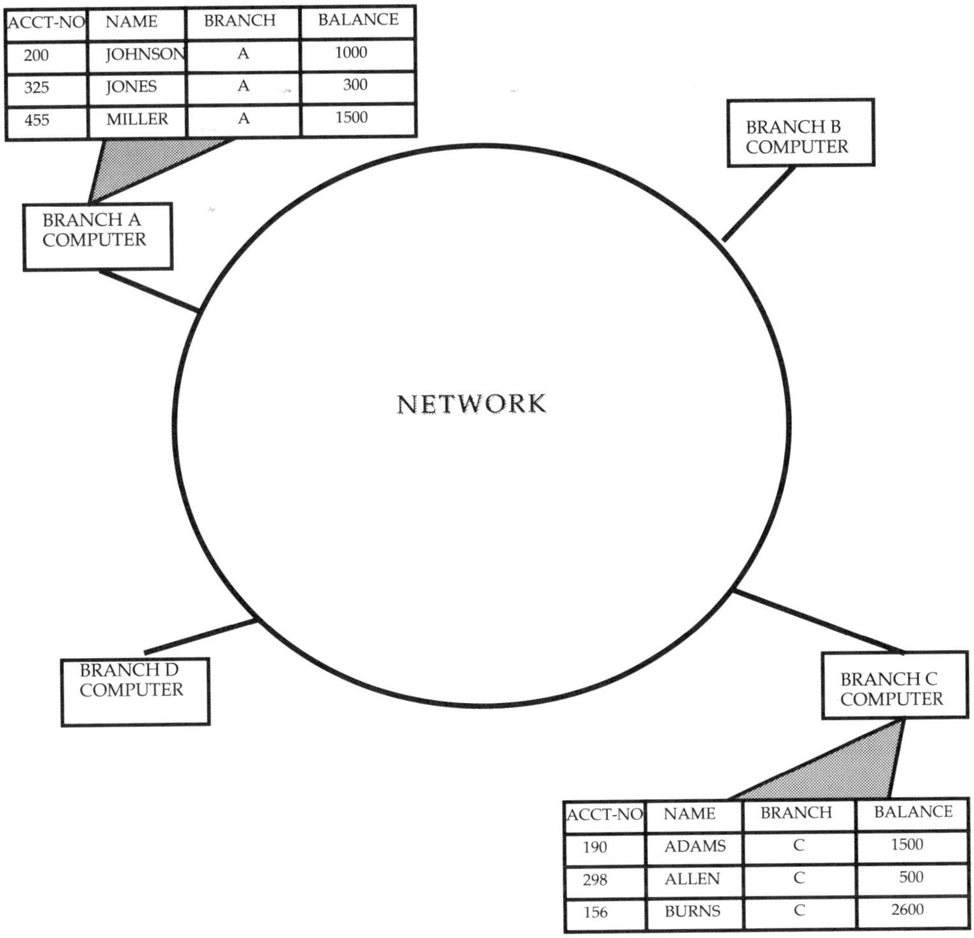


| ACCT-NO | NAME | BRANCH | BALANCE |
|---|---|---|---|
| 200 | JOHNSON | A | 1000 |
| 325 | JONES | A | 300 |
| 455 | MILLER | A | 1500 |

| ACCT-NO | NAME | BRANCH | BALANCE |
|---|---|---|---|
| 190 | ADAMS | C | 1500 |
| 298 | ALLEN | C | 500 |
| 156 | BURNS | C | 2600 |

A vertical partioning of a database means some columns of a table are stores at one site and other columns are stores at another. An illustration of how this concept might be used in a manufacturing company is shown in Figure 10.7.

Figure 10.7 shows the table for an entity PART. Some of the data in this table is used by engineering and other data by manufacturing. The data is distributed to their respective departmental computers.

The original relation or base table can be obtained by a join of the two partioned tables. The distributed DBMS handles the data at different locations as if it were one table. Location becomes transparent to the user.

It should be noted that horizontal partioning supports decentralized organizations where as vertical partioning supports a functional division of labor. The disadvantages of partioning whether horizontal or vertical are: (1) Inconsistent access time - when data from several locations is required access time can be significantly different from local access, (2) Backup vulnerability - if data is damaged at one site then the system cannot switch to another site for the desired data since there is not replication. Data may be lost if proper backup procedures are not followed at each site.[12]

FIGURE 10.7 *An Example of Vertical Partitioning in a Distributed Database*

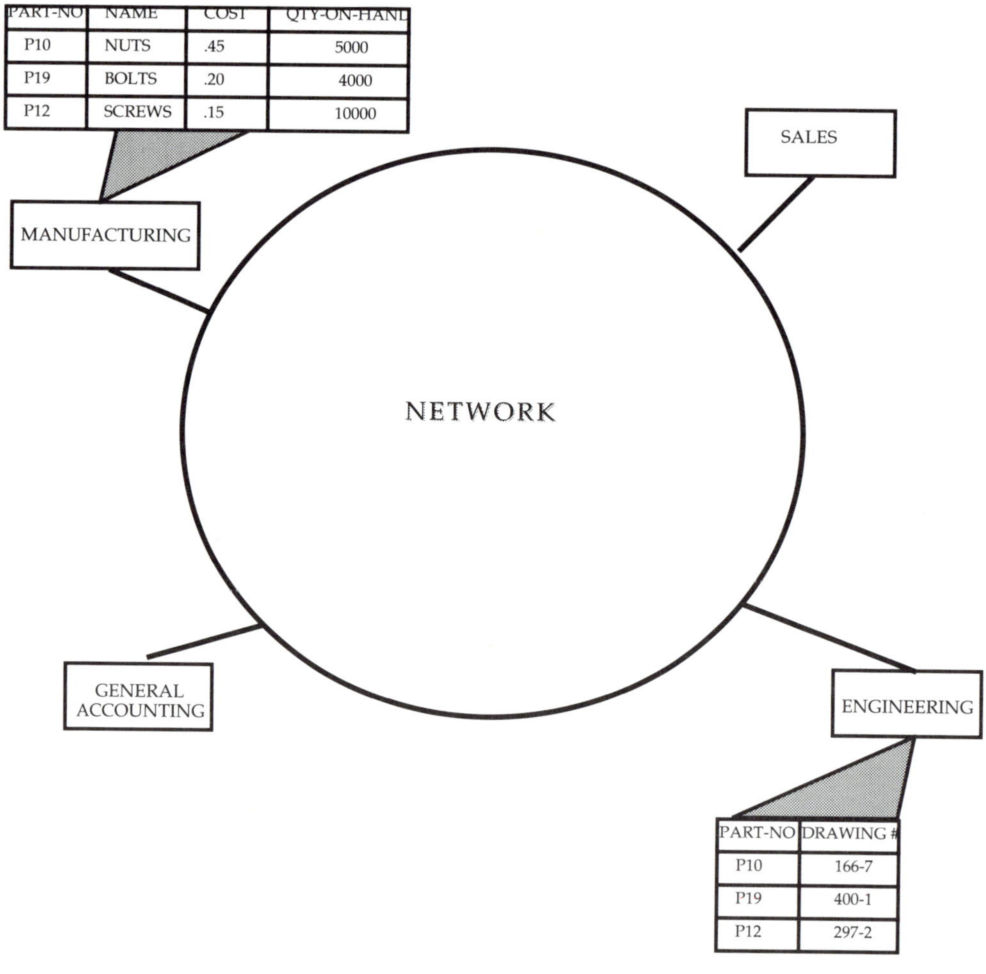

A third alternative, the replicated database, allows each site to store a complete copy of the database. It, however, requires a synchronized approach to updating the database stored at different sites. This approach is not appropriate for high volume transactions environments because it requires changes in the database to be broadcast to other sites. However, this approach has a high degree of reliability, since reasonably current data can be accessed from any site. This concept is illustrated in Figure 10.8.

FIGURE 10.8 *An Example of Replicated Approach to Distrbuted Databases*

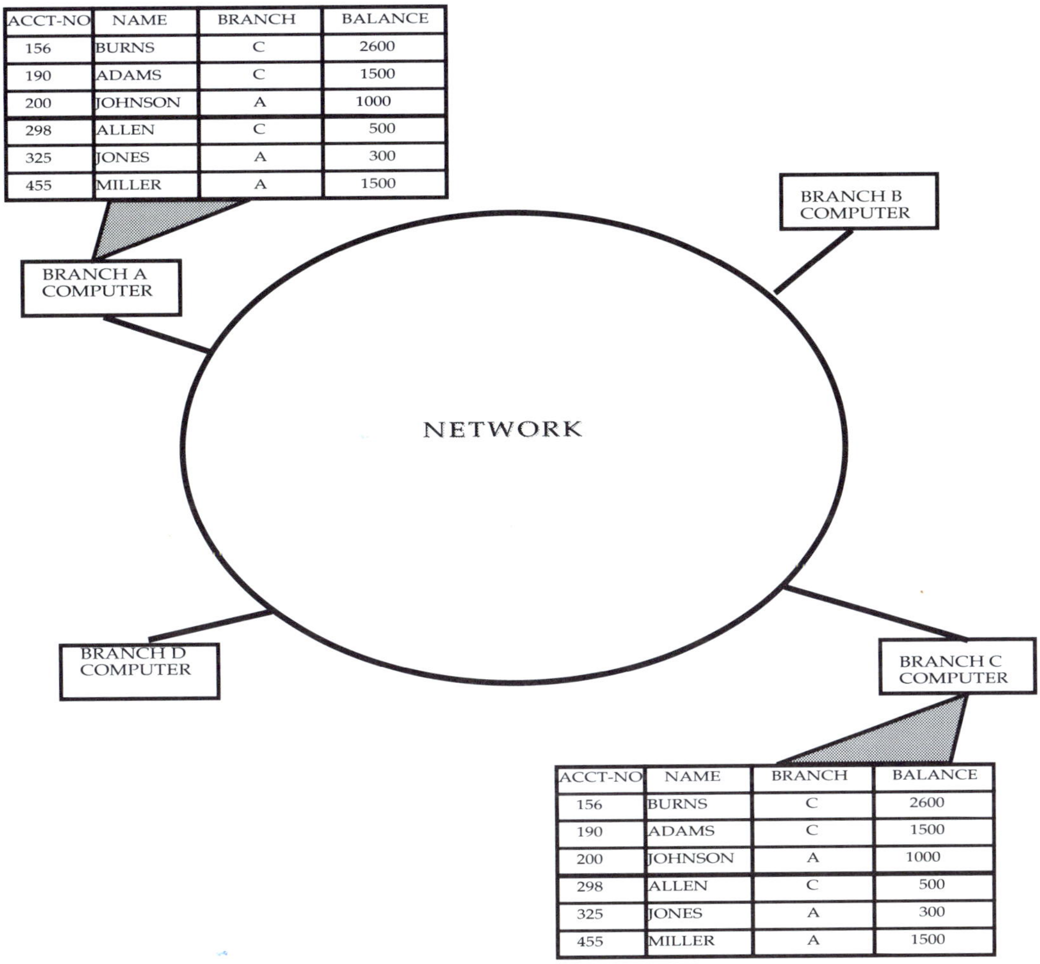


| ACCT-NO | NAME | BRANCH | BALANCE |
|---|---|---|---|
| 156 | BURNS | C | 2600 |
| 190 | ADAMS | C | 1500 |
| 200 | JOHNSON | A | 1000 |
| 298 | ALLEN | C | 500 |
| 325 | JONES | A | 300 |
| 455 | MILLER | A | 1500 |

| ACCT-NO | NAME | BRANCH | BALANCE |
|---|---|---|---|
| 156 | BURNS | C | 2600 |
| 190 | ADAMS | C | 1500 |
| 200 | JOHNSON | A | 1000 |
| 298 | ALLEN | C | 500 |
| 325 | JONES | A | 300 |
| 455 | MILLER | A | 1500 |

The disadvantage of a replicated database is the increased processing overhead on update. It requires that all copies of the database are consistent, otherwise updating errors may occur. Therefore, when an update at one site occurs, the change must be broadcast to all sites containing replicas, which results in increased overhead. This solution also requires a complex concurrency-control mechanism. Concurrency control avoids the problem of two simultaneous transactions changing an account and thus creating inconsistent replicas.

The fourth distributed database alternative is referred to as a clustered system. This approach combines the partioned and replicated alternatives. A clustered system has a unique subset of part of the database as well as redundant copies of some files or subsets of files.

An example of a clustered system would be a regional sales office, which maintains records for customer in that region, and also has a copy of the credit file from the home office. The credit file, which is maintained at the home office is accessible by the regional sales office. Typically, the replicated portion of the database would be updated by the central database system; the partioned part would be maintained locally .

## OBJECTIVES OF DISTRIBUTED DATABASE

The objective of a distributed database is to give each site the responsibility for the data stored at that site. Ideally, this would allow some local autonomy. Local autonomy fosters a sense of ownership of the data at the local site which increases the concern for maintaining data quality and integrity.

Distributed databases reduce data communications traffic by storing the data of the site where it is most frequently used. This approach also makes it convenient to consolidate the data across different sites.

Ideally, a distributed system would be transparent to the user. The concept of data independence means that data could be accessed without knowing the details of location and representation.

## LIMITATION OF DISTRIBUTED DATABASE

Distributed database is not a mature technology. Current solutions are usually confined to one vendor's DBMS running on a given computer system.[13] The adoption of SQL as a standard will allow a mix of heterogeneous products to function in a distributed network environment.

While several vendors have released distributed database management systems, these products allow multisite querying but not multisite updates. Multisite updates is an extremely complex task and may not be available for some time. Current heterogeneous distributed DBMS products support a distributed read (query) capability but not a distributed write (update) capability.

Braude cautions that:

> Distributed DBMS is totally uncharted waters and nobody really understands the implications for database integrity, file recovery and restart recovery....Just in terms of the file and data integration mechanisms that must be put in place, the problem is awesome.[14]

Software development in a distributed database environment is more complex and thus more costly. There is more potential for bugs in the system and increased processing overhead to achieve intersite coordination compared with centralized systems.

Despite these limitations distributed database is an emerging technology which is coming because it serves real needs. While current solutions are partial implementations of a true distributed database they offer desirable features that many organizations can exploit.

## Guidelines for Managers

DISTRIBUTED PROCESSING WITH MICROPROCESSORS, LANs, and relational database servers represents a strategic opportunity to achieve mainframe performance with a flexible, low-cost alternative. Distributed database on the other hand is still an emerging technology.

## Guidelines for MIS Professionals

THE POWER AND FUNCTIONALITY OF MICROPROCESSORS CAN no longer be ignored by MIS professionals. The synergism of microprocessor-based work stations, LANs, and relational database servers provides low cost processing with the simplicity of a relational database.

## Key Terms

Peer-Coupled Network
Two-Tiered Network
Three-Tiered Network
Connectivity
Asynchronous Transmission
Synchronous Mode
ASCII
Extended Binary Coded Decimal Interchange Code (EBCDIC)
Protocol Conversion
Local Autonomy
Terminal Emulation
File Transfer
Data Extraction
Software Upload
Database Machines
Microprocessor-based Workstations
Centralized Database
Partitioned Database
Replicated Database
Clustered System
Concurrency Control

## Review Questions

1. Does distributed processing lead to simpler systems design? Explain
2. What are some of the difference between mainframe, mini and micro-computers which have lead to connectivity problems?
3. Why are file transfer systems a less than satisfactory solution to the micro to mainframe connection problem?
4. Discuss the various security features of an integrated data dictionary.
5. What are the advantages and disadvantages of relational database technology as it relates to distributed networks?
6. Why is a replicated database inappropriate for a high-volume transaction environment?
7. How does the concept of data independence fit with distributed processing?
8. Explain how distributed databases help to achieve both centralized and decentralized data processing.
9. What are the disadvantages of replicated data in a distributed database?

10. Describe a situation in which a vertical partitioning of the manufacturing company's database would be a benefit.

**Case Study**

## GENERAL HOSPITAL

Before 1981, the federal medicare program paid 100 percent of the total cost of treatment. When national health care costs climbed to 10 percent of the U.S. gross national product in 1981, however, an alarmed Congress took action to control these costs. Among other reforms, they instituted a standard cost reimbursement program for medicare, to be phased in over the next few years. This system was based on the concept of diagnostic related groups (DRGs).

Illnesses and treatments were classified into 467 DRGs, each of which has associated with it a standard cost. (Provisions were made for adjusting these costs for inflation and other factors.) When a medicare patient was admitted to a hospital, he or she would be classified into a DRG. The amount medicare would reimburse the hospital was fixed by the DRG standard cost, regardless of the actual costs incurred. If the hospital bill was greater than the DRG standard, the hospital had to absorb the difference; if the hospital actually spent less than standard, they kept the difference as profit.

After several years of operating in this new environment, General Hospital was faced with seriously declining profits. At a healthcare industry trade show, Nancy Wilson, General Hospital's chief administrator, met Bob Fry. Bob was at the trade show representing Utilization Management Services, Inc. (UMS) located in Omaha, Nebraska. He and several other entreprenuers had seen the need for management information systems for the healthcare industry. The company developed and is currently marketing a utilization review system.

Utilization review is the process of analyzing the cost of providing patient care. Specifically, hospitals are interested in comparing costs actually incurred against what is considered standard cost for a particular illness or treatment. UMS's system helps hospital administrators obtain timely answers to the following questions:

- In what areas (DRGs) are our costs significantly above or below the standards?
- What is our cost performance by departments?

- What is our cost performance by insurer?
- Are cost overruns or underruns related to the physician who provides the primary care?
- Are there any identifiable trends over time?

UMS will license the software/hardware system or hospitals can access the system in a timesharing mode. The hardware system consists of a local area network of microprocessor-based workstations and file servers. The software is based on relational database technology which allows the user to manipulate data within a table or tables without programming knowledge. The entire database is resident on a file server. Users retrieve data from the file server.

Several weeks after the trade show, Bob Fry submitted a proposal to Nancy Wilson. Nancy immediately forwarded a copy to Jerry Smith, Director of General Hospital's DP department, for his review. On the day of the board meeting, Jerry called Nancy to tell her he would not support the acquisition of UMS's Utilization Review System.

1. Why would General Hospital's DP staff oppose the installation of UMS's Utilization Review System?
2. One of the most critical factors affecting performance in the distributed processing system is placement of the data. Which of the four methods of database placement: centralized, partitioned, replicated or clustered does the UMS system utilize? Why are the advantages and disadvantages of this placement methodology?
3. Why do so many users, such as Nancy Wilson, turn to outside computer services, to acquire timesharing or special software packages?

# 11

# Telecommunications and Networking

*"Implicit in the mandate for an overall network architecture (and a central architect responsible for same) which derives from a strategic plan that incorporates business priorities, available and emerging technologies, and operational conditions."*

*James Herman et. al.*

## Overview and Objectives

RECENT TECHNICAL ADVANCES IN TELECOMMUNICATIONS have given organizations a number of alternatives for transmitting data. These new technologies have also created new business opportunities and lower cost alternatives for existing business activities. The unprecedented event of deregulation of the telephone industry also has many implications for organizations using telecommunication systems.

In this chapter, we will examine the fundamentals of data communication: The distinction between voice grade and broad band channels; the impact of the switch from analog to digital transmission of telephone messages.

Telecommunication alternatives include satellites, microwave systems, and fiber optic network. We will analyze the advantages and disadvantages of these alternatives.

Network alternatives have also emerged due to new technology. We will compare local-area network choices and their characteristics. We will examine wide-area networks and determine the advantages of private and public networks.

AFTER READING THIS CHAPTER YOU SHOULD BE ABLE TO:

- Explain the data transmission alternatives.
- Indicate the impact of deregulation of the telephone industry on data communications.
- Describe the local area network alternatives and some of the advantages and disadvantages of each.
- Define the need for network management as opposed to waiting for the telephone companies' services.

## Introduction

ONE MIGHT ASK THE QUESTION, WHY IS DATA COMMUNICATION necessary or desirable for an organization? In reply, several examples might be cited of organizations using applications that were not feasible prior to the availability of widespread data communications. Airline reservation systems were the first application utilizing data communications. Some recent examples are:

1. Nationwide newspapers - *The Wall Street Journal, USA Today,* and the *New York TImes* are available nationwide the day they are printed. This is possible because of printing facilities located throughout the country linked by data communications to their

editorial offices. The editorial offices of *The Wall Street Journal* are located in New York. Full page images of the newspaper are converted to digital signals and transmitted to a satellite 22,300 miles above the equator. The satellite transmits a signal to a dozen printing plants, which is then converted by laser beam technology to press plates. The paper is printed during the night and distributed to local markets.

2. Nationwide retail banking - Several networks of Automatic Teller Machines (ATMs) provide banking services on a regional, and in the case of Citibank, a national basis. While there are currently some legal constraints on interstate banking, the banks have plans for expansion of their services to include deposits and debit cards as regulatory constraints are relaxed.

The examples above are strategic uses of communication networks. They represent new opportunities to expand or existing business develop new businesses based on the new capabilities of this technology. There are several other less glamorous examples of how this technology is currently being used by business organizations:

- Order entry systems permit customers at remote locations to place orders. This capability to serve customers in remote locations is also the idea behind airline reservation systems and ATMs.
- Distributed processing, which permits firms with remote manufacturing and sales facilities to monitor the performance of these operations and keep up-to-date records.
- Networks which allow personal computers to gain access to mainframe databases for purpose of analysis.
- Local area networks for electronic mail and other office automation functions.
- Data communication links which permit people to work at home and transmit their work via telecommunication links to the office.
- Software development on small economical computers which is uploaded to large mainframes via networking.
- Developing networks of small economical computers into a coherent system. This allows a firm to place computers closer to the end user without losing coordination and control.
- Sharing expensive software and peripheral devices for users of personal computers.

## Telecommunication Fundamentals

IN THIS SECTION WE WILL EXAMINE SOME OF THE FUNDAMENTALS of data communications.

### Classifying Telecommunication Services

Telecommunication channels are the means of transmitting data between one location and another. The usual types of telecommunication channels are telegraph lines, telephone lines, microwave systems and satellites. Some limited use has been made of waveguide communication links. Optical fiber cables have proven to be a high speed, high capacity alternative to copperwire networks.

- Voice grade channels are ordinary telephone lines. They can transmit data at rates of 300-9600 Baud. For our purposes, we assume that a baud is a bit per second. Dial-up data communication services will support up to 300-2400 Baud. Dedicated lines or leased lines are often required for transmission rates of 4800-9600 Baud. Leased lines do not require dialing because they physically connect equipment at each end of the communication line.
- Broad-band channels have data communication transmission speeds in excess of 9600 Baud. These speeds can be achieved on a variety of communication links, including digital communication channels, microwave systems, satellite and optical-fiber networks. The advantage of broad band channels is that they transmit information much faster than voice grade channels. They are also much more suitable for transmitting images, which have much higher information content. This is shown in Table 11.1.

TABLE 11.1 *Information Density*

| MESSAGE TYPE | BITS |
|---|---|
| A color television frame | 1 million |
| A document page in facsimile form | 200,000 |
| A newspaper-quality photograph | 100,000 |
| A document in computer code | 10,000 |
| A typical airline reservation | 200 |
| A fire or burglar alarm signal | 40 |

### ANALOG TO DIGITAL

Any information can be sent over a telecommunication channel in two different forms: analog and digital. Analog refers to a wave form that resembles an electrocardiagram. A digital signal is a stream of on/off pulses. Both types are illustrated in Figure 11.1.

FIGURE 11.1 *Analog vs. Digital Transmission*

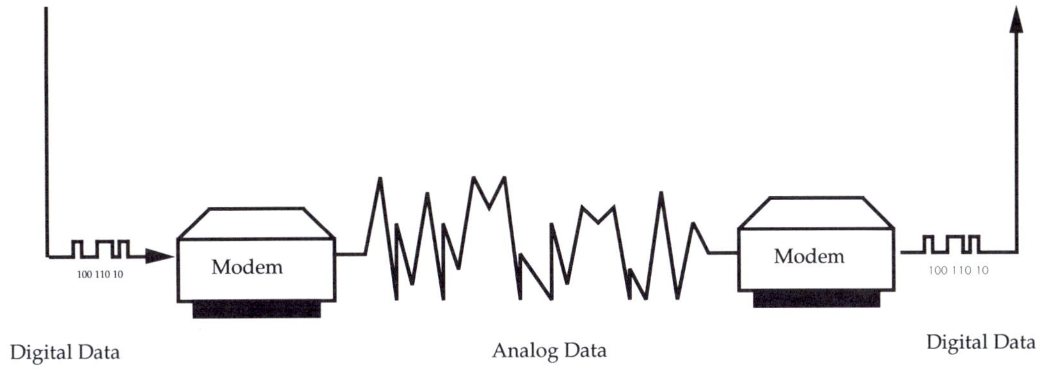


Digital transmission has several advantages over analog:

1. Significantly higher transmission speed
2. Lower error rates
3. More economical
4. Ability to transmit voice, data, and images.

Telephone companies in the United States are switching from analog to digital technology in the transmission and switching of telephone messages. Digital transmission permits two-way transmission of data at a rate of 56,000 Baud. Currently, analog transmission is limited to 9600 Baud. This should have a dramatic effect on land based data communication costs.

The migration of telephone companies from analog transmission to digital will eventually enable all types of information—voice, data, and image—to be transmitted on a single public network. Currently, data and image transmission are often accomplished using private networks or public packet switching networks

## Environmental Changes in Telecommunications

### DEREGULATION OF TELECOMMUNICATIONS

After 75 years, the telephone industry was changed from a regulated monopoly to a competitive industry. The Bell System was broken into two groupings: 1) the 22 local Bell operating companies; and 2) AT&T. The 22 Bell operating companies provide local telephone service, sometimes referred to as dial tone. AT&T consists of long distance service; Western Electric, the manufacturing arm of the old Bell System; and Bell Laboratories, the respected research organization of AT&T.

The 22 Bell operating companies have been organized as eight regional holding companies. These firms are free to purchase equipment and long distance service from any source, not excluding AT&T. They are forbidden by the divestiture agreement from manufacturing equipment. One of the effects of breaking up the Bell System will be a growing and competitive market for telephone equipment. Deregulation and advancing technology are expected to increase the number of phones in use and the number of purchased outright. New features are being added to make telephones the hottest consumer electronic product since video games and the personal computer. The battle for the telephone equipment market will continue at the consumer level as well as the business systems level.

The market for long-distance communication services, including voice, video, data, and facsimile, is experiencing the effects of deregulation and divestiture. Several more years of turbulence in the market place is expected before stability returns. Individuals and organizations will continue to have a broader array of data communication choices, many of which were unheard of a few years earlier.

## TECHNICAL INNOVATION

Technical innovation was the driving force behind deregulation. As other forms of telecommunications became economically feasible, existing telecommunication carriers using earlier technology became vulnerable. Small innovative firms were able to leapfrog the previous generations of telecommunications technology and telephone rates which subsidized rural subscribers to undercut AT&T in volume markets. The courts either had to declare that AT&T was a government sanctioned monopoly or opt for competition and innovation in telecommunications.

The major innovations in telecommunications have been satellites, microwave systems, and fiber-optic transmission media. These are examined in the next section.

## MICROWAVE SYSTEMS

Microwave systems transmit a high-frequency radio wave. They provide much faster transmission rate than is possible with telephone lines. Microwave systems transmit data on a line-of-sight beam between towers spaced 20 to 25 miles apart. For long-distance transmission, the signal is amplified and retransmitted to the next station. A microwave system is illustrated in Figure 11.2.

FIGURE 11.2 *Microwave System*

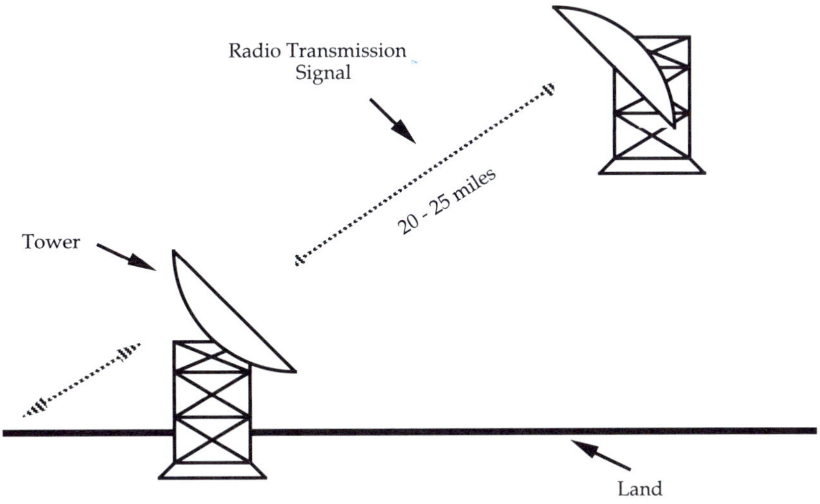


Microwave systems are widely used by common carriers for long distance telephone service and by private users for local or regional communications. Microwave systems are a cost-effective solution for many organizations; their main disadvantage is distortion, induced by weather conditions, and foreign-objects interference with the path of the microwave transmission.

## COMMUNICATIONS SATELLITES

Communications satellites are a special case of a microwave- relay transmitter. They are positioned in a geosynchronous orbit 22,300 miles above the earth, which keeps the satellite over the same part of the earth at all times. Satellites serve as relay stations for signals transmitted from earth.

The principle advantage of satellites is long-distance communications service where low cost and reliability are required. They have several other advantages, including the following:

1. Broadcast capability. A satellite transmission can be received at multiple locations. Applications such as teleconferencing and electronic mail can use this capability.
2. Distance Insensitivity. The costs of satellite communications are not dependent upon the distance between the transmitting and receiving stations.
3. Networking. In contrast to other alternatives, a satellite provides an immediate network for any site with a transmission and receiving station. A satellite integrates voice, data, and image communications among all earth stations. All stations have a simultaneous link to other stations. A satellite transmission system is illustrated in Figure 11.3.

FIGURE 11.3
*Satellite Transmission*

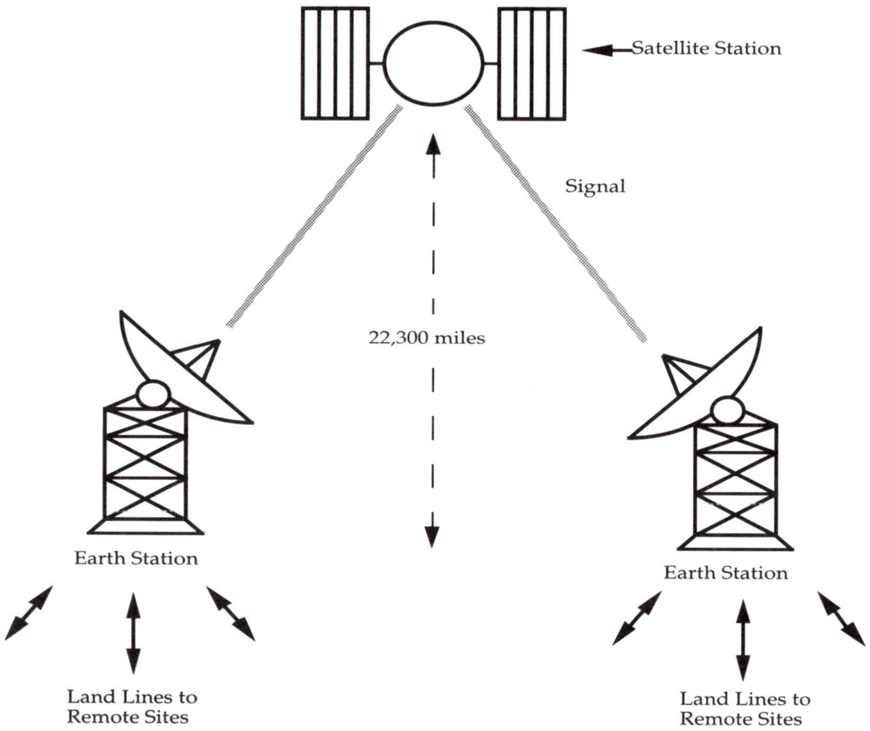

There are, however, some disadvantages of satellites. Among these are:

1. Propogation delay. Although the microwave signal travels between the sending and receiving station at the speed of light, the distances are so great that there is a slight delay in the signal. This delay introduces an undesirable element into interactive communications. This may cause problems with timing and data throughput if special compensating devices are not used.
2. Cost of earth stations. The cost of satellite transmission stations has declined dramatically. The first earth station cost $50 million to build, but the cost has now declined to less than $100,000.

Satellite transmission is ideally suited to the transmission of large batches of data in one direction at a time. For example, large retail chains with many dispersed locations transmitting data between those retail locations and a central site can use satellite transmission effectively.

The space shuttle now makes it possible to place much larger and more powerful satellites into space. The effect of this development has been two-fold: (1) the cost of facilities to receive and transmit satellite signals has been reduced; and (2) the capacity of the satellite itself has been increased, thus lowering the costs for users.

## Fiber-Optic Transmission Systems

Fiber-optic technology is based upon the ability of glass fibers to conduct light over long distances with little loss of signal. An incoming electrical signal is converted to light pulses by a laser or light emitting diode (LED) and transmitted over a fiber-optic cable. At the other end of the cable, a photodetector converts the light signal back to an electrical signal.

A single glass fiber, approximately half the diameter of a human hair, can transmit data about a thousand times faster than a microwave. Fiber-optic cables provide substantial savings in weight and size as well as a dramatic increase in carrying capacity compared with copper wire cables. A half-inch-thick fiber-optic cable can carry 50,000 channels, compared to about 5,500 channels on a standard coaxial cable.

There are several other inherent advantages in fiber optics including the following:

1. No electrical current. This is particularly advantageous where the potential of a spark would constitute a hazard. Examples include flammable or explosive environments such as grain elevators, petro-chemical plants and petroleum refineries.
2. No interference. Electrical signals transmitted over a copper wire are subject to electro-magnetic interference and radio-frequency interference. Interference can cause erroneous data transmission or serious systems malfunctions.
3. Secure communications. Transmission of a signal on a copper wire generates an electro-magnetic or radio frequency signal. This signal makes it possible to intercept or *bug* this communications medium. Stealing information from a fiber-optic cable would require a physical tap which would produce a noticeable signal loss, ensuring detection.

However, there are some disadvantages of fiber-optic cables. First, they require a point-to-point connection. Second, it is difficult to tap a fiber-optic cable at an intermediate point. The difficulty of making taps has limited its potential for office automation applications.

## Local-Area Networks

LOCAL AREA NETWORKS MAKE IT POSSIBLE FOR MULTIPLE USERS to share access to a computer resource without the necessity of either a direct cable connection between each device or a dial-up telephone link. The advantages and disadvantages of each alternative are summarized in Table 11.2.

TABLE 11.2

*Advantages and Disadvantages of Data Communications Alternatives*

| | ADVANTAGES | DISADVANTAGES |
|---|---|---|
| DIRECT CABLE CONNECTION | 1. High-speed communication link<br>2. User will not encounter busy signal | 1. Limited distance<br>2. High cabling costs<br>3. No sharing of scarce resource |
| TELEPHONE LINK | 1. No distance limitations<br>2. Several users may share scarce resource<br>3. Relatively inexpensive | 1. User may encounter a busy signal<br>2. Relatively slow transmission rate<br>3. Inconvenience of dial-up access<br>4. High cost of modems |

| | ADVANTAGES | DISADVANTAGES |
|---|---|---|
| LOCAL-AREA NETWORK | 1. High-speed communication link<br>2. Highly flexible in handling different types of devices<br>3. User will not encounter busy signal<br>4. Accomm odates growth | 1. Some distance limitations<br>2. Technology not widely understood |

A local-area network (LAN) is designed to link computers to each other and to peripheral devices so that they can exchange information. These low-cost networks are most commonly used to connect personal computers within a building or several nearby buildings. Typical peripheral devices are file servers and laser printers. Typical local-area networks linked by gateways are shown in Figure 11.4.

FIGURE 11.4 *A Typical Local Area Network (LAN)*

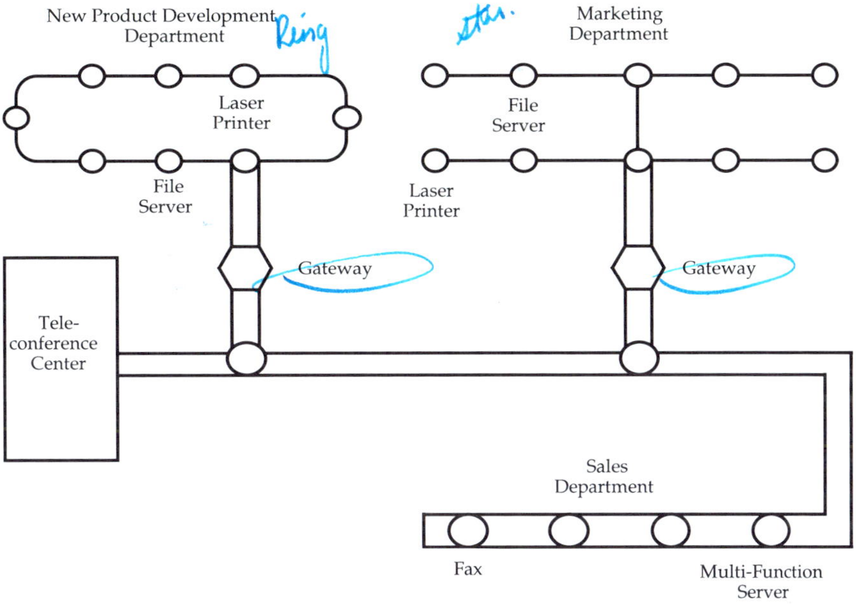


A file server may be a specialized device with 50 megabytes or more of disk storage, or it may be a general purpose computer dedicated to that function. The rationale behind file servers is that they provide greater security and lower software licensing costs. Devices such as tape drives are frequently used to back up data and programs.

A network gateway connects the LAN to the corporate-wide area network or commercial networks. This enables users of the LAN to exchange information with sources outside the network.

A network gateway connects the LAN to the corporate-wide area network or commercial networks. This enables users of the LAN to exchange information with sources outside the network.

Laser printers are high-quality printers that can print graphics and type in several fonts at a quality level that rivals commercial typesetting. These printers are an integral component of desktop publishing.

Several alternative local-area networks using different approaches are currently available. These alternatives have tradeoffs of performance, cost, flexibility, and reliability. The tradeoffs make the acquisition decision for a local-area network quite complex.

The key characteristics of LAN's are configuration, transmission media, network line control, and transmission method.

## LAN CONFIGURATION ALTERNATIVES

STAR - A star network links each device or node in the network to a central controller. The most common example of a star configuration is a network based on a PBX (private branch exchange) system. The primary advantage of this configuration is that it uses existing telephone lines. The disadvantages of the star configuration are its dependence on the central controller and it requires more cable than other LAN configuration alternatives. A star configuration is shown in Figure 11.5.

FIGURE 11.5
*A Star Network Configuration*

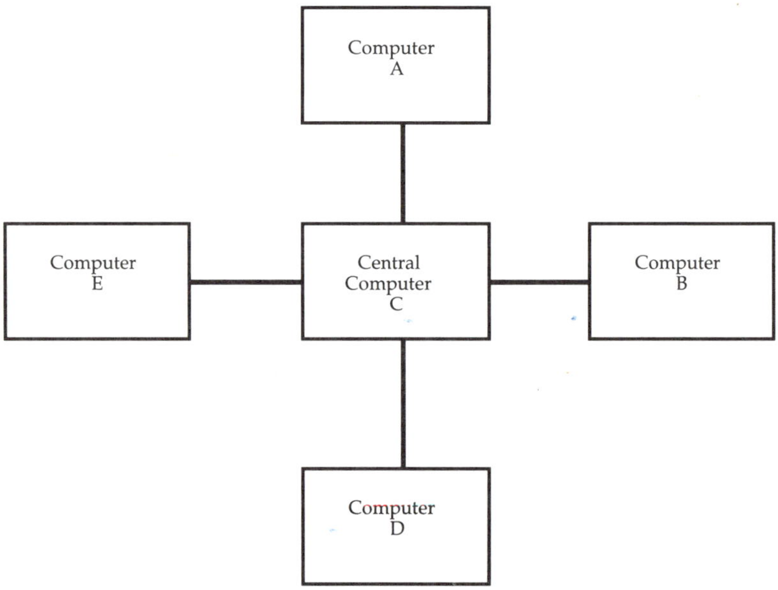

RING - Ring networks are formed by a cable connecting device, in a loop. The device that controls the ring is part of the loop. The advantage of the ring configuration is its relatively low cost. Its disadvantages are reliability and transmission capacity. Ring networks require that all nodes be operational for the network to function. They are not suitable for anything but data and the attachment of new nodes requires configuration of the ring. A ring configuration is shown in Figure 11.6.

FIGURE 11.6
*A Ring Network Configuration*

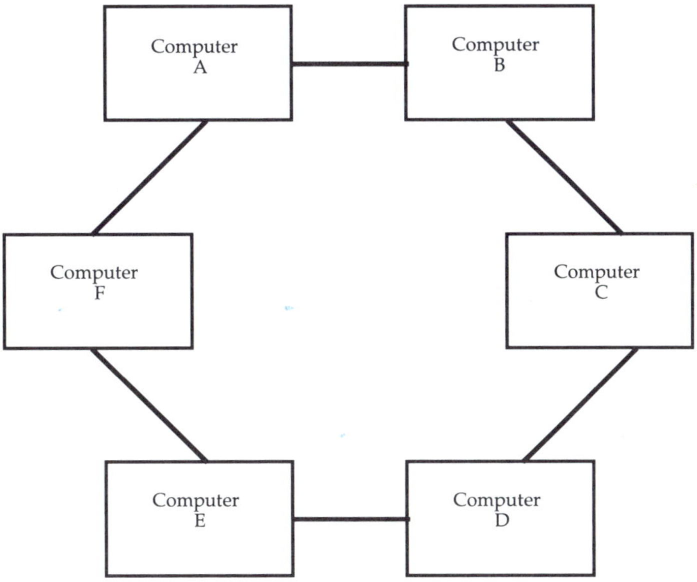


BUS - A bus requires a single length of cable to which various network devices are connected. It has no controller and is usually unaffected by the failure of any node or nodes. Bus configurations do require the use of an intelligent device to manage network communications. The principle advantage of the bus configuration is its reliability. If a broadband-based transmission method is chosen, it is suitable for data, voice, and image transmission. It is also quite flexible in attaching new devices. This configuration is illustrated in Figure 11.7.

FIGURE 11.7
*A Bus Network Configuration*

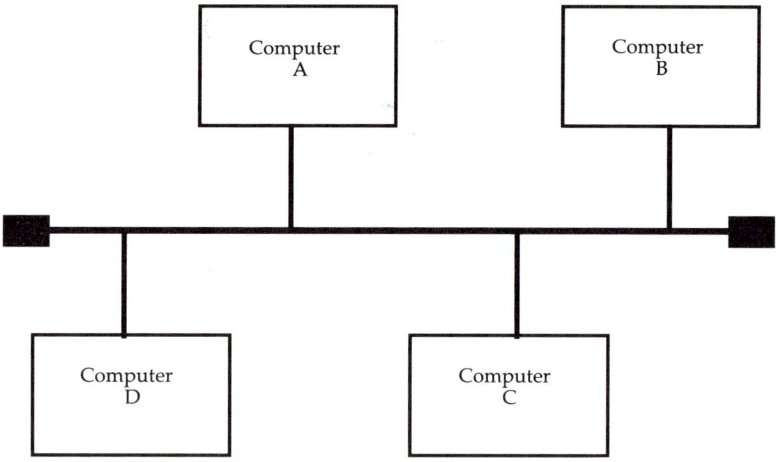


## LAN TRANSMISSION MEDIA

The alternatives for transmitting data, voices and images in a LAN are: 1) twisted pair cable, 2) coaxial cable, and 3) fiber-optic cable. These alternatives differ in cost, transmission capacity, and flexibility.

A twisted-pair cable consists of two pairs of insulated copper wires. The principal advantage of twisted pair is the low cost of installation. In fact, a telephone system using twisted pair cables is present in most offices. This system can potentially provide the transmission medium for a LAN.

The disadvantage of twisted pair is transmission capacity typically 1200-10,000,000 Baud (1.2 mbps to 10 mbps). This is suitable for transmission of data and voice, but not for image transmission. Twisted pair is also more susceptible to electrical interference than other LAN transmission mediums.

Coaxial Cable (COAX) has been widely used for cable television. Depending on the grade of COAX, it will transmit data at the rate of 3 to 400 mbps. The advantages are its transmission rate and freedom from electrical interference. The disadvantage of COAX is the expense of installation.

Fiber-optic cable is made up of glass filaments which transmit light pulses. The advantages of fiber-optic cable are its capacity, up to 50 gigabits per second (gbps), and its freedom from electrical interference. (A gigabit is one billion bits per second.)

These LAN transmission alternatives are shown in Figure 11.8.

FIGURE 11.8
*LAN Transmission Alternatives*

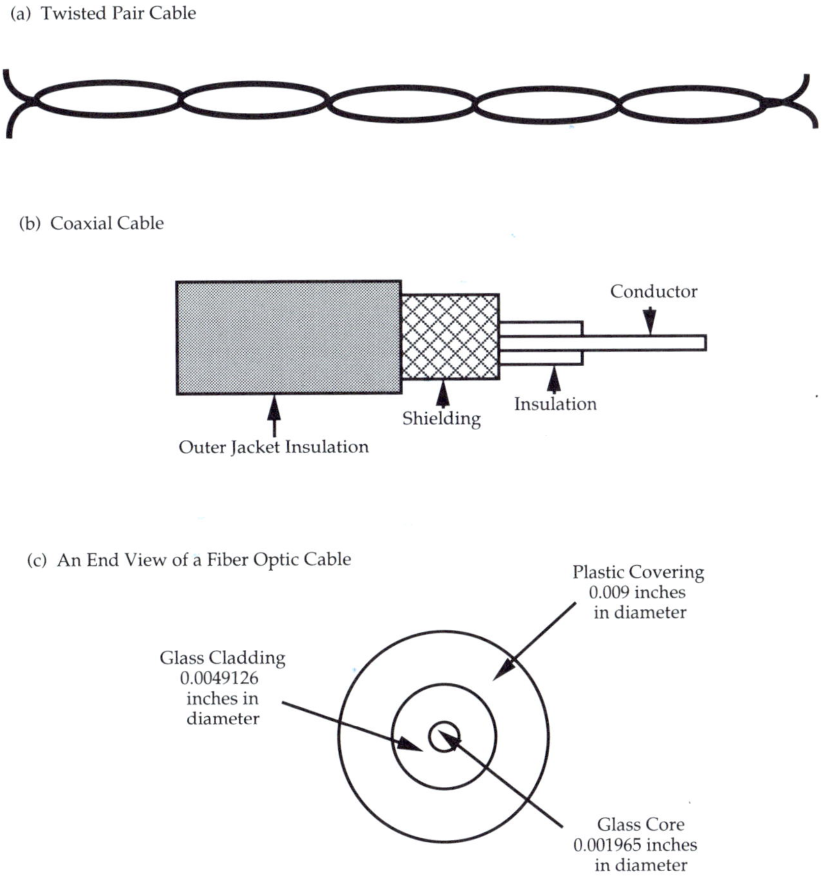


## NETWORK LINE CONTROL

There are three modes of network line control. These are 1) contention (also known as CSMA/CD), 2) token passing, and 3) polling. Network line control involves the use of procedures and signals to control the transmission of messages.

Contention network line control might be thought of as a network where nodes compete for access to the network. In effect, a node "listens" before transmitting a message. If the network is busy, the node waits for a random period and then listens again. If the network is idle, the node transmits the message and listens to detect if a collision occurred with another message. If it detects a collision, it transmits an error message, waits a random interval, and retransmits the message.

Contention line control is popular in bus networks. The advantage of contention line control is reliability. Failure of a node does not make the network inoperative. Contention line control is quite flexible in changing the configuration of the network. The disadvantages of contention line control are centered on the unpredictability of access. Consequently, it is unsuitable for real time voice and image transmission.

Token passing allows a node to transmit a message when it has received a control message which allows it to transmit. If a node has no message, it transmits the control message to the next node. If it has a message, it transmits the message and then passes the token to the next node. The advantage of a token passing network control is that access delay is predictable. The disadvantages of token passing is that it tends to degrade performance with the addition of nodes. Furthermore, the network must be reconfigured for adding or subtracting nodes. Polling requires the use of a central computer which polls each node asking if it has a message to transmit. If yes, a message is transmitted. If no, it moves to the next node. The advantage of polling is that it can often use existing wiring; the disadvantage is its dependence on a central controller.

## TRANSMISSION METHOD

There are two alternatives for network transmission: baseband and broadband. Baseband is the simplest alternative. It has a single communications channel which is shared by the attached devices. Only one message can be transmitted at a time. Baseband can be implemented for twisted pair and coaxial cable. Transmission is generally limited to data; baseband is not a suitable medium for real time voice and image transmission.

Broadband uses a single cable to transmit multiple messages. This is accomplished by transmitting messages over the cable at different frequencies. The receiving device must tune the appropriate channel to receive the message.

Broadband may have three types of channels: dedicated, shared, and switched. A dedicated channel connects two devices and functions exactly as a hardwired cable connection. Shared channels are operated much like baseband systems. They allow only one message at a time to be transmitted on a channel. Baseband networks may be a subset of broadband networks. Switched channels are temporary connections which are dedicated during the period of data transmission. Switched channels are suitable for real time voice and image transmission. An illustration of broadband and baseband transmission is shown in Figure 11.9.

FIGURE 11.9 *Baseband and Broadband Transmission*

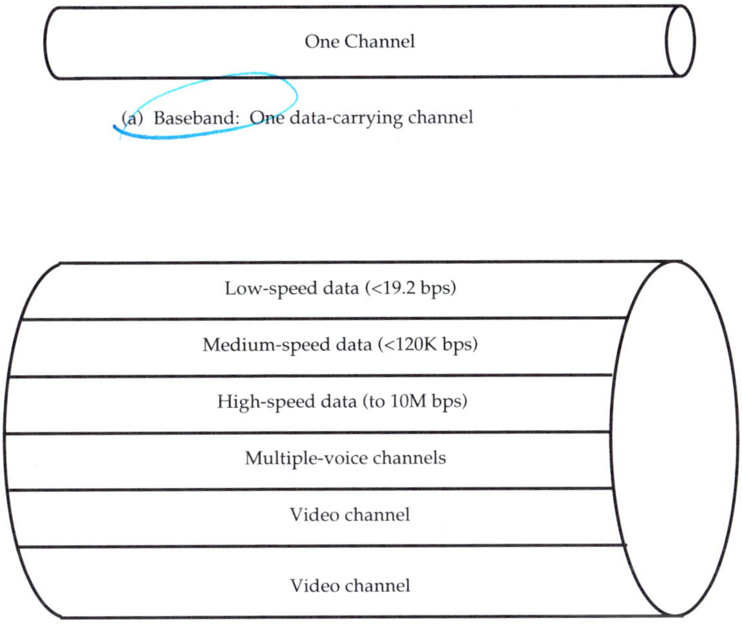


(a) Baseband: One data-carrying channel

(b) Broadband: Multiple data-carrying channels

## PBX AS LOCAL AREA NETWORK

The typical business office utilizes a private-branch telephone exchange (PBX), which provides an internal telephone system and also interfaces with the local telephone company. The PBX allows an individual to dial other offices without using the switching facilities of the telephone company. While the PBX system has so far been limited to telephone services, new PBX systems provide the ability to route and display telephone messages, memos, and other documents on new electronic telephone terminals. Some manufacturers believe that the telephone will be replaced by specialized terminals. The PBX may also provide a mechanism for interconnecting a broad variety of information processing devices in the future. If this is accomplished, the PBX becomes a local-area network alternative and a vehicle for implementing office automation.[2]

## REPRESENTATIVE LAN PRODUCTS

There are several trade-offs in selecting a local area network. These are cost, transmission speed, flexibility, and growth potential.

IBM's token ring, introduced in 1986, uses as the name suggests a ring topology and token passing as the method of network line control. It also uses a twisted pair for a transmission medium and is a baseband network.

A twisted pair is easy to install and inexpensive but limits applications to voice and data transmission; image transmission would require greater transmission capacity. The use of token passing means that network access is predictable. However, as more workstations are added to the network, each has a longer wait to get on to the network. Predictable access is important in applications such as process control, but may be less important in typical business communications.

The IBM token ring should succeed in the lower end of the market. However, it is not suitable for large numbers of workstations spread out over several building complexes.

Ethernet is not actually a product but a standard developed by Digital Equipment Co., Intel and Xerox. As a standard, Ethernet is supported by more than 150 companies. Xerox's XCZZ is a typical Ethernet product: it is a bus topology with CSMA/CD access method, uses coax, and is also a baseband network. A bus topology is more flexible in adding additional workstations than a token ring. It also is more reliable, since it is not subject to failure if a component of the network fails.

The disadvantage of CSMA/CD is unpredictable access, which makes it unsuitable for applications which require specific and consistent access to the network. On the other hand, it is probably better suited than token ring to a mix of file transfer and interactive inquiry traffic.[1]

Dr. Robert Metcalfe, who is generally credited with inventing Ethernet predicted the future of LANs until the year 2000. His views are contained in Issues and Controversies.

## Issues and Controversies

## The Future of Local Area Networks

Ethernet, a local area network (LAN), was invented in a memo written on May 22, 1973 at Xerox's Palo Alto Research Center. The fifteenth anniversary of this event makes it appropriate to venture some LAN predictions out to the year 2000.

In making predictions two things must be remembered: first, the future does not happen by chance but can be shaped by conscious effort. Second, while almost anything can be achieved eventually, timing is critical.

### ETHERNET IS NUMBER ONE

One might take the position that Ethernet is the only LAN needed for the foreseeable future. While it's an extreme position it has a degree of merit and indeed a certain charm. However, the continuing evolution of networking applications and the underlying technologies makes it necessary to have a portfolio of networking technologies.

Ethernet, a 10 megabit per second (mbps), LAN standard was proposed in 1980. By 1981 products compatible with the proposed standard were being shipped. Beginning in 1982, Ethernet was adopted as a standard by the world's major standards organizations.

Ethernet (IEEE 802.3) has become the most widely installed LAN. One company, 3 COM, alone by 1987 had shipped over 500,000 direct Ethernet connections. Why then do we need any other LANs?

### APPLETALK: TIMING IS EVERYTHING

Appletalk is a nonstandard slowed down version of Ethernet that is built into the Apple Macintosh. It is easy to use and inexpensive. Appletalk, which is about 1/40th of the speed of Ethernet, is too slow for all but the smallest of LANs. It is just right, however, for the tens-of-thousands of Macintosh workgroups consisting of three to ten members. Appletalk is second only to Ethernet in number of installations and will remain useful on the very low end through the year 2000. Timing is everything.

### IBM'S TOKEN RING

IBM has been using token-passing technology for several years. It is therefore surprising that the IBM token ring was about five years behind Ethernet. Unfortunately for the computer industry IBM did not adapt the Ethernet standard back in 1980. Instead it chose to develop its own LAN which has no technical advantages over Ethernet. The effect has been to divide industry efforts.

Few propaganda campaigns can match the absurdity of token ring advocates' attempts to convince LAN buyers that Ethernet's 10 mbps is some how slower than token ring's 4 mbps. Furthermore, the advantage of Ethernet's five year lead time has been greatly underestimated by analysts predicting that IBM's token ring will soon overtake

**Ethernet. Still it is not controversial to predict that the IBM token ring will be among those LAN's dominating until the year 2000, if for no other reason than to provide a gateway to the IBM environment.**

**FDDI**

**FDDI (Fiber Distributed Data Interface) is a new LAN technology capable of loads of 100 mbps. It is projected to cost $10,000 per workstation, more than ten times the current cost of Ethernet. Since most LANs do not currently need the capacity of existing Ethernet and token ring networks the near term future of FDDI will most likely be limited to serving as a backbone or bridging LAN among Ethernet and IBM token rings.**

**TOO MANY LAN STANDARDS**

**There are dangers in too many LAN standards. Too many standards reduces the volume of sales for existing standards which increases costs and reduces the interoperability which decreases the volume of these standards. One additional standard, MAP, the General Motors sponsored standard for manufacturing automation, is expected to succeed mainly because it uses OSI protocols.**

Adapted from "Networking Predictions," Robert M. Metcalfe, Connect (Winter 1988), pp. 20-22.

## Wide-Area Networks

WIDE-AREA NETWORKS ARE NETWORKS DESIGNED TO SERVE telecommunications needs over a broad geographic area. In the past, these networks have been designed to serve an environment of individuals communicating with the computer from a terminal. the transmission was characterized by a character-by-character transmission over a long period of time. Future network requirements will require computer-to-computer communications, transmission of images, and complete files. This mix of applications will require a network with a wider bank width.

### PRIVATE NETWORKS

A private network does not mean that a firm builds its own telecommunications system with microwave links and installs its own switching system. While some private networks do have these elements, most private systems are a mix of in-house equipment and facilities, and transmission lines leased from a common carrier.

Frequently, private networks consist of separate networks for voice and data. Many firms, however, have integrated voice, data and facsimile transmission on their private networks, mainly on a time sharing basis.

## PUBLIC TELEPHONE NETWORKS

The most commonly used wide area networks are the common carriers switched telephone networks. Voice grade telephone circuits are frequently time-shared among voice, data and facsimile. Organizations with communications requirements that require greater capacity can use dial up services such as Wide Area Telephone Services (WATS). Here again firms can use the same network for voice, data and facsimile transmission.

## PACKET SWITCHING NETWORKS

Public telephone networks are too slow and too expensive for high volume data transmission. A private network on the other hand is vulnerable to failure. If a line fails it can isolate portions of the network. Critical applications, therefore, require backup facilities.

Packet switching networks are a third alternative. They can be accessed in all major cities and they provide high speed data transmission. The carrier assumes responsibility for day to day management of the network and in the event of failure provides alternative routes.

A packet switching network is illustrated in Figure 11.10. The figure shows three messages which are broken into packets. The packets are transmitted and the messages reassembled when received.

While the data transmission rate is less than private networks they offer a cost effective solution to a user with intermediate volume. The carriers prefer packet switching networks because they allow shared use of the carrier's facilities.

## ISDN

The latest idea in wide-area networks is ISDN or integrated services digital network. This service is a worldwide digital network capable of handling voice, data, text and images. ISDN is a concept which evolved from existing telephone networks, and is designed to provide a public network as easy-to-use as the telephone. As indicated earlier, telephone companies world-wide are in the process of converting their analog transmission to digital. This will enhance their bandwidth and enable telephone networks to handle images as well as voice and data. The advocates of ISDN believe it will encompass or make obsolete all preceding network technologies. While this concept shows promise, its ultimate impact is unknown. In the mean time, it bears watching.

FIGURE 11.10 *Packet Switching Network*

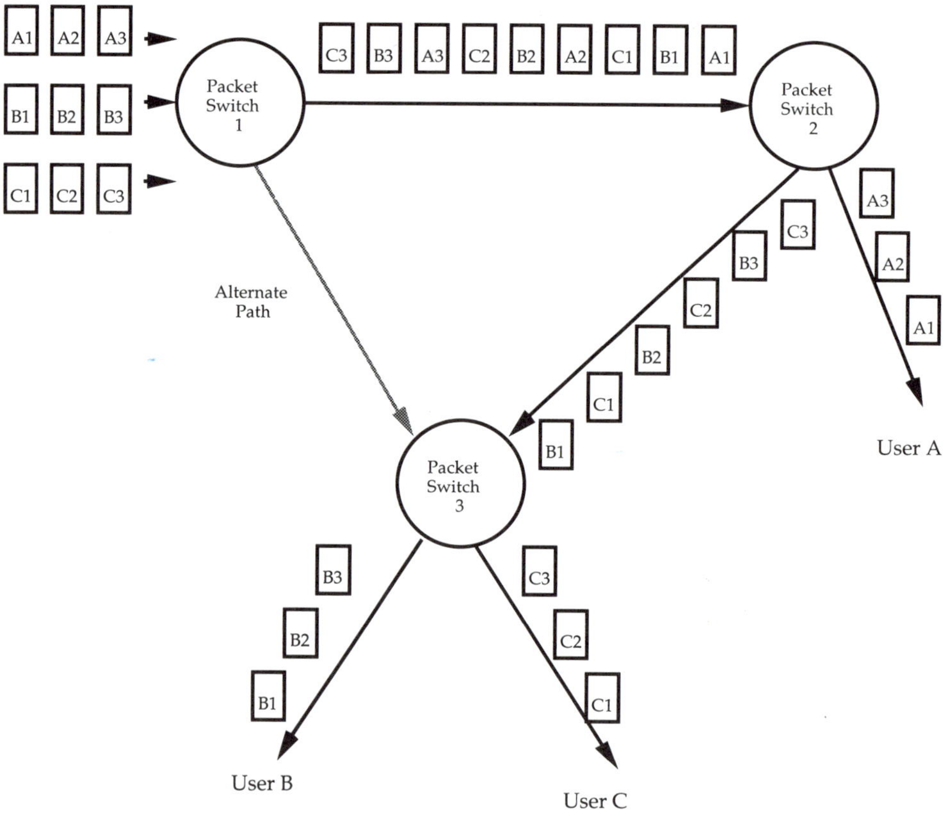


## Network Administration

IN MANY ORGANIZATIONS MULTIPLE INCOMPATIBLE NETWORKS have been put in place to handle different networks. For example a terminal is attached to an order entry network; a specialized word processing terminal to a word processing network; personal computers to a local area network; a managerial workstation to an electronic mail and decision support network and finally, specialized terminals are available in a department to access an external data network.

The difficulty with this redundancy is that many of these terminals deliver duplicate functions and few of them can access other networks. This duplication leads to the frustration of the users of data networks, excessive cost, and redundant information storage.

To introduce some coherence into network planning requires two related developments: (1) a network administrator should be appointed to coordinate network planing and use, and (2) top management should recognize the potential strategic uses of networks by making available to the network administrator the business strategy. As has been pointed out earlier in the chapter, competitive uses of information systems technology are frequently external to the firm. The opportunities to create new products, provide better service and lock in customers can result in far better returns on investment than the usual cost reduction focus of an MIS department.

An analysis of the relationship between a telecommunications and business strategy will inevitably lead to a plan for future telecommunications growth. This plan will point the direction towards the type of information exchanges that will be required, the geographic areas to be covered, and the external entities with whom information will be exchanged.[3]

This plan should address how office automation, decision support systems and transaction processing functions will be supported. It should be conscious of the need to provide communication links with customers, suppliers, and other external entities.

## Guidelines for Managers

NETWORKS ARE IMPORTANT TO STRATEGIC USES OF INFORMATION technology. The strategic uses of communication networks are expected to grow as telecommunications and computer hardware costs continue to decline. New technologies which make transmission and storage of images less costly will create new business opportunities.

Networks are also required to exploit the low cost computing made possible by microprocessor technology. To take advantage of these low-cost computers traditional mainframe and terminal architectures can be replaced by networks of microprocessor-based workstations and database servers.

Use of networks will be possible only if an organization plans for it and acquires the necessary personnel to implement them. Personnel knowledgeable about networks are scarce and retraining existing personnel might be a better strategy than attempting to hire someone outside the organization.

## Guidelines for MIS Professionals

NETWORKS ARE A KEY TECHNOLOGY FOR THE 1990S. INFORmation systems professionals who wish to remain effective must take advantage of new networking capabilities. They should also learn how to link low cost microprocessor-based workstations into networks. Initially, these networks may be devoted to one type of processing but gradually they are expected to evolve toward networks integrating transaction processing, decision support and office automation.

## Key Terms

| | |
|---|---|
| Voice Grade Channel | Broadband Channel |
| Baseband Channel | Dedicated Lines |
| Leased Lines | Analog Signal |
| Digital Signal | Private Telephone Networks |
| Public Telephone Networks | Public Packet Switching Network |
| Microwave | Satellites |
| Propogation Delay | Fiber Optic Cable |
| Local Area Networks (LANs) | File Server |
| Network Gateway | Laser Printer |
| Star Network | Ring Network |
| Bus | Twisted Pair Cable |
| Coaxial Cable | Contention (CSMA/CD) |
| Token Passing | Polling |
| Private-Branch Telephone Exchange (PBX) | Wide-Area Networks (WATs) |
| Integrated Digital Services Network (ISDN) | Baud Rate |

## Review Questions

1. Which type of channel is more suitable for transmitting images? Explain your answer.
2. Name some of the advantages of digital over analog transmission.
3. Discuss how technological innovation has brought about a period of change in telecommunications.
4. How can propogation delay, as it relates to satellite communications, cause problems in terms of interactive communications?
5. Discuss the differences between fiber-optic cable and copper wire or coaxial cable.
6. Identify two disadvantages of fiber-optic cables.
7. How are local area networks commonly used today and what types of peripheral devices are connected?
8. List four characteristics of local area networks which should be taken into consideration before acquiring a LAN.
9. Why is contention line control popular in bus networks?
10. A PBX represents what type of line configuration?

## Case Study

### SEEDS-BY-MAIL

Seeds-By-Mail is a startup company located in Rolling Hills, Wisconsin. The president, Ed Miller, and two founders have deciced to capitalize on the boom in home gardening by becoming a mail order discount outlet for seeds, bulbs and gardening supplies. Business at Seeds-By-Mail has been rapidly growing and a decision has been made to expand. The first phase of the expansion will include the installation of a mini-computer where all inventory, pricing and customer information will be stored. Ed and his partners also wish to automate the order-entry and customer service functions by linking ten workstations and one laser printer to the mini-computer. They have identified the following as key requirements for their proposed network: (1) the network will be used to transmit data only; (2) the network must be reliable; failure of one device will not make the network inoperative; (2) the network must be flexible in terms of adding nodes; (3) installation of the network should be relatively low in cost; and, (4) the network should support a transmission speed of between 1200 and 9600 baud.

1. Given this information, Ed Miller wants to know which network configuration, transmission media, line control and transmission method will best serve Seeds-By-Mail's needs.
2. How would your recommendations be impacted if the transmission requirements included voice and image as well as data?
3. What types of issues should Ed and his partners address in order to adequately plan for the future growth of telecommunications and networking at Seeds-By-Mail?

# 12

# Managing End-User Computing

*"Why should MIS stand between the information and the users?"*

*Ron Cipolla*

## Overview and Objectives

END-USER COMPUTING HAS BEEN DRAMATICALLY TRANSformed in the 1980's by the introduction and proliferation of the personal computer; the PC and its accompanying software have changed the scope and definition of *end-user computing*. End-users have become more self sufficient and increasingly are demanding access to mainframe data and to external databases. With this transformation, however, has come confusion and anarchy, as management techniques lagged behind exploding technology and the pluralism and democracy inherent in end-user computing has eroded management control and standardization.

Along with this phenomenon of change, there are tremendous opportunities (and pitfalls) for management: harness this new energy and direct it towards contributing to the growth and effectiveness of the firm, or drown in a sea of confusion and frustrated potential.

The key issue for management is how to effectively manage this growing phenomenon. The potential disaster in not managing this activity are clearly explained.

AFTER READING THIS CHAPTER YOU SHOULD BE ABLE TO:

- Define the purpose of an Information Center
- Describe the functions of the Information Center
- Explain the need for end-users to access mainframe databases
- Explain the difficulties of integrating end-user computing with information systems transaction processing systems

## Introduction

SINCE THE INTRODUCTION OF THE IBM PC IN 1981, END-user computing (EUC) has emerged with such great force as to challenge MIS departments as the dominant form of corporate computing. Several authorities have observed signs of this transition in organizational computing:

- Benjamin notes that end-user computing utilized 25% of the computing budget of Xerox Corp. in 1981; by 1990, end-user computing is projected to account for 75% of the budget.[1]
- Rockart and Flannery predict that MIS departments may soon become junior partners to *user-developed and -operated* computing.[2]
- Peterson sees MIS departments evolving towards the supporting role of data custodians.[3]

Clearly, the energy and growth in corporate computing has been at the level of the individual user, not at the MIS department level.

There are a variety of reasons why end-user computing has shown such dynamic growth. The first is the personal computer phenomenon: PCs have become affordable, powerful and easy to use. As a result, they have become popular and their use widespread. For example, International Data Corporation counted 39 computer keyboards per 100 office workers in 1985; it predicts that by 1990 this figure will reach 78 per 100 workers.[4] Most of these computer keyboards are connected to personal computers.

A second reason for the growth in EUC has been the development of user-friendly software. *Non-techies* resistance to new technology has gradually eroded as simple, easy-to-understand programs "humanized" the PC. The spreadsheet software package, for example, has become a familiar part of the office environment.

Finally, MIS departments have not met the needs of end-users. For many of their applications, end-users find that the tools, methods and processes used by the MIS department are inappropriate[5] End-users have been opting for quicker, smaller-scale solutions, often on a do-it-yourself basis.

Many end-users now have the ability to develop their new applications more quickly and at less expense than information systems professionals. In most organizations with active EUC the finance, marketing and operations staff are far more adept at spreadsheet and financial planning software than MIS personnel. Faced with a problem, an end-user's attitude is likely to be, "Why have the MIS department get involved when I could do the job over the weekend on my PC? If they get involved it would cost me $25,000 and I would have to wait three months."

There are two primary needs that are satisfied by EUC that were not met by traditional MIS departments. The first is *access* to transaction data and the second is software and hardware that is easy to use for *analysis*.

## END USERS

Ten years ago, end-user computing (EUC) was mostly limited to the *slide-rule* crowd: scientists, engineers, and mathematicians. Now it has spread throughout organizations, becoming prevalent among managers, professionals and clerical employees. In a study in the early 1980's, Rockart and Flannery identified the following types of end users:

1. Nonprogramming end users - Use menu driven applications or a well defined set of procedures.
2. Command level users - Utilize 4GLs and Query languages to access data.
3. End-User Programmer - Use both 4GLs and procedural languages to develop applications for their personal use.
4. Functional Support Personnel - Sophisticated functional support personnel who develop applications within their functional area. For example, accountants who develop applications for the accounting department.
5. End-User Support Personnel - Personnel usually assigned to central EUC support organization.
6. MIS programmers who program in end-user languages.

Rockart and Flannery show that end-users are a diverse group who need multiple software tools and strongly differentiated training. They found a major source of end-user dissatisfaction was a tendency to target training on the most sophisticated segment of end-users.

In general, end-users can be divided into two groups. Those who need to access data and those who perform analysis. These two groups are not entirely separate. There are end users who need access to data and perform analysis.

## DATA EXTRACTION

Rockart and Flannery noted in their study that there was a widespread feeling among end-users that information systems departments had dropped the ball in making data accessible. They refer to this condition as a *data extraction gap*: end-users being unable (or able only with great difficulty) to gain access to transaction data. Several solutions are available to help end-users cross that gap and gain access to production data:

1. Direct access by end users into production databases using query languages

2. Extracted production data loaded into a relational database for end user access
3. End-User languages such as Focus or RAMIS II
4. File transfer software
5. Terminal emulation software

These solutions are roughly ranked in the order of their desirability from the perspective of end-users. The last two alternatives are generally unsatisfactory because they are cumbersome. The third alternative, the use of end-user languages such as Focus and RAMIS II, is common in firms using hierarchical databases such as IMS. These languages, while easier to use than 3rd Generation languages such as COBOL, still require considerable expertise to extract transaction data and therefore are less desirable than the first two alternatives. This view is confirmed in When Things Go Right.

**When things go right**

## Icons Simplify Data Access at Chevron

Some managers believe that if they could get access to data on the mainframe their problems would be solved. For several years, Chevron had used what most experts would consider a user-friendly 4GL to access corporate data. This approach proved too difficult for the average end user.

Instead of using the tools, the executives and financial analysts would tell programmers what they needed. Using the 4GL tools, the programmers would obtain the required data in the form of printouts. The users would then key in the data to their spreadsheets.

This approach proved cumbersome, unproductive, error-prone, and untimely. When Chevron merged with Gulf, some of the Gulf managers grew impatient with Chevron's methods and began to ask for more flexible data access tools.

Chevron stumbled across the Metaphor system, which is designed for data access and interpretation. The Metaphor system is implemented on a workstation which combines a graphical interface, a file server, a local-area network, a database machine, and application software.

Data is accessed using a mouse to select icons representing one or more programs or routines. Chevron has been so pleased with the user-friendly interface that they have purchased 100 workstations. Don Matto, Director of MIS at Chevron estimates the system has increased revenues by $500,000 and cut costs by $75,000 per year by eliminating the need for programmer support of end users.

Adapted from Philip J. Gill, "Merger Helps Propel Easier Data Manipulation of Chevron Chemical," Computerworld, April 10, 1989, p. SR/8. Chapter 14 - Managing End-User Computing

The first two solutions have proven to be preferable for end-users and MIS professionals: both allow end-users to extract transaction data from relational databases without professional assistance. The difference between them is that the first solution, direct access using query languages, allows end-users to extract data from a *production* database whereas the second creates a separate database for the sole purpose of end-user queries. This requires a duplication of hardware and software. It has been referred to as the *two database solution*: one for production and the other for end-user queries.

Each solution has its accompanying advantages and disadvantages. For example, the advantage of a separate end-user database is that the performance of production applications are unaffected by end-user queries and production data does not necessarily have to be structured to the standards of a shared subject database environment. The result is that users obtain the accessibility of a relational database. On the down side, though, separating the database means that change and additions to the production database are not immediately represented in the end-user database; this means that for highly sensitive or volatile data environment, the two-database solution is not appropriate.

## Managerial Approaches to Personal Computing

THERE ARE THREE MANAGERIAL STYLES THAT AN INFORMATION systems department can adopt with respect to end-user computing: authoritarian, free rein, and an information center.[6]

### THE AUTHORITARIAN APPROACH

The authoritarian approach attempts to dominate end-user computing. In its extreme form it may even prohibit the purchase of personal computers. The justification for this domination is frequently couched in terms like data security, documentation standards, compatibility and budgets. Whatever the rationale this approach is doomed to failure. The reasons for failure of the authoritarian approach are legion, including: (1) application backlogs, (2) end user dissatisfaction, (3) the economics of personal computing, (4) user-friendly PC packages, and (5) ingenuity of end-users in by-passing enforcement rules.

Many end-users have valid complaints against authoritarian policies which prohibit them from acquiring PCs or from using external databases. Information systems departments, attempting to control end-user participation often have backlogs of two to four years for new applications. The point is, they aren't without blame.

The economic arguments against PCs has been destroyed by the reversal of economies-of-scale. The *least* expensive computing is now done on PCs. And due to technological improvements, the economic advantages of the PC are expected to grow in the near future.

In addition, the documentation standards that are maintained by information systems departments for large transaction processing systems are not pertinent to most personal computing applications. These applications are likely to be of a one-of-a kind, ad hoc nature.

Many end-users have been adept at circumventing policies which require MIS department approval of PC purchases. Personal computers have been acquired with a wide variety of imaginative budgeting strategies. In practice the policies that lead to information systems domination of personal computing are rarely effective because the end-user population does not feel they are sound.

In sum, the authoritarian approach to end-user computing management, a left-over from the heyday of the mainframe, is fundamentally flawed. It fails to acknowledge that the trend toward end-user computing is inherently democratic, and that the management style must be consistent with this trend.

## THE FREE REIN APPROACH

This approach is the philosophical opposite of the first: it is a *hands-off* policy. The free-rein approach attempts to shed responsibility along with authority, saying, in effect, "They created their own mess now let them live with it." However, *not deciding*, is in fact a decision, one which frequently creates anarchy and confusion.

The main difficulty with the free rein approach is its short-sightedness. Uncontrolled proliferation of personal computers of different brands running different software packages is creating an incompatible collection of equipment that will require great effort to integrate.

At its extreme, the free-rein approach becomes management by non-management. In reality a decision to give a blank check to end-users to purchase personal computers and software packages without guidance ignores consideration of other information systems priorities. End-users need training, consulting services and standards. They need a consistent interface to access mainframe databases. These considerations are ignored with the free rein approach.

## THE INFORMATION CENTER APPROACH

The term *information center* was coined by IBM. It refers to an organizational unit responsible for providing training, assistance and consulting services to end-users. The original concept was a defensive reaction by IBM to keep end-users on mainframe time sharing systems as opposed to PCs. Later, as IBM embraced the PC, the concept of the information center has broadened its role to include support for end-users on PCs. The latest thinking on information centers is that they should support all four of the major end-user technologies, which are: (1) time sharing, (2) personal computers, (3) networking, and (4) office automation. These technologies are closely related and end-user support for them should be coordinated.

The information center approach attempts to provide freedom to the end-user within a set of guidelines. Typically these guidelines include a statement of the types of hardware and software that will be supported by the organization. This allows training and consulting services to be developed for a limited array of alternatives. It also allows networks to be developed to allow communications across the organization. These services would be difficult, if not impossible, to provide in an environment without limits.

The information center recognizes the balance between the individual's need for freedom of choice and the organization's need for order. The individual is motivated to select a computer and the appropriate software for the application of their choice within the bounds of information center policies. These bounds are established in the interests of the organization as a whole.

The contrast between effective management and ineffective management of end-user computing is discussed in When Things Go Right/When Things Go Wrong.

## When things go right/ When things go wrong

# Power to the People

End-user computing, which enables end-users to develop their applications, is potentially the greatest development in the computer field. Although personal computers have penetrated every corner of the organization, and although people have become more knowledgeable and enthusiastic about them, in many organizations end-user computing has been less effective and more expensive than anticipated.

A study of end-user computing in 17 large companies revealed that 11 had serious problems. Six of them, however, had effective end-user computing.

The 11 companies with problems in end-user computing had some common symptoms. Four of them laid out large sums for end-user computing before they had even drawn up a budget for it.

- One financial services company purchased micros from eight different vendors. Furthermore, it had service contracts with five vendors. Service delays were common and up to 10% of installed machines were inoperable at any point in time.
- After a spreadsheet problem surfaced this same firm found that it was using nine different word processing packages. Because end-user support was provided on only one of them, the firm estimated it lost 8000 hours of productive time for employees learning by trial and error.
- A bank bought three 4th generation language packages which cost in excess of $200,000 in licensing fees. It was found that one $50,000 would have met the need.
- An insurance company supported more than 20 PC packages. The training group alone invested more than $30,000 in labor to support them. It was later estimated that five packages would have met the need.

In trying to limit computer costs, 7 out of the 11 firms with ineffective end-user computing resorted to *hard* controls. These controls, which included MIS department approval for PC purchases, were ineffective. The users in these companies devised ingenious ways to circumvent the hard controls. One MIS department conducted an audit and found 1500 unapproved PCs. These companies also encountered huge cost overruns.

In contrast, the firms with successful end-user computing used *soft* controls. They set standards for all PC purchases. They also standardized an operating system, spreadsheets, word processing packages, and 4GLs.

The successful firms provided training only on approved software. They distributed new releases and trained end-users in good development methodology. Soft controls were found to cost less, limit proliferation, incompatibility and maintenance problems.

Adapted from J. Daniel Couger, "E Pluribus Computum," Harvard Business Review, (September-October, 1986), pp. 89-90.

## The Information Center

THE CONCEPT OF THE INFORMATION CENTER HAS EVOLVED with new technological developments such as personal computers, networking and 4GLs. What is constant is the commitment to make end-users self sufficient. In his book, Megatrends, John Naisbitt identified one of the major trends of our society as "From Institution Help to Self-Help."[6] Information centers are consistent with this movement towards independence and self-sufficiency; they have caught the vision and are attempting to "teach people to fish rather than giving them fish."

### BASIC INFORMATION CENTER SERVICES

The basic information center services will vary from one organization to another but several services are common to most information centers:

TRAINING: This service is usually offered in the form of courses taught by the information center staff and include the following:

- Survey of Data Processing
- PC Orientation
- Courses that are designed to train users to use a specific package, e.g., LOTUS 1-2-3

CONSULTING AND ASSISTANCE: These services are of two types (1) assisting end-users with problems encountered in developing an application and (2) assisting end-users in designing a new application, if necessary.

PRODUCT EVALUATION: Information center employees are knowledgeable about software and hardware alternatives. To provide effective training and consulting services most information centers have standardized on one or two personal computers and a small group of software packages.

MARKETING: To be successful an information center must assume an aggressive stance in marketing its services. Many information centers publish newsletters which keep end-users up-to-date on new software packages, class schedules, and interesting new projects.

DATA EXTRACTION: The information center personnel extract data from database and file-management systems and present the data in useable formats.

QUERY FACILITY: Information centers should encourage end-users to do their own retrieval and processing using user oriented languages.

DATA INTEGRITY AND SECURITY: The need for data integrity and security should be reinforced by information center personnel.

The personal computer is the driving force behind a new definition of end-user computing. Until quite recently, the connection between end-user computing, decision support systems and office automation wasn't recognized. In office automation for example, the personal computer has now been recognized as the basic building block around which an automated office is built.

This redefinition of end-user computing is expanding the role of the information center as the organizational unit designed to support end-user computing. Some of the new areas are networking, data base access and office automation. While some of these new responsibilities are controversial they are closely related to current information center activities.

## Linking Information Centers and MIS

TWO BROAD AND SOMETIMES CONTRADICTORY TRENDS— on the one hand, end-user involvement with developing applications and interfacing with MIS departments and, on the other hand, rapid changes in information technology—are currently coexisting, creating several concerns which demand increased attention of MIS managers:[7]

1. Data Administration - As data becomes recognized as a corporate resource it requires more centralized coordination. Much of this coordination is accomplished by the self-imposed discipline of data administration and operation of a database management system. Among the responsibilities of a data administration department is insuring that data is consistent, accurate and complete. These responsibilities also require that data is timely, so that all parties are viewing the same data at a given time. Data administration relates to end users by assisting them to access data. This can be accomplished through training and information assistance. The data administration staff is also responsible for data security, which requires a determination of end user access requirements and how these can be implemented. The use of *user views* is particularly applicable both for simplifying access

to database tables and for limiting access to certain columns or rows within a table.

2. Development Support - New development tools and methodologies have frequently received too little management attention. The result has been little or no training, and poor follow through. The full potential of these innovations is frequently not realized due to inadequate implementation. The solution is an organizational unit charged with the responsibility of coordinating the activities relating to implementation of development and productivity tools. This properly gives increased emphasis to implementing these new technologies. While the primary focus of a development center is usually information systems professionals, some organizations encourage end-users to develop applications.

3. User Support - The end-user revolution started with terminals and time sharing but accelerated with the advent of PCs and the associated software. The impact of this change has touched every information systems department. The problems of using personal computers productively can be addressed effectively through training and consulting services. As PC users become more sophisticated, they begin to see the possibilities of tapping mainframe databases. Access to a database eliminates tedious data entry, and improves the consistency, accuracy, and timeliness of data.

The three areas of increased responsibility can be viewed as a triangle as shown in Figure 12.1.

The data support center is shown at the top of the triangle and supports both the development support center and the information center. The relationship between these three areas is discussed in Issues and Controversies.

## Issues and Controversies

### The Temporary Role of the Information Center

**The goal of an information center should be to eliminate the need for its existence. But because the task of an information center consultant is so time-consuming, satisfying, and so greatly needed, it is difficult to get an information center staff to see beyond that role.**

**As the general level of computer competence grows and application software becomes easier to use, information centers should broaden their scope. The end-user orientation which has been the center's greatest strength may wind up to be its greatest weakness.**

The information center should treat the organization as a user who needs assistance to get the most value from information technology. Ironically, as information centers developed strategies and found tools for end-users, these discoveries were rarely shared with or accepted by MIS departments.

When the types of tools found in an information center are aimed at MIS professionals, the result is sometimes called the development center. The name of this game is to use the power of the computer itself against its own complexity. Assuming this broader role will lead to the eventual disappearance of the information center.

As valuable as the information center's role is to distribute knowledge of computing, it will become increasingly important for it to help unify the organization's approach to data management. The mandate of many information centers seems to be "to know your tools" but are tools more important than nuts and bolts? By concentrating on the data, the information center can help develop an effective enterprise-wide information system. It is towards this end that information centers should be directed.

To the information center managers of today I would say: Plan to put yourself out of business - and give yourself a big raise when you succeed.

Adapted from Richard Makita, "Satisfying MIS and Users," Computerworld (October 8, 1986), pp. 39-42.

FIGURE 12.1

*Three Areas of Increased Attention for MIS Managers*

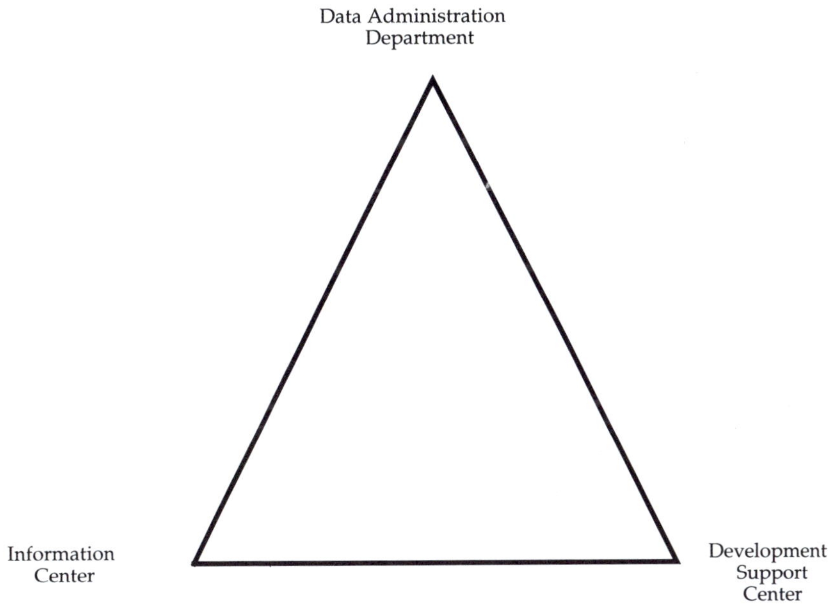

## Benefits of End User Computing

THERE ARE SEVERAL BENEFITS OF AN EFFECTIVELY MANAGED end-user computing program. These benefits are real but somewhat intangible.

### INCREASED UNDERSTANDING OF COMPUTER TECHNOLOGY

The growing body of end-users is producing some interesting side effects. MIS departments are finding their clients far more sophisticated and demanding than they have experienced in the past. While initially this change has produced some conflict, in the long run it will enhance the effectiveness of MIS departments who are able to tap the organizational experience of more knowledgeable clients.

This increased understanding of computer technology is leveraged in two important payoff areas: (1) using computers for competitive advantage and (2) improving organizational effectiveness.[7]

### COMPETITIVE ADVANTAGE

Most market opportunities are discovered by professionals and managers "in the trenches" who also have an understanding of new enabling technologies. The diffusion of information technology is ensuring that competitive uses of this technology are being discovered by people close to the problem.

Most of these discoveries do not have a major impact on the organization because corporate excellence is not usually the result of one "bold strategic stroke" but the cumulative effect of a large number of minor organizational improvements.

### IMPROVED ORGANIZATIONAL EFFECTIVENESS

We live in the age of the knowledge worker. Improving the tools of knowledge workers makes them more productive. It also creates a larger body of managers and professionals with the ability to access, use and distribute good management information. Good information is vital in an environment of turbulent change.

Some of the tools required to make managers and professionals more effective are addressed in the next section.

## Personal Computer Workstations

IN THE NEAR FUTURE, THE PERSONAL COMPUTER WILL BE REDEfined as a managerial workstation. The concept is drawn from the engineering work station. Some of the following functions might be included in a managerial workstation.[8]

1. Financial planning software
2. Word processing for preparing reports
3. Access to corporate data base by use of a query language
4. A graphics package
5. Access to external databases such as Dow Jones or Dun and Bradstreet
6. Access to CD-ROM database

Financial planning software packages are the most popular software used on personal computers. They are essential components of the software complement for the managerial workstation.

Word processing software is also an essential component. Increasingly, word processing is integrated with graphics capabilities to provide desktop publishing capability. Word processing also enhances productivity by minimizing the reliance of managers and professionals on clerical help.

Query languages allow end-users to extract data from corporate databases. This will generally require a personal computer software package that interfaces with a mainframe database management system (DBMS). Another approach is to purchase a personal computer version of a mainframe DBMS. This allows a seamless interface to the mainframe.

A graphics package is desirable to develop high quality presentation graphics. There are several personal computer packages that provide a user-friendly package for developing multiple color graphs, charts, and diagrams.

Managers and professionals frequently need access to external data bases for research purposes. There are a growing number of external on-line databases. These might be divided into three categories:

- Financial
- General Business/Research
- Special Purpose (i.e. legal, environmental)

The Dow Jones News Retrieval is the best known financial database. It offers the following services:

- Price quotes from the New York and American stock exchanges as well as over the counter quotations.
- Text of the *Wall Street Journal* and *Barrons*
- News, sports and weather.

Dialog Information Services dominates the general business research category with over 250 databases in the areas of business, government, current events, law, medicine, science, technology and environment.[9]

Access to these software components is desirable to bring the concept of the managerial workstation to reality. The key difference between a PC and a workstation is that workstations are connected to a network. The current generation of PCs will be superceded by PCs more suitable for the role of a workstation. This will require a multi-tasking operating system, graphics, windows, icons and memory mapped displays. The new computers will permit a user friendly interface which can show information in the *what you see is what you get* (WYSIWYG) form.[10]

THE DEVELOPMENT OF APPLICATIONS BY END-USERS IS CONtroversial. Many MIS departments are willing to allow end-user development of applications that are used only by the department that developed them, but draw the line for applications being used for two or more departments.

There is also the difficulty of defining the difference between ad hoc analysis and applications. Ad hoc analysis at the extreme is a one-of-a-kind analysis with no thought of developing a reusable "program". An application, on the other hand, assumes an ongoing activity which is used frequently. If end-user application development is encouraged, there must be a commitment to quality control. This issue is addressed in Issues and Controversies.

## Issues and Controversies

# Certification of End-User Systems

While there are enormous benefits to end-user computing, it is easy to identify some potential problems. The advantages of end-user involvement in computing are so great, however, that it is expected not only to continue but to proliferate.

The task for MIS departments is to solve the problems of end-user involvement in developing computer systems rather than denying end-user access to development tools. One attractive solution to this problem is the certification of end-user-developed systems.

For systems developed solely for a single department there is no problem. It is a manager's prerogative to use the tools that, in the manager's judgment, are required to run his department. If the tools selected by the manager are not subject to appropriate development discipline, the result will be poor departmental performance.

It is when an end-user system is applied beyond the department in which it was originally developed that problems often emerge. Often software developed by end-users lacks edit controls, documentation and these flaws are not apparent until it becomes an application used by more than one department. At this point it often affects the firm as a whole.

What follows the lack of discipline in building end-user systems is the distinct possibility of organizational failure based on faulty information. The underlying data may very well be correct, but if the process used in transforming the data to information is faulty, the result will be flawed.

Certification is based on two assumptions. First, some systems require certification if the firm is to make decisions with a degree of confidence and accuracy. Second, certification offers benefits to the developer. Both concepts must be satisfied if the certification program is to be successful.

Systems that require certification are those that affect areas beyond the department that developed the system. Other departments become vulnerable to interpretations and views of the developing department.

The second assumption is equally important - that the end-user perceives benefits in seeking certification. One benefit is escaping the burden of support. It allows them to take advantage of the MIS department assuming responsibility for reporting, security and backup. The acceptance of a system is an external validation of the developer's efforts. This recognition is a powerful motivation for certification.

With a little imagination one can see that end-user systems will gradually replace systems developed by MIS departments. The systems department function will be reduced to certifying end-user developed systems. The primary role of MIS departments will be data custodians.

Adapted from Robert Peterson, "Giving End-Users the MIS Seal of Good System Building," Computerworld (June 1, 1987), pp. 83-86.

## ADVANTAGES OF END-USER APPLICATION DEVELOPMENT

One of the primary advantages of end-user application development is the ability of the user to develop the application in a timely manner instead of waiting out—and adding to—the MIS department backlog. The user develops the application when it fits the need, rather than fitting the priorities of the MIS department.

Typically, the development time is reduced because the user does not have to spend time communicating his/her needs to others. This saves considerable analysis and design time compared with the MIS department using the conventional life cycle.

Finally, end-user satisfaction with the finished system is usually good because he/she developed the solution. This reduces the *not invented here* syndrome.

## PROBLEMS WITH END-USER APPLICATION DEVELOPMENT

One of the problems with end-user development is that it may generate excessive unplanned use of computer systems. This is a particular problem if end-users compete with production applications for computer time. Database query languages, in particular, when placed in the hands of untrained users, can use excessive computer time. Much of this problem can be avoided by training end-users, providing information center assistance for difficult problems and perhaps by certifying end-users.

MIS departments also fear application development by end-users because they believe end-users would use inferior development methods. Users are more likely to produce applications that lack documentation, data editing and error control mechanisms. They are also less knowledgeable about appropriate application testing. Application certification as described in Issues and Controversies would seem to be an appropriate solution for this problem.

End-user developed systems may lack the documentation necessary for them to be used and maintained by others. They may also be idiosyncratic, reflecting the biases and style of the developer or simply inappropriate for use by someone other than the designer. When turnover occurs this can render them unusable.[11]

## Managing End-User Computing Development

IN 1979 RICHARD NOLAN WROTE AN INFLUENTIAL ARTICLE IN the *Harvard Business Review* in which he identified six stages of growth in the MIS function.[12] While not originally intended to apply to end-user computing, the article seems to capture the dilemma of managing end-user computing.

Nolan identified six stages of development including:

1. Initiation
2. Contagion
3. Control
4. Integration
5. Data Administration
6. Maturity

Managers of end-user computing and information centers are concerned with recognizing which stage the organization is in and applying the appropriate management strategy to develop end-user computing effectively.

Early on, the appropriate strategy is a marketing strategy to make end-users aware of the benefits of end-user computing. Draconian controls at this stage are counter-productive. Initially the management approach should probably be limited to soft controls which encourage standardization.

Initially end-users might be encouraged to use the information center in an experimental manner without any charge to the user's budget. This temporary lapse of control achieves another objective—nurturing innovation. End-user computing begins to penetrate the firm's functional areas, i.e., manufacturing, marketing, accounting, and personnel.

During stage three, *control*, end-users are made more accountable by charge outs for the Information Center's services. There begins to be an awareness of the limitations of the free standing PC and much discussion of data communication and database technologies. The indifference of end-users to data control and application development standards complicates these discussions of movement towards integration by the use of networks and database technology.

In stage four, *integration*, the end-users gain access to mainframe data but find difficulty in using it because of inconsistent data formats, cumbersome access tools, and data redundancy. The end-users begin to press MIS for consistent interfaces, query languages, and relational database technology.

In stage five there is a focus on data administration, and the beginnings of the recognition that data is a corporate resource which should be managed. Data administration gives support to both MIS professionals as well as end-users.

Stage six involves alignment of the goals of end-user computing with those of the firm. The firm begins to practice Information Resource Management.

## Guidelines for Managers

MANY ORGANIZATIONS REGARD END-USER COMPUTING AS A free-standing process with little need to integrate it with traditional MIS departments. End-user computing is growing and becoming increasingly important to integrate with conventional MIS. This integration will impact both end-user computing and traditional MIS departments. Information resource management is a framework that will unite transaction processing and end-user computing.

## Guidelines for MIS Professionals

MIS PROFESSIONALS SHOULD RECOGNIZE THE IMPORTANCE OF end-user computing. This is a phenomenon that will not go away and requires some adjustments on the part of MIS departments. Indeed, some experts believe that information centers have provided an excellent model for introducing new technology in MIS departments.

## Key Terms

End-User Computing
The Free Rein Approach
Time Sharing
Networking
Data Administration
User Support
Managerial Workstation
The Authoritarian Approach
Information Center
Personal Computers
Office Automation
Development Support
Knowledge Worker
Application Certification

## Review Questions

1. Define End-User Computing and explain the forces which have fueled its growth.
2. Identify several reasons for the failure of the authoritarian approach to managing end-user computing.
3. Name the four major end-user technologies which an information center should support.
4. Discuss how information centers are consistent with societal trends of independence and self-sufficiency.
5. Compare and contrast the services provided by the Information Center with those provided by the Data Support Center.
6. What are the two payoffs associated with end-user's increased understanding of computer technolog?
7. Name five of the functions which might be included in a managerial workstation.
8. What is the key difference between a personal computer and a managerial workstation?
9. According to the definitions provided in this chapter, which of the following are ad hoc analyses and which are applications? Explain your answer.
   a. A program which computes total inventory stocking costs for each product.
   b. A program which computes bi-montly payroll.
   c. A spreadsheet program that forecasts profit if advertising were increased 10 percent and sales growth was 16 percent.
   d. A model whose output serves as a tool for establishing optimal staffing levels for a fast-food restaurant.
   e. A program which compares budgeted costs to actual costs by department on a monthly basis.
10. Discuss the advantages and disadvantages of end-user application development.

## Case Study

### ACME RENT-A-CAR

Early this year, Sarah Hansen, got a call from a friend, Richard Hoffman, who is a division chief financial officer of Acme Rent-A-Car, a Fortune 500-size company. "I just came from a planning meeting where two of our managers made presentations," he said. "Both used spreadsheet programs on their personal computers to produce the numbers, and each of them came up with a completely different prediction."

Richard continued, "The program occurred when the analysts entered the actual results into their models by copying data from printouts—one used a week-old report, the other used a revised report he got that day. To make it worse, there were at least two data entry errors in the copying. Maybe the only real solution to problems like this is to take away all the personal computers and software used in our organization."

"No, I don't agree," Sarah told him. "Your story isn't an argument against using personal computers; it's proof that they haven't been used enough."

This situation is typical in many companies. The most common problem new personal computer users have encountered is that while they may be using the same spreadsheets, they are not necessarily working with the same data.

1. Which managerial approach to managing end-user computing was Richard advocating? Will it work? Why or why not?
2. Which of the basic services provided by an Information Center would have helped resolve the problem described by Richard?
3. What are some of the potential problems of increased access of mainframe databases by end-users? How can these potential problems be avoided or controlled?

## Suggestions for Further Reading

R. Ryan Nelson, End-User Computing (John Wiley and Sons, 1989)

*This is an excellent collection of journal articles on end-user computing. The articles are balanced and current. The book also contains a bibliography on end-user computing.*

# 13

# Decision Support and Expert Systems

*"The end products of managers*

*work are decisions and actions."*

*Peter Drucker*

## Overview and Objectives

DECISION SUPPORT SYSTEMS ARE A RELATIVELY NEW APPROACH for applying computers to managerial problems. The characteristics of decision support systems are an emphasis on direct involvement of the users, ease of use and flexibility. This chapter examines both the concept of a decision support system as well as describing applications.

Expert systems are an application of artificial intelligence to practical problems. Expert systems emulate the reasoning process of a human expert in a narrow area of expertise. Expert systems are being applied to a broad range of problems but the supply of knowledge engineers is limited and the response from educational institutions has been slow.

AFTER READING THIS CHAPTER YOU SHOULD BE ABLE TO:

- Describe the difference between transaction processing and decision support systems.
- Discuss the model building process.
- Illustrate the difference between structured and semistructured decisions.
- Discuss the role of management in building and using decision support models.
- Discuss the types of problems that can be addressed by expert systems.
- Explain the differences between decision support and expert systems

## Decision Support Systems

DECISION SUPPORT SYSTEMS (DSS) ARE FUNDAMENTALLY DIFferent from transaction processing which has dominated the computing scene for the past 30 years. Decision support systems provide information that is required for management decision making whereas the objective of transaction processing is to automate clerical activities. This difference in objectives is illustrated in Figure 13.1.

Decision support systems represent a synergism between man and the computer. As an information processor a human being excels the computer in: 1) recognizing logical relationships between seemingly unrelated events or phenomena, 2) organizing data into meaningful information, 3) conceptualizing alternatives, and 4) adapting as the situation changes. The computers advantages in information processing are: 1) computational speed, 2) accuracy, 3) ability to retain and retrieve rapidly detailed historical records, and 4) the ability to deal with complexity. Decision support systems combine the problem solving capability of a human being with the computational speed and accuracy of the computer.

FIGURE 13.1
*Decision Support Systems Versus Transaction Processing Systems*[a]

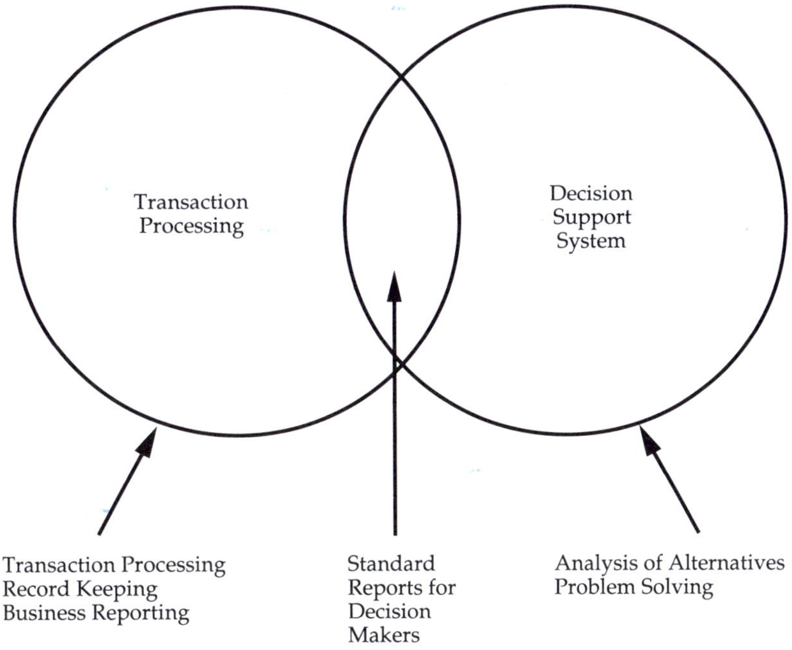


| <u>Transaction Processing</u> | <u>Decision Support Systems</u> |
|---|---|
| Passive use | Active use |
| Clerical activities | Line, staff and management activities |
| Oriented toward mechanical efficiency | Oriented towards overall effectiveness |
| Focus on the past | Focus on the present |
| Emphasis on consistency | Emphasis on flexibility and ad hoc utilization |
| | Model building |

[a]Steven Alter, Decision Support Systems: Continuing Practice and Continuing Challenges, (Reading, Mass.: Addison-Wesley Publishing Co., 1980), p. 2.

Sprague and Carlson have suggested that decision support systems consist of: (1) dialog, (2) data, and (3) modeling. Dialog consists of the interaction between the user and the computer. Ideally this interface should be interactive and easy to use. Data refers to access to a wide variety of data—the accessibility of data has been a consistent theme throughout the text. It can be summarized as follows: relational database technology if properly implemented will make data readily accessible to end-users. This contribution of database technology to decision support systems is not always recognized.

Modeling refers to the ability to apply a broad range of analytical models to data. The model building process is the critical process in using decision support systems.

## Model Building

MODELS ARE FREQUENTLY USED IN DECISION SUPPORT SYSTEMS to analyze complex situations. Models might be defined as representations of something else. An equation can represent the relationship of costs and revenues. Models represent something else either in the way the model behaves or by symbolic representation of the properties of the object being modeled. The usual purpose of model building is to use the model for experimentation and analysis.

Model building begins with some understanding of the system being modeled. This understanding, however, is incomplete or there would be no reason to build a model. For example, a designer of an airplane typically knows a great deal about the relationship of airplane shape and aircraft performance. Through experimentation a designer refines his understanding of the relationship between the shape and performance of an aircraft by testing a model aircraft in wind tunnel.

Model building consists of two complementary processes—abstraction and simplification. Abstraction consists of representing the essence of something without duplicating it. A photograph of a human being is a realistic representation of the appearance of an individual. A caricature or cartoon representation of that same person is more abstract. Pictures and cartoons represent only the appearance of an individual, to get some insight into an individual's values or behavior might require a biographical sketch or a description of his/her behavior in different situations. Abstraction requires the ability to isolate relevant features in an object being modeled and to be able to represent these features in a model.

Simplification in model building is required because of the complexity of representing reality in a model. For example, a model of a projected income statement typically omits details that are not material. A model builder selects those features that are critical to make the model representative. This process of simplification saves both time and cost in building models. Obviously simplification and abstraction can be overdone to the point that a model is an oversimplified representation of the real thing and decisions based on model performance would be questionable.

The validity of a model is measured by the extent of which the model accurately represents the qualities of the real object. Validity is usually measured by testing the model in the real word as indicated in Figure 13.2.

FIGURE 13.2

*The Modeling Process*

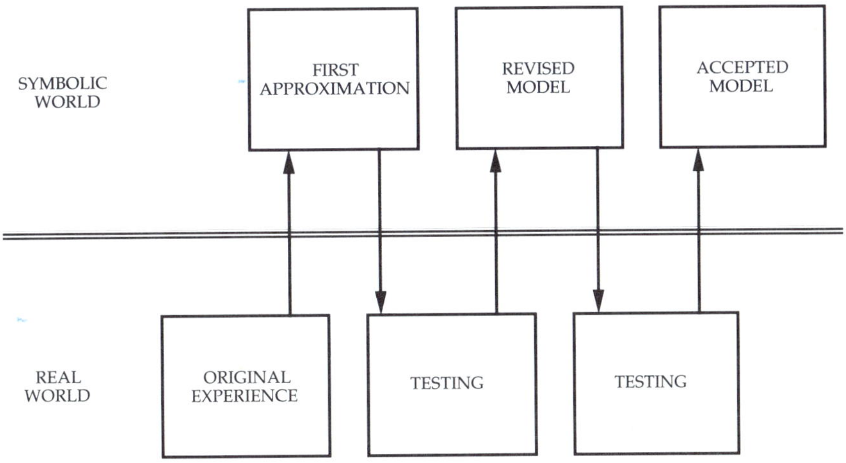


The concept of model building in decision support systems is closely related to prototyping in application development. What they have in common is an iterative process that involves a series of successive refinements. The difference is that the purpose of prototyping is to allow users to experience the look and feel of a proposed system whereas model building is more concerned with simplification and abstraction. The processes of simplification and abstraction are required in model building to manage complexity.

## Semi-structured Decisions

DECISIONS MAY BE CATEGORIZED AS STRUCTURED OR UNSTRUCTURED. Unstructured decisions are characterized by personal judgment and difficulty of quantification. Examples of an unstructured decision would be selection a new employee, determining which of two advertising campaigns would be most effective and deciding which of several R and D projects should receive increased emphasis. Unstructured decisions are referred to as nonprogrammed decisions by Simon. The term nonprogrammed suggests this type of decision lies outside the boundary of Decision Support Systems.

Structured decisions do not require managerial attention. These decisions usually involve situations where the factors that influence a decision are well understood and the computer or a clerk can make the decision based upon a decision rule or a simple model. An example of this type of situation would be a decision as to how much of a particular inventory item should be ordered.

Between these two decision extremes lies what can be referred to as semi-structured decisions. In a semi-structured decision environment the user initiates and controls the problem-solving process. The users values and judgment determine the alternatives examined as well as the interpretation of results. Users need models and computational assistance to facilitate this process.[1]

Some decisions which at first glance appear to be structured upon closer examination turn out to be semi-structured. A treasurer of a major corporation allowed two student acquaintances to build a linear programming model to determine how to invest excess short term cash. After comparing the LP solutions with 6 months of historical data the students concluded the model would have generated $1,750,000 of additional interest. The treasurer asked the students, "What would happen if interest rates in London suddenly rose?" The students answered that the model would *optimally* ship all the firm excess cash to London. The treasurer's response was that the hypothetical rise in interest rates may have been the result of investors anticipating devaluation of the pound. Under these circumstances the LP solution might have been disastrous.

The students recognized the validity of the treasurer's viewpoint and attempted without success to fix the model. The treasurer on the other hand, later recognized that the LP model would make better decisions than he could in investing short term cash for most weeks but occasionally made very bad decisions. The treasurer eventually decided it would be helpful to run the LP model and review the results. If no special problem or factors existed he would implement the LP solution.

The treasurer learned that a computer model and human judgment were more effective in combination than either would be alone. The students learned that what appeared to be a structured problem actually was semistructured.[2]

Decision support systems concentrate on a middle ground between unstructured problems in which decisions are best made by those with informed judgment and structured which can be made by a computer or by a decision rule from a table. Semi-structured decisions can best be solved by a man-computer team.

## Decision Support Usage Pattern

MUCH OF THE EARLY WRITING ABOUT COMPUTERS AND DECISION making envisioned executives working with computer terminals. Early experiments with executives using computer systems were mostly unsuccessful. Executives in the 1960's and 1970's were either intimidated by the computer or they were unwilling to learn the detail necessary to interface with the computer. More recent experience has been more positive. Personal computers and user-friendly software have removed many of the barriers associated with executive computer use.

Decision support systems do not require that an executive actually use the computer. While this model of usage is encouraged other patters of usage have evolved. Alter has identified four modes of usage.[3]

1. Subscription Mode - The decision maker receives regularly scheduled reports that are obtained by consolidating and abstracting data submitted by someone other than the decision maker.
2. Terminal Mode - The decision maker employs an on-line terminal to query a database and/or use analytical software.
3. Clerk Mode - The decision maker frames the questions to be answered but directs someone else to do the necessary computer tasks. The decision maker may be involved with other work until an answer is obtained.
4. Intermediary Mode - The decision support system is used by an intermediary who performs the analysis and prepares a report. The decision maker may not be aware of how the report was prepared.

These modes of decision support usage are defined in Figure 13.3.

FIGURE 13.3

*Patterns of System Usage From the Decision Maker's Viewpoint*[b]

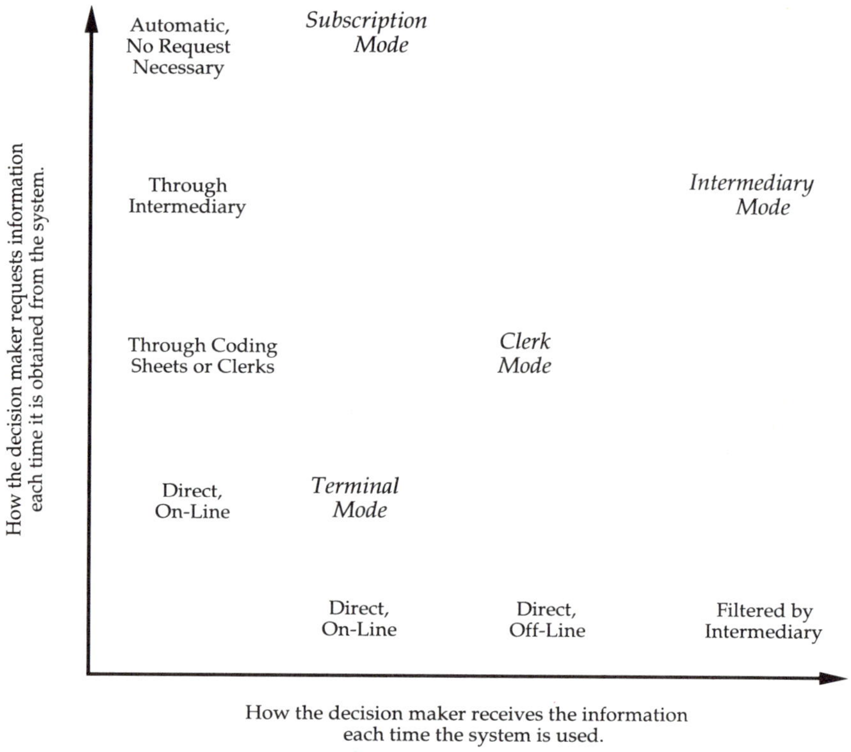


[b]S. A. Alter, Decision Support Systems: Current Practices and Continuing Challenges. (Reading, Mass.: Addison-Wesley, 1980), p. 111.

Over time decision makers may change their preferred mode in using decision support systems. As decision makers become more comfortable with personal computers or terminals they may become more directly involved.

There is a small but growing group of executives who have developed what Rockart and Tracy refer to as Executive Information Systems.[4] Executive Information Systems (EIS) may be thought of as a decision support system tailored for chief executives.

## Executive Information Systems

INCREASED GLOBAL AND DOMESTIC COMPETITION HAS DEcreased the response time for strategic decisions. This has made many executives hungry for information. Typically this information has been provided by middle managers but competitive pressures have led to corporate belt-tightening which has led to cutbacks at many firms. These cutbacks have directly impacted middle management.

These changes have fueled the demand for executive information systems (EIS) which replace the functions formerly performed by middle managers. EIS require a much different approach to computer interfaces and man/machine interplay than those used for decision support systems. These systems typically use a heavy emphasis on graphics, speed, and a minimum of computer commands to shield executives from technical details. They rely on mice and touch screens to minimize keyboard input.

The distinction between DSS and EIS is that EIS emphasizes current operations whereas DSS focuses on the future. Decision support systems offer sophisticated modeling languages that enable an analyst to build strategic planning and forecasting models that deal with the future of the organization. Executive information systems is a display technology which allows an executive to develop static reports and graphs to review and analyze current operations.

Many EIS provide relational database tools for gathering data across many hardware platforms. This requires a common interface across the various databases that provide information for an EIS. SQL can perform this function for relational DBMS but does not interface with hierarchical and network DBMS.

EIS are particularly useful for organizations which have rapidly changing market conditions, or where operations are critical to organizational success. Executives in these organizations want systems that allow them to read and display the data stored in the database.

Typically, an EIS includes a database, a support organization, and appropriate software. The support organization provides training, and ongoing assistance or *coaching*. In short, the support organization appears to be an information center for executives.

## Types of Decision Support Tools

### SPREADSHEETS

The growth of spreadsheets as a decision support tool has been explosive. They have become the most commonly used data analysis package. The name spreadsheet is derived from the fact that the program is formatted as a row and column worksheet and accepts data and computational formulas in this format.

The most popular spreadsheet is Lotus 1-2-3 which has become a defacto standard. There are several clones of 1-2-3 which have the look and feel of this package. Today there are dozens of packages being used for budgeting, forecasting, and other financial planning applications as well as countless other applications such as a professor's grade book.

While spreadsheet packages were originally limited to personal computers there are now minicomputer and mainframe versions as well. However, spreadsheet packages are still closely associated with personal computers. An example of a spreadsheet application is found in Figure 13.4.

FIGURE 13.4

*A Typical Spreadsheet Application*

| | A | B | C | D | E | F | G | H |
|---|---|---|---|---|---|---|---|---|
| 1 | | | | | | | | |
| 2 | | | | Sales Report | | | | |
| 3 | | | | Design-A-Sign, Inc. | | | | |
| 4 | | | | 1985 to 1987 | | | | |
| 5 | ------ | ------ | ------ | ------ | ------ | ------ | ------ | ------ |
| 6 | | | Year | Sales | Product No. | | | |
| 7 | ------ | ------ | ------ | ------ | ------ | ------ | ------ | ------ |
| 8 | | | 1985 | $2,450 | X-143N | | | |
| 9 | | | 1985 | $3,000 | Y-873L | | | |
| 10 | | | 1985 | $2,340 | X-657G | | | |
| 11 | | | 1986 | $4,900 | X-143M | | | |
| 12 | | | 1986 | $3,750 | Y-873L | | | |
| 13 | | | 1986 | $2,800 | X-657G | | | |
| 14 | | | 1987 | $5,800 | X-143M | | | |
| 15 | | | 1987 | $6,300 | Y-873L | | | |
| 16 | | | 1987 | $4,500 | X-657G | | | |
| 17 | ------ | ------ | ------ | ------ | ------ | ------ | ------ | ------ |
| 18 | ------ | ------ | ------ | ------ | ------ | ------ | ------ | ------ |
| 19 | | | Total | $35,840 | | | | |
| 20 | | | | | | | | |

Spreadsheet software is seductive. Once users have mastered it they tend to use it for a broad variety of tasks. Some authorities worry that these packages are being used for applications that other packages could do better. The use of spreadsheet templates for applications requiring heavy revision or auditing may not be appropriate.

The difficulty with spreadsheets is the difficulty of detecting errors and the lack of documentation. To resolve these problems many firms have insisted on a central group responsible for coordinating a technical review, documentation, and dissemination of templates.

For some types of problems, particularly those involving very large models, users may find financial modeling software to be superior. This type of software is self documenting, performs functions such as goal seeking and makes it easier to consolidate several models.

## QUERY LANGUAGES

More recently the development of Query Languages has enabled end-users to extract data for ad-hoc information requirements. Ad hoc information is information required for a specific purpose. An example of an ad hoc query is found in Figure 13.5.

FIGURE 13.5

*A Five-Year Product History Would be Generated in Response to This Ad Hoc Query*

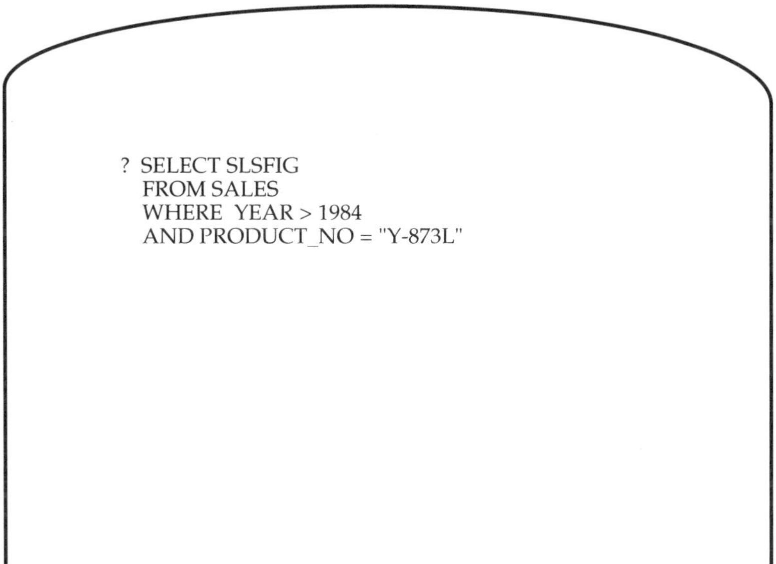

## STATISTICAL ANALYSIS SOFTWARE

Statistical analysis software provides an analytical tool for the analysis of data. Representative statistical analysis packages are SAS or SPSS. Statistical analysis software might incorporate a graphics module to present data in the form of a bar graph, pie chart or line graph.

## FINANCIAL PLANNING SOFTWARE

Financial planning decision support systems may use either personal computer based spreadsheet packages or financial planning languages to perform various types of financial planning. Spreadsheet packages are suitable for a wide spectrum of financial planning applications. More complex financial planning applications may require a financial planning language. A case study using a financial planning language is found later in this chapter.

## LINEAR PROGRAMMING PACKAGES

Linear programming packages are used to develop normative models. A normative model is one that suggests an optimum course of action or the best possible result that can be obtained. Linear programming packages develop an optimal solution to a set of constraints which represent limitations of resources or capacity.

Linear programming packages are frequently used in an iterative fashion by changing the assumptions of the model. This allows a model builder to analyze the effects of various assumptions on the model output.

## SIMULATION LANGUAGES

Simulation languages can be used to simulate the effects of various decision alternatives. Simulation models used in organizations are typically dynamic; that is, they represent the behavior of a system over time. Some financial modeling languages have incorporated some elements of simulation and are able to perform risk analysis simulations. Simulation languages are applicable for a broader range of applications including simulating the effects of queing, inventory systems, and production operations.

### APPLICATION SPECIFIC PACKAGES

Application specific packages are limited to a specific application. They may be purchased or developed internally. Application specific packages differ from the previous tools in the breadth of applications they address and the flexibility that they afford a user.

An example of this type of tool is a lease payment computational package used by leasing companies or banks to determine periodic-lease payments. Input may include the desired after tax return, payment pattern and tax considerations. The package determines the payment per period required to bring the target return to the firm. This type of model may appear at first glance to be structured but the judgment and skill of the user are important to achieving a good solution.

## Financial Planning - A Case Study

ONE OF THE MOST IMPORTANT INNOVATIONS IN DECISION Support Systems has been the development of financial planning languages. these languages enable non-dp managers to build and solve models in an interactive experimental manner.

The ease of use of these models is suggested by a survey of users. A survey of one commercial financial planning language (IFPS) users found that 44% of the models were developed by middle and upper level managers. These planning languages are examples of special purpose non-procedural languages.

To illustrate the use of planning languages the following example shows the development and use of a projected (pro forma) income statement. In developing this model several analytical steps were required which may not be obvious to the reader. A starting point of this analysis was the current income statement for Wonderworks Bicycle Company which is found in Figure 13.6. These analytical steps include some of the following:

1. Determination of historical growth rates of equipment sales and service revenue.
2. Determination of the ratio of various expenses to total revenue.
3. Determination of ratio of taxes to income before taxes.
4. Analysis of expense items unrelated to growth in total revenue.

FIGURE 13.6
*Current Income Statement for Wonderworks Bicycle Company*

Wonderworks Bicycle Company

Income Statement

For the Year Ending December 31, 1988

| | |
|---|---|
| Revenues | |
| Equipment Sales | $200000 |
| Service and Other Revenues | 25000 |
| Total Revenue | $225000 |
| Costs and Expenses | |
| Cost of Equipment Sales, Service and Other Revenues | $115000 |
| Research and Development Expense | 35000 |
| Selling, General and Administrative Expenses | 35000 |
| Interest Expense | 2400 |
| Total Costs and Expenses | $187400 |
| Earnings Before Taxes | $ 37600 |
| Income Tax | 15020 |
| Net Income | $ 22530 |

### *Problem Statement: Project the Income Statement of Wonderworks Bicycle Company for 5 Years Into the Future*

To accomplish this task an analysis of historical sales growth rates and judgment of future growth rates would be required. Furthermore the model builder must decide the appropriate relationships of different planning items. In figure 13.7 is a set of assumptions for the Wonderworks Bicycle Company.

A set of planning equations was also developed to implement the model. These equations are found in Figure 13.8.

The actual planning language implementation (IFPS) is found in Figure 13.9. Notice the simplicity and the ease of use of this planning language.

The report generated by the model is found in Figure 13.10. If a formal report format is desired the language has formatting capabilities.

FIGURE 13.7

*Assumptions for Wonderworks Bicycle Company*

Wonderworks Bicycle Company

Assumptions

| | |
|---|---|
| Bicycles Sold Annual Growth Rate | 20% |
| Service Revenue Annual Growth Rate | 35% |
| Cost of Sales and Service Annual Growth Rate | 15% |
| Percent Selling, General & Admin. Expense | |
| Year 1 | .20 |
| Year 2 | .20 |
| Year 3 | .22 |
| Year 4 | .22 |
| Year 5 | .25 |
| Interest Expense | 2400 per year |
| Research and Development Expense | 35000 per year |
| Taxes | 40% of earnings before taxes |

FIGURE 13.8

*A Set of Planning Equations*

Wonderworks Bicycle Company

Planning Equations

Equipment Sales = Equipment Sales * (1 + Equipment Sales Growth Rate)

Service Revenue = Service Revenues * (1 + Service Revenue Growth Rate)

Total Revenue = Equipment Sales + Service Revenue

Cost of Sales and Service = Cost of Sales and Service * (1 + Cost of Sales and Service Growth Rate)

Research and Development Expense = $35,000

Selling, General & Admin. Expense = Total Revenue * Percent Selling Expense

Interest Expense = $2400

Total Costs and Expenses = (Cost of Sales and Service + Research and Development Expense + Selling, General and Admin. Expense + Interest Expense )

Earnings Befores Taxes = Total Revenue - Total Costs and Expenses

Income Tax = Earnings Before Taxes * .40

Net Income = Earnings Before Taxes - Income Tax

**FIGURE 13.9**

*I.F.P.S. Statements to Build and Generate a Projected Income Statement*

(a) The model in IFPS

```
MODEL WONDER  VERSION OF  01/29/90  14:26
10  * WONDERWORKS BICYCLE COMPANY
20  * PRO-FORMA INCOME STTEMENT
30  *
40  COLUMNS 1989-1993
50  *
60  * REVENUES:
70  BICYCLES SOLD = 1000, PREVIOUS BICYCLES SOLD * 1.20
80  SELLING PRICE = 200.00
90  EQUIPMENT REVENUE = BICYCLES SOLD * SELLING PRICE
100  SERVICE REVENUE = 25000, PREVIOUS SERVICE REVENUE * 1.35
110  TOTAL REVENUE = EQUIPMENT REVENUE + SERVICE REVENUE
120  *
130  * COSTS AND EXPENSES:
140  PERCENT SELLING EXPENSE = .20, .20, .22, .22, .25
150  COST OF SALES AND SERVICE = 115000, '
160     PREVIOUS COST OF SALES AND SERVICE * 1.15
170  RESEARCH AND DEVELOPMENT EXPENSE = 35000, '
180     PREVIOUS RESEARCH AND DEVELOPMENT EXPENSE
190  SELLING GENERAL ADMIN EXPENSE = 35000, TOTAL REVENUE * '
200     PERCENT SELLING EXPENSE
210  INTEREST EXPENSE = 2400, PREVIOUS INTEREST EXPENSE
220  TOTAL COSTS AND EXPENSES = SUM(COST OF SALES AND SERVICE '
230     THRU INTEREST EXPENSE)
240  *
250  EARNINGS BEFORE TAXES = TOTAL REVENUE - TOTAL COSTS AND EXPENSES
260  INCOME TAX = EARNINGS BEFORE TAXES * .40
270  NET INCOME = EARNINGS BEFORE TAXES - INCOME TAX
END OF MODEL
```

(b) The IFPS statements to run the model

```
? SOLVE
MODEL WONDER  VERSION OF  01/29/90  14:26 -- 5 COLUMNS 14 VARIABLES
ENTER SOLVE OPTIONS
? WIDTH 80, 25, 9, -1
? ALL
```

**FIGURE 13.10**

*Output Report Generated from the I.F.P.S. Model in Figure 13.9*

| | 1989 | 1990 | 1991 | 1992 | 1993 |
|---|---|---|---|---|---|
| WONDERWORKS BICYCLE COMPANY | | | | | |
| PRO-FORMA INCOME STATEMENT | | | | | |
| | | | | | |
| REVENUES: | | | | | |
| BICYCLES SOLD | 1000 | 1200 | 1440 | 1728 | 2074 |
| SELLING PRICE | 200 | 200 | 200 | 200 | 200 |
| EQUIPMENT REVENUE | 200000 | 240000 | 288000 | 345600 | 414720 |
| SERVICE REVENUE | 25000 | 33750 | 45563 | 61509 | 83038 |
| TOTAL REVENUE | 225000 | 273750 | 333563 | 407109 | 497758 |

FIGURE 13.10

*Continued*

| | 1989 | 1990 | 1991 | 1992 | 1993 |
|---|---|---|---|---|---|
| COSTS AND EXPENSES: | | | | | |
| PERCENT SELLING EXP | .2000 | .2000 | .2200 | .2200 | .2500 |
| COST OF SALES AND S | 115000 | 132250 | 152088 | 174901 | 201136 |
| RESERACH AND DEV | 35000 | 35000 | 35000 | 35000 | 35000 |
| SELLING GENERAL ADMIN | 35000 | 54750 | 73384 | 89564 | 124439 |
| INTEREST EXPENSE | 2400 | 2400 | 2400 | 2400 | 2400 |
| TOTAL COSTS AND EXP | 187400 | 224400 | 262871 | 301865 | 362975 |
| EARNINGS BEFORE TAXES | 37600 | 49350 | 70691 | 105245 | 134783 |
| INCOME TAX | 15040 | 19740 | 28277 | 42098 | 53913 |
| NET INCOME | 22560 | 29610 | 42415 | 63147 | 80870 |

The report shown here represents one set of assumptions. Typical use of this type of planning tool would involve multiple runs using various sets of assumptions. This language is interactive which allows the user to generate alternatives very quickly.

Planning languages usually incorporate simple decision models within the language. Suppose the user wanted to know what level of net income would be generated by a 20% increase in service revenue. In IFPS this is implemented with the goal what if command. Figure 13.11 illustrates the results of a what if session.

FIGURE 13.11

*A "What If" Command in I.F.P.S.*

User/System dialog to change assumptions and print three lines containing total revenue, total costs and expenses and net income

```
? WHAT IF
MODEL WONDER  VERSION OF  01/29/90  14:26 — 5 COLUMNS 14
VARIABLES
WHAT IF CASE 1
ENTER STATEMENTS
? SELLING PRICE = 200, PREVIOUS SELLING PRICE * 1.10
? SERVICE REVENUE = 25000, PREVIOUS SERVICE REVENUE * 1.20
? SOLVE
ENTER SOLVE OPTIONS
? TOTAL REVENUE, TOTAL COSTS AND EXPENSES, NET INCOME

***** WHAT IF CASE 1 *****
2 WHAT IF STATEMENTS PROCESSED
```

| | 1989 | 1990 | 1991 | 1992 | 1993 |
|---|---|---|---|---|---|
| TOTAL REVENUE | 225000 | 294000 | 384480 | 503194 | 659032 |
| TOTAL COSTS AND EXP | 187400 | 228450 | 274073 | 323003 | 403294 |
| NET INCOME | 22560 | 39330 | 66244 | 108114 | 153443 |

A goal seeking feature allows the user to determine the effects on other variables of achieving a specified goal. For example, how many bicycles must be sold to break even—other things being equal. This is shown in Figure 13.12.

FIGURE 13.12

*Goal Seeking in I.F.P.S.*

User/System dialog to execute goal seeking — altering bicycles sold each year to achieve breakeven (net income = 0)

```
? GOAL SEEKING
GOAL SEEKING CASE 1
ENTER NAME OF VARIABLE(S) TO BE ADJUSTED TO ACHIEVE PER-
FORMANCE
? BICYCLES SOLD
ENTER 1 COMPUTATIONAL STATEMENT(S) FOR PERFORMANCE
? NET INCOME = 0

***** GOAL SEEKING CASE 1 *****
```

| | 1989 | 1990 | 1991 | 1992 | 1993 |
|---|---|---|---|---|---|
| BICYCLES SOLD | 812 | 827.6 | 855.1 | 860.2 | 909.1 |

Planning languages are an excellent example of the type of man-machine interaction that is characteristic of Decision Support Systems. They exhibit the properties of flexibility and ease of use. They focus on effectiveness and emphasize a focus on the future. Finally, they focus on managerial activities and are actively used by managers. Planning languages are a key software package in an information center which was discussed in the previous chapter.

## Expert Systems

EXPERT SYSTEMS ARE COMPUTER-BASED SYSTEMS THAT ARE DEsigned to simulate the reasoning process of one or more experts. Expert systems can be though of as computer programs that act as a consultant for decision making.

One of the earliest expert systems to gain creditability as a practical tool was an expert system developed at Stanford — MYCIN. MYCIN was designed to aid physicians in the diagnosis and treatment of meningitis infections. It was designed to provide attending physicians with the advice comparable to that of a specialist in bacteremia and meningitis infections.

Within a well-circumscribed area the best of expert systems are able to perform their specialized tasks as well or better than human experts can. However, expert systems do not learn, they are limited to using the facts and rules of thumb that they are *taught* by human experts.

The component parts of an expert system are rules, an inference engine and data. These components are illustrated in Figure 13.13.

FIGURE 13.13

*Components of an Expert System*

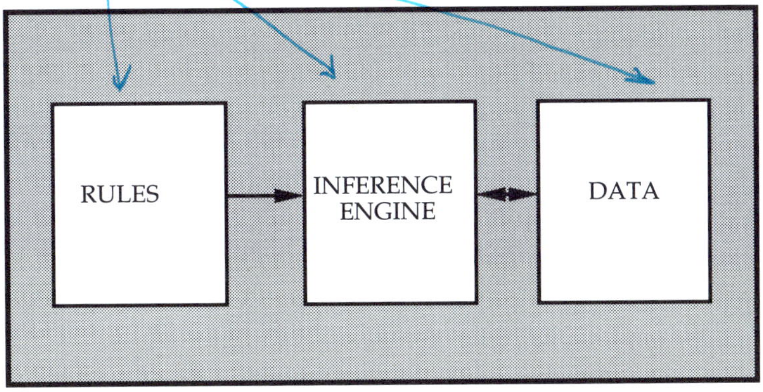


The rules represent the expert's knowledge which is stored in a knowledge base. The inference engine examines the existing facts and rules. Secondly, it determines the order in which inferences are made. In doing so it may engage the user in dialog.

Expert systems lack common sense and cannot reason by analogy. They are not designed to solve problems that go beyond the domain for which they are conceived. They are unsuited for solving poorly defined problems that are wide-ranging in scope such as analysis of a potential legal problem. Most problems of this kind require common sense and the ability to reason by analogy—qualities that expert systems do not possess.

On the other hand, expert systems are not biased nor do they jump to conclusions and maintain that conclusion in spite of contradictory evidence. They consider all the relevant alternatives and don't have bad days.[5]

## EXPERT SYSTEMS VERSUS DECISION SUPPORT SYSTEMS

Turban and Watkins have pointed out several differences between decision support systems (DSS) and expert systems (ES).[6] A DSS supports a human who makes decisions while an ES acts as an advisor. A DSS is used for broad organization-wide problems whereas an ES is used as an advisor to an individual.

DSS problems tend to be broad and complex while an ES is confined to a much more structured and limited domain. As a result DSS are more suitable for ad hoc and unique situations, while ES are more suitable for repetitive decisions. These differences and others are summarized in Table 13.1.

TABLE 13.1 *Differences Between Expert Systems and Decision Support Systems*[c]

| ATTRIBUTES | DSS | ES |
|---|---|---|
| Objectives | Assist human Decision maker | Replicate a human advisor and replace him/her |
| Who makes the recommendations (decisions)? | The human and/or the system | The system |
| Major Orientation | Decision making | Transfer of expertise (human-machine-human) and rendering advice |
| Major query direction | Human queries the machine | Machine queries the human |
| Nature of support | Personal, groups, and | Personal and groups |
| Data manipulation method | Numerical | Symbolic |
| Characteristics of problem area | Complex, broad | Narrow domain |
| Type of problems treated | Ad-hoc, unique | Repetitive |
| Content of Database | Factual knowledge | Procedural and factual knowledge |
| Reasoning capability | No | Yes, limited |
| Explanation capabili | Limited | Yes |

[c]Efraim Turban and Paul R. Watkins, "Integrating Expert Systems and Decision Support Systems," MIS Quarterly (June 1986), p. 123.

Expert systems are also characterized by an interactive dialogue which consists of questions and answers about the problem to be solved. While typically the expert system asks the questions and the user answers; the roles may be reversed and the user may ask the expert system why a given line of questioning is relevant. An illustration of an expert system dialog is shown in Figure 13.14.

FIGURE 13.14

*An Example of an Expert System*

```
ENTER THE NAME OF THE PATIENT
?A
PATIENT AGE
?62
PATIENT SEX
?M
ECG INTERPRETATION
?N
BP < 100/60
?N
CHEST X-RAY INTERPRETATION
?N
PAIN EXCRUCIATING
?N
HISTORY OF TRAUMA
?N
PAIN ANGINA
?Y
ONSET < 48 HOURS PRIOR TO ER VISIT
?Y

THE FOLLOWING TREATMENT IS
RECOMMENDED

OXYGEN
IV LINE
ADMIT
```

Whereas decision support models are computational, expert systems are logical. Input to expert systems may range from yes or no, unknown, technical terms or numeric answers.

## EXPERT SYSTEMS AND ARTIFICIAL INTELLIGENCE

Artificial intelligence is a discipline that attempts to emulate the human brain with computers. The goal is to duplicate human thought processes, communication, vision, and motor skills with a computer. There are three branches of artificial intelligence: 1) natural languages, 2) robotics, and 3) expert systems. The first area is concerned with developing computer programs that can read, speak and understand language as used in ordinary conversation. The second branch of artificial intelligence is concerned with developing robots that can *see* and *feel* so as to observe and respond to changes in their environment. The third branch is concerned with developing programs that use the symbolic knowledge of experts to make decisions.

Expert systems are built by *knowledge engineers* who capture an expert's knowledge. Since some expert systems contain knowledge that is useful but hardly the equivalent of a human expert, some knowledge engineers prefer the term *knowledge systems* instead of *expert systems*.

Artificial intelligence as a discipline is broad and theoretical. Expert systems on the other hand are narrow and applied. Many regard this shift in focus from generic problem solving techniques to an indepth focus on specific problem solving as the major conceptual breakthrough in artificial intelligence during the past 15 years.[7]

## TYPES OF PROBLEMS ADDRESSED BY EXPERT SYSTEMS

Harmon and King suggest that expert systems are useful for three broad categories of problem solving: 1) diagnosis/prescription, 2) planning, and 3) design.[8] Table 13.2 illustrates the three types of problem solving addressed by expert systems.

TABLE 13.2

*Types of Problem Solving Behavior Addressed Expert Systems*[d]

| PROBLEM SOLVING CHARACTERISTIC | DIAGNOSIS/ PRESCRIPTION | PLANNING | DESIGN |
|---|---|---|---|
| Alternate Names | Structured selection, classification | Constraint satisfaction | Discovery |
| Example | Diagnosis of an an infectious disease | Planning a project | Designing an integrated circuit |
| Input | Conditions, answers to inquiries | Goals, limitations, means | Goals, limitations means |
| Knowledge | Expert uses rules-of-thumb simple calculations | Constraints, templates, heuristics | Constraints, templates, heuristics |
| Output | Solutions, heuristics, simple calculations | Planning heuristics, templates constraints | Discovery heuristics constraints |

[d] Adapted from Paul Hormon and David King, Expert Systems, (New York: John Wiley and Sons, Inc., 1985), p. 94.

They also show the overwhelming majority of expert systems that have been built and the tools to build them are for diagnosis/prescription. In listing the commercial tools available for building expert systems only two are considered to be good for planning and none for design. This is shown in Table 13.3.

TABLE 13.3

*Types of Problem Solving Typical of Various Expert System Tools*[d]

| TOOL | DIAGNOSIS PRESCRIPTION | PLANNING | DESIGN |
|---|---|---|---|
| EMYCIN | X | | |
| ES/P Advisor | X | | |
| Expert-Ease | X | | |
| INSIGHT | X | | |
| M.1 | X | | |
| Personal Consultant | X | | |
| EXPERT | X | | |
| KES | X | | |
| OPS5 | X | X | |
| S.1 | X | | |
| TIMM | X | | |
| ART | X | | |
| KEE | X | X | |
| LOOPS | X | | |

[d]Adapted from Hormon and King, op. cit., p. 95.

The difficulty in addressing planning problems with expert systems is the tools currently available tend to lack support for what knowledge engineers refer to as *nonmonotonic reasoning*. Nonmonotonic reasoning is reasoning from tentative facts which may be retracted at a later stage of planning. The decisions and their consequences based on these *facts* must be withdrawn. The difficulty is not changing the *facts* but in tracing the decision consequences of the earlier set of facts and retracting them.[9]

## Development of Expert Systems

EXPERT SYSTEMS CAN BE DEVELOPED BY THREE GENERAL APPROACHES: purchase of an expert system package, development using an expert system shell, and custom development.

Expert systems have been developed for a number of specific applications. Some of these are sold as packages. Examples of expert system application packages are a credit card advisor which checks the completeness of a credit card application, determines the credit worthiness of an applicant, and suggests a credit limit; and a life insurance underwriting advisor which evaluates applicants for life insurance, assessing such factors as occupation and health, and suggests risk ratings and premium quotations.

A second approach to developing an expert system is using a software package that uses a predetermined strategy for building an expert system. Using an expert system shell the user has to supply the knowledge base to the system. The knowledge base includes two basic elements: (1) facts—which describe the problem situation and the theory relating to the problem area and (2) the rules or heuristics which represent the underlying decision criteria.

The final approach is unconstrained by the structure of an expert system shell but requires greater effort to build an expert system because it uses a programming language such as LISP, Prolog, or FORTRAN to build an expert system from scratch.

## Applications of Expert Systems

### SELECTING EXPERT SYSTEMS PROJECTS

Application selection is vitally important to success with expert systems. Expert systems are ideal for highly structured, repetitive decisions. They are usually confined to problems with a very narrow domain because building and maintaining a large knowledge base is resource intensive. Defining the domain of expert systems is critical since they have fragile behavior at the boundaries. A system doesn't give the right answer if the question is not confined entirely within a specified domain. This presents problems for managerial decisions since they are often based on broad interdisciplinary knowledge.

Some other criteria for selecting expert system projects would include the following:[10]

1. Problems which are not too simple (10 decision rules or less) or too complex (perhaps 200+ rules). Complex problems pose problems for current computer hardware and reasonable project completion time. Simple problems can ordinarily be handled by human experts.
2. Problems which cannot be solved by mathematical modeling techniques.
3. Problems where there is sufficient information to select a course of action and there is general agreement by experts on decision rules.

## CURRENT APPLICATIONS

Baroid's Mudman is an expert system being used in industry. Baroid invented drilling mud, a lubricant used in drilling oil wells, during the 1920s. Baroid has over 65 years of experience with drilling mud. This experience is embedded in the knowledge of mud engineers.

When drilling mud is sold to an oil firm a mud engineer is assigned to each drilling site. It takes about three years to develop a mud engineer. No decision support models are universally applicable to the problems faced by a mud engineer.

Mudman uses pattern matching and decision rules to diagnose drilling problems. It serves both the client and the mud engineer in extending the know-how available from human experts.[11]

Southwestern Bell Telephone Company has used an expert system called Automated Cable Expertise (ACE) to diagnose cable maintenance problems since 1982. This system is different from most expert systems in that it can sift through massive amounts of data to identify problems. It detects recurring patterns and may request additional data to test against its expert-derived rules. The result is that ACE can identify problems much earlier than human experts.[12]

IBM uses an expert system AOS (Automated Operations System on 3031) to run thirteen mainframes with one computer operator instead of the usual thirteen at its command center in Kawasaki, Japan. This system will be a common feature on future computer systems.[13]

An expert system to schedule truck deliveries has been developed by Fisher and Jaikumar of Dart, Inc. The model incorporates information about distance, loading capacities, time constraints, quality of roads, maximum allowable speeds, and other factors affecting delivery. Among the users are Air PRoducts and Chemicals, Exxon, Hershey Foods, Edward Don, a restaurant supplier, and DuPont. Users report efficiency has increased up to 10 percent.[14]

United Airlines has implemented an expert system with outstanding results. This system is described in When Things Go Right.

**When things go right**

## United Airlines' Innovative Use of Expert System Technology

**United Airlines has implemented a gate assignment display system (GADS) for assigning arriving aircraft to specific gates at Chicago's O'Hare and Denver's Stapleton Airports. The system is designed to assist gate controllers in making gate assignments in light of rapidly changing conditions brought about by bad weather, mechanical failure, and the domino effect of multiple delays.**

**The system makes gate assignments based on the size and capacity of the arriving plane, characteristics of the gate itself, constraints based on previous gate assignments (e.g., two 747 may not be assigned to adjacent gates) and the connecting flights of arriving passengers. GADS utilizes not only a knowledge base built on the accumulated experience of gate controllers but also taps the database for information about arriving airplanes, previous gate assignments and passengers' connecting flights.**

**The system was developed by Texas Instruments and required eight man years of effort over two years and cost $1.2 million. United Airlines claims the system saves $300,000 per month by reducing the cost of delays.**

Adapted from Harvey Newquist, "The Real Thing," Business Software Review (March 1988) pp. 53-58.

## NEAR TERM APPLICATIONS

Nissan is working on expert systems assistance for the mechanic. Automobile service has become so diversified and complex, especially with the incorporation of more electronic devices in automobiles, that it has become very difficult for mechanics to stay abreast of new developments. An expert system would guide the mechanic through the maze of possible diagnoses to reach the correct decision.[15]

The Bank of New England is developing expert systems to replace personnel in areas such as foreign exchange and credit services. It has begun to implement expert systems for consumer loans.[16]

## THE FUTURE OF EXPERT SYSTEMS

While it is clear that the application of expert systems to business problems is growing it is also clear that major improvements in the ease of use and the ease of implementation of expert systems technology is required before it becomes commonplace. That is to say that expert systems technology has great promise in a wide variety of business applications but these solutions must be cost effective.

There is a major shortage of qualified expert systems professionals. Qualified knowledge engineers and knowledge based systems designers are not being trained in sufficient numbers to meet the demand. Furthermore, the training effort lacks a systematic focus to address the needs of managers and information systems professionals. Expert systems training is often presented in jargon and excessive technical detail that does not address the interests and needs of managers.

The current involvement in expert systems is mostly a big company phenomena. Defense contractors have major projects which are aimed at integrating expert systems with weapon systems.

## Guidelines for Managers

DECISION SUPPORT SYSTEMS HAVE EMERGED WITH GREATER power in the past decade. This has been largely an end-user phenomena. Management should assure that suitable decision support tools are available and that training is available for end-users who desire and need help.

Expert systems are suitable for simulating the reasoning process of a human expert. This technology is new and there is a major shortage of qualified expert systems professionals.

## Guidelines for MIS Professionals

MIS PROFESSIONALS CAN SUPPORT DECISION SUPPORT SYSTEMS by assisting in standardizing on a few decision support tools and making transaction data accessible.

Expert systems represents a new technology that will be integrated with conventional information technology and represents a new challenge to MIS professionals.

## Key Terms

| | |
|---|---|
| Decision Support Systems | Transaction Processing |
| Dialog | Data |
| Modeling | Abstraction |
| Simplification | Validity |

| | |
|---|---|
| Prototyping | Structured Decision |
| Unstructured Decision | Semi-structured Decision |
| Executive Information Systems (EIS) | Spreadsheet Software |
| Query Languages | Statistical Analysis Software |
| Financial Planning Software Packages | Linear Programming |
| Simulation Languages | Expert Systems |
| Artificial Intelligence | Natural Languages |
| Robotics | Nonmonotonic Reasoning |

## Review Questions

1. Which of the following are examples of decision support systems and which are transaction processing?
   a. Cost Forecast Spreadsheet
   b. Cost Variance Diagnosis
   c. Monthly Production Statistics
   d. Profitability Reporting
   e. Attendance Report
2. What are the three components of a decision support system?
3. Discuss the relationship between the concepts of abstraction simplification and validity as they relate to model building.
4. Compare and contrast model building and prototyping.
5. Name the four modes of executive usage of decision support systems.
6. Discuss the advantages and disadvantages of using spreadsheet software for decision making.
7. Compare and constrast expert systems and decision support systems.
8. List the three categories of problem solving for which expert systems are useful.
9. Define Nonmonotonic Reasoning.
10. Should DSS be viewed as a threat by MIS professionals? Discuss.

**Case Study**

## FIRST RIVERSIDE BANK

Since the early 1980s, the First Riverside Bank has been known for its innovation. It was first in the city to offer credit cards and automatic teller machines (ATMs). It also developed a sophisticated computerized financial accounting system and an advanced transaction cost accounting system.

Against this background, in mid-1985, the bank found itself in trouble. Daily operations were characterized by excessive short-term borrowing to support the expanding loan portfolio. The situation was not responding to traditional management practices, and the underlying reasons were not obvious.

To tackle the problem, the top management team at the bank decided to implement a set of tools that would hopefully meet the challenge of the situation. The statement of management needs was straightforward: Something to help manage the bank at the top level, especially in the areas of profit planning and liquidity analysis.

Specific tasks called for the development and implementation of a financial planning system by the MIS department that would provide reporting, analysis and forecasting. The components of First Riverside Bank's financial planning system are as follows:

- Data: At the end of each month, summary accounting data are extracted from the general ledger system. The data are then added to the historical database which maintains up to three years of monthly figures. In addition, 12 periods of future data in the same format are maintained. These data are developed from the forecasting and simulation capabilities.
- Reports and Analysis: Each month, the system produces a full set of summary financial statements. The current monthly actual data are compared with the forecast, budget and actual for the previous year. The system also produces a series of special reports which analyze critical areas of the bank. Of particular importance is the interest rate-volume-mix analysis, and an analysis of each major segment of the bank—retail or consumer sector, public sector and commercial sector.
- Forecasts: The reports outlined above are also available for each of the coming 12 months which are forecast by the system. Independent variables may be entered by management or generated by statistical techniques with management override capability. The

bank may expand the horizon as far into the future as it desires on a monthly or quarterly basis.

The top management team is unaminous in its praise of the system; indeed the most important benefit is that it has helped make the bank more profitable. The decisions that led to the profit turnaround radically revised the financial structure of the bank. For example, based on an analysis management decided to curtail installment loan growth until additional sources of retail funds were found and to sell a sizable portion of the real estate and construction loan portfolios.

Over the past five years, the financial planning system has grown and evolved. Today, the president and each of the five vice-president's have personal computer workstations which provide them with direct access to the financial planning system.

1. Describe First Riverside Bank's pre-1985 approach to information systems. Describe the bank's current approach to information systems.
2. Summarize the impact that the financial planning system has had on the bank?
3. What decision support usage patterns has the bank employed over the years?

## Suggestions for Further Reading

Paul Harmon and David King, Expert Systems: Artificial Intelligence in Business (John Wiley and Sons, Inc., 1985).

*A highly readable explanation of the basic ideas behind expert systems. It explains not only the types of problems that expert systems will solve but also the limitations of expert systems technology.*

# 14

# ffice Automation: Improving Vhite-Collar Productivity

*"Farmer, laborer, clerk: That's a brief history of the United States."*

*John Naisbitt*

## Overview and Objectives

IN THIS CENTURY, AUTOMATION OF FARMS AND FACTORIES HAS led to dramatic increases in productivity in major occupational categories. However, similar productivity improvement has yet to affect white-collar workers. Office automation has potential as a tool for achieving this end. In this chapter, we will emphasize the often overlooked importance of including managers and professionals, as well as clerical workers, in office automation.

The major components of office automation include: word processing, electronic filing, desktop publishing and electronic mail. We will compare word processing on personal computers with word processing on general purpose computer systems and dedicated word processors, and examine their respective advantages and disadvantages.

Significant new technological developments, such as electronic filing, desktop publishing, image processing, and electronic mail/message systems, have the potential to transform the way in which office work is done. We will also examine the development of local-area network technology to facilitate the integration of office automation components.

AFTER READING THIS CHAPTER YOU SHOULD BE ABLE TO:

- Explain the white-collar productivity problem;
- Describe the components of office automation;
- Explain the advantages of various word-processing alternatives;
- Indicate the state of development of other office automation components;
- Discuss the critical role of local area networks for introducing office automation.

## White-Collar Productivity

PRODUCTIVITY IS WHAT YOU GET OUT COMPARED TO WHAT you put in. Improvement in labor productivity is the driving force behind the development of an economy as it evolves from a rural society to an advanced industrial economy.

The transformation of the U.S. labor force from an agrarian society to an industrial world power took place in a relatively short period of time. In 1820 more than 70% of the work force was farmers, by 1920 it was 40%; today, farmers constitute less than 3% of the labor force.

The manufacturing of goods occupied nearly 40% of the working population in 1920; today it is approximately 20%. During the 1960s, the decade of our greatest growth, the productivity in manufacturing increased 80%, and farm productivity increased 62%, while white collar productivity increased a mere 4%.[1] In the U.S., much of the recent economic stagnation has been incorrectly blamed on the blue collar worker. The above statistics point to the fact that the great opportunity for productivity improvement lies with clerical, managerial, and professional workers.

> "The occupational history of the United States tells a lot about us. For example, in 1979 the number one occupation in the United States, numerically, became clerk, succeeding laborer, succeeding farmer. Farmer, laborer, clerk - that is a brief history of the United States...."
>
> "The second largest classification after clerk is professional, completely in tune with the new information society, where knowledge is the critical ingredient. The demand for professional workers has gained substantially since 1960, even more dramatically than the rising need for clerical workers."[2]

The number of white collar workers currently employed is a reflection of the demand for knowledge workers in a knowledge-intensive society. It also reflects the poor record of productivity improvement with this group of workers. In agriculture and manufacturing, improvements in productivity led to dramatic declines in the number of workers in these categories.

White collar workers are composed of three distinct groups: 1) clerical personnel, 2) professionals, and 3) managers. It is estimated that white-collar workers are paid 60 percent of the total wages, salaries and benefits paid in the United States. Clearly, productivity improvement programs should not neglect white-collar workers. Furthermore, since managers and professionals are paid 80 percent of all white collar salaries, it would be a mistake to focus office automation solely on clerical workers. Indeed, many observers feel the greatest potential for productivity improvement using office automation is with managers and professionals.[3]

Achieving improved productivity with office automation has proved to be at least as difficult as factory automation. Office automation works best when it reorganizes the way work is done in an office. Simply automating existing tasks provides little productivity improvement.

There is another view that suggests that office automation should be directed at improving effectiveness not improving productivity. This point of view is expressed in Issues and Controversies.

## Issues and Controversies

### Office Automation or Office Information Systems?

**Henry Ancona, Vice President of Digital Equipment's Business and Office Information Systems does not believe in office automation. "I don't believe in automating offices. I believe in providing information to offices...."**

**Ancona believes that the goal should be to make offices function more effectively. To be more effective there must be a free flow of information. People are interested in solutions not the delivery vehicle. Computers and networks are vehicles to deliver information.**

**Office automation implies cost reduction or efficiency. It falls in the same category as the vision of the paperless society which never materialized. By increasing the effectiveness of organizations through better flow of information revenues can be increased.**

Adapted from Corey Sandler, "Digital VP Ancona: `I Don't Believe in Automating Offices'," Digital News (May 16, 1988), p. 107.

## Office Automation Components

OFFICE AUTOMATION IS JUST NOW EMERGING AS A NEW FORM of information processing. Its principle components are word processing, electronic filing, desktop publishing, and electronic mail/message systems. At this point in time office automation is still in the development stage. While parts of an office automation system exist and are being used, they have not yet been integrated into a unified system. One of the enabling technologies for office automation, local area networks, are still relatively new.

### LOCAL AREA NETWORKS

Local area networks will make it possible to tie together a variety of office automation devices, including personal computers, graphics terminals, laser printers, and a variety of office automation devices, as well as mini- and mainframe computers.

The broadband capabilities of a local-area network are required, for example, to transmit the image of a document. A typical page would need 250,000 bits to encode it in facsimile form. If transmitted over a voice-grade phone line, it would require half a minute to transmit a single page. Voice and image transmission call for a transmission medium with high capacity or broadband.

Office automation will require a local-area network to make it a reality. At present, there are several competing local-area network technologies but the two leading candidates appear to be Ethernet and IBM's Token Ring.

## WORD PROCESSING

The term *word processing* was introduced by IBM in conjunction with its first word processing product, the Magnetic Tape Selectric Typewriter - MT/ST. The most recent products show more similarity to computers than to typewriters. Word processing is the automation of text preparation, letters, reports, and narrative material; it includes input, editing, formatting, output, and printing. Word processing attempts to improve upon what typewriters have traditionally done: produce high quality text quickly. Word processing machines, however, have several capabilities that go beyond those of an ordinary typewriter. Some of the capabilities are explained in Table 14.1.

TABLE 14.1
*Word Processing Capabilities*

| | |
|---|---|
| TEXT EDITING | Creating, inserting, or deleting text characters. |
| GLOBAL TEXT EDITING | A feature that allows a word processing operator to make changes in an entire document, e.g., substitute one word for each occurrence of another word in a report. |
| AUTOMATIC PAGINATION | Word processor automatically breaks text into page size increments and numbers the pages. |
| PROPORTIONAL SPACING | Space allocated to individual characters is proportional to their width. |
| JUSTIFICATION | Alignment of right hand margin. |
| SPELLING CHECKER | A word processing program that checks the spelling of each word in a document against a dictionary and flags misspelled words. |

| | |
|---|---|
| DOCUMENT MERGING | This feature enables a form letter to be merged with another file containing variable information such as name, address, etc. The form letter which is referred to as the primary document includes special field codes which insert variable information during the merge process. |

Word processing is available in three modes: 1) dedicated word processor, which may be either single terminals or multiple terminal systems; 2) personal computers; and 3) word processing applications on general purpose computers.

Dedicated word processors are used exclusively for word processing. They are essentially computers that run a single program — a text processing program. In the past, dedicated word processor systems were the standard by which other word processing alternatives could be judged. The keyboard and other components of a dedicated word processing system are specifically designed for word processing, whereas in other cases, the systems are designed for general purposes.

Word processing software on personal computers has improved dramatically to the point that the best packages are functionally superior to dedicated word processing systems. This development is ominous for the future of dedicated word processing systems.

It appears that dedicated word processing systems are not cost effective in comparison with personal computers. Dedicated word processing systems are being replaced by personal computers or departmental mini-computers with integrated office automation systems.

The advantages and disadvantages of various word processing alternatives are described in the Table 14.2.

TABLE 14.2
*Word Processing Alternatives*

| ALTERNATIVE | ADVANTAGES | DISADVANTAGES |
|---|---|---|
| PERSONAL COMPUTER | 1. Inexpensive | 1. Generic keyboard may require multiple strokes for some functions |
| | 2. Usually easy to use | 2. Duplication of equipment |

| ALTERNATIVE | ADVANTAGES | DISADVANTAGES |
|---|---|---|
| | 3. User may create his/her own document at keyboard | |
| | 4. Can integrate word processing with other functions | |
| DEDICATED WORD PROCESSOR | 1. Several users can share printers, etc. | 1. Not integrated with organization database |
| | 2. Keyboard designed for word processing | 2. Requires either dictation or hand written copy for creating a document |
| | 3. Cost | |
| INTEGRATED WP/DP APPLICATION | 1. Access to organizational database | 1. Response time may deteriorate during peak usage periods |
| | 2. Can integrate WP and DP applications | 2. Computer failure will shut down WP |

While many managers resist having personal computers in their office, the new generation of middle managers increasingly views the personal computer as a necessary tool. Professionals especially may desire word processing capabilities. The author is acquainted with several college professors who type all their own tests and manuscripts on a personal computer. Managers and professionals who use word processing in preference to shared secretarial support may increase their own productivity and reduce the demand for secretarial services.

Word processing may have only marginal impact on the productivity of the typical secretary who types correspondence. It should have much greater productivity impact on typists who type forms such as legal documents or engineering reports. This is because, in the latter case, large portions of the report may be *boiler plate*, or text from previous reports. Correspondence is typically unique, although a form letter sent to a large number of individuals would be an ideal candidate for word processing.

Word processing is the foundation of office automation. It is highly desirable, however, to integrate word processing with other office automation functions. Desktop publishing and image processing in particular are closely related to word processing. These tools make it possible to integrate text with images such as graphs, pictures, and drawings.

## DESKTOP PUBLISHING

Desktop publishing, which began on Apple's Macintosh computer, has now migrated to the IBM PC. Page composition software, laser printers, and a Macintosh-like graphics interface are necessary ingredients to implement this new technology on the PC.

Desktop publishing is attractive to corporate publishing departments, small firms such as instant printers, and copy shops, as well as individual free-lance writer and designers. It can be used for developing newsletters, business forms, and other applications requiring both words and graphics in complex page layouts. While the quality of desktop publishing is not yet comparable to sophisticated computer typesetters used by professional designers, people with a minimum of training have been able to produce attractive, well designed publications.

The centerpiece of desktop publishing is page composition software. This software allows a user to pull together text and graphics and to format the content into page layouts with columns, captions, and so forth. Most page composition software will interface with word processing software, graphics packages, and font editors. Interfacing with these software packages extends the functionality of the page-composition program.

Page-composition software will usually dictate which software packages and peripheral devices can be used. For this reason, page-composition software should be purchased before acquiring other desktop-publishing components.

Laser printers are the most commonly used printer for desktop-publishing. These devices have a resolution of 300 dots per inch (dpi) and can print eight pages per minute. For higher resolution, a typesetter can provide resolutions of 1200 to 2400 dpi.

The future of desktop publishing is discussed in Issues and Controversies.

**Issues and Controversies**

## The Future of Desktop Publishing

Freedom of the press, the cynic said, is guaranteed only to those who own one. This remark was made some twenty years ago when publishing technology was very expensive - typically a good electronic typesetting and layout system cost several hundred thousand dollars. The advent of desktop publishing has changed all that. Anyone with a Macintosh has freedom of the press to the fullest extent.

Not since Benjamin Franklin's day have individuals had such power to be their own authors, typesetters and publishers. Small publishing firms offering a rich and diverse set of publications are springing up all over the country. Many of the culturally significant publications would never have emerged had it not been for desktop publishing.

Desktop publishing is a lot more than just pretty memos and newsletters. For example, most academic, technical and scientific publishers operate on thin margins. This means that these publishers often have to reject worthwhile manuscripts for budgeting reasons. The cost savings and efficiency of desktop publishing enable them to publish more books, and reports in a timely fashion than was possible with traditional printing methods.

Literature benefits from desktop publishing as well as science. As small publishing houses emerge because of desktop publishing, more aspiring writers can get published. Writers will have more options for publishing their poetry, short stores, plays, novels, and essays. Even though this may lead to a lot of junk getting published, some real gems will be found in the rubbish.

Don't be fooled that desktop publishing is a passing fad. The potential market for desktop publishing is enormous and is just beginning to be tapped. Desktop publishing will grow by leaps and bounds and make further encroachment on the domain of traditional publishers. Publishing is the largest U.S. manufacturing industry. Over the long term desktop publishing will become the dominant technology.

Adapted from "Gutenberg's Desktop" by Fredric E. Davis, MacUser (August 1988), pp. 11-16.

## IMAGE PROCESSING

Image processing is the creation, storage, retrieval, and reproduction of images created either by digitizing photographs, pictures, and diagrams, or by the interactive creation of these images with graphics software. This is not a new technology. The space program, for example, has used image processing technology to capture, transmit, and display images of Saturn, Mars, and Jupiter.

An image is captured by a scanning process which digitizes an image and represents the color and intensity of an image by a series of digital measurements. These digital measurements can be stored and regenerated as an image formed with rows of small dots.

Facsimile machines, which have been available before the turn of the century, and have been associated with law enforcement and the newspaper industry, were an early but crude example of image processing. A facsimile machine can be considered as the conceptual equivalent of a copy machine, which is capable of transmitting an image to a distant location, where the image is reproduced. Facsimile machines were not widely adopted until recently, because they have been slow and the image produced had relatively poor resolution. New faster data transmission allows fax machines to produce images with much higher resolution.

Most firms today have copy machines. Copy machines or their functional equivalents may provide the starting point for emerging technologies which will tie together the storage, transmission and reproduction of an image. Copy machines provide the capabilities for reproducing text as well as diagrams and pictures. Coupled with local area networks and an electronic file and retrieval capability, a copy machine could provide high quality reproductions of images that are stored and accessed by the computer. If the local image processing network is tied to a long distance network via satellite or other broad band media, the image could be reproduced at a remote point.

Ideally, image processing capabilities would include the ability to manipulate an image. Some desired features would include: 1) the ability to crop an image; 2) a capability of enlarging an image; 3) an ability to shrink an image; and, 4) the capacity to combine stored images with computer-generated graphics. These capabilities are already available with the MacIntosh computer system by Apple.

The difficulty in implementing image processing is to integrate it with other components of office automation. New technology which will facilitate the storage and transmission of images is now in sight.

Storage of images has been a particular problem because of the mass of information required to reproduce an image. Current practice is to use computer files to store text information, and paper or microform reproductions of paper documents to store images.

## ELECTRONIC FILING - RECORDS AUTOMATION

Currently, there are two basic approaches to information storage and retrieval: (1) magnetic disk storage, which has fast access times but relatively limited capacity; and (2) archiving, which relies on micrographics technology (microfilm and microfiche) to store film images of paper documents. The difficulty with archival methods is slow access time.

OPTICAL STORAGE TECHNOLOGY: Optical storage technology is an alternative to standard magnetic storage particularly for storing images. A finely focused laser beam can be used to cram at least 50 times more data per square inch than magnetic storage devices. The optical disk is also a better medium for distribution because they can be stamped out like cookies in a factory while magnetic disks still have to be duplicated byte by byte and track by track.[4]

CD-ROM: The compact disk read only memory (CD-ROM) is a close relative to the audio compact disk of the 1980s. Storage capacity on a compact disk is over 500 megabytes which is the equivalent of 25,000 pages of text or 1500 floppy disks.[5] The contents of a CD-ROM are fixed at production time usually by stamping from a master. A master disk may cost $3000 to $5000 to produce while duplicates can be made for $5 to $10.[6]

The CD-ROM as a storage medium has several advantages in addition to low cost. First, data on a CD-ROM cannot be destroyed by dust or fingerprints that can cause head crashes in current computer technology. The disk head mechanism does not touch the disk. Data should be usable for as long as the laser beam can be reflected from the surface.

Despite the fact that the CD-ROM has a very large storage capacity at low cost they have some limitations. The principle limitation is data cannot be erased, added to or edited. Another limitation is the lack of accepted standards for CD-ROM drives and interfaces between the computer and the drive. There is also no standard for organizing data on CD-ROM disks which is needed to allow software developers to develop software that would allow users to search and manipulate the data stored on CD-ROM disks.[7]

The characteristics of CD-ROM (massive storage, durability and security) make it an excellent medium for databases. Frequently, subscribers can access data on CD-ROM for less than the cost of on-line or magnetically stored data.

An example of the cost advantage of CD-ROM is the financial information available from Disclosure Information Group. They provide copies of 10K, 10Q, and 20F forms filed by over 10,000 firms with the SEC. This information is available on CD-ROM, plus he use of a CD player for $4000 per year. The same information, when accessed on line with a PC from Dow Jones or Compuserv, would typically cost $2000 to $3000 per week.[8]

New uses of CD-ROMs are being developed. British Airways has stored the entire maintenance manual for the Boeing 757 on CD-ROM. American Airlines is adding information to CD-ROMs to allow users of its SABRE reservation system to display photographs of hotel accommodations, including hotel rooms, on the same screen now used for flight and fare information.[9]

WORM: The write once ready many times (WORM) optical disk is another promising technology. It differs from CD-ROM in that the user can create images. Creating an image on the WORM optical disk results in irreversible physical changes to the surface of the disk. The WORM has many of the same disadvantages as the CD-ROM.

Capacity of WORM disks ranges from 1 gigabyte (1 billion bytes) per side for 8-inch disks to approximately 10 gigabytes per side for 14-inch disks.[10] The physical durability of the medium together combined with its enormous storage capacity make it a great alternative to huge filing cabinets or microfilm for storage of documents that should not be destroyed.

ERASABLE OPTICAL DISK: The erasable optical disk is a developing technology and is just coming to the market. It will provide at least ten times the storage capacity of magnetic media and can be erased either section by section or an entire disk at a time.

Optical disks are not intended to replace magnetic disks or archival storage methods, but to supplement these methods with a new technology that provides some benefits of both. As detailed in Table 14.3, optical disks are expected to be used for applications where access time is important and the volume of information is too great for magnetic-disk storage. Look-up applications will most likely use CD-ROM technology and the other applications WORM technology.

Optical disk capabilities are expected to be used for a variety of applications which require too-frequent access for archival storage methods and are too expensive to implement on magnetic-disk media. Magnetic disk media are currently not practical for storing images, a function suitable for optical disks.

TABLE 14.3 *Potential Applications of Optical Disk*

| LOOK-UP APPLICATIONS | CENTRAL INFORMATION APPLICATIONS | W/P APPLICATIONS |
|---|---|---|
| Catalogs | Bank information files | Correspondence records |
| Phone directories | Government files | Document storage |
| Credit information | Utility customer records | |
| Bank signatures | Engineering drawings | |
| Parts lists | Medical records management | |
| Newspaper files | Motor vehicle accident reports | |
| Dictionary | | |
| Thesarus | | |
| Legal or medial reference library | | |

The need for automated document storage and retrieval is indicated by a number of factors: 1) a large and rapidly growing document collection; 2) legal and regulatory requirements to retain records; and 3) increasing liability for faulty records.

The creation, storage, and retrieval of paper documents is expensive. Estimates place the cost of creating a letter at $6 - $18. American business firms have created and stored approximately 342 billion documents;[11] about 90% of these documents are stored in file cabinets.[12] It is estimated that the number of documents stored grows 25% per year,[13] and the cost of housing and maintaining a four drawer file cabinet is $800 per year.[14]

While optical disk technology is a promising solution to solving the storage problem, some records storage problems can be solved with micrographic technology coupled with the computer. These methods would be applicable for records which require infrequent access.

Electronic filing, like word processing, may appear to be a technology which would have the most impact on clerical workers. However, most experts believe it will have a greater impact on the productivity of professionals and managers by making information more accessible. Time studies point out that 25% of all managers' time is spent on information retrieval.[15] Thus, electronic filing systems may impact the productivity of managers to a greater extent than that of clerical workers. This is also true of electronic mail systems.

## ELECTRONIC MAIL/MESSAGE SYSTEMS

Electronic mail is a computer based system for transmitting messages. The message is created on a computer terminal and transmitted via a computer network to the intended recipient. Each user of the electronic mail system has a computer-stored *mailbox* to hold messages. Automatic distribution of messages is one advantage of this method.

A computer-based electronic mail/message system may incorporate features such as an agenda or scheduling system. An agenda/schedule facility would allow a user to look ahead for schedule of future activities or generate a current agenda. Using this feature, a user could do the following:[16]

- Block out periods of reserved time;
- Generate scheduled activities;
- Issue reminders;
- Establish priority items;
- Store and retrieve special information;
- Execute desk calculator functions.

An alternative to electronic mail is an electronic voice message system. This alternative allows the user to store and forward a telephone message to the receiver's mailbox. The message is stored as a digital pattern which can be distributed to a specific receiver or a prespecified mailing list. The recipient then plays back the message.

The principle advantages of electronic mail/message systems compared with conventional alternatives are the low cost of message preparation and the speed of distribution. In addition, the message is retained until the recipient desires to receive it. This prevents the frequent interruption of telephone messages and the game of *telephone tag*.

An electronic mail/message system is a device to improve the productivity of managers and to reduce the need for internal memos and correspondence. While electronic mail is not used for external correspondence, it allows managers to enter internal memos and interdepartmental correspondence directly without secretarial support. It also provides management with improved communication and scheduling capabilities.

## ELECTRONIC DATA INTERCHANGE

Transactions between businesses are traditionally transmitted by mail. Electronic Data Interchange (EDI) connects buyers and sellers by electronic transmission of purchase orders, invoices, confirmations, payment and administrative messages.

The advantages of EDI are that it saves time and money. Time is saved by transmitting message electronically instead of through the mail. Money is saved by avoiding data entry from paper documents.

The automobile industry is using EDI to purchase parts *just in time* for manufacturing. This avoids inventories and the paperwork associated with inventories. EDi is used to coordinate the daily exchange of goods.

EDI requires that the format in which information is sent and received are identical. Data elements must be placed in the same position on the form. Furthermore, both organizations must use the same number to identify products.

There are a number of third party firms that provide electronic transmission services to link buyers and sellers. This is a fast growing component of office automation that has real potential for increasing productivity.

## Management Concerns in Office Automation

MANAGERS IMPLEMENTING OFFICE AUTOMATION MUST GUARD against, on one extreme, automating complex manual systems, and, on the other extreme, creating narrow assembly-line-type jobs. The new technology provides both an opportunity for improved productivity and the risk of creating a set of bad jobs. The middle ground between automating an existing system and the alternative of creating a clerical assembly line should be found.

Some organizations have implemented word processing by establishing word processing pools. Secretaries who have been assigned to a word processing pool may resent the factory atmosphere and the loss of personal contact with managers. This problem parallels the establishing of typing pools when typewriters were popularized. Typing pools were soon abandoned in most organizations because they fostered poor morale, poor quality work and a lack of responsibility. These problems are particularly prevalent when a large number of users share a word processing pool. The advantages of a central pool can often be achieved by using smaller pools serving a smaller number of users.

Most observers believe that small groups of secretaries and managers make better decisions about office organization than office automation experts. The history of factory automation should suggest that workers, managers, and their organizations fare better under an approach that recognizes workers' contributions, creates whole jobs, and keeps workers motivated. A classical case of office automation is discussed in When Things Go Right.

**When things go right**

## Citibank's Implementation of Office Automation for Letter-of-Credit

The experience of Citibank in New York illustrates the "high tech-high touch" concept introduced by John Naisbitt in his book Megatrends. Citibank's "letter-of-credit" department is also a showcase example of office automation implementation. A letter of credit is a complicated guarantee by a bank of a customer's credit. For example, a manufacturer in Mexico City might desire a letter of credit to buy machine tools in Cincinnati. Prior to automation, preparation of this letter of credit often involved 50 clerks in a half dozen departments. These clerks often maintained duplicate files. Processing a letter of credit usually involved large sums of money, and because so many clerks were involved, there was substantial potential for error.

Once issued, the letter of credit would frequently require amendment. For example, a $500,000 loan for machinery might be paid out in $100,000 installments for five shipments. If one shipment was more or less than $100,000, the entire letter had to be amended.

Each clerk was an expert in some aspect of issuance or amendment. In the event something went wrong, the customer had a difficult time deciding who to talk to. Citibank decided to reorganize the entire department, despite the skepticism of some of the clerks. "You can't take 20 years of my experience and teach it to everybody else in six months," one clerk said. But within six months, the retrained clerks were able to issue a complete letter of credit using the computer to call up the necessary information and file the results.

The revamped letter-of-credit department was able to function with 55 clerks as opposed to 142 before reorganization. Job satisfaction also increased substantially, and Citibank rewarded the clerks' increased productivity with a sizeable boost in pay.

The computer obviously contributed to improvements in the letter-of-credit department. However, reorganization was possible prior to automation. Indeed, the clerks were taught the new process on paper before the new equipment was brought in.

The clerks began to deal with customers directly. Before the change, clerks never knew how their work affected customers,

**but afterward. they expressed satisfaction in seeing the overall picture. Customer contact brought about a change in the "work-station professional's" dress. Their jeans disappeared and traditional banking attire became more common.**

Adapted from Jonathan Schlefer, "Office Automation and Bureaucracy," Technology Review, (July 1983), pp. 32-40.

The great promise of the office automation concept will not be fully realized for some time. The marketing campaigns of the office automation vendors neglect to mention the problems of implementation and the difficulties of integrating various components. Implementation problems are to be expected when using new technology that changes the way an office functions. It is a familiar story. Initially, users have difficulty defining their needs and vendors cannot pinpoint them either. Office automation will arrive later than most observers originally thought, and it will take some time to pull it together in a unified package.

## WHITE-COLLAR PRODUCTIVITY: THE BENEFITS OF SIMPLICITY

As our economy becomes increasingly service-oriented, there are fewer opportunities for substituting capital for labor. Some experts believe that office automation represents the last and best hope for improvements in white-collar productivity. However, more than two decades of computerization have yielded few measureable effects on white-collar productivity.

The difficulty may be that we have automated inefficient systems. For example, during the 1960's, Citibank grew rapidly and tried to cope with the flood of paperwork by buying huge computers and adding thousands of clerks. By 1970, Citibank's backroom operations employed over 10,000 people, and customers raged about delays, errors, and the difficulty of getting mistakes corrected. The backroom was organized by function: all check encoding was done in one place, and data-entry functions in another. Responsibility for errors was lost and it was nearly impossible to get them corrected.

The solution was to replace the functional division of labor with small groups responsible for processing a particular type of transaction. For example, one group was given the responsibility of transferring funds from abroad. One person frequently performed all the steps required. Errors could be found quickly and corrected. Responsibility was clear and services improved; the backroom staff was reduced by a resounding 40%.

The lesson is that we must not automate functions that shouldn't exist in the first place or systems that can be dramatically simplified. First simplify; then automate. Ten years ago, work simplification was applied almost exclusively in manufacturing. Today, it is widely used in white-collar productivity programs.

## ELIMINATION OF WASTE

In manufacturing, the Japanese have been successful using the philosophy of Just-in-Time (JIT). Although many individuals regard JIT as a methodology to eliminate inventory, it is more than an inventory control technique. It is an aggressive philosophy which stimulates workers to identify and eliminate sources of waste. Waste can be defined as any activity that does not add value to the product or service.

In an administrative setting, there are several tasks that fit this definition of *waste*.[17] Such tasks include: batching, filing, mailing, transmitting, rush orders, routing, prioritizing and proofing. Office automation should not be applied until *waste* activities are examined. Those that are unnecessary should be eliminated. Some *waste* activities are necessary evils; billing does not add value to the product or service, yet it is necessary if one desires to be paid.

## WANKING AND BUREAUCRACY

The Australian slang word for intellectual work with no practical value is *wank*. While we have no equivalent term in our American vocabulary, the word describes a real problem often made worse by computers.[18]

> "If you take a traditional bureaucracy and give it computers," says Paul A. Strassman, "then instead of generating 30 useless pieces of paper, you generate 300. You may be worse off."[19]

Computers and office automation both can be powerful amplifiers of *wanking* and bureaucracy. Computers provide an intellectually stimulating environment for university graduates who want to remain aloof from the *grubby* concerns of making a profit. Office automation appeals to bureaucrats who create rigid procedures and forms to fill in.[20] To avoid *wanking* and bureaucracy managers must insist that computers are used for productive purposes.

## Guidelines for Managers

OFFICE AUTOMATION IS AN EXTENSION OF PERSONAL COMPUTING into the office. The requirements for success in office automation are integration, connectivity, consideration of human factors, and simplicity. MIS professionals will have a key role in integration of office automation with transaction-processing and decision-support systems.

## Guidelines for MIS Professionals

OFFICE AUTOMATION HAS PROVEN TO BE MORE DIFFICULT TO implement than originally envisioned. Some of the difficulties include integration problems and the failure to simplify systems before automation. Improvements in white-collar productivity as the result of office automation require careful analysis of existing systems, simplification and—finally—automation. This must be done in a way that is consistent with Naisbitt's notion of *high tech—high touch*.

## Key Terms

- White Collar Workers
- Office Automation
- Word Processing
- Electronic Filing
- Image Processing
- Electronic Mail/Message Systems
- Local Area Network
- Boiler Plate Language
- Desktop Publishing
- Page Composition Software
- Image Processing
- Copy Machine
- Electronic Filing/Records Automation
- CD-ROM
- Write Once Read Many Times (WORM)
- Erasable Optical Disk
- Just-In-Time (JIT) Methodology

## Review Questions

1. Discuss some of the capabilities of word processing machines which go beyond those of an ordinary typewriter.
2. Define Image Processing.
3. Which common office machine may provide the starting point for emerging technologies which will tie together the storage, transmission and reproduction of an image?
4. What are the two current approaches to information storage and retrieval?
5. Compare and contrast CD-ROM, WORM and Erasable Optical Disks.
6. What three factors are creating a need for automated document storage and retrieval?
7. What types of applications will most likely use CD-ROM?
8. Discuss the difference between an electronic mail and an electronic message system.
9. Why do attempts to automate complex office functions frequently result in 0% productivity increases?
10. Discuss why office automation has proven to be more difficult to implement than originally envisioned.

## Case Study

### PREMIER FOODS, INC.

Jim Harris, Regional Sales Manager for Premier Foods, Inc., a grocery wholesaling firm, had just returned from a 3-day trip to the northern region where he had talked to sales representatives about delivery problems with the fresh produce line. The meetings had been productive, and Harris really felt he now understood the problems that these delivery delays caused in the field.

As Harris walked into his cramped office in the company's downtown Chicago headquarters building, he knew immediately that this was not going to be a pleasant week. For one thing, his desk was covered with 25 or 30 pink phone messages from salespeople, customers, and several senior managers. For another, Harris' secretary was on the phone with the president's secretary, and it sounded like they were scheduling an important meeting with the president and all of the marketing people.

When Harris scanned the messages he realized that several needed his immediate attention. In one case, a sales representative on the West Coast needed a quotation before lunch. This meant he would have to pull out all the files on the particular grocery items being quoted, calculate all of the prices, and get any discounts approved before phoning a figure to Los Angeles. He obviously couldn't send the written quote in time, but maybe if he devoted his entire morning to that problem, he might be able to telephone a response before the deadline.

Unfortunately, the next message Harris looked at was from his boss, who needed the revised budgets for the company's new line of canned goods before the 2 p.m. meeting. Harris still needed to make a few corrections to these budgets, and then his secretary would need to type the final report. This was certain to take her most of the morning, leaving him on his own with the L.A. quote.

In addition to these two impossible tasks, however, the phone rang. "Just what I need," thought Harris, "another interruption."

1. How could Jim Harris benefit from an electronic message system? Would there be any disadvantages?
2. Providing a manager or professional with access to an electronic mail/message system is an application that is difficult to rigorously cost-justify. Why do you think this is so?
3. What other office automation technologies might help Jim Harris get his quote to the West Coast by noon?

# 15

# Manufacturing Information Systems

*"Meanwhile a naive fatih in technological silver bullets diverts manufacturers from the hard work of rebuidling North Amierica's indistrial base, and tempts them into alarming, high-risk forays toward the factory of the future."*

*Timothy N. Warner*

## Overview and Objectives

MANUFACTURING REPRESENTS THE LATEST OPPORTUNITY TO use information technology for competitive advantage. Computer integrated manufacturing (CIM) promises lower costs, improved quality and greater flexibility in adapting to change. Applying information technology on the factory floor has encountered several problems including difficulty in integrating free standing systems and elusive benefits.

Domestic manufacturers' widescale use of computers has not made them more competitive in world markets. Foreign competition is generally producing higher quality goods, with less workers and less inventory than domestic manufacturers and making significantly less use of computers.

This situation calls for a reexamination of how computers are being used in manufacturing. Currently computers are used in manufacturing primarily for inventory control, cost accounting, and production planning. Frequently, we have automated existing systems which are complex and inefficient. In contrast, our oversees competitors have simplified production systems and have obtained significant competitive advantages.

This chapter examines how computers are currently used in manufacturing and recommends computer applications that will bring substantial strategic benefits.

AFTER READING THIS CHAPTER YOU SHOULD BE ABLE TO:

- Discuss the current uses of computers in manufacturing
- Explain the new manufacturing technologies
- Identify the areas of manufacturing computer use with a high payoff
- Describe the strategic advantages of the *factory of the future*
- Explain how database technology and local-area networks are vital to computer-integrated manufacturing.

## The Current Manufacturing Environment

IN SPITE OF THEIR MORE WIDESCALE USE OF COMPUTERS THAN their foreign competitors, the inferior performance of domestic manufacturers has become a major issue. Cyert warns that U.S. manufacturing firms have three options "automate, emigrate, or evaporate."[1] This assessment is accurate in its recognition of the need for change, but may be too narrow in its prescriptions.

What types of changes are required to survive as a *world-class manufacturer*? What contribution will information technology and MIS professionals make to the factory of the future? This chapter addresses these questions. The necessity of change for domestic manufacturers can be illustrated with a comparison.

Japanese and Western European manufacturers seem able to produce higher-quality goods with less workers and less inventory than comparable U.S. firms. A Honda plant in Marysville, Ohio produces 875 automobiles per day. A Jeep factory in Toledo, about a 100 miles away, produces 750 vehicles per day. The Honda plant has 2,432 workers and occupies 1.7 million square feet. The Jeep plant has slightly more than twice the number of workers and occupies more than three times the space of the Honda plant.[2] Honda is recognized as a world-class manufacturer of automobiles. Its products are recognized for their high quality by consumer groups and trade publications. This comparison shows a domestic manufacturer uses substantially more employees, and floor space to produce slightly less vehicles.

## MRP

One of the most pervasive manufacturing information systems is material requirements planning (MRP). MRP focuses on order planning and control: when to release orders and for what quantity.

MRP systems are complex information systems requiring expensive hardware, software, and skilled people. They are designed to have material or parts delivered or produced when required for the next production task. To succeed, an MRP system requires the coordinated efforts of several functions. These include purchasing, forecasting, production control, and materials management. Vendor cooperation is also required.

An MRP system requires the following information: (1) a master production schedule, (2) a bill of materials, and (3) parts inventory. A master production schedule shows the number of units of each product that are to be produced for each time period for the planning horizon. Ideally, this plan is developed in consideration of the coordinated overall operations in the firm.

A bill of materials or product structure file contains information that identifies the components of a product. An example of a product structure tree is shown in Figure 15.1.

FIGURE 15.1 *Product Structure Tree*

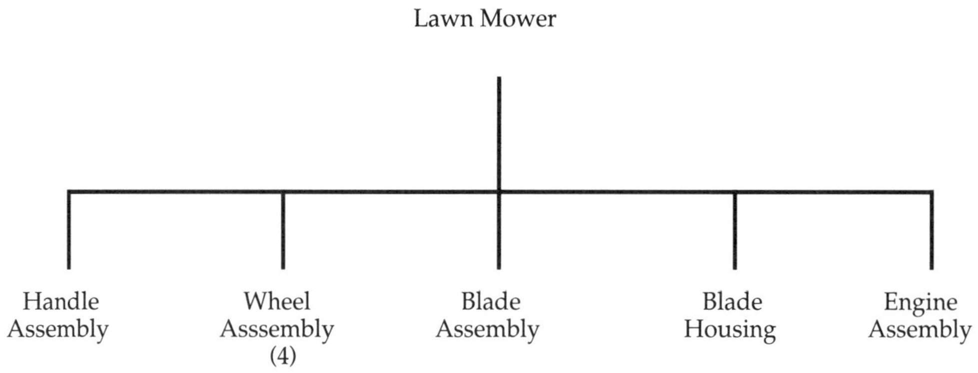


For example, a lawnmower requires four wheels, handle, blade assembly, blade housing, and engine assembly. The planned production volume of each product is exploded to reflect the components required for each production period. This requires multiplying the number of units to be produced by the number of component parts. If, for example, 100 lawnmowers are to be produced in a period, the number of wheel assemblies required would be 400. This outcome is referred to as gross requirements.

Lead time for a component represents the time between when an order is placed and when it arrives. Planned order releases take into account lead time, the time required between replacement of an order and its delivery. The lead time for each component of a lawnmower is shown in Figure 15.2.

FIGURE 15.2 *Planned Lead Times*

| Part | Weeks |
| --- | --- |
| Assemble Lawn Mowers | 1 |
| Purchase Wheels | 1 |
| Assemble Engine | 3 |
| Assemble Handle | 1 |
| Purchase Blade Assembly | 1 |
| Purchase Blade Housing | 2 |

The parts inventory is used to determine the net requirements. Net requirements is computed by subtracting scheduled receipts (open orders) and inventory on hand from gross requirements. This process is illustrated in Figure 15.3.

FIGURE 15.3 *Materials Requirements Plan*

| | Week | | | | | |
|---|---|---|---|---|---|---|
| | 1 | 2 | 3 | 4 | 5 | 6 |
| Lawn Mowers | | | | | | |
| Gross requirements | -- | -- | -- | -- | 200 | 150 |
| On-hand/scheduled receipts | 50 | -- | -- | -- | -- | -- |
| Net requirements | -- | -- | -- | -- | 150 | 150 |
| Planned order releases | -- | -- | -- | 150 | 150 | -- |
| Wheels (4) | | | | | | |
| Gross requirements | -- | -- | -- | 600 | 600 | -- |
| On-hand/scheduled receipts | 100 | -- | -- | -- | -- | -- |
| Net requirements | -- | -- | -- | 500 | 600 | -- |
| Planned order releases | -- | -- | 500 | 600 | -- | -- |
| Engine Assembly | | | | | | |
| Gross requirements | -- | -- | -- | 150 | 150 | -- |
| On-hand/scheduled receipts | 75 | -- | -- | -- | -- | -- |
| Net requirements | -- | -- | -- | 75 | 150 | -- |
| Planned order releases | 75 | 150 | -- | -- | -- | -- |
| Handle Assembly | | | | | | |
| Gross requirements | -- | -- | -- | 150 | 150 | -- |
| On-hand/scheduled receipts | 25 | -- | -- | -- | -- | -- |
| Net requirements | -- | -- | -- | 125 | 150 | -- |
| Planned order releases | -- | -- | 125 | 150 | -- | -- |
| Blade Assembly | | | | | | |
| Gross requirements | -- | -- | -- | 150 | 150 | -- |
| On-hand/scheduled receipts | 50 | -- | -- | -- | -- | -- |
| Net requirements | -- | -- | -- | 100 | 150 | -- |
| Planned order releases | -- | -- | 100 | 150 | -- | -- |
| Blade Housing | | | | | | |
| Gross requirements | -- | -- | -- | 150 | 150 | -- |
| On-hand/scheduled receipts | 25 | -- | -- | -- | -- | -- |
| Net requirements | -- | -- | -- | 125 | 150 | -- |
| Planned order releases | -- | 125 | 150 | -- | -- | -- |

The experience with MRP has been mixed. Some firms have experienced great success with MRP. Steelcase, Inc., an office furniture manufacturer, has improved its delivery performance, and dramatically improved its inventory turnover ratio. Success with MRP requires management commitment, training and discipline.

There have been quite a few failures with MRP. One of its critics believes that it is too complex. This view is discussed in Issues and Controversies.

**Issues and Controversies**

## A Simple System is Sometimes Best

**There are apparent American cultural biases that tend to favor complex solutions. American manufacturing firms commonly use an elaborate and expensive inventory control system that requires computers. This system, known as Materials Requirements Planning (MRP), requires bills of materials, lead-time estimates, inventory records, and master production schedules.**

**This method of inventory control computes the gross requirements for each component part, subtracts the inventory or scheduled receipts of the item, determines the required vendor lead time and determines when the order should be placed. The complexity of this technique can be visualized if one recognizes the combinations created by the number of component parts, different products and different variations of these products.**

**The success of MRP systems has not been very good. It is estimated that $10 billion dollars has been spent on MRP systems in the U.S. and only 25% of these installations are successful.**

**In contrast, the Japanese have had great success with a simple manual system relying on a card which instructs the supplier or the person representing the immediate upstream process to refill an order. The order quantity is a standard size known to both parties. In place of a complicated master plan, the system works by having each link in the productionchain order know what is required to complete the production schedule from the preceding link.**

Adapted from Robert E. Cole, "Target Information for Competitive Performance," Harvard Business Review (May-June, 1985), pp. 100-109.

Many manufacturers have made a false start toward improving productivity by installing MRP or the even more ambitious MRP II. Only a very small percentage has been successful. The difficulty has been complexity. The complexity has resulted from expanded product lines, functional plant layouts and the policy of storing and retrieving materials between production stages. The outcome has been a mountain of data which must be scaled to raise productivity.[3]

Companies have to break old habits to take advantage of new manufacturing technology. Automation is a process of discovering how to simplify the entire manufacturing process. There is considerable evidence that the best firms are not using MRP anymore.[4]

### INVENTORY CONTROL

Inventory control systems are very common in manufacturing. Inventory systems are common for raw materials, component parts, semi-finished goods and finished goods. The computer has expanded our ability to keep track of inventories.

Have these inventory systems enhanced our ability to compete in manufacturing? Our major competitors, the Japanese, regard inventory as waste and ordinarily do not maintain inventory systems for raw materials, component parts, and semi-finished goods. The Japanese have demonstrated that parts inventories and semi-finished goods inventories are not essential and are usually not desirable. Without inventories, sophisticated information systems are not needed for inventory tracking.

Inventory systems for finished goods are necessary to provide customer convenience. Some of these systems are highly sophisticated incorporating demand forecasting tools for each item. Many of these systems employ lot sizing formulas, which are used to determine production lot quantities. Some manufacturing firms have simplified the production process and increased their flexibility to the point that the manufacturing process can parallel the demand pattern. In this situation lot sizes can be as small as one.

The important question in inventory systems is: What inventories should we maintain and manage? Too often in the past we have maintained inventory systems that gave us no substantial benefit.

## Simplicity—The Key to Improved Production Performance

SIMPLICITY IS THE KEY TO IMPROVED MANUFACTURING PERformance. Simplification can bring about substantial gains in productivity with little or no capital investment. It prepares a factory for automation; it also avoids the common error of automating complex and inefficient production processes, which rarely give a satisfying outcome. Computers have a place in manufacturing only after simplifying materials flow and production processes. This is consistent with the philosophy of systems engineering which suggests that system improvement is the objective not just system automation.

Several years ago Ford Motor Company found that it had hundreds of accounts payable employees while its Japanese partner Mazda had only a few. By allowing warehouse workers to verify incoming supplies, Mazda simplified the accounts receivable function. Ford followed suit, reducing the number of people required to verify receipts—and cutting costs.[5]

As embodied in the *just in time* (JIT) production system pioneered by the Japanese, simplicity means reducing the number of suppliers; eliminating work in-process; reducing set-up times; reducing parts inventories; and increasing the responsibility of the worker for product quality and for maintaining the machinery.

Unfortunately, many managers think JIT is a distraction from what they really need to become more competitive—automation. Not only do managers want a high tech solution, but they also want a *big-hit-high-tech* solution that will solve their productivity problems for the next 20 years.[6]

## REDUCING SET UP TIMES

Set up time represents the amount of time required to change over a production facility from one product to another. Reducing set up time is the most important objective in simplifying the flow of materials and of production processes. Long set up times mean long production runs and large stocks of finished goods. Minimal set-up times mean a manufacturer can produce small lots and reduce finished goods inventory. The ideal set-up time is *zero*, which enables a firm to produce in lots of one. The Allen Bradley contactor production line is a good example of the benefits of achieving this objective. The Allen-Bradley factory is discussed in "When Things Go Right."

**When things go wright**

## Allen-Bradley's Assembly Line of the Future

Allen-Bradley, a Milwaukee manufacturer of industrial controls, has developed a computerized assembly line that can make different versions of a product at mass-production speeds, even in lots of a single unit. According to John C. Rothwell, no one else has achieved "the dream of the Japanese," which is "to make goods flow like water." While other firms have the ability to customize their products they cannot do it automatically without slowing down or stopping their assembly lines.

This assembly line produces contactors (devices that stop and start electric motors) and relays which are used in industrial electric motors. These products, while not as complex as automobiles or farm equipment, require 26 automated assembly stations.

The contactors and relays are assembled in a plastic casing about the size of a pocket transistor radio. Printed bar code labels are pasted on each casing, tell each station which of nearly 200 different parts to install in

**what combination. The products are all assembled, boxed and sorted by customer order automatically. The four technicians who stand by to monitor the line and unclog jams are rarely needed.**

**This assembly line is a showcase example of computer-integrated manufacturing (CIM). It integrates robots, conveyors, bar code scanners, and specialized equipment built by Allen-Bradley.**

**The results enable Allen-Bradley to boast that no competitor anywhere can beat them on price and quality. The line produces 600 units per hour with an elapsed time of 45 minutes from start to finish. This capability allows Allen-Bradley to deliver finished product the next day. It also allows them to eliminate most of their finished goods and parts inventory. The firm manufacturers everything it needs for contactors and relays except springs, coils, and screws. Springs are obtained from a local supplier on a just-in-time basis. The technicians load the assembly line with just enough raw materials and parts to take care of the next day's run.**

Adapted from Gene Bylinsky, "A Breakthrough in Automating the Assembly Line," Fortune (May 26, 1986), pp. 64-66.

## MINIMIZING THE NUMBER OF SUPPLIERS

Reducing the number of suppliers allows a firm to develop a long term relationship with its suppliers, a practice JIT practitioners believe results in improved quality. It also minimizes the number of transactions with suppliers and gives the supplier enough volume that they find it economical to make frequent deliveries—one or more times per day.

Frequent deliveries by suppliers eliminates the need for parts inventories stored in a stock room. JIT practitioners have vendors delivering parts directly to the assembly line. This eliminates parts inventories and the movement and paperwork associated with parts inventories.

## IMPROVING QUALITY

The principle benefit of JIT is greater productivity, but most Japanese firms using it also practice a complementary concept of total quality control (TQC). This concept embodies the value of *making it right the first time*, as well as worker (as opposed to quality control staff) responsibility for quality. The manager of Honda's Marysville plant expressed it as follows: "Don't accept bad parts, don't make bad parts and don't ship bad parts."[7]

## REDUCING TRANSACTIONS

The breakdown of U.S. manufacturing costs shows that materials cost 55%, direct labor 10% and overhead 35%.[8] Direct labor is no longer the major cost of production. New production strategies must be directed at other more substantial cost components. Expeditors, inspectors, and materials handling personnel are components of overhead costs. Just-in-time production eliminates the need for these personnel. Automating these functions is unnecessary and wasteful.

In the post-WWII era, the major change in manufacturing has been the increase in automation, resulting in a reduction in direct labor costs but greater overhead costs for depreciation, maintenance, and technical staff. Current accounting and information systems, with few exceptions, have not kept up with this change and are attempting to focus on further reducing direct labor costs. The result has been a rapid growth in overhead costs. Miller and Vollmann show that these overhead costs are directly related to the volume of transactions.

Transactions relating to overhead costs include the following:[9]

1. Logistical transactions—transactions related to the movement of materials from one location to another.
2. Balancing transactions—transactions that attempt to ensure that materials, labor, and capacity are in balance with demand.
3. Quality transactions—transactions which include quality control, identification, and certification of specifications, and procurement.
4. Change transactions—transactions which update information systems to accommodate engineering changes, changes in schedules, standards, materials specifications, and bills of material.

Managing transactions is the key to controlling overhead costs. JIT minimizes transactions by simplification, with particular impact on logistical and balancing transactions. This benefit of JIT is often overlooked in place of more visible effects such as reduced inventories.

## GROUP TECHNOLOGY

Group technology is an old concept which is now receiving more interest as a component of flexible manufacturing systems and JIT production. The first step is to identify parts with similar characteristics and group them into *part families*. Similarity is determined by processing characteristics. The general size and shape of a part family should be the same so that the equipment of the same type and capacity can be used in manufacturing members of the parts family.

The key to group technology is a classification and coding scheme designed to capture the geometric characteristics of parts. This geometric data is stored in a database and is routinely used for selection and analysis. Information about parts is accessible through a variety of query and analysis programs.

Group technology isn't a matter of buying new equipment, it's a matter of using existing equipment in a more efficient way. Most manufacturing plants use a functional layout, grouping similar machines together. This results in wasted time moving material from one department to another. This layout is depicted in Figure 15.4.

FIGURE 15.4

*Functional Layout of Gear-Making Plant*[a]

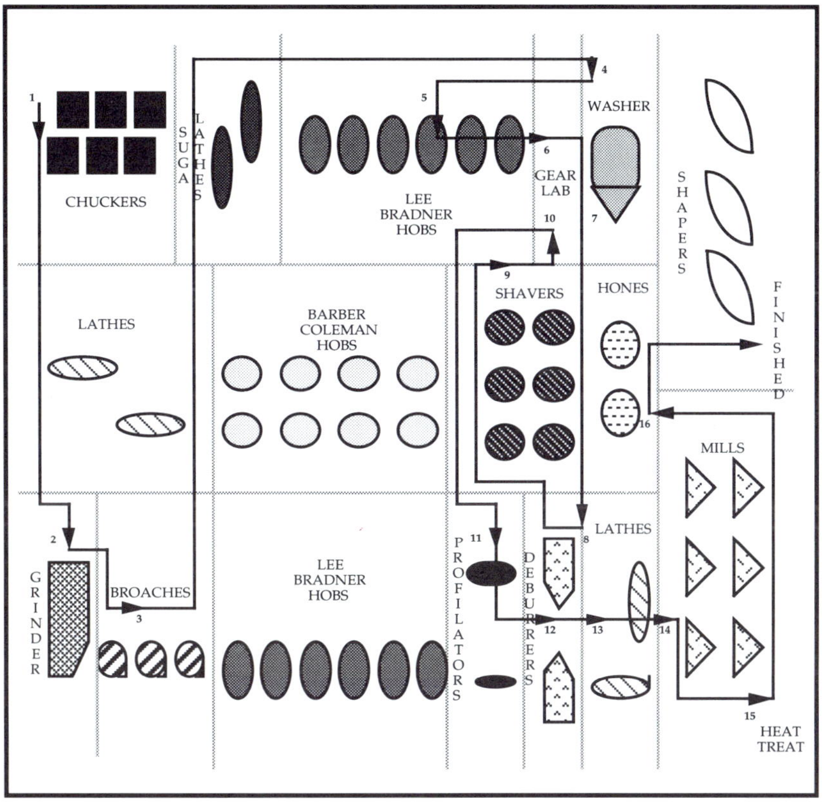


[a]Trends in Information Technology, 3rd Edition © Arthur Andersen and Co., 1987, p. 76. Used by permission.

The second step in applying group technology is to arrange the equipment required for manufacturing a part family into cells. Typically, the configuration of a group technology cell is U shaped, which permits one person or robot to tend a number of machines without moving very far. The result of group technology organization is a group of small plants (cells) within a plant.

The benefits of group technology are reduced set up times, simplified work flow, and reduced work in process. The disadvantages are the expense of classifying parts into families, the expense of repositioning equipment, and some possible duplication of equipment.

The alternative group technology layout speeds up the production process, minimizes material movement and saves floor space. In group technology a cell is dedicated to a part family. Set up is simplified because of similarities between parts. This configuration is illustrated in Figure 15.5.

FIGURE 15.5

*Group Technology Layout of Gear-Making Plant*[b]

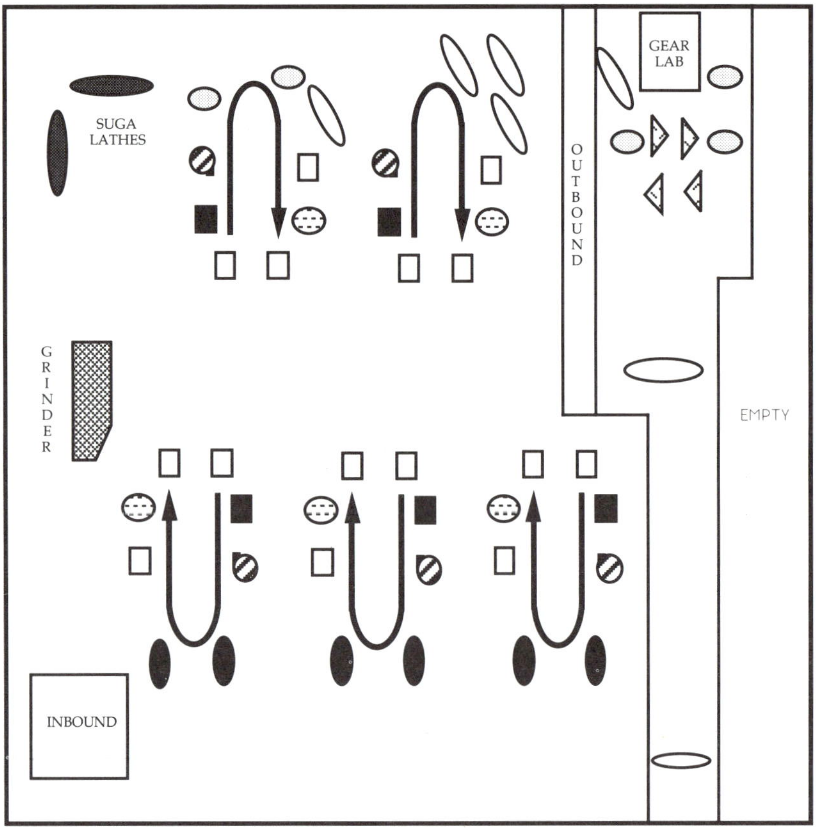


[b]Trends in Information Technology, 3rd Edition © Arthur Andersen and Co., 1987, p. 76. Used by permission.

Group technology is a method of building little *focused factories* or a *plant within a plant*. By focusing on the production of part families it simplifies manufacturing. Group technology is also complementary to JIT and automation.

Schoenberger believes that continual and rapid improvement is necessary for firms to excel in today's manufacturing environment. This is possible if they apply the lessons of simplicity. He indicates the benefits of simplicity are:

1. Better maintenance with less maintenance personnel.
2. Better quality with fewer quality control personnel.
3. Better accounting with fewer accountants.
4. Better production control with fewer production controllers.
5. Better materials management with fewer materials staff.[10]

## Automation - New Manufacturing Technologies

EFFECTIVE FOREIGN COMPETITION HAS BEEN THE CATALYST FOR rapid changes in manufacturing technology. Firms have also recognized the importance of manufacturing as a competitive weapon. Technology has frequently been viewed as a means of achieving lower manufacturing costs. The difficulties of implementing and integrating new manufacturing technologies are often underestimated, and consequently, the results have frequently been disappointing.

There are, however, several promising new manufacturing technologies. Robots are one of the most visible of these new developments.

### ROBOTICS

Robots are programmable machines which perform materials handling and other production tasks. The distinction between a robot and other automated manufacturing equipment is the robots' capacity to be reprogrammed. This makes them more flexible than other alternatives. Robots are particularly useful for tasks that are uncomfortable or dangerous for human beings to perform. Some of these tasks include painting, welding, positioning, assembly, changing fixtures and tools, and drilling. Robots may also be useful for tasks that human beings find repetitive and boring.

A new generation of robots incorporate a vision system that enables the robot to perform a wider variety of tasks. These new capabilities include the ability to sort through a variety of parts to select the right one, inspection of a part for dimensional accuracy and the ability to pick up a randomly positioned part without damaging it.

## COMPUTER-AIDED DESIGN / COMPUTER-AIDED ENGINEERING

Computer-aided design (CAD) is a computer based system that improves engineering design productivity. It uses an engineering workstation to automate the design process. The capabilities of CAD systems include geometric modeling, stress and strain analysis, drafting, storing specifications, and simulation of a mechanism's parts. This allows several design alternatives to be explored.

GEOMETRIC MODELING: Geometric modeling systems use computer graphics and processes to create and modify engineering designs. The CAD system allows the designer to describe a part in terms of lines, angles, and shapes. These specifications are used to develop a visual representation of the object being designed.

The simplest CAD systems represent objects in two dimensions with solid lines sometimes referred to as wire frame models. More sophisticated representations show three dimensional images using dashed lines to represent the portion of the object which would be hidden. Some CAD systems will show three dimensional solids in color to represent a part.

The output of a geometric modeling process is mathematical specifications which describe the shape and size of the object. This data is stored in a database shared with other engineering design processes.

AUTOMATED DRAFTING: Automated drafting systems are used to create hard copy engineering drawings from the specifications created by the geometric modeling process. Automated drafting systems replace manually-drafted engineering drawings, and usually result in significant productivity gains.

Automated drafting systems can produce a drawing of a part from different perspectives by rotating it. This flexibility gives the viewer a more realistic idea of how the object would actually appear.

COMPUTER-AIDED ENGINEERING: This process is an analytical step which assists the CAD designer. Analysis features of CAD systems compute surface area, weight, volume, center of gravity and the moment of inertia. More advanced CAD systems can compute strain calculations, heat transfer characteristics and can simulate the dynamic behavior of the part being designed.[11] This capability allows the designer to examine various design alternatives and make tradeoffs. The objective of design evaluation is to improve the performance of a part, substitute another less expensive but satisfactory material or to simplify the steps required to manufacture a part.

## COMPUTER-AIDED MANUFACTURING

Computer-aided manufacturing (CAM) is the use of computers to control automated equipment on the factory floor. CAM has replaced an older technology referred to as numerical control. Numerical control allows a machine to operate automatically through the use of a set of coded instructions. Until recently, these instructions were coded on paper tape which directed the operation of the machine much like a player piano roll.

A CAM system using data generated by a CAD system can quickly and accurately generate the instructions for computer-controlled factory equipment. This makes a manufacturing process highly flexible by reducing set-up times; in other words it permits the manufacture of small batches, shortening lead time and reducing inventory.

## BAR CODING

Bar coding is a technology that has been around for some time but has only recently been applied in manufacturing. Most of us have encountered bar coding in the form of UPC codes in grocery stores. Many grocery stores have laser scanners which read the bar code, identifying the price, the manufacturer, and the product. This technology is highly reliable; a U.S. Department of Defense study shows only four errors in reading over a half million labels averaging 24 characters each.[12]

While the bar code technology has been widely applied in warehousing and packaging, only recently has it received much attention in the manufacturing process. Allen-Bradley uses bar codes to identify different products on the assembly line. The bar code label tells all the machines on the assembly line which operations to perform. Flexible assembly machines respond to bar codes to make nearly instantaneous changes (set-ups) without slowing production. For example, when a bar code tells a screwdriver assembly that a larger version of the product is approaching, it positions itself accordingly.

Allen-Bradley found that the key to producing in lots of one is finding a way to identify products on the line so the line would not have to be slowed or stopped for set-up. The breakthrough came when engineers decided to identify products with bar codes.[13]

## COMPUTER-AIDED PROCESS PLANNING

Process planning is concerned with determining the sequence of manufacturing operations required to produce a given part or product. While this task has traditionally been performed by manufacturing engineers there are potentially great differences of opinion among process planners as to what constitutes an *optimal* method of production.

Computer-aided process planning is a major opportunity area for automation and integration. Process planning typically consumes nearly 50% of a company's manufacturing engineering staff and drives all downstream functions. It is usually dependent on the expertise of a few key people and its results are inconsistent.[14]

Computer-aided process planning (CAPP) offers a number of potential advantages over manual process planning. A CAPP generated sequence of manufacturing operations, referred to as a route sheet, is more likely to be consistent, logical, and optimal than a manually generated alternative. In addition, CAPP increases the productivity of process planners, reduces the time required to produce a route sheet, and the output is neater and easier to read than manually written route sheets.

**Integration - Linking *Islands of Automation***

CURRENT MANUFACTURING TECHNOLOGIES ARE OFTEN USED as *stand-alone* applications. Examples would include numerical control machines, robots, MRP and CAD. Many of these components of computer integrated manufacturing have substantial benefits but are less effective as *islands of automation* than as part of an integrated whole.

The objective of CIM is to integrate these stand-alone applications into the factory of the future. Two of the key technologies for accomplishing this integration are local area networks (LANs) and database management systems.

## MANUFACTURING DATABASE

Database management systems (DBMS) provide a mechanism for integrating engineering, manufacturing operations, and manufacturing administration applications. The relationship of these three functional areas is shown in Figure 15.6.

FIGURE 15.6

*A Computer Integrated Manufacturing System (CIM)*

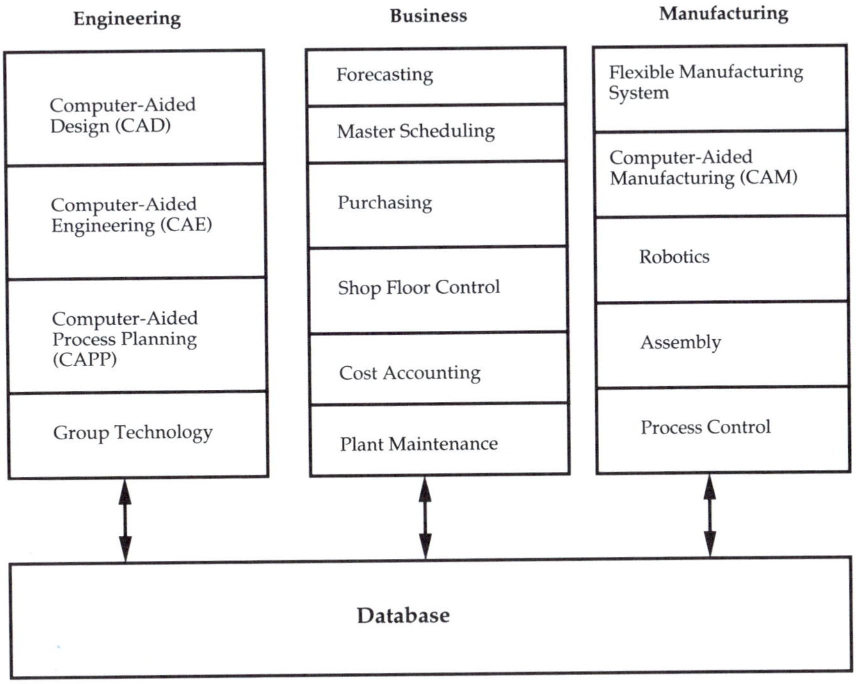


A computer integrated manufacturing system provides a shared database that makes it possible to link engineering, manufacturing operations, and manufacturing administration information systems. Bentley Nevada, an industrial instrumentation manufacturer, found the key to success with CIM was a single, unified database that would serve all departments, not just engineering. Weyerhaeuser, the integrated lumber and paper firm, also found that a shared database was critical to its success with CIM.[15]

Engineering systems develop two types of data critical to a computer integrated manufacturing: (1) product data and (2) process data. Product data is the data developed by a CAD system. It is data about the objects to be manufactured. It consists of text, alphanumeric and geometric data. For example, it may consist of a part number, a part description, and geometric data describing the configuration of the part.

The object of a part database is to develop a mechanism for organizing, storing and retrieving designs. This enables an engineer designing a new product to use an existing standard part instead of creating a new one.

Process data includes data describing the sequence of production steps and the gross machining requirements at each step. This enables a CIM facility to cope with the complexity of a multiple product environment and to reconfigure it for different parts.

The language used in CAD is primarily geometry-based with the results from a designer stored in computer form as points and equations. This data allows lines, arcs, and circles to be combined and displayed as representations of finished parts. CAM, however, has a different language. Terms like *hole*, *notch*, *slot*, and *groove* have meanings in a manufacturing environment. These attributes of parts are used to interpret geometric drawings and make manufacturing process decisions. One of the major challenges of CIM is to represent part features in a common language in a data structure that is accessible to either CAD or CAM applications.[16]

Manufacturing operations data is data which defines the machine instructions required to manufacture a part. This is the equivalent of numerical control tapes. Operations data would include the instructions for integration of all components of a CIM system.

Manufacturing administration requires data information about the accounting function including cost accounting, accounts receivable, and payroll. It also includes data describing purchasing, finished good inventories, and forecasting.

The basic concept of computer integrated manufacturing (CIM) is to develop an automated factory linked to a computer-aided design and engineering facility. A system such as this would enable a firm to manufacture high quality one-of-a-kind products almost overnight.

Currently, automation exists in the factory primarily in isolated *islands of automation*. CAD systems are unable to communicate with numerically controlled milling machines, each machine requires a different set of commands. It's as if a user were trying to play a piano with the instructions that give the fingering for a clarinet. To resolve this problem common interface and communication standards are required which will permit different types of factory systems to communicate with each other.

GM has recognized the difficulty of developing a coherent system from incompatible machines and is attempting to solve the communication problem with Manufacturing Automation Protocol (MAP). This development will encourage machine tool manufacturers to adhere to the defacto MAP standard.

## MAP

A major problem in developing the factory of the future is to link the islands of automation. The difficulties of integrating the various machines that comprise the factory of the future has been a major barrier to Computer Integrated Manufacturing (CIM).

General Motors has sponsored a project to develop a local area network suitable for the production floor. Manufacturing Automation Protocol (MAP) is setting a standard for communication between equipment on the factory floor.

In technical terms, MAP is a local area network which uses a bus topology, and a token passing access methodology. This makes it suitable for the factory floor, where predictable access to the computer is highly desirable. MAP is less suitable for office use, so business functions such as procurement, inventory control, etc. would most likely use another local area network.

## Use and Misuse of Computers in Manufacturing

SCHOENBERGER, IN HIS BOOK *WORLD CLASS MANUFACTURING*, points out that computers are frequently misused in manufacturing. He says that

> ...compared with the rest of the world, American manufacturers make more use of computers in managing maintenance, quality, accounting, production control, and materials.
>
> As we have seen, WCM (World Class Manufacturing) causes each of these functions to be simplified and reduced. Data processing is cut at the same time....It is

> no small irony that I hear about this kind of action most often in companies that produce and sell computers.
>
> The computer does have a bright future in the factory. That future is mostly in direct process control and not so much in information systems to support staff and management.[17]

Schoenberger's point is that we have automated complex administrative manufacturing systems and the results haven't been very satisfying. He suggests we will get far better results by first simplifying our manufacturing systems and then applying computer automation to activities where it is appropriate. Some of the activities in which the computer may play a central role are premanufacturing activities.[18]

## PREMANUFACTURING

Schoenberger believes the computer is of particular value for what he terms major events. Major events include new products, new orders, new rates of production, new processes and new product designs.

ORDER ENTRY: GM of Canada has instituted a program in which suppliers receive their orders by a direct computer to computer linkage. Furthermore, GM has given many of these suppliers access to its computers for the purpose of examining the inventory records for those parts which the vendor supplies. This linkage assists in establishing a cooperative partnership between GM and its suppliers.

DESIGN: Computer-aided design (CAD), and computer-aided engineering (CAE) assist in increasing the productivity of engineers designing new products or modifying old products. The computer allows designers to access a database of standard parts, so as to avoid adding unnecessary new parts.

MASTER PRODUCTION SCHEDULE: A master production schedule is useful even for a repetitive manufacturing environment. For regularly scheduled products, the final assembly schedule is equivalent to a scheduled production rate. The bill-of-materials processor is also useful to determine the production rate for component materials.

Cut-over: For repetitive manufacturing a materials requirements planning (MRP) type program is useful for determining the cut-over date for each component when the production rate is changed. Between production rate changes, the MRP program would not be useful for routine work order scheduling, since JIT would take over.

Purchasing: Some firms use bar codes on shipments from suppliers to confirm receipt of regular orders and initiate payment by accounts payable.

## Process Control

Computers have a big role in process control in industries which use continuous processing. Organizations processing water, gases, chemicals, ores, foods, rubber, flour, spirits, cements, petroleum, paints, milk and drugs are typically highly automated and frequently operated under computer control.

Robots, numerical control machine centers, and flexible manufacturing systems operate under the supervision of a computer. The computer permits these machines to be reprogrammed to make different products. The flexibility of numerical control machine centers and flexible manufacturing systems are typically limited to similar products.

## Materials Management

The conventional wisdom of materials management leads to double handling of inventories and elaborate inventory control systems to keep track of inventory. Double handling occurs when the firm receives inventory and places it in the storeroom. Later, the storeroom receives a materials requisition and moves inventory from the storeroom to the assembly line. Not only is the physical double-handling of inventory unnecessary, so are the transactions recognizing this change-in-inventory status. This paperwork sequence entails considerable overhead expense.

In contrast, many firms avoid not only physical double handling of inventory and the associated transaction costs, because materials are delivered just in time for production and are never recognized as inventory. Savings include less space to store inventories; less equipment to handle it; less inventory accounting; and less physical inventory controls.

## A Contingency View of Automation

GENERALLY SPEAKING, MANUFACTURING CAN BE DIVIDED INTO three stages: an assembly stage, a sub-assembly stage, and the component stage. Automobiles are assembled in plants, for example, that are designed to produce finished products from sub-assemblies. Sub-assemblies would be engines, transmissions, frames, and bodies.

Sub-assemblies manufacturing may involve several stages. An automobile engine which is considered a sub-assembly requires sub-assembly components including a carburetor, starter, fuel pump, alternator, and a water pump.

Component manufacturing is concerned with producing parts for sub-assemblies. For an automobile engine components would include: pistons, piston rings, cam-shafts, valves, connecting rods, and crankshafts.

It can be argued that components' product life cycles are longer than sub-assemblies and sub-assemblies' longer than finished goods. Flexibility in moving from one generation of products to another is highly desirable for finished goods. Robots and other components of CIM may take considerable time to set up for new products. Thus, it makes more sense to focus automation efforts on the most stable components of production—components and sub-assemblies.[19]

There are some obvious exceptions to this generalization. G.E. has automated its appliance assembly operations reducing the manufacturing cycle for dishwashers from five days to several hours and boosted market share from 30% to 40%. G.E.'s highly successful efforts at automation has cut employment at their Appliance Park complex from 19,000 to 10,000 and boosted output.[20]

Process industries which produce products or commodities with long product life cycles would be excellent targets for automation. Examples of these would be chemicals, and food products such as pasta and cereal.

## Advantages of the Factory of the Future

THE ADVANTAGES OF THE FACTORY OF THE FUTURE ARE LOWER costs, increased flexibility, and improved quality. CIM decreases use of raw materials by reducing scrap and defective products, increases the ability of the firm to make late design changes, and reduces manufacturing errors. Allen-Bradley found that its success with CIM led to more flexibility as well as reduced inventories and better quality.[21] In the past, manufacturing was based on the assumption that large production lots produced low costs. This resulted in long production runs, rigid product specifications, and large finished goods inventories.

The economics of the factory of the future are quite different. It can be just as cheap to produce a variety of products as it is to produce a single product. Using flexible automation, it does not matter whether twelve identical units are produced or a dozen different products.

## FLEXIBILITY

Flexibility refers to the ability of an organization to respond to changes in market demand. These changes can involve a change in product design, product mix, or product volume. There are great benefits in flexibility. One of the primary benefits is that the firm can manufacture the mix of products which correspond with customer demand resulting in great savings in inventory.

Product variety and customization is less important to consumers than quality and low price and this means mass production. Flexibility is important, therefore, not so much for customization but in the changeover from one mass-produced product to another.[22]

## QUALITY

Quality refers to the fitness of a product for its intended use; it can often be more important than price as a competitive weapon. Most authorities on quality agree that the key to quality is to *make it right the first time*.

Automated production is more reliable, more accurate, and more predictable than manual production alternatives. This leads to improved quality.

## DELIVERY

Delivery refers to the ability of the manufacturing organization to deliver its product to the customer when desired. In the past, this was accomplished by maintaining finished good inventories.

The factory of the future may be located close to the customer. Smaller distributed factories may avoid shipping and inventory-holding costs by locating near population centers and not producing the product until an order is in hand.

## COST

Some manufacturing experts believe that CIM would enable countries with high labor costs to leapfrog their low cost competitors. Because labor costs with CIM are minimal, it would reverse the competitive advantages of cheap foreign labor in favor of quick turnarounds and low inventories. The ideal location of a CIM factory would be in the market where its products are sold. This would minimize shipping and warehousing costs.

What is delaying the arrival of the factory of the future? A mixture of managerial caution and *islands of automation*. CIM represents a long term commitment and major changes in organization and culture. The implications of this concept will uproot traditional precepts in manufacturing, marketing, finance, and business planning.

Several firms that have tried and failed to implement CIM, failed because they attempted to apply a *quick technical fix* to an inefficient production system. The key to success is to first simplify and then automate. Automating complex and inefficient production systems is much more difficult than introducing CIM to one that has been simplified.[23] John Deere, the agriculture equipment manufacturers implementation of CIM is described in When Things Go Right.

**When things go right**

## CIM at Deere

**At John Deere, CIM may be the answer to a double whammy. Deere, like other manufacturers, has been buffetted by the ill economic winds that have created the *rust belt*, and its marketplace still lies at the heart of the depressed corn belt.**

**Farmers have had a difficult time surviving, much less purchasing giant harvestors that can cost in excess of $100,000 each. This shrinking market has forced Deere to innovate.**

**Deere started their CIM implementation process by streamlining their factory floor operations. This simplification process happened before they began selecting software and hardware.**

**Deere implemented a group technology (GT) system. The object of the GT system was twofold; first, to avoid creating duplicate part designs and second, to create manufacturing cells. Deere found that developing a new part cost $8,000**

**before it was actually manufactured.**

**The GT program was implemented by rearranging the plant floor into manufacturing cells which included different types of machines according to the kinds of products they produced. This required grouping together milling machines, drilling machines, and boring machines into GT cells. The result was a 70% reduction in the number of departments a part had to go through, and a 25% reduction in the number of machines required. During the first 18 months of operation, the GT system saved more than $9 million.**

**Deere was the first manufacturer to use MAP in production mode, creating a manufacturing cell that used a combination turret press/laser machine to cut sheet metal into hundreds of shapes and to punch a variety of holes into these shapes. This machine creates an annual return on investment of up to 34%.**

Adapted from Robert Knight, "Plan First, Then Use CIM," Software News (December 1987), pp. 61-65.

Information technology will play a key role in transforming manufacturers into world class competitors. But not now, at least for most firms. They are faced with the difficult task of improving their production processes before injecting a dose of information technology.[24]

## Guidelines for Managers

MANAGERS MUST BEWARE OF THE BELIEF THAT INFORMATION technology can solve all of their manufacturing problems. Success with information technology will come after simplification of manufacturing processes, followed by automation and then by integration. Powerful new integrating technologies are available to allow engineering, manufacturing, and administration to share data. Automation and integration are an incremental process not an event.

## Guidelines for MIS Professionals

INFORMATION SYSTEMS PROFESSIONALS ARE NOT USUALLY familiar with manufacturing. Information systems professionals should become familiar with the manufacturing environment and resist the temptation to believe that an inventory control package will make manufacturing competitive. Success will be found in implementing the computer in direct process control applications such as CAD/CAM or CAPP with less emphasis on inventory control, cost accounting, and production control.

## Key Terms

Materials Requirements Planning (MRP)

Inventory Control Systems

Just-In-Time (JIT)

Total Quality Control (TQC)

Group Technology

Part Families

Focused Factories

Robotics

Computer Aided Design (CAD)

Computer Aided Engineering

Geometric Modeling

Automated Drafting Systems

Computer Aided Manufacturing (CAM)

Bar Coding

Computer Aided Process Planning (CAPP)

Computer Integrated Manufacturing (CIM)

Materials Management

Manufacturing Automation Protocol (MAP)

Local Area Networks (LANs)

Premanufacturing

Database Management Systems (DBMS)

Process Control

World Class Manufacturing (WCM)

## Review Questions

1. What is the major difficulty that has caused mixed results in terms of improving productivity for many U.S. manufacturers?
2. What is the most important objective in simplifying the flow of materials and production processes?
3. Explain the two types of data critical to computer integrated manufacturing.
4. Compare and contrast group technology layout with functional layout.
5. What force has been the catalyst for rapid changes in manufacturing technology?
6. What is the difference between a robot and other automated manufacturing equipment? What are the tasks for which robots are particularly well suited?
7. Discuss the advantages that computer aided process planning (CAPP) offers over manual process planning.

8. Define Manufacturing Automation Protocol (MAP). MAP represents a possible solution to what problem?
9. How can JIT techniques improve materials management?
10. Discuss the four main advantages of the factory of the future.

**Case Study**

## ALLEN-BRADLEY: MANUFACTURING SURFACE MOUNTED CIRCUIT BOARDS

Allen-Bradley built a successful CIM plant in Milwaukee to build contactors and relays. But, contactors conform to worldwide standards and seldom change. When Allen-Bradley began to plan its printed-circuit board plant it realized it would be a far more difficult task than manufacturing contactors. The plant was to be designed for assembling 350 different boards and producing a total of 10,000 boards per month. Furthermore, there was a need to integrate constantly changing design elements. To insure competitive advantage it was important to cut the time needed to design the complex surface mounted circuit boards and place them into production.

Before CIM it took up to three weeks for CAD drawings to pass through a number of manual steps which determined machine selection, sequence and produce the punched tape instructions for the machines which manufacture circuit boards. The solution was to have the CAD groups extract engineering information and place it in four standard database tables. The four tables describe printed circuit board positioning, physical shape, pin connections and the electromechanical characteristics of components. These four tables provide a standard interface between CAD and CAM. The information in these tables is used to generate programs that assemble and test circuit boards. Furthermore, it allows manufacturing to purchase new CAM equipment without affecting the engineering design process or engineering to alter the CAD system without affecting manufacturing. The result has been a reduction in the time for new designs to be placed in production from weeks to a few hours. Furthermore, the plant can manufacture a batch of boards from start to finish in a single day compared with 15 days using the previous semi-automatic process.

Another advantage of Allen-Bradley's CIM process has been the achievement of near-zero defects in product quality. This result has reduced scrap, warranty, replacement, and repair expenses. Customer satisfaction has improved and Allen-Bradley expects to have less need to rework products and reduce inspection.

Adapted from Dennis Livingston, "Pulling It All Together," Mini-Micro Systems (September 1988), pp. 110-117.

1. What is lead time and why is it important?
2. What does this illustrrate about the benefits of CIM?
3. What was key to integrating CAD and an automated factory?

## Suggestions for Further Reading

Trends in Information Technology, 3rd Edition (Arthur Andersen and Co., 1987)

*This is a handbook for managers who must understand information technology in a competitive context. The chapter on trends in computer integrated manufacturing is of particular interest. It points out that CIM implementation should follow a simplication phase.*

# 16

# Computers and Society

*"The new source of power is not money in the hands of the few, but information in the hands of the many."*

*John Naisbitt*

## Overview and Objectives

THERE IS CONTINUING DEBATE ABOUT THE MERITS OF A POST industrial society or, as some have dubbed it, *the information society*. Does an economy have to give up its manufacturing sector to make the transition to a society dominated by services, knowledge workers and creative professionals?

Thirty years ago Leavitt and Whisler predicted that information technology would create centralized organizations and reduce the requirement for middle managers. We shall investigate whether these, and other changes have in fact been brought about. Specifically, what changes in organizations and society can be attributed to information technology?

AFTER READING THIS CHAPTER YOU SHOULD BE ABLE TO:

- Describe the characteristics of a post industrial society.
- Explain the effects of information technology on organizations.
- Discuss the impact of information technology on middle management.
- Illustrate the connection between human assets and information technology.
- Discuss the special problems of information ethics.
- Explain some of the hazards to information security created by information technology.
- Explain how information technology has created new business opportunities for entrepreneurs.

## The Post Industrial Society

DANIEL BELL HAS ARGUED THAT CHANGES IN THE ECONOMY, technology, and the occupational system have transformed the U.S. economy from an industrial society to a post-industrial society.[1] He suggests that we may recognize a post-industrial society by several criteria: the first is that a majority of the work force is no longer engaged in agriculture or manufacturing, but in services.

The second criterion is the growth in professional and technical occupations. In 1979, the number-one occupation in the United States, numerically, became clerk, succeeding laborer, succeeding farmer. The second largest occupational classification is professional, completely in tune with the information economy. Professional workers are almost all information professionals—lawyers, doctors, teachers, programmers, system analysts, engineers, architects, accountants, and nurses.[2]

A third criterion is the dominance of theoretical knowledge. Drucker explains this criterion as follows:

> In 1910 steel was the economic measurement - and the steel industry was based squarely on skill rather than on knowledge. If all the men of knowledge at work in a nation in 1900 had suddenly been taken away, the economy would hardly have noticed the difference. Knowledge was then ornamental, economically speaking, rather than functional. Today it is the foundation and measurement of economic potential and economic power.[3]

Advocates of the post industrial society have argued that the American economic future is assured by a smooth shift into services. As Gary Becker, a professor of economics and sociology writes: "Strong modern economies do not seem to require a dominant manufacturing sector."[4] This is the argument made by a prominent politician, that computer related service jobs will replace the manufacturing jobs lost to foreign competition.

## Issues and Controversies

### Understanding a New Economy

**The U.S. economy is adjusting to the most profound change since the industrial revolution. No longer do the majority of workers produce goods and commodities. In 1981 the Labor Department predicted that by 1990 71% of the work force would be in services. However, the shift was even more dramatic than anticipated, with 75% working in the service sector by 1987.**

**In spite of the reality of the new economy, many of us continue to think in terms of the old one. We still think of the U.S. as an industrial economy. This tendency is reinforced by problems in the industrial sector. In the first six years of the 1980's, the U.S. lost 2.6 million manufacturing jobs. Even in high-tech industries, the U.S. has lost market share in 7 of 10 sectors. Our bilateral trade deficit with Japan in electronics is likely to exceed our automobile deficit.**

**Solving these problems requires an understanding that the new economy is as different from the industrial economy as the industrial economy was from the agricultural economy that preceded it. It is easy to become distracted by the arguments of smoke-stack politicians and labor leaders on the one hand, and high-tech proponents on the other. Catchy slogans such as "Big Mac vs. Big Steel" do not contribute much to our understanding.**

**Economists have traditionally valued the production of goods**

**over the production of services. This has led to the myth that service work does not produce anything of economic value.**

**The reality is:**

- **Most service work is not what we think it is. Information jobs such as programmer, teacher, accountant, manager, and technician are all service occupations.**
- **Information/Service Production is increasingly a high-capital/high-technology activity. Service firms are in the midst of a technological revolution. For example, in 1982 they invested $140 billion in new technology.**
- **Information/Service industries are essential to a strong industrial sector. Robots made smart by business software and "expert systems" using artificial intelligence are two examples of services which are required to make American manufacturing competitive.**
- **Information/Service activities can narrow the trade deficit. The world market in services is estimated at $700 billion. Technological developments have created opportunities in telecommunications, data processing and information services.**

**Prior to this technological revolution, a doctor or engineer who desired to see his services in Pakistan or Brazil had to be there. Now engineers in San Francisco transmit architectural drawings to Pakistan. Doctors in New York can diagnose patients in Brazil using CAT-scan and X-Ray satellite transmissions.**

**We are in the midst of an economic revolution. We have become the world's leading service/information economy, yet we remain the largest industrial and agricultural economy. This revolution cannot happen until we have a revolution in thought.**

Adapted from "Understanding a New Economy" by Ronald K. Shelp and Gary W. Hart, The Wall Street Journal (December 23, 1986), p. 18.

An unemployed auto, steel, or machine-shop worker will find little hope in this line of thinking. But for those able to master the new information technology the future is bright. Computerized automation may enable the U.S. to recover lost manufacturing jobs.

## ARGUMENTS AGAINST THE POST INDUSTRIAL SOCIETY

The idea that a post-industrial society will provide continued growth and a high standard of living has been criticized. Cohen and Zysman point out this view ignores the linkage between high-paying service jobs and manufacturing.

Cohen and Zysman argue that if high tech is to sustain a scale of activity that matters to the economy, a country must manufacture high-tech products, not just invent them. There are several recent inventions, including semiconductor memory, VCRs, and compact discs, which were invented in America but manufactured elsewhere. The resulting rewards flow mainly to the country which manufacturers them. This pattern suggests a weakness in managing technology.

Furthermore, they argue that semiconductors, machine tools, computers and robotics which are required for national defense would be prohibitively expensive for an economy without a strong and broad manufacturing sector.[5] The linkage between high-paying service jobs and manufacturing on the one hand and the need to maintain manufacturing for national defense on the other are the two principle arguments against the post-industrial society.

Another important question to be asked about a post industrial society is: "Will a post industrial society provide sufficient economic growth to maintain and enhance the standard of living enjoyed in the latter stages of an industrial society?" This question must be answered before we abandon the benefits of an industrial society.

## Impact of Information Technology on Enterprise

### CHANGING ORGANIZATIONAL STRUCTURES

About 30 years ago, Leavitt and Whisler predicted that information technology would transform organizations with two major effects: (1) Information technology would create centralized organizations with highly structured jobs for all but top management, and (2) there would be a reduction of middle management jobs. More recent observations by Drucker and others cast serious doubt on the first prediction and generally support the second.[6]

Information technology is creating what Drucker refers to as the *New Organization*. Information technology is changing the role of middle managers and bringing about a radical restructuring of the firm's middle ranks, shrinking them drastically in many firms.[7] Just as mechanization brought about by the industrial revolution changed organization structures, radicalized workers and created widespread social and economic change, information technology is producing unforeseen changes.

Why is this change occurring nearly 40 years after the introduction of commercial computers? The answer is that early applications of information technology simply used the computer to automate clerical tasks. Large numbers of clerks were displaced but absorbed elsewhere in a growing economy. Now the computer is being used to generate information, a function performed in the past by middle managers.

The primary function of middle managers is to serve as relays—human amplifiers for the faint unfocused signals that are broadcast indiscriminately by a pre-information organization. As top managers begin to see that much of the information generated by middle managers can be obtained more quickly, thoroughly and with less effort by computers, they have begun to perceive middle managers as redundant.[8]

This perception is strengthened by foreign competition. Executives are beginning to realize that only the leanest and fittest of firms will survive world class competition.

Drucker suggests that the information-based organization requires far more specialists than the traditional organization. However, these specialists will be directly involved in operations, not in headquarters staff. Furthermore, the need for staff specialists — individuals who advise, counsel and coordinate — shrinks drastically in the *New Organization*.[9]

The Ascendency of Line: The original purpose of staff personnel was to gather information that executives needed for decision making. More often than not, staff continued its role long after the need was gone. Instead of being eliminated, staff were given the responsibility of monitoring operations in marketing and manufacturing. The unintended result was a layer of management which frequently second-guessed line managers and vetoed technological changes thought to be too risky.[10] Now it is recognized that much of the information needed by top management can be gathered more quickly and efficiently by a computer. The resulting reduction of layers of middle management makes the organization more responsive to change.

The elimination of layers of middle managers has resulted in the ascendency of line managers. Line managers, particularly first line managers, whose power has been eroded by staff, are now making marketing and manufacturing decisions. Line managers in growing numbers have decided that information systems are too important to be left to computer technicians. Many line managers are now managing information technology for competitive advantage in their organizations.

Strategic information systems tend to be multi-organizational, and multi-functional, which makes line leadership imperative. The conception of these systems requires the kind of strategic business understanding which exists primarily at senior levels. Furthermore, implementation of these systems requires significant organizational change—change that is beyond the ability of MIS departments to effect.[11]

TASK-FOCUSED WORK TEAMS: The information-based organization will accomplish its work largely in task-focused teams consisting of specialists from different functions working together as a team. The manager's role in this structure is to define the goals of the team as a whole and for each specialist individually; and to develop feedback mechanisms that allow each member of the team to exercise self-control by comparing actual performance with performance expectations.[12]

One might ask, how will a manager evaluate the performance of a specialist? Drucker uses the example of a symphony orchestra to explain this. There are probably few orchestra conductors that are proficient horn players; however, the conductor and the horn player use a common score.[13] It tells the conductor what to expect and when. The point is that a manager must be knowledgeable enough about the work of the specialist to tell good work from poor performance.

A specialist in a task-focused team must also take information responsibility. The key to information responsibility is the answer to the question: Who in the organization depends on me for the information? The list will include both superiors and subordinates, but the most important names will be colleagues with whom they must coordinate.

## CHANGING ORGANIZATIONAL BOUNDARIES

Information technology will alter the legal and physical boundaries of the firm—a development which may cause the lawyers some heartburn. There is growing recognition that information technology makes it possible to link an organization electronically with customers, suppliers, and financial institutions. Networks designed to transmit data, voice, and images will grow steadily as recognition of their strategic potential increases. These networks will create new relationships between firms and their suppliers and customers. Pacific Intermountain Express, a big truckling firm, allows its customers to access its computers so they can check on the status of an order. Electronic transmission of orders (EDI) between a firm and a supplier requires a level of coordination and collaboration that is unusual. This environment may also change the relationship from an adversarial to a cooperative one.

The advantages of EDI goes well beyond the savings realized from not preparing documents manually. The real benefit of EDI is time. Shortening the lead time, the time between when an order is placed and when it arrives, reduces the level of safety stock required, and permits smaller economic order quantities. Ultimately EDI results in better inventory management.[14]

Information networks may also become an alternative to vertical integration. A company that might formerly have acquired a key supplier to gain greater control over raw materials may, in the future, opt instead to track the supplier's performance by computer.[15]

The growing networks of debit card systems are another example of interorganizational information systems. Debit card systems use a plastic card similar to a credit card to transfer funds from a consumer's account to a retailer's account to pay for purchases. Both online and offline debit card systems exist, the difference being that online systems guarantee payment during the transaction whereas offline systems do not. National grocery chains, oil firms, and fast food chains have established POS (point of sale) systems which accept debit cards. Some observers feel debit cards have great strategic potential.[16]

## SHIFT FROM CAPITAL TO HUMAN RESOURCES

The shift from an industrial society to an information society shifts the focus from capital to human resources. An information society's critical resources are information, knowledge and creativity. There is only one source of these resources—human beings.

An information society also shifts management's focus from manual and clerical workers to knowledge workers, which, in turn, will limit the power of traditional management; knowledge workers resist the authoritarian management style that business adopted from the military. Human assets, as independent entities, not only go home every night, they may join the competition. In an information society the real competition is in creating a work culture that is both attractive and productive.

Maintaining the value of human assets will require a continuing commitment to training. Indeed, retraining may become as important as initial training. Knowledge is the critical resource in a technology intensive economy as described in Issues and Controversies.

## Issues and Controversies

### Knowledge is Power

Contrary to popular opinion progress in computers is on the brink of dramatic acceleration. This is due to three major developments in the computer industry.

The first breakthrough is artificial intelligence. In the last few years scores of firms have developed products that manipulate symbols, deal with uncertainty, use rules and inferences in solving problems and simulate human intelligence on expert systems.

The significance of this development might be better understood with an analogy. Suppose all engineering and mathematical problems had to be solved with a calculator or a slide rule. The computer industry has been using similar inflexible tools. Computers are now capable of using common sense and the experience of experts in solving problems.

The second development is the silicon compiler. This enables an engineer with a $50,000 workstation to design a computer chip. Manufacturing can be accomplished by any of scores of semiconductor firms around the world with modern chip making facilities.

The third breakthrough is the abandonment of the cherished von-Neumann computer architecture in favor of parallel processing. Imagine a grocery store with a single checkout station. In spite of efforts to speed up checkout customers would have to que up to be processed and other functions and employees would be idle much of the time, limited by the speed of the checkout station. Parallel processing in effect allows multiple checkout stations.

The effect of these three developments will be a dramatic increase in computer efficiency by a factor of thousands. Carver Mead, of the California Institute of Technology, predicts a 10,000 fold increase in cost-effectiveness of information technology during the next decade.

The effect of these converging developments can be summed up with a cliche: Knowledge is power. Today knowledge is not *a* source of power, it is *the* source of power.

**In the past power was derived from control of natural resources, territory, taxes, military manpower, national currencies, and trade surpluses. These things will no longer control power or will be less effective in conferring power.**

**The most immediate impact of this effect is already evident in the value of natural resources. The silicon chip is made of sand, one of earth's most abundant resources. The value of raw materials in pots and pans is approximately 80%, in automobiles 40% and in integrated circuits less than 2%. Within five years, a few pounds of sand, transformed as a fiber optic cable will carry as much information as a ton of copper wire.**

**The effect of these developments will be tremendous advances in computational power at a small cost. This will allow entrepreneurs to exploit the power of knowledge while economizing on capital in effect mixing sand and ideas to generate wealth and power.**

Adapted from George Gilder, "Vital Breakthroughs - And a Dash of Sand - Will Propel Technology," Information Week (January 19, 1987), pp. 42-43.

## FLEXIBILITY

There is a growing recognition that the business environment of the 90s will require firms to reduce product development cycles and move from design to finished product in less time than they have in the 80s. Information technology will be the key to improved flexibility.

The Limited, the speciality retailing firm, tracks consumer preferences every day by monitoring POS terminal sales. It identifies items that are selling well and transmits orders by satellite to plants in the U.S. and the Far East. If new designs are required, it transmits facsimile illustrations with the order. The goods are then collected in Hong Kong and flown to the U.S. in a chartered 747. Within 48 hours of arrival at the distribution center, apparel is on its way to one of the Limited's 3200 outlets. Within 60 days of the order, the apparel goes on sale—compared with competitors who place orders six months or more in advance.[17] This is an example of the competitive advantage gained through reducing product development cycles.

IBM has halved the development time for a mainframe from three years to eighteen months. Honda and Toyota can take a car from concept to market in three years versus five years for GM. Ford has reduced the product cycle to four years and is shooting for three.[18]

Information technology is one reason things can happen faster. Improved simulations have allowed IBM to skip two prototype stages in developing new integrated circuits. Improved flexibility and shortened development cycles have become competitive weapons.

### ENTREPRENEURIAL ACTIVITY

Information technology, particularly microcomputer technology, has spawned a great deal of entrepreneurial activity. This technology, according to Gilder, favors small companies, entrepreneurs, inventors, and creators at the expense of large centralized organizations.[20] The low cost of microcomputers has allowed individuals and small businesses to compete with large businesses in tasks that were formerly beyond their reach. Entrepreneurs have been much quicker than large firms to exploit this new technology. They have recognized that microcomputers can now perform tasks that formerly required expensive mainframes. From semiconductor design to software development, microcomputers are enabling entrepreneurs to compete with larger established firms that are committed to centralized mainframe computers rather than decentralized microcomputers.

## Management of Technology

ONE OF THE CONSISTENT THEMES IN CRITICISMS OF AMERICAN management is that managers really have little or no technical understanding of the business they manage, but have essentially mastered only the field of finance. Therefore managers set about managing the corporation with little or no understanding of the "nuts and bolts of the business." The result is a failure in management of technology.[21]

This failure to manage technology effectively is a symptom of the widening gap between managers and day-to-day operations. *Business Week* suggests that this leads to the "hollowing" of the corporation, a condition created when a firm loses its critical skills and becomes only a shell of its former self.[22]

In contrast to professional managers, entrepreneurs often regard the firm as an extension of their own values, beliefs, and family; company founders tend to feel a deep sense of obligation to their customers and employees. They frequently create a corporate culture that survives their tenure. Entrepreneurs, in contrast to professional managers, tend to manage for long term results and to really understand the technical realities of day-to-day operations.[23]

## Computer Crime and Malicious Mischief

INFORMATION TECHNOLOGY HAS CREATED NEW HAZARDS which managers need to recognize and combat by taking measures which minimize the threat to the firm. These hazards include computer crime and malicious mischief. A list of potential threats to computer systems, excluding acts of nature such as fire, floods and earthquakes and possibly power failures, might include the following:

1. Virus and Other Malicious Software
2. Wiretaps and Electronic Eavesdropping
3. Sneak Attacks by Hackers
4. Employee Tampering

### COMPUTER CRIME

Disgruntled former employees have been the source of much damage. In one case a programmer who resented authority and who boasted he had never paid taxes was fired by a Ft. Worth securities firm. Before leaving, the programmer planted a program to wipe out the firm's record of commissions earned. While it was detected within a few days, over 168,000 records were lost.
In another case, an employee was fired by the Wollogong Group, a software firm. Two months later she was detected logging on to the firm's computer. A police raid on her apartment revealed that software worth millions of dollars had been illegally copied.[24]

Failure to change passwords was a contributing factor to both of these cases of tampering by former employees. Allowing an unauthorized individual in a sensitive area of the bank contributed to the Security Pacific National Bank fraud by Stanley Mark Rifkin. This famous case is discussed in When Things Go Wrong.

## When things go wrong

### The Security Pacific National Bank Fraud

**Stanley Mark Rifkin was a computer consultant who had done some work at the Security Pacific National Bank's home office in Los Angeles. Rifkin, a bachelor in his early 30s, earned a modest but steady income in his consulting business. In some**

**ways, he felt unfulfilled and dissatisfied with the level of recognition he had achieved and the failure of his relationships with women. He began to plan how to steal several million dollars from Security Pacific National bank.**

**On October 25, 1978, Rifkin entered the home office of the bank, posing as a consultant hired by the Federal Reserve bank to improve funds transfer. No one at the bank checked his credentials. He was allowed to enter the wire transfer room where he observed clerks making funds transfers. During this time he asked questions and made notes about the funds transfer procedure. Using a public telephone in the bank, he was able to call the wire transfer room and give them the required codes to transfer $10.2 million to a Swiss bank.**

**Rifkin then flew to Zurich where an American diamond broker purchased over $8.1 million worth of diamonds for him from the Russians. Then he flew back to the U.S. and went through customs without them detecting the diamonds.**

**Arriving home, Rifkin went to his attorney to have him dissolve his consulting business. Unable to contain himself, he confided that he had stolen several million dollars from Security Pacific and paid the attorney in diamonds as compensation for his work. The attorney went to the FBI, who began to investigate.**

**An FBI agent went to Security Pacific Bank to check out the attorney's story. Initially the bank denied that a fraud had occurred but several days later called the FBI to confirm that it had lost more than $10.2 million. Shortly afterward, Rifkin was arrested and convicted.**

Adapted from Bruce Henderson and Jeffrey Young, "The Heist," Esquire (May 1981), pp. 36-47.

Wiretaps and electronic eavesdropping are other hazards of modern telecommunication systems. Fortunately, new technologies such as fiber optics are less susceptible to wiretaps and eavesdropping. Cryptography, which codes transmissions is being used more often as electronic funds transfer becomes more common. Inexpensive chips are available to encode and decode transmissions. These chips are changed periodically to make it very difficult for someone to crack the code.

Hackers, a term often used to describe computer enthusiasts, have been less of a problem for business organizations than for defense and research organizations. Some hackers have invaded sensitive files to gain access to restricted information; a German hackers club has been particularly aggressive in gaining access to sensitive information and using news media contacts to publish it. Recently, this club gave the German news media government information about the Chernobyl nuclear disaster that was at odds with what the government was telling the media.

## COMPUTER VIRUS

A computer virus is a program that multiplies by *infecting* other programs and modifying them to include a copy of itself. With this ability to spread *infection*, a virus can spread from computer to computer, and program to program damaging both programs and data.

A program that is infected looks like an ordinary program to an unsuspecting user. The virus is usually activated by the computer's internal clock—the virus waits dormant for the right moment to wreak havoc. A typical mode of spreading infection uses a floppy disk. On a personal computer a virus can spread from one disk to another, to the computer's memory and by data communication to other computers.

Viruses are difficult to eradicate because they can reinfect programs that have been cleaned up. Back-up copies of software are also not guaranteed to be virus-free—the virus can lie dormant in a backup copy. The usual solution to a virus infection is to shut down a computer and rebuild its files from scratch. Programs should be reloaded from the original manufacturer's copy.

The motivation of the creators of computer viruses is not clear. Drew Davidson, a programmer in his early 20s from Tucson, created a Peace virus which flashed an innocuous greeting on the screen. While criticizing other virus creators, he admits he created the virus to call attention to his programming skills. A less friendly virus was created in Pakistan and is discussed in When Things Go Wrong.

**When things go wrong**

## The Pakistan Brain Virus

**In Lahore, Pakistan, a shop called the Brain Computer Store was selling copies of brand-name software for as little as $1.50. Visiting computer buffs found this too good a bargain to pass up. Programs such as Lotus 1-2-3 and Wordstar were purchased by scores of Americans during a two-year period in 1986 and 1987.**

**They took away a lot more than a bargain-priced copy of software. Hidden in nearly every copy was a piece of software that some**

**consider the world's most sophisticated computer virus. Before long, the virus found its way onto at least 100,000 floppy disks. The virus, which often destroyed data, left behind a calling card—a message which began—Welcome to the Dungeon. The message was signed by the store's proprietors, the Alvi brothers, Amjad and Basit.**

**The brothers, self-taught computer experts, originally created the virus to protect their custom programming business. They wanted a means of "infecting" and unauthorized user's computer, disrupting their operations and forcing them to come to the Alvi brothers for repairs.**

**The Alvi brothers began to make bootleg copies of American software packages, selling them at steep discounts. Pakistani customers were given virus-free copies; but foreign customers, particularly Americans, were often given contaminated versions. The Alvi brothers confused rationale for this practice was that Pakistani law does not protect software copyrights therefore local citizens are not pirating software. Americans, on the other hand, are software pirates and must be *punished*.**

**The Alvi brothers stopped selling virus-ridden software sometime in 1987, satisfied that they had taught the bargain-hunting bootleggers a lesson. No one knows how much damage was wrought by the Pakistan Brain Virus, but observers agree that it was an impressive piece of work.**

Adapted from Philip Elmer-DeWitt, "You Must be Punished," Time (September 26, 1988), p. 66.

## Information Ethics

Information technology has created new ethical issues for those who create and use information systems. Developing a new standard of ethical behavior as it applies to information systems is neither easy nor natural. Information ethics are difficult to define and perhaps even more difficult to get information systems professionals to adopt. Relying on good people to behave in an ethical manner in the absence of guidelines can be dangerous. Information technology has created new challenges in applying ethical standards in a clear and consistent way to our behavior. One of the reasons for this challenge is the way in which information technology has altered relationships.

### Information Technology and Relationships

Ethics is concerned with our relations with others and their property. Information technology tends to depersonalize our interactions with others; interactions can take place without a personal relationship.

Personal relationships tend to make us more sensitive to ethical behavior.

Information technology alters relationships by separating the parties. An individual contemplating mischief can hide behind an electronic bulletin board. The victim may be anonymous too. The creator of a computer virus may know who the first target is, but where the virus goes and who it affects after that are beyond his control.

Thus, information technology can weaken positive ethical tendencies in relationships with others and strengthen negative tendencies. It would seem that positive action must be taken to offset such action. Management should define and reinforce information ethics.

## Intellectual Property Rights

Intellectual property rights are concerned with the creative efforts of others. Traditionally, intellectual property rights have been protected by patent and copyright. These traditional protections have been inadequate in protecting software and other intellectual property associated with information technology.

Basic ethical principles of the right of ownership and the right to benefit from one's creative efforts should hold true for intellectual property as well as tangible property. The unauthorized copies of software that exist in both the private and public sectors are one example of widespread breaches of these principles.

## The Conflict Between Secrecy and Sharing

People tend to accumulate and protect tangible property. With information and software, our inclination is to communicate and share. In doing this, we often forget the individual's right to privacy, and the software developer's right to benefit from his efforts. The human tendency to forget confidentiality, to be helpful, to trade information, and to establish a relationship can be harmful if practiced in violation of other individuals' rights to privacy or intellectual property.

## Individual Integrity and Professionalism

The solution for unethical behavior such as computer crime or computer viruses is clearly greater individual integrity and professionalism on the part of information systems professionals. Longer-established professions have established codes of conduct and defined ethical standards in order to govern themselves.

A profession is recognized not only as a group that has mastered a body of knowledge, but one that uses that knowledge and skill in ways that benefit society. Many professions have a code of ethics which upholds a standard of ethical behavior; they regard practice in a profession as a privilege which can be terminated for unprofessional conduct.

## Guidelines for MIS Professionals

MIS professionals need to be reminded of the ethical nature of professionalism. Professional societies, educational institutions, and the firms in which information systems professionals practice can reinforce these principles. One such code of ethics is examined in Issues and Controversies.

## Issues and Controversies

### Code of Ethics

The Institute for Certification of Computer Professionals, which awards the Certificate in Data Processing (CDP) and the Certified Systems Professional (CSP), has published the following about the code of ethics for holders of the certificate in data processing.

Holders of the Certificate in Data Processing are a select group of people who have qualified for and successfully completed an examination assessing their grasp of the knowledge considered by recognized experts as important to data processing and information management.

By choosing to seek this certification, the CDP holders have demonstrated their concern for the continuing development of high standards of personal and professional conduct. The Certification Council, the governing body for the CDP Program, has consistently throughout its existence recognized the need for a set of personal and professional standards to support and identify CDP Holders as a group dedicated to the quest for knowledge and competence, to ethical behavior and social responsibility, and to the advancement of data processing and information management."

#### Code of Ethics for Holders of the Certificate in Data Processing

The holder of the Certificate in Data Processing, consistent with his obligation to the public at large, should promote the understanding of data processing methods and procedures using every resource at his command.

The holder of the Certificate in Data Processing has an obligation to his profession to uphold the high ideals and the level of personal knowledge certified by the certificate. He should encourage dissemination of knowledge pertaining to the development of data processing.

**The holder of the Certificate in Data Processing has an obligation to serve the interests of his employer and clients loyally, diligently, and honestly.**

Excerpted from "Examination Announcement," Institute for Certification of Computer Professionals, 1988.

Educational institutions have too often emphasized the beauty and wonder of information technology without an accompanying appreciation for social responsibility. Some critics have charged that educational institutions have created a *nerd syndrome* common to students of science and information technology: these students exhibit a prankish bent that is a reflection of immature social and ethical standards.

Individual integrity can be fostered by a careful selection process and an organizational climate that supports individual and organizational integrity. The key is not greater organizational control but having employees accept and internalize a set of standards that embody information ethics.

## Key Terms

Post Industrial Society
Linkage
Changing Organizational Structures
Changing Organizational Boundaries
Flexibility
Management of Technology
Computer Virus
Information Ethics
Intellectual Property Rights
Professionalism

## Review Questions

1. What are the characteristics of a post-industrial society?
2. What is the relationship between high paying service jobs and manufacturing?
3. What impact are computers having on organizational structures?
4. How does an information society shift the focus of scarce resources?
5. What are some of the problems in managing technology?
6. How has information technology created ethical issues?
7. What is a profession?

## Suggestions for Further Reading

George Gilder, "The Revitalization of Everything: The Law of the Microcosm," Harvard Business Review, (March-April, 1988).

*The author argues that the microprocessor will have a revolutionary impact on computer architectures and mainframe computer manufacturers but perhaps more importantly it will create an era of entrepreneurialism in the U.S. The law of the microcosm means that the microprocessor enables the individual to perform tasks previously thought to be the domain of large, centralized organizations.*

Stephen S. Cohen and John Zysman, Manufacturing Matters: The Myth of the Post-Industrial Economy, (Basic Books, 1987).

*This book argues that a post-industrial economy based on services is unrealistic. Furthermore the authors contend that most of the high-paying information technology jobs are closely linked to manufacturing.*

# *Appendix*

# Database Design

*"The industry is well into the era of data base technology after having implemented the first decade incorrectly....After more than a decade of hard lessons learned in developing data base technology, it is now time to present effective solutions to the professionals responsible for building data bases."*

*Robert Holland*

## Overview and Objectives

DATABASE DESIGN IS CRITICAL TO SUCCESSFUL DATABASE implementation and use. Good database design will provide a stable structure that responds to new user requirements and does not require continual redesign. It should enable the firm to develop new applications quickly in response to changes in the environment. Good database design provides data that is accessible to end users. Properly designed a database will exhibit the properties of data independence, data integrity and minimal data redundancy. These benefits, however, are dependent upon proper database design.

AFTER READING THIS APPENDIX YOU SHOULD BE ABLE TO:

- Define entities, attributes, and logical user views
- Explain the meaning of cardinality
- Show how entities and relationships are defined
- Normalize simple logical user views
- Explain the cannonical synthesis process
- Explain the importance of normalization in achieving data independence
- Describe the function of an automated database design tool

## Introduction

DATABASE DESIGN HAS GENERALLY BEEN VIEWED FROM THREE different perspectives: (1) a conceptual model, which represents an enterprise view of data; (2) a logical model, which represents the view of the user or of individual applications; (3) a physical model, which represents the perspective of how the database is implemented and physically stored on a mass-storage device. Physical database design is concerned with efficient retrieval and updating of data as well as details of data integrity and recovery.[1] This three-level architecture is shown in Figure A.1.

This chapter is concerned with the first two levels of database design. Physical database design is normally the responsibility of a database administrator. The position of database administrator includes responsibility for DBMS performance and efficient utilization of storage space. Whereas conceptual and logical database design require an understanding of the enterprise and the ability to work with people, physical database design requires a solid technical background. Normally, physical database design is started after conceptual and logical design are completed.

FIGURE A.1 *Database Architecture - Three Tiered Approach*

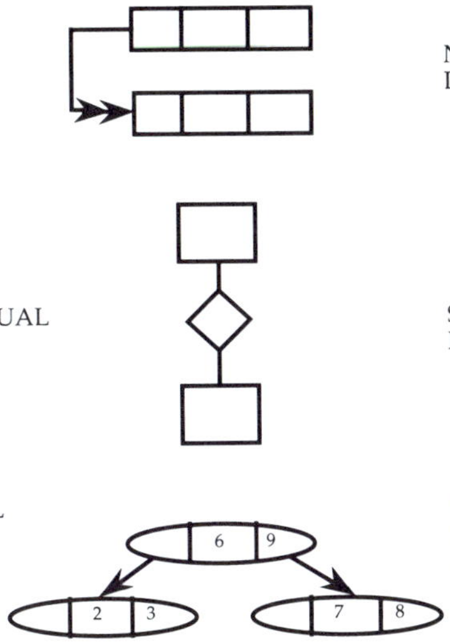

| Database Design Perspective | Related Concepts | Objective |
|---|---|---|
| LOGICAL | Normalization<br>Logical User Views | Indentify attributes<br>Simplification<br>Accessability |
| CONCEPTUAL | Subject Database<br>Information Architecture | Provide structure<br>Stable data model<br>Minimize Redundancy |
| PHYSICAL | Indexes<br>Pointers<br>Access Methods | Performance<br>Backup<br>Recovery |

## Conceptual Database Design

CONCEPTUAL DATABASE DESIGN IS CONCERNED WITH DEFINING the entities of an enterprise and their relationships. While there is general agreement about the scope and objectives of conceptual database design, there are many different diagramming conventions for representing entity relationships. The first task in conceptual database design is to identify the entities of the organization.

### ENTITY IDENTIFICATION

Entities constitute the objects and events about which an organization stores data. Entities are things which can be identified as nouns. These objects and events must be important enough to the organization for it to desire to store information about them. Some objects and events in an enterprise are trivial and do not warrant keeping track of them.

Entities should be given a name that is a singular noun. Typical entities in a university would include:

Student
Instructor
Class
Classroom
Course
Semester
Course-Offering

Individual entity occurrences can be identified by an attribute which is a primary key. For example, a student may be uniquely identified by a student number.

Conceptual data modeling is a top-down process which requires an indepth understanding of the enterprise and its functions, processes and activities and the related entities. Managers and professionals should be involved in the process of entity identification as well as later stages of conceptual database design.

## ENTITY RELATIONSHIP DIAGRAMS

Entity relationship diagrams document the entities of the organization and their relationships. This step in database modeling provides a conceptual framework for later stages in database modeling.

An entity relationship diagram for the entities order and customer is shown below in Figure A.2.

FIGURE A.2

*Two Different Entity Relationship Diagramming Conventions*

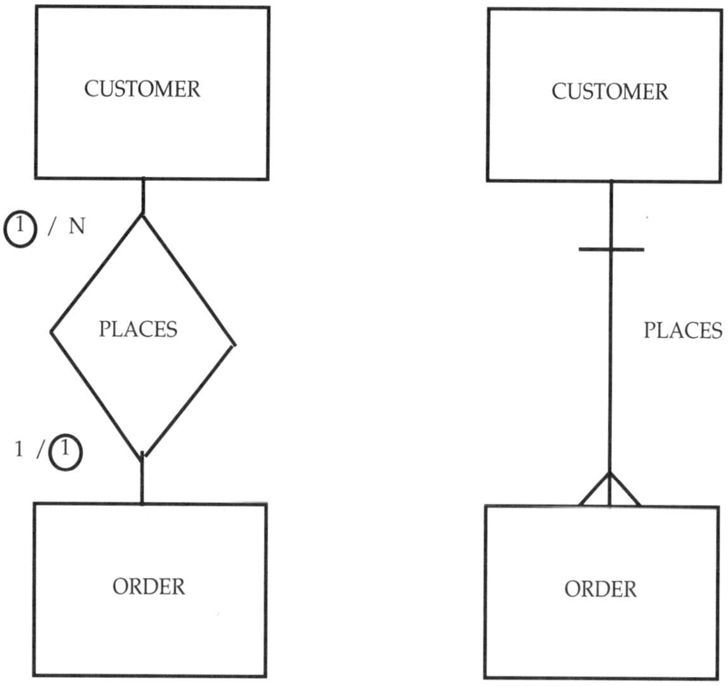


(a) Conventional Chen Diagram

(b) Automated Data Modeling Tool

This diagram is shown in two different entity relationship diagramming conventions. The diagram on the left is a conventional Chen diagram while the diagram on the right is a method used by several automated data modeling tools.

The relationship between the two entities is shown in the diamond-shaped polygon on the left and is written on the line connecting the two entities on the right. A relationship is a verb. This relationship captures the meaning of the association between the two entities. It is possible to have more than one relationship between two entities. For example, a customer may cancel one or more orders. This would be shown as two separate lines connecting the two entities. This is shown in Figure A.3.

FIGURE A.3

*An Example of More than One Relationship Between Entities*

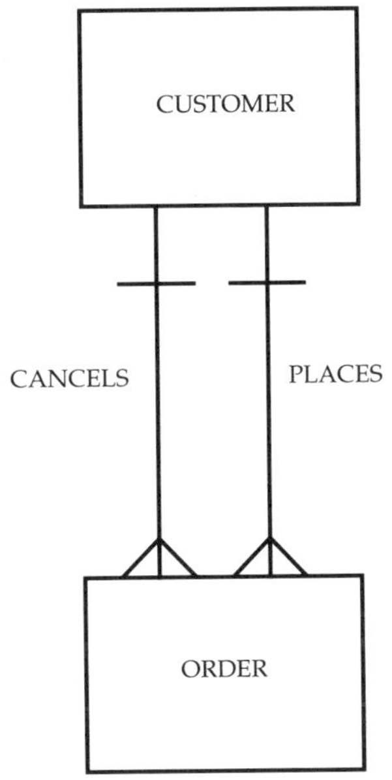


The other piece of vital information in Figure A.3 is how many orders are associated with a customer and vice versa. The diagram shows that a customer can have one or many orders, but an order has only one customer. This information is referred to as cardinality. Cardinality refers to the number of occurrences of one entity that are associated with a single occurrence of another entity. The conventions for showing cardinality with automated tools are shown in Figure A.4.

**FIGURE A.4**

*The Conventions for Showing Cardinality with Automated Tools*

1:1 Association

- A identifies B.
- B is functionally dependent on A.
- For one occurrence of A there is always one and only one occurrence of B.

1:M Association

For one occurrence of A there are one or multiple occurrences of B.

Optional 1:1 Association

For one occurrence of A there is zero or one occurrence of B.

Optional 1:M Association

For one occurrence of A there are zero, one, or multiple occurrences of B.

Labeled Associations

A label may be written on an association. This is normally done when two associations with different meanings exist between the same two data-item types.

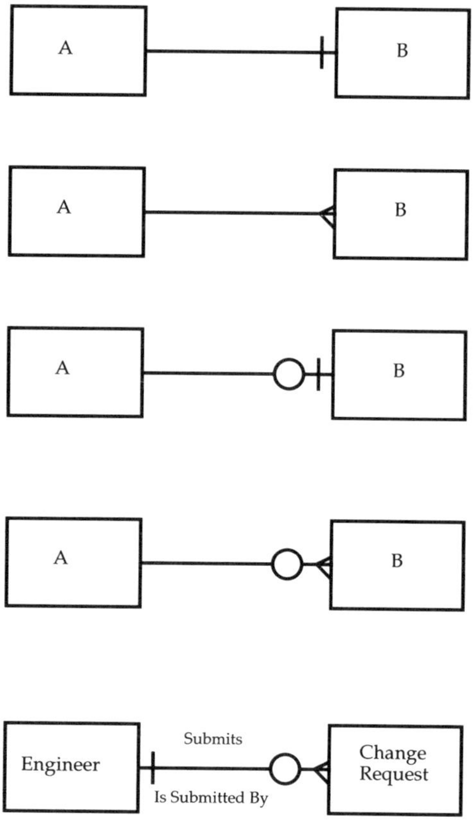


Entity relationship diagrams can be determined by constructing a sentence. This is shown below:

| SUBJECT | VERB | PREDICATE |
|---|---|---|
| Customer | places | order |
| Purchase_order | contains | purchase_order item |
| Product | stocked | product_stock |
| Warehouse | holds | product_stock |
| Student | registers | class |

The subject and predicate of this sentence are entities and the verb represents a relationship.

If a subject is associated with but one object, the relationship is said to be a binary relationship. If more than one object, then it is an N-

ARY relationship. An example of an N-ARY relationship is shown in Figure A.5.

FIGURE A.5
*An Example of an N-ARY Relationship*

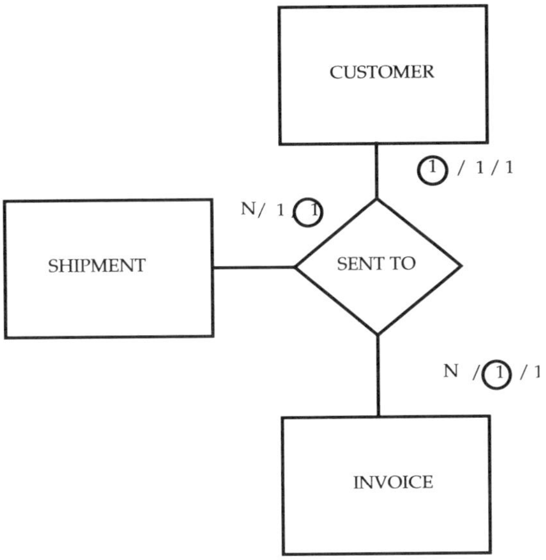


One of the biggest controversies in entity relationship modeling is what to do with many-to-many associations between two entities. The controversy concerns whether a relationship may have attributes. For example, the relationship between Order and Item is many-to-many. This is shown in Figure A.6.

FIGURE A.6
*Entity Chart Showing Many-to-Many Association Between Order and Item*

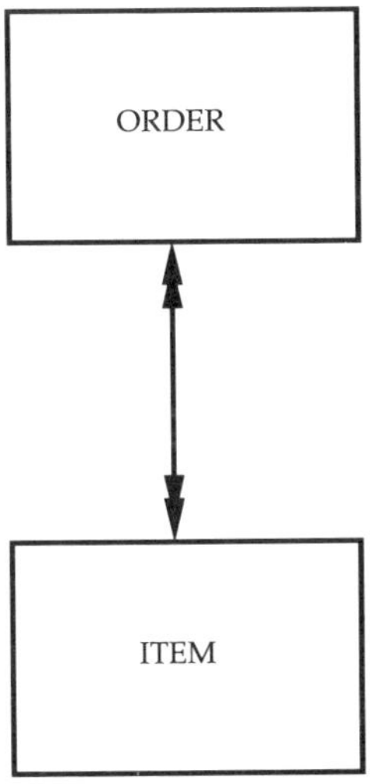

Many-to-many associations almost always have intersecting attributes. Quantity ordered is an attribute of the relationship of Order and Item. One school of thought resolves this dilemma by creating what is known as a weak entity—Order-Item—and attaches the attributes. The other school of thought says that relationships can have attributes and shows them as attached to the relationship. This is shown in Figure A.7.

FIGURE A.7
*Entity Chart Showing a Relationship With Attributes*

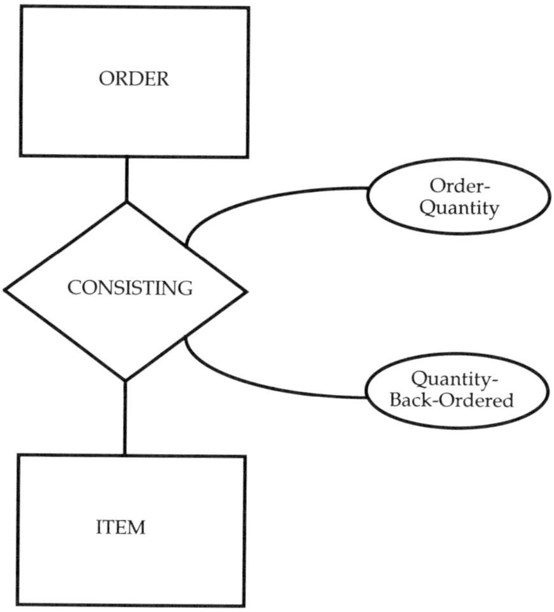


Finally, entity relationship modeling must deal with entity subtypes. Entity subtypes can be identified by asking the question: Is there an occurrence of this entity that will have different attributes than other occurrences? If the answer is yes, there may be an entity subtype. An automated tool representation of an entity subtype is shown in Figure A.8.

A conventional entity relationship modeling representation of an entity subtype is shown in Figure A.9.

**FIGURE A.8**
*An Entity Hierarchy Diagram*

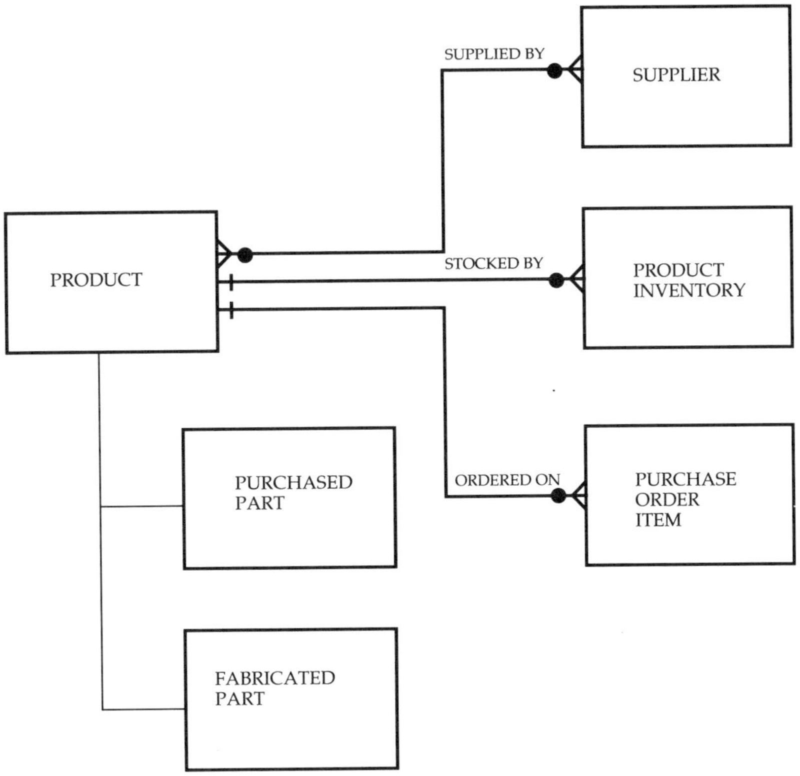


**FIGURE A.9**
*Entity Supertype and Subtypes*

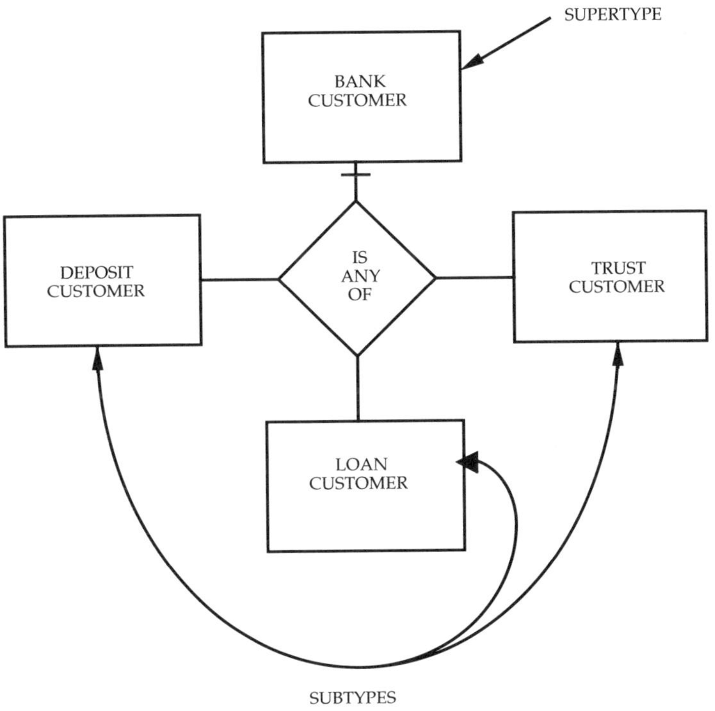

An entity relationship diagram provides a conceptual framework for database design. While there is some divergence of opinion, the entity relationship model is frequently extended by identifying the primary key for each entity. Some advocates of entity relationship diagrams believe the process should be further extended by identifying the attributes of each entity. The entire data modeling process would then become a top down implementation process.

## Normalization

NORMALIZATION AS A CONCEPT IS CONCERNED WITH DETERMINING which data elements are to be stored in a table. If we are to successfully implement the supermarket approach to data organization as discussed in Chapter 3, we must understand the concept of normalization.

The concept of normalization underlies the data modelling process.[2] Normalization attempts to get data grouped together in a form that is able to accommodate future change.[3] Normalization is beneficial in a file processing environment as well as a database environment.

Data exists in the real world as sets of related data elements. These sets of data elements are often found on invoices, payroll registers, way bills, and various reports. Often these complex data structures have not been simplified, or "normalized." Unsurprisingly, unnormalized data groupings have frequently been implemented in data files. Data groups implemented as unnormalized groups can cause data integrity problems in the future.[4]

In spite of the obvious advantages of normalization, as late as 1983, only a small proportion of corporate databases existed in normalized form. An even smaller proportion of data files have been normalized. Some corporations, however, have implemented normalization as a standard for all datastores.[5] This policy anticipates a switch to data base and facilitates it.[6]

We have introduced the concept of an entity. Entities have characteristics which are known as attributes. Examples of attributes are customer name, item description, and order quantity. A primary key is the attribute that uniquely identifies an instance of an entity.

## Bubble Charting

THE RELATIONSHIP BETWEEN DATA ELEMENTS CAN BE GRAPHIcally represented. There are several methods for doing this, one of which is bubble charting. Bubble charts show the relationship between an entity and its attributes. In a wholesaling firm, for example, some entities would be customer, item, supplier, order, and salesperson. Each entity has attributes that characterize it. Attributes would include: item number, description, price, and quantity on hand. Item number, for example, has only one item description associated with it. Thus, item number is a key.

The following standard symbols are used when representing a user view as a bubble chart as shown in Figure A.10.

FIGURE A.10
*Bubble Charting Symbols*

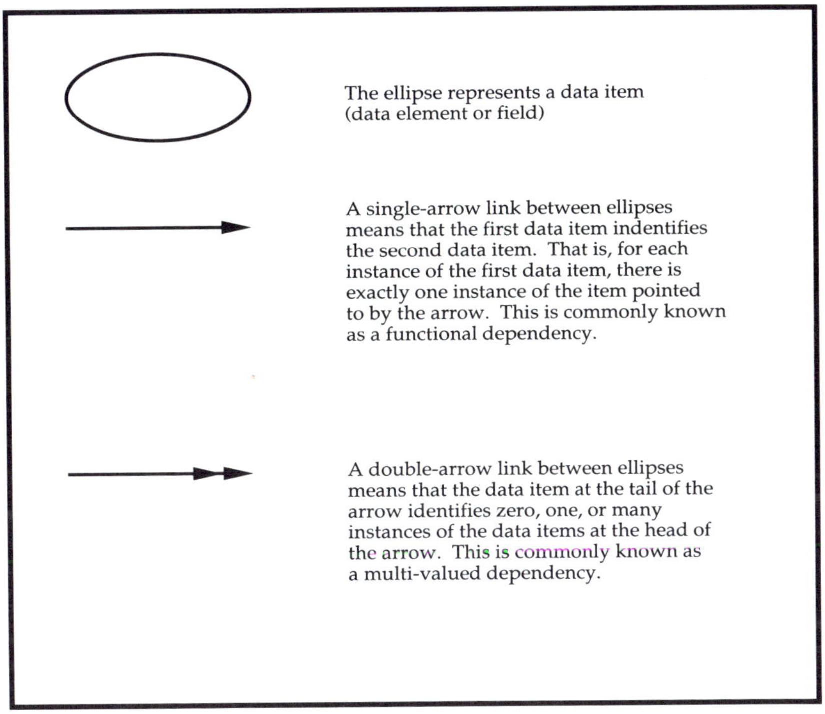


Any ellipse (bubble) on a bubble chart may represent either a key or an attribute, as described as follows:

| | |
|---|---|
| Primary key | A bubble with one or more single-arrow links leaving it. |

| | |
|---|---|
| Attribute | A bubble with no single-arrow links leaving it. |
| Secondary key | A bubble with double-arrow links leaving it, but no single-arrow link leaving it. (Note that a secondary key is also an attribute.) |
| Concatenated key | A primary key made up of more than one data element. It is represented as a single bubble. |

## DATA ASSOCIATION

Associations between data elements are represented by arrows. A single-head arrow between student number and grade-point average means that there is only one grade point average associated with a student number. Student number is said to be the primary key as shown in Figure A.11.

FIGURE A.11
*An Example of a One-to-One Relationship Between Data Items*

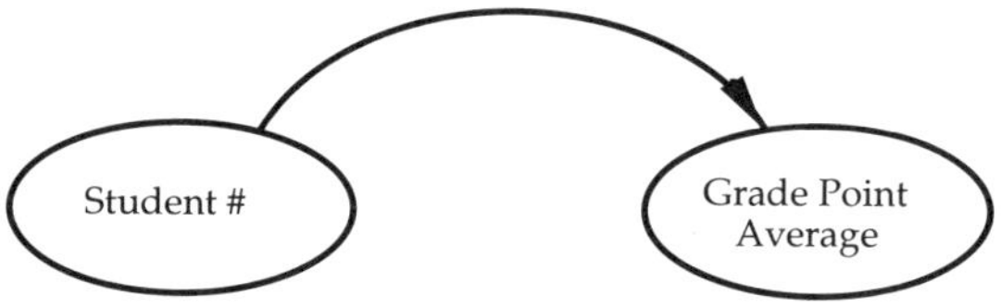


While a student can have but one grade-point average at a time, he may have zero, one or many instructors. This relationship is represented with a double arrow in Figure A.12.

FIGURE A.12
*An Example of a One-to-Many Relationship Between Data Items*

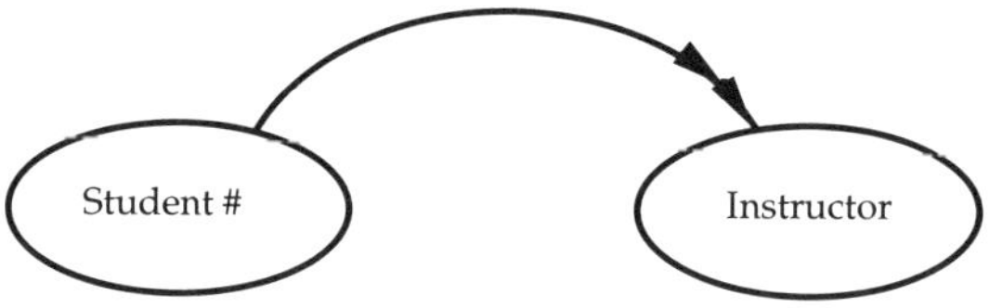

We can combine both of these views into one diagram. The combined chart is shown in Figure A.13.

FIGURE A.13
*A Combined View*

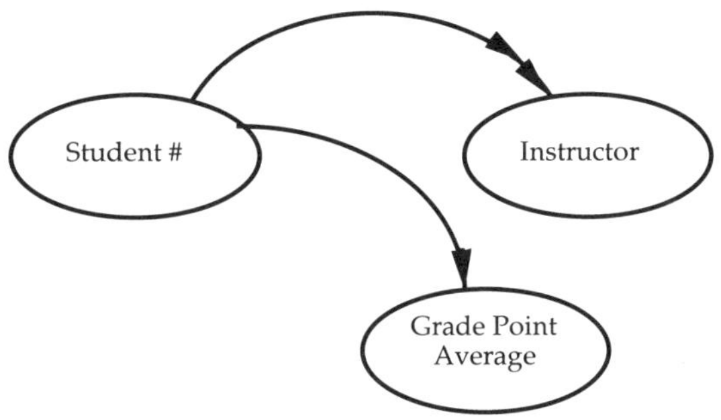


This diagram represents both views of the data, and from this chart, either of the two previous views could be derived. Effective data modeling synthesizes the various user views of data. User views of data in actual applications are likely to be much more complex than the charts represented above.

Between any two data items there can be arrows in both directions. This is shown in Figure A.14.

FIGURE A.14
*An Example of a Reverse Association Between Data Items*

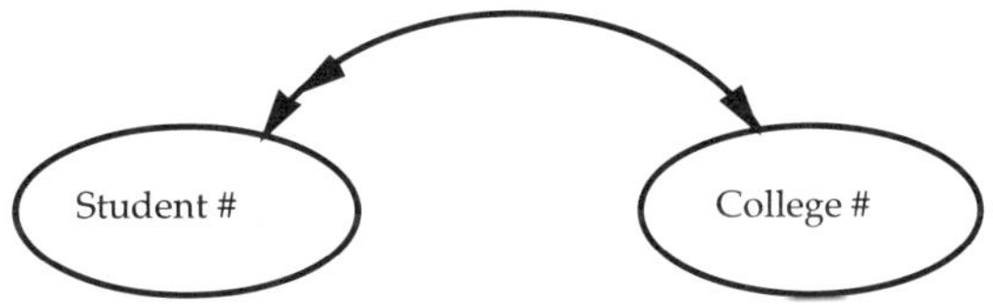


Note that each student is associated with but one college (one-to-one) but each college may have many students (one-to-many).

The association shown would allow a university to determine which college a student is registered in. It would also be possible to determine which students are registered in a given college. As a general rule, reverse associations are shown only between primary keys.

Data elements can be grouped into collections of related data elements or data groups. A data group may also be known as a *record*, a *segment*, or a *tupple*. A data group can be represented as a rectangular bar containing the names of the data elements as shown in Figure A.15 or it can be represented as a bubble chart.

FIGURE A.15
*Two Different Representations of a Data Group*

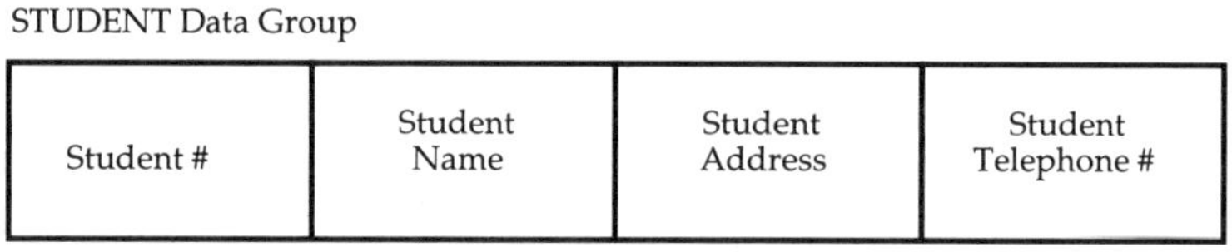


(a) A Rectangular Bar

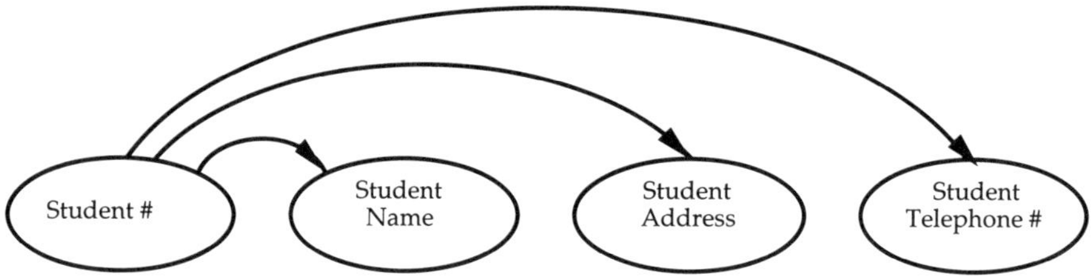


(b) A Bubble Chart

The relationship of data groups can be shown by single head arrows and double head arrows. This is illustrated by Figure A.16.

FIGURE A.16
*The Relationship Between Data Groups*

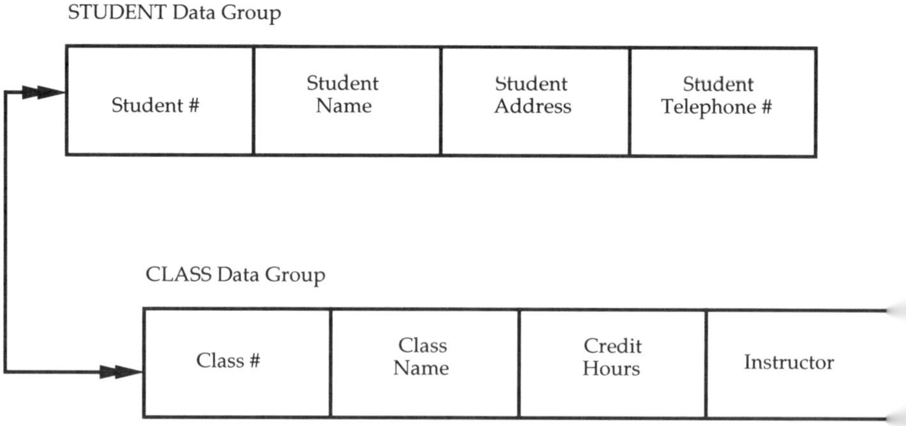

This diagram shows that each student may have several classes and each class may have several students.

Frequently, it is advantageous to develop bubble charts directly from a logical user view without going through the process of normalization first. The resulting bubble chart must be in third-normal form, however. Logical-user views may be represented as forms, input-screens, and requests.

## NORMALIZATION AND BUBBLE CHARTING FROM A LOGICAL USER VIEW

Date and Wilson developed a technique for normalization which assumes that entities and their keys are easy to recognize in the application environment.[7] Normalized data can be represented as normalized data groups or as a bubble chart, depending upon one's preferences.

This process is shown in the following example. A logical user view is shown in Figure A.17. In this particular case the logical user view is represented by a form. If a form is not available, it might be advantageous to first make a list of the data elements which are associated with a logical user view. Items like page number would not be included as data elements, since a page number is not stored in the database nor is it calculated from other data elements.

The second step is to recognize the data elements which uniquely identify the entities associated with a logical user view. The entities associated with this logical user view are order, department, and item. The data elements which identify these entities are respectively Purchase-order #, Department #, and Item #. See Figure A.18 for an illustration of this process.

The next step is to determine the relationships between the entities and sketch these on the form. For example, an order involves a single department, but a department may have many orders. The resulting relationships are shown in Figure A.19. The relationship between orders and customers is many-to-one. The relationship between orders and items is a many-to-many relationship.

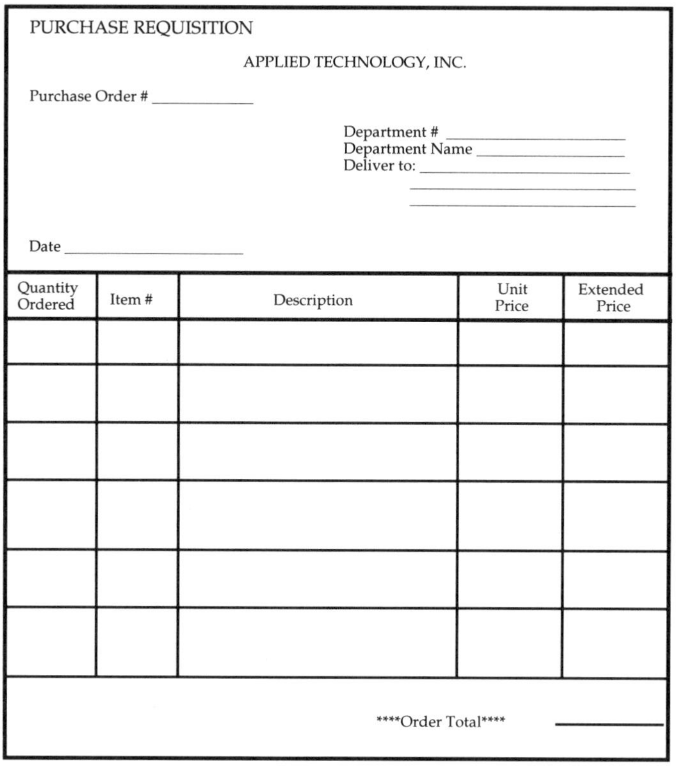
PURCHASE REQUISITION

APPLIED TECHNOLOGY, INC.

Purchase Order # ____________

Department # ____________
Department Name ____________
Deliver to: ____________

Date ____________

| Quantity Ordered | Item # | Description | Unit Price | Extended Price |
|---|---|---|---|---|
| | | | | |
| | | | | |
| | | | | |
| | | | | |
| | | | | |
| | | | | |

****Order Total**** ____________

FIGURE A.17
*A Logical User View*

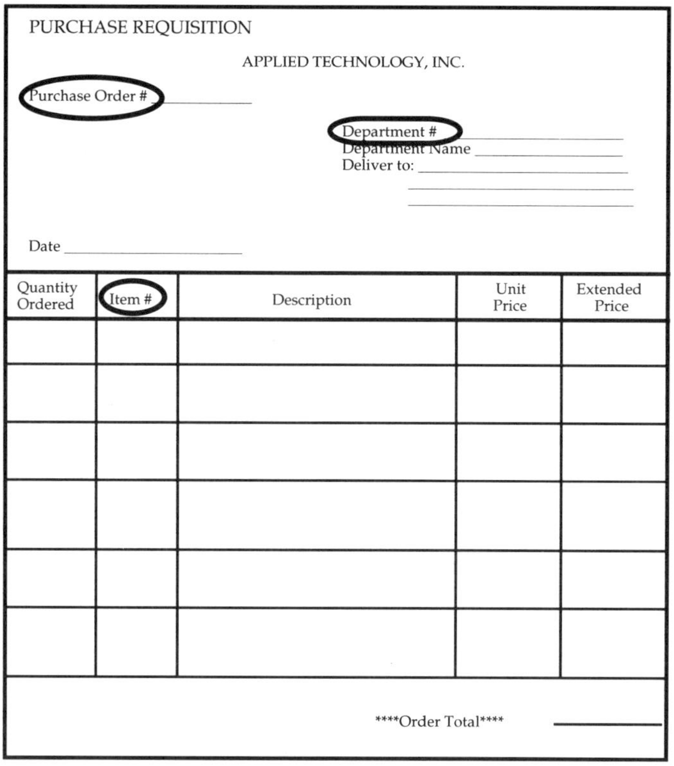
PURCHASE REQUISITION

APPLIED TECHNOLOGY, INC.

Purchase Order # ____________

Department # ____________
Department Name ____________
Deliver to: ____________

Date ____________

| Quantity Ordered | Item # | Description | Unit Price | Extended Price |
|---|---|---|---|---|
| | | | | |
| | | | | |
| | | | | |
| | | | | |
| | | | | |
| | | | | |

****Order Total**** ____________

FIGURE A.18
*Identification of Entities*

FIGURE A.19
*Entity Relationships*

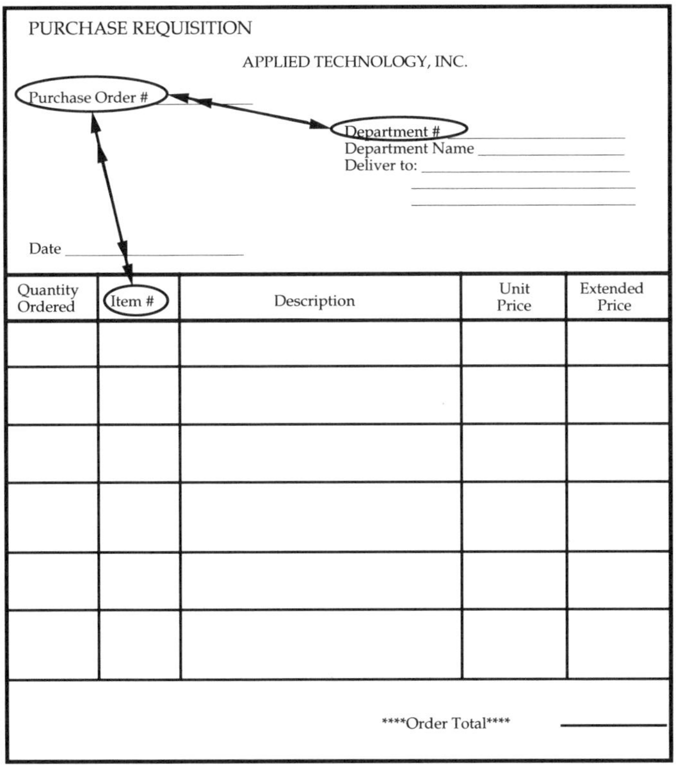


Many-to-many relationships must be resolved in a bubble chart. There can be many items per order and many orders for each item. This relationship is shown in Figure A.20.

FIGURE A.20
*A Many-to-Many Relationship*

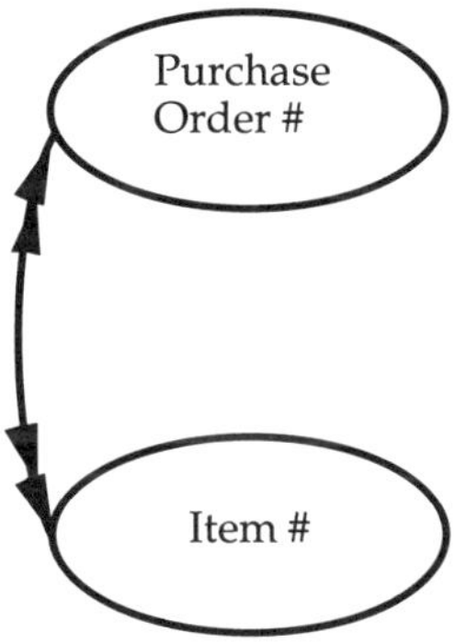

A many-to-many relationship is resolved by a concatenated key. The term concatenation refers to joining together. A concatenated key incorporates both of the primary keys in a single concatenated key. A concatenated key is shown in Figure A.21. The purpose of creating a concatenated key is not obvious at this point. Later, the student will find that some attributes need to have both keys to identify them.

FIGURE A.21

*Resolution of a Many-to-Many Relationship*

The many-to-many relationship is resolved with a concatenated key. The concatenated key has a many-to-one relationship with each of the original primary keys. With many-to-many relationships resolved, a bubble chart showing primary keys of the logical user view is complete. This is shown in Figure A.22.

To complete the bubble chart we must find which attributes are functionally dependent on a primary key. The term functional dependence refers to which primary key identifies one instance of the attribute. For example, a Department # will identify a specific Department-Name.

FIGURE A.22
*Logical User View With Primary Key Relationships*

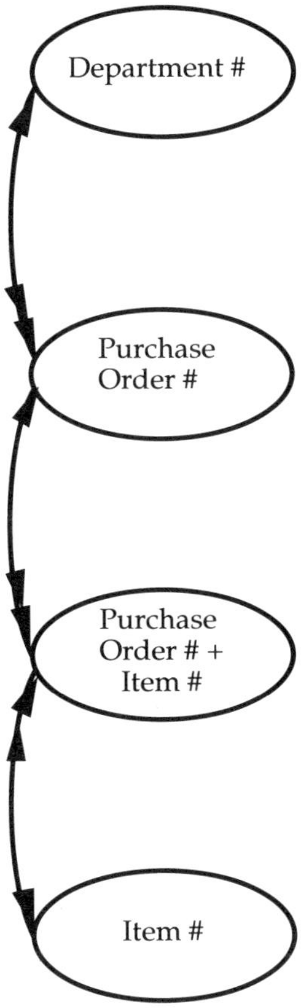


The remaining attributes from the form are as follows:

| ATTRIBUTE | FUNCTIONALLY DEPENDENT UPON |
|---|---|
| Department-Name | Department # |
| Deliver-to-Address | Department # |
| Order-Date | Purchase-Order # |
| Order-Total (D)* | Purchase-Order # |
| Qty-Ordered | Purchase-Order # + Item # |
| Unit Price ** | Purchase-Order # + Item # |
| Extended-Price (D) | Purchase-Order # + Item # |
| Item-Descriptio n | Item # |

*(D) Derived data - may not be in database

**Assumes different departments may get different prices.

Once the functional dependence of the remaining attributes has been determined, the bubble chart can be drawn. The bubble chart is shown in Figure A.23.

FIGURE A.23 *Bubble Chart for Order Form*

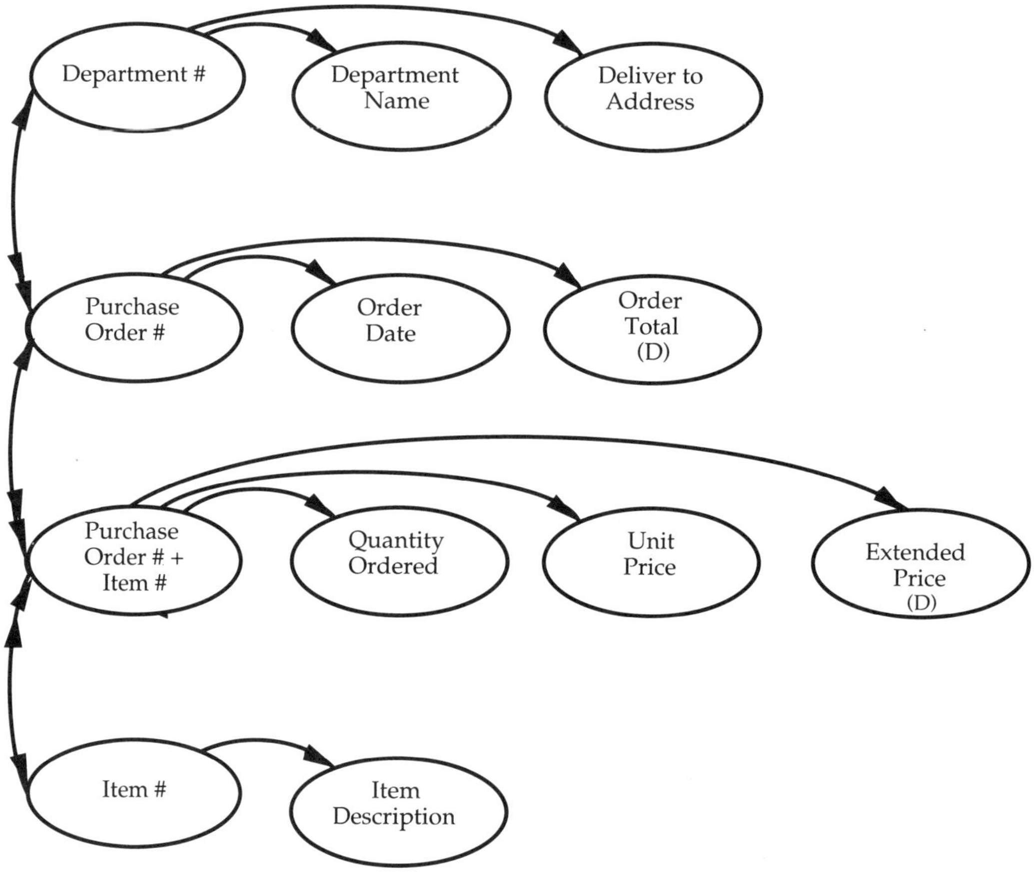


The final step is to add foreign keys to the bubble chart. A foreign key is defined as an attribute in one data group which is a key in another data group. In the relational database model related data groups are linked either by concatenated keys or by foreign keys. A foreign key is used in the absence of concatenation.

For example, Department # is the key of the data group shown in Figure A.24.

FIGURE A.24
*DEPARTMENT Data Group*

As shown earlier, the relationship between the DEPARTMENT data group and the PURCHASE ORDER data group is one-to-many as shown in Figure A.25.

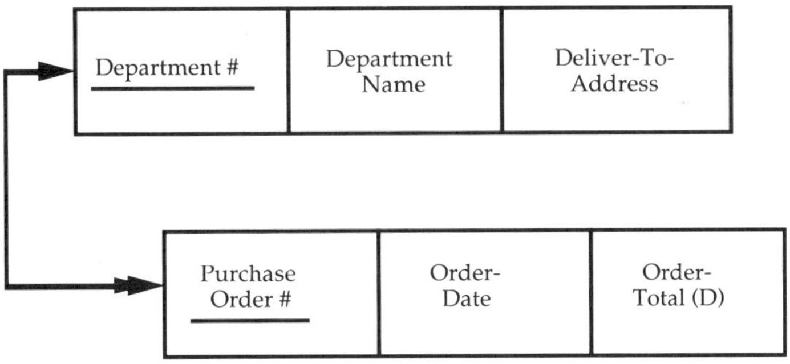


FIGURE A.25
*The Relationship Between the DEPARTMENT Data Group and the PURCHASE ORDER Data Group*

As was shown earlier, the relationship between this data group and the order data group is one-to-many as shown below in Figure A.25.

As shown in Figure A.26, Department # is added as a foreign key in the PURCHASE ORDER data group because it is a key in another

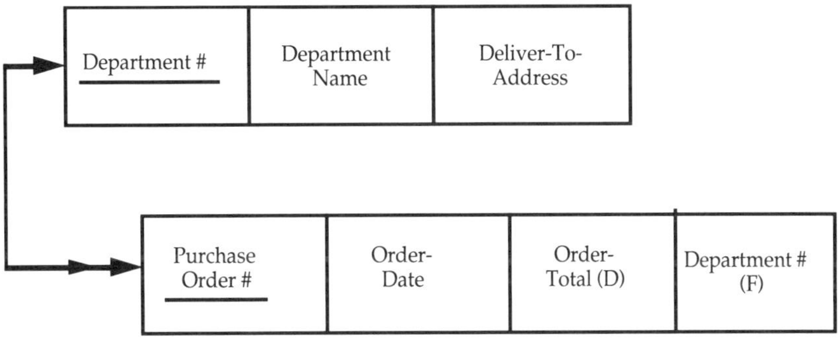


FIGURE A.26
*Department # is a Foreign Key in the PURCHASE ORDER Data Group*

data group. In contrast to other database models, the relational database model uses values in data groups rather than physical pointers to represent relationships.

The completed bubble chart is shown in Figure A.27.

FIGURE A.27 *Bubble Chart With Foreign Key*

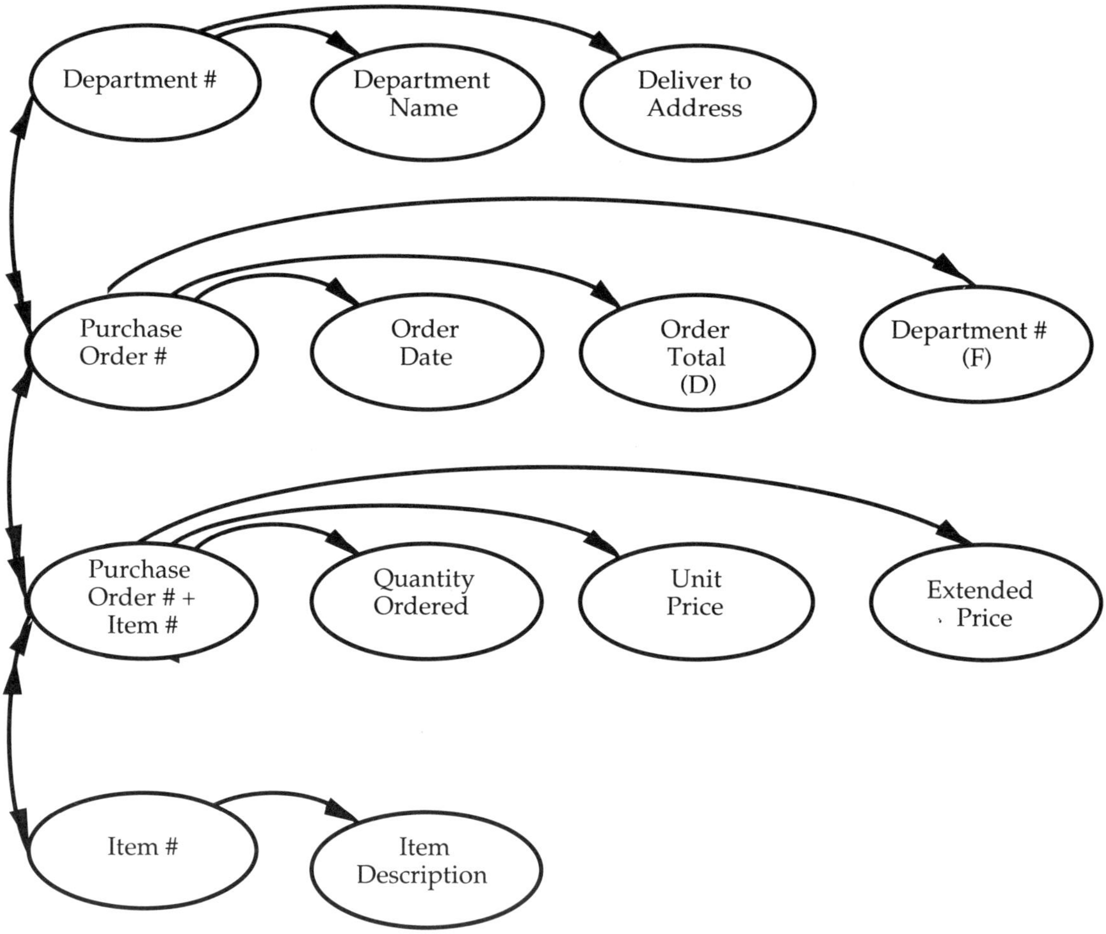


The bubble charting process can be summarized as follows:

1. Identify logical-user view
2. Identify entities in view.
3. Draw key bubbles.
4. Draw associations between keys.
5. Resolve many-to-many associations.
6. Determine functional dependence of remaining attributes.
7. Add attributes to keys.
8. Add foreign keys.

If the bubble charting process is done correctly, the resulting bubble chart will be fully normalized. The bubble charting approach works well for most logical user views, some views however, might be normalized more easily with the three step process.

## A Three Step Normalization Process

NORMALIZATION MAY BE CONCEPTUALIZED AS A THREE-STAGE process which changes unnormalized data to third-normal form. Unnormalized data is recognized by the presence of repeating groups. A repeating group is a field or group of fields that can take on more than one value in a single record. Unnormalized data with a repeating group is shown in Figure A.28.

FIGURE A.28 *Unnormalized Data With Repeating Groups*

| Purchase Order # | Dept. # | Dept. Name | Item # | Description | Quantity | Unit Price |
|---|---|---|---|---|---|---|
| 204 | 522 | Payroll | W-1 | Pencils | 6 | .15 |
| 204 | 522 | Payroll | Q-66 | Pens | 24 | .59 |
| 406 | 601 | Admin. | Z-28 | Paper | 1 | 4.00 |
| 406 | 601 | Admin. | Q-66 | Pens | 18 | .59 |
| 326 | 773 | Finance | R-101 | Glue Stick | 100 | .69 |

Unnormalized records or data groups can be changed to first-normal form by removing the repeating group into a new data group. A record without a repeating group is already in first-normal form.

The key of the new data group is the key of the original data group concatenated with a key from the repeating group. A concatenated key is two or more data elements that are required to uniquely identify the entity associated with the new data group. Figure A.29 shows how this is accomplished. Note that Item *, which is from the repeating group, and Purchase-Order # make up the concatenated key.

FIGURE A.29 *First Normal Form: No Repeating Groups*

| Purchase Order # | Dept. # | Dept. Name |
|---|---|---|
| 204 | 522 | Payroll |
| 406 | 601 | Admin. |
| 326 | 773 | Finance |

| Purchase Order # | Item # | Description | Quantity | Unit Price |
|---|---|---|---|---|
| 204 | W-1 | Pencils | 6 | .15 |
| 204 | Q-66 | Pens | 24 | .59 |
| 406 | Z-28 | Paper | 1 | 4.00 |
| 406 | Q-66 | Pens | 18 | .59 |
| 326 | R-101 | Glue Stick | 100 | .69 |

While repeating groups are eliminated in first normal form, there are still problems to be resolved. Specifically, there are anomalies present which would cause problems in inserting, deleting, and updating data. Referring to the data group at the right of Figure A.29, the following problems can be observed.

| ANOMALY | EXAMPLE |
|---|---|
| Insertion | You cannot enter an item description until a pur chase order number is assigned. |
| Deletion | If you delete an order you delete the description of the item associated with that order. |
| Update | If you desire to update an item description you must search for every record that contains that item. |

These anomalies are caused by redundancy, which creates potential data integrity problems. To move towards resolution of these anomalies, we must get the data in second-normal form.

To get data in second-normal form requires an understanding of the concept of functional dependence. Functional dependence refers to data elements which are uniquely identified by other data elements. This concept is shown in Figure A.30. As shown in Figure A.30, Item # identifies a single value of Description. Description is said to be functionally dependent upon Item #. In contrast, it takes both Purchase-Order # and Item # to uniquely identify Quantity and Unit Price. The reason for this is that both price and quantity will vary on different orders.

FIGURE A.30
*Functional Dependence*

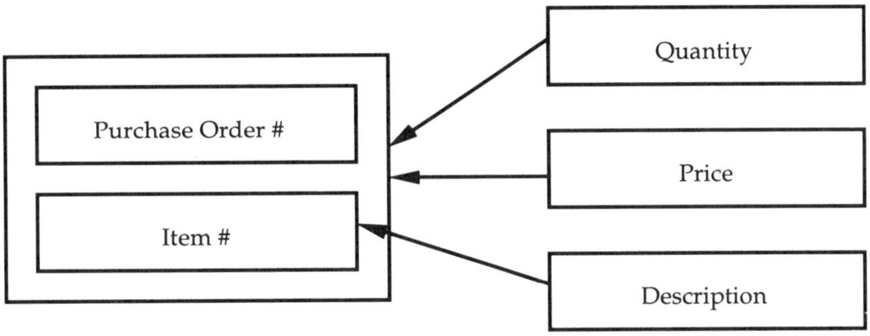


Functional dependence is the concept behind second normal form. Data groups in first-normal form with a single key are already in second-normal form. Data groups with concatenated keys must be examined to determine if all data elements are functionally dependent on the whole key. Those not functionally dependent on the whole key form a new data item group again as shown in Figure A.31.

FIGURE A.31
*Second Normal Form: Fully Functionally Dependent on Whole Key*

| Purchase Order # | Dept. # | Dept. Name |
|---|---|---|
| 204 | 522 | Payroll |
| 406 | 601 | Admin. |
| 326 | 773 | Finance |

| Purchase Order # | Item # | Quantity | Unit Price |
|---|---|---|---|
| 204 | W-1 | 6 | .15 |
| 204 | Q-66 | 24 | .59 |
| 406 | Z-28 | 1 | 4.00 |
| 406 | Q-66 | 18 | .59 |
| 326 | R-101 | 100 | .69 |

| Item # | Description |
|---|---|
| W-1 | Pencils |
| Q-66 | Pens |
| Z-28 | Paper |
| R-101 | Glue Stick |

Note that the key of the new data group is the data element which was part of the concatenated key and upon which the other data elements are functionally dependent. The original concatenated key is retained with any data items that are functionally dependent upon it.

There are still problems in second-normal form. The data groups show on the left of Figure A.31 is in second-normal form because it is in first-normal form and doesn't have a concatenated key. This data-item group still has insertion, deletion, and update anomalies as shown below:

| ANOMALY | EXAMPLE |
|---|---|
| Insertion | You cannot enter any information about a customer until the customer places an order. |
| Deletion | If you delete the last order a customer placed you delete information about the customer. |
| Update | If you want to update information about a customer you must find every data group with the same customer number that you wish to update. |

The redundancy present in second-normal form can cause problems of potentially inconsistent data. These problems are resolved in third normal form.

Changing data structures from second-normal form to third-normal form requires the identification of transitive dependencies or hidden keys. A data element that is functionally dependent upon a non-key data element must be removed into a separate data group. The key of the new data group is the non-key element that identifies other data elements in the group. It should be noted that the new key remains in the original data group as a non-key element. This is illustrated in Figure A.32.

The steps required to reach normalization are summarized in Figure A.33.

A data structure in third-normal form an be identified by asking this question: Are all data elements functionally dependent on the key, the whole key, and nothing but the key?[8]

We have shown normalization as a three-step process, and for beginners it is useful to visualize it in that manner. Experienced data modelers, however, can go to third-normal form immediately. There has been some investigation of normal forms beyond third-normal form, but as a practical matter, most authorities stop at third-normal form.[9]

FIGURE A.32
*Third Normal Form: No Hidden Keys*

| Purchase Order # | Dept. # |
|---|---|
| 204 | 522 |
| 406 | 601 |
| 326 | 773 |

| Dept. # | Dept. Name |
|---|---|
| 522 | Payroll |
| 601 | Admin. |
| 773 | Finance |

| Item # | Description |
|---|---|
| W-1 | Pencils |
| Q-66 | Pens |
| Z-28 | Paper |
| R-101 | Glue Stick |

| Purchase Order # | Item # | Quantity | Unit Price |
|---|---|---|---|
| 204 | W-1 | 6 | .15 |
| 204 | Q-66 | 24 | .59 |
| 406 | Z-28 | 1 | 4.00 |
| 406 | Q-66 | 18 | .59 |
| 326 | R-101 | 100 | .69 |

FIGURE A.33
*Summary of the Steps Required to Reach Normalization*

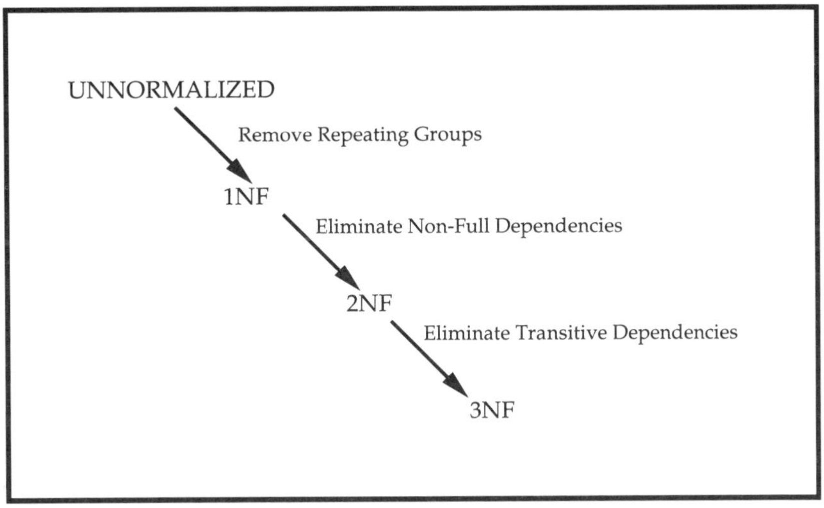

Bubble charting and normalization are complementary processes. In some cases, the data modeler will find it easier to first normalize and then construct a bubble chart. In other cases, it will be easier to construct a bubble chart and then determine if it is properly normalized. The author has found that logical user views with several repeating groups are easier to tackle by first normalizing and then bubble charting. Most situations, however, lend themselves to bubble charting.

## Canonical Synthesis

ONE OF THE MOST FUNDAMENTAL CONCEPTS OF DATABASE IS data sharing by multiple applications. This avoids redundancy and consequent data-integrity problems. The data requirements for each application can be shown as a bubble chart. Data structures of this type are referred to as logical-user views. Several related logical-user views are combined to make up a subject database.

Logical-user views for a payroll application and a personnel record application would obviously have some data elements in common. These logical-user views may be combined manually or they may be combined by an automated tool. The advantages of an automated tool are as follows:

1. It provides an automated mechanism for documenting database design.
2. An automated tool simplifies corrections or additions to an existing design.
3. Errors in the design may be detected by the automated design tool.

To illustrate the use of an automated database design tool, three logical-user views will be integrated. The first is the bubble chart of the order-form illustrated in Figure A.33. Two additional logical-user views, shown as bubble charts, are a Purchasing Department Report and a Budget Analysis Report which are represented in Figure A.34.

The input for the data-modeling tool is shown in Figure A.35. The input identifies both the name and the relationships of data elements.

FIGURE A.33 *Bubble Chart of Order Form*

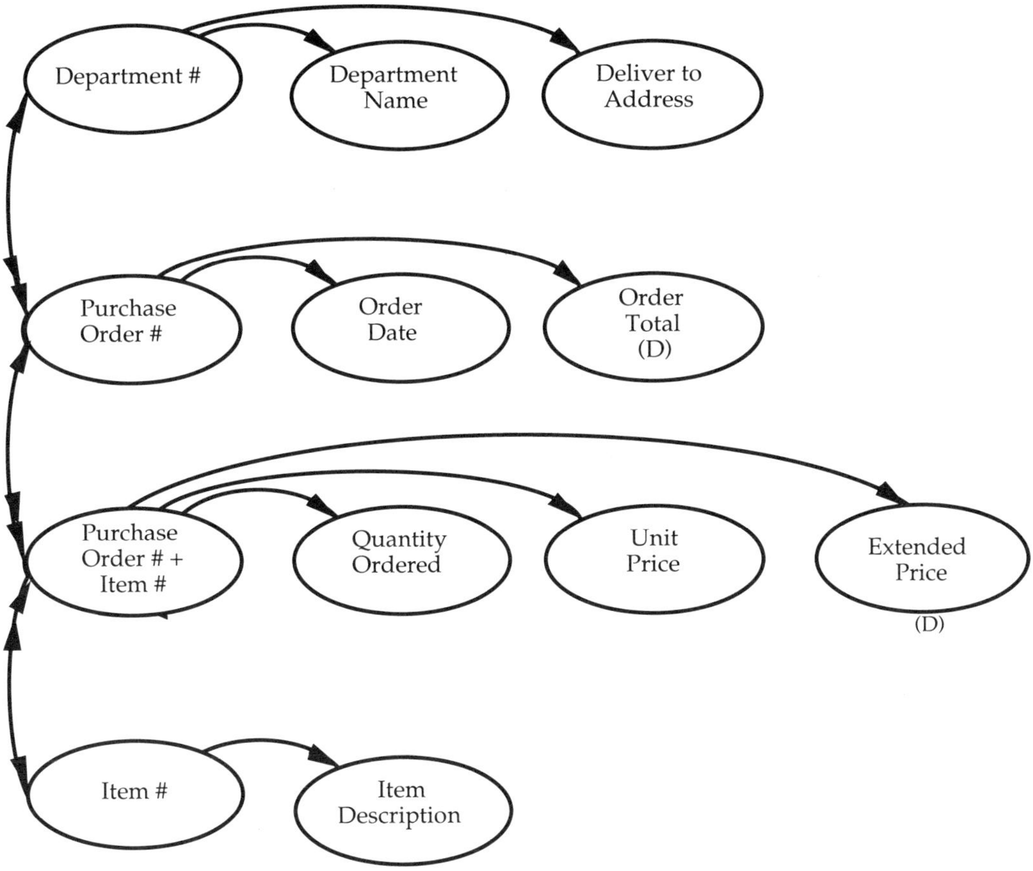


FIGURE A.34 *Logical User Views Before Synthesis*

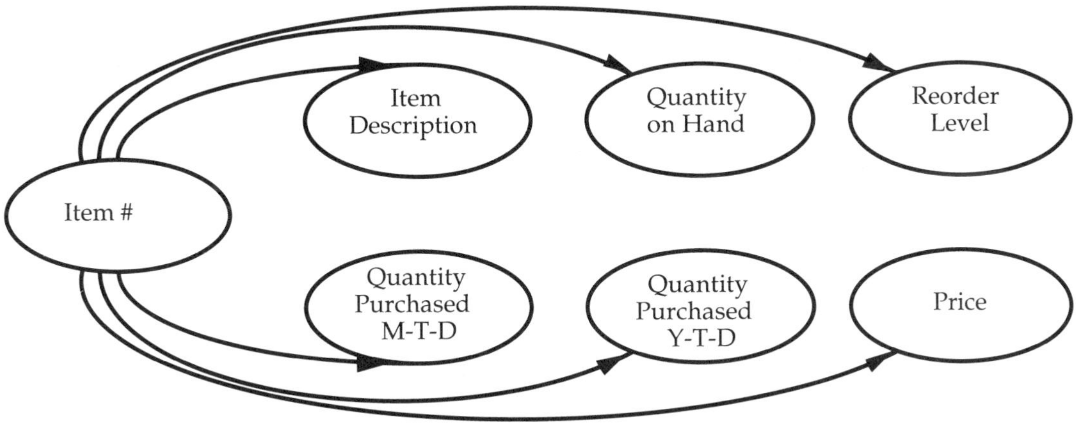


(a) Bubble Chart of Purchasing Department Report

FIGURE A.34 *Continued*

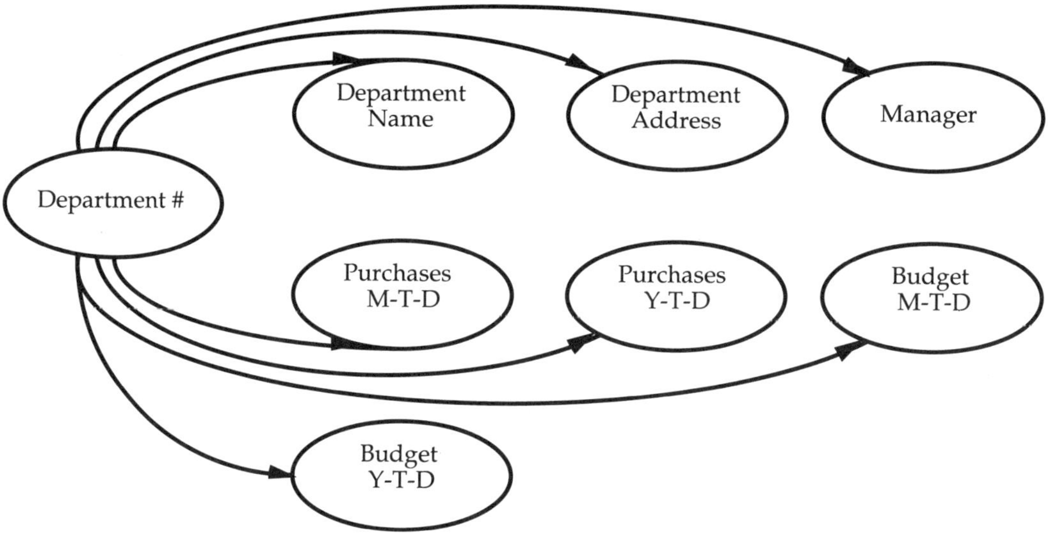


(b) Bubble Chart of Budget Analysis Report

The first character identifies the type of entry or relationship. This is illustrated below:

| FIRST CHARACTER | MEANING |
|---|---|
| V | Logical user view |
| K | Primary key |
| L | Data item group label |
| 1 | An attribute of previous key with a one to one relationship |
| M | An attribute with zero, one or many values |
| C | Concatenated key—data element is concatenated with previous element. |

Note that keys are entered both as a primary key and as attributes of other keys with which they have relationships.

The output is an integrated model which incorporates all three logical user views. The output is shown in Figure A.36. The tool has several parameters which can be controlled by the database modeler to secure the desired result. It incorporates several error-detection and modeling-logic features, which are especially helpful to the novice database analyst.

FIGURE A.35
*Input for Data ModelingTool*

```
V, ORDER-FORM
K, DEPT-#
L, DEPARTMENT-DETAILS
1, DEPT-NAME
1, DEPT-ADD
M, ORDER-#
K, ORDER-#
L, ORDER-DETAILS
1, DEPT-#
1, ORDER-DATE
1, ORDER-TOTAL
M, ORDER-#
C, ITEM-#
K, ORDER-#
C, ITEM-#
L, ORDER-LINE-DETAILS
1, QTY-ORD
1, UNIT-PRICE
1, EXT-PRICE
1, ORDER-#
1, ITEM-#
K, ITEM-#
L, ITEM-DETAILS
1, ITEM-DESC
M, ORDER-#
C, ITEM-#
V, PURCHASING-REPORT
K, ITEM-#
1, ITEM-DESC
1, QTY-ON-HAND
1, REORDER-LEVEL
1, QTY-PURCHASED-MTD
1, QTY-PURCHASED-YTD
1, ITEM-PRICE
V, BUDGET-ANALYSIS-REPORT
K, DEPT-#
1, DEPT-NAME
1, DEPT-ADD
1, MANAGER
1, PURCHASES-MTD
1, PURCHASES-YTD
1, BUDGET-MTD
1, BUDGET-YTD
```

There are several automated database design tools including Data Base Design Aid, FACETS, Design Manager, and Data Designer. The tool illustrated in this chapter is Data Designer.

Automated database modeling tools might be compared with word processing and spreadsheet software; all of these software packages facilitate functions that can be done manually, but are easier with automated tools.

FIGURE A.36

*Output From Automated Design Tool*

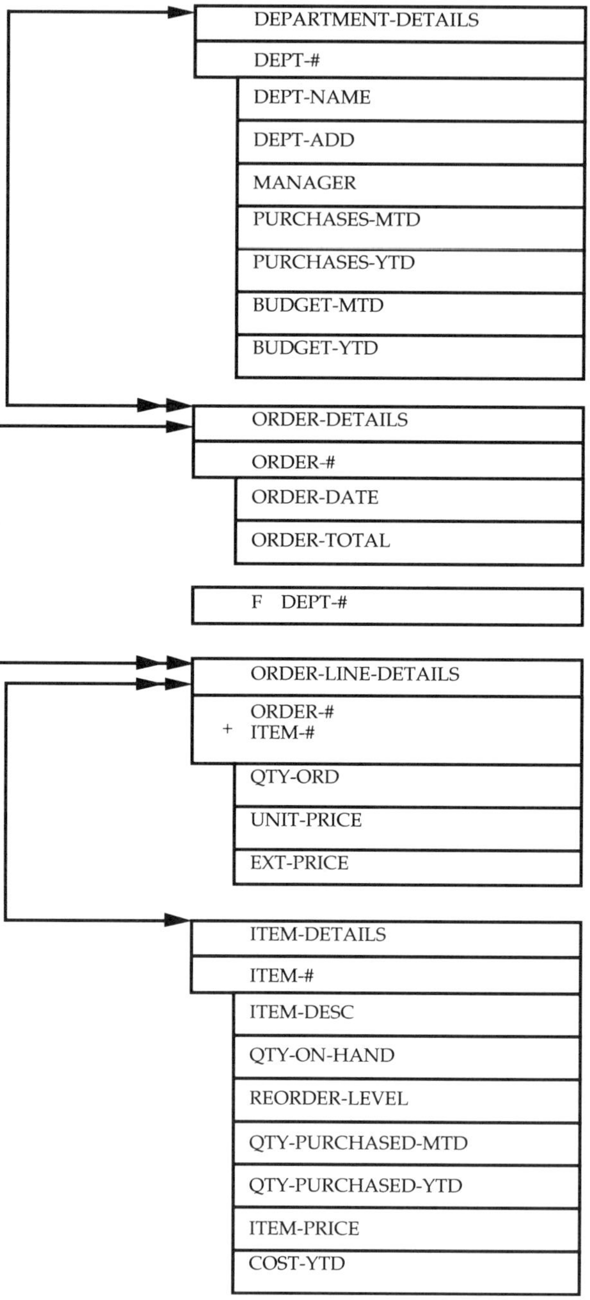

There are some obvious relationships between a logical data model and how data is physically stored. Generally speaking, an entity becomes a table in the DBMS, a one-to-many relationship becomes a foreign key and an attribute becomes a column in a table; a many-to-many relationship requires a separate table.[10] The function of foreign keys and concatenated keys is to provide navigational links between related tables.

The database design strategy discussed in this chapter has been described as top down/bottom up. Bill Durell is critical of this methodology in Issues and Controversies.

## Issues and Controversies

## The Fallacy of Top Down/Bottom Up Design

Information Resource Management (IRM) has brought about a recognition that logical data analysis and design should precede physical database design and implementation. This recognition was created by an number of factors including the following:

- The costs of computer hardware have steadily declined. This has made the issue of physical database design with its emphasis on database optimization and performance less significant.
- The increasing cost of software development ha placed more emphasis on designing data structures that are flexible, modular and extensible. This has been done to reduce future costs associated with database redesign and reorganization.
- Since information is recognized as an organizational asset should we not employ measures to improve data quality and accessibility?
- The widespread adoption of the relational model has emphasized the importance of logical design based on the relational model.

While there is widespread agreement on the need for logical data modeling there is no concensus on how it should be done. There are three basic methodologies: 1) bottom up, 2) two-pronged approach, and 3) top down.

### The Bottom Up Method

The bottom up method starts with the identification of data elements. These data elements are classified in two categories: 1) keys and 2) attributes. A bubble chart diagram is drawn showing the association of these data elements. These diagrams are drawn on a userview by userview basis. These charts are combined in a process called canonical synthesis. Data elements with a common key represent logical record types.

### The Two-Pronged Approach

The two pronged approach appears to be the most commonly used method. This method begins with top down analysis followed by bottom up design. The top down phase consists of entity identification, definition, and classification. This is followed by the bottom up process described above. The logical record types identified in this stage are fit into the entities identified in the top down phase.

THE TOP DOWN METHOD
This method begins by identified entity super groups or subject databases. These are broken down into entities following the rules of normalization. When this process is complete the result is logical record types.

THE DISADVANTAGES OF THE BOTTOM UP

1. It makes the assumption that today's data processing system will satisfy the needs of tomorrow's shared database.
2. It assumes that the data elements in today's userviews will be the same as the new data elements.
3. This approach assumes you can name and design data elements without an information model.
4. It requires the data analyst to deal with a tremendous number of data elements.
5. It is time consuming and labor-intensive.
6. Without the benefit of an information model it is difficult to understand the scope of the bottom up activity.
7. The bottom up tool requires an automated tool to manage the complexity of hundreds or thousands of data elements.
8. The bottom up approach often creates redundant data elements and unnecessary primary keys.
9. This approach does not consider future information needs.

DISADVANTAGES OF THE TWO PRONGED APPROACH
This approach suffers from many of the same problems as the bottom up approach. The initial top-down entity analysis does provide a framework of an information architecture before the bottom analysis is begun.

CONCLUSION
The strictly top down approach is clearly superior. Using the top down method the identification of entities and logical record types can be achieved in less time and at less cost than either of the two other methods. Employing the top down approach will develop a fully normalized database model and eliminate the need for the bottom up logical design phase.

Adapted from Bill Durell, "The Fallacy of Top-down Bottom-up Design," Database Newsletter (May/June 1986), pp. 1-15.

## Guidelines for Managers

DATABASE DESIGN REQUIRES MANAGERIAL LEADERSHIP AND involvement. The process of database design requires an understanding of data relationships which are often determined by organization policy or by business practice. Management and end-users are in the best position to define these relationships; their involvement is vital to database modeling efforts.

Success with 4th database technology requires more than the acquisition of software and hardware. It requires a new method of developing software which rests on a foundation of database design.

## Guidelines for MIS Professionals

DATABASE DESIGN IS THE FOUNDATION UPON WHICH SUBJECT database applications are developed. Computer professionals should prepare for this new environment by acquiring skills in database design, including normalization, canonical synthesis, and entity relationship modeling. Data administrators usually train others in normalization and supervise the initial database design project.

## Key Terms

Conceptual Model
Logical Model
Physical Model
Entity
Primary Key
Attributes
Top Down Process
Entity Relationship Diagram
Binary Relationship
N-ARY Relationship
Weak Entity
Entity Subtypes
Entity Supertypes
Normalization
Data Elements
Repeating Group
First-Normal Form
Concatenated Key
Redundancy
Data Integrity
Second-Normal Form
Functional Dependence
Third-Normal Form
Transitive Dependence
Bubble Chart
Secondary Key
Data Group
Logical User View
Many-to-One Relationship
Many-to-Many Relationship
Foreign Key
Canonical Synthesis
Subject Data Base
Automated Database Modeling Tool
Cardinalities

## Review Questions

1. Obtain a logical user view for a credit card statement of account, a phone bill, or some other common document. Using the bubble chart diagramming syntax introduced in this chapter, draw a data model from the entities and relationships found on the document by first identifying the primary keys for the entities.
2. Draw the association between the primary keys you identified in Question 1.
3. Resolve the many-to-many relationships in the model you developed in answering Question 2.
4. Add nonkey attributes to the model you developed in answering Question 3.
5. Identify the foreign key attributes in the model you developed in answering Question 4.
6. How does the conceptual schema differ from the logical database design?
7. How does the logical database design differ from the physical database design?
8. What is the difference between transitive dependence and functional dependence? Give an example of each.
9. Contrast the following terms:
   a. Unnormalized relation; normalized relation
   b. Full dependence; partial dependence
   c. Insertion anomaly; deletion anomly
   d. Primary key; foreign key
   e. Supertype; subtype
10. Classify each of the following relations as unnormalized, 1NF, 2NF, or 3NF (state any assumptions you make).
    a. EMPLOYEE (EMPLOYEE#,EMPNAME,JOBCODE)
    b. EMPLOYEE (EMPLOYEE#,EMPNAME {JOBCODE,#YEARS})
    c. EMPLOYEE(EMPLOYEE#,EMPNAME,JOBCODE,JOB DESCRIPTION)
    d. EMPLOYEE (EMPLOYEE#,EMPNAME,PROJECT#,HRS-WORKED)

**Case Study**

## THE UNITED STATES AIR FORCE

The Air Force training program resembles the curriculum of a university, except that its program is much larger than the average civilian institution. The training program includes more than 5,000 Air Force skills supported by some 500 courses. Each year, approximately 50,000 classes are held and over 250,000 Air Force personnel are trained.

The purpose of Air Force education and training is to provide enough skilled and knowledgeable people to meet Air Force requirements. To achieve this goal, program managers rely on complex procedures to determine skill requirements, plan training programs, schedule courses and classes, recruit qualified men and women, and train those people.

An Air Force study identified several deficiencies in a sequence of training events that begin when the Air Force recruits and enlists an individual and end when the individual is assigned to an Air Force unit. The study concluded that many organizations in the training process lacked adequate information to identify problems and support critical decision making. As a result, organizations made decisions without realizing the impact on the activities of other organizations. Many examples of inadequate information were directly attributed to deficiences in data processing support.

At the time, data processing support for training came from a number of independent subsystems that had evolved in increments over many years (Figure S5.37 shows the primary sources of data). The earliest applications were oriented toward record keeping, and each subsystem developed unique applications to support a specific organization mission.

The first subsystem was a small hierarchical database that contained class schedules and enrolled students. The hierarchy duplicated a number of data elements, such as class-related items.

The second subsystem was a standard batch processing design that consisted of two primary master files—one for courses and one for classes. Both master files used repeating groups of data to store information about skills and students.

The third subsystem, designed to manage Air Force skills, used a flat file of very large skill records. The skill record contained repeating groups of 12 months of courses and each month contained repeating groups for six classes. Although the skill subsystem performed a critical and very specialized function, it duplicated the entire class schedule in the second subsystem.

1. What are some of the problems that could be avoided by designing and implementing a centralized database?
2. Define the functions, processes and activities of the Air Force Training program.
3. Define the entities and draw an E/R diagram.

FIGURE S5.37 *Primary Sources of Air Force Training Data*

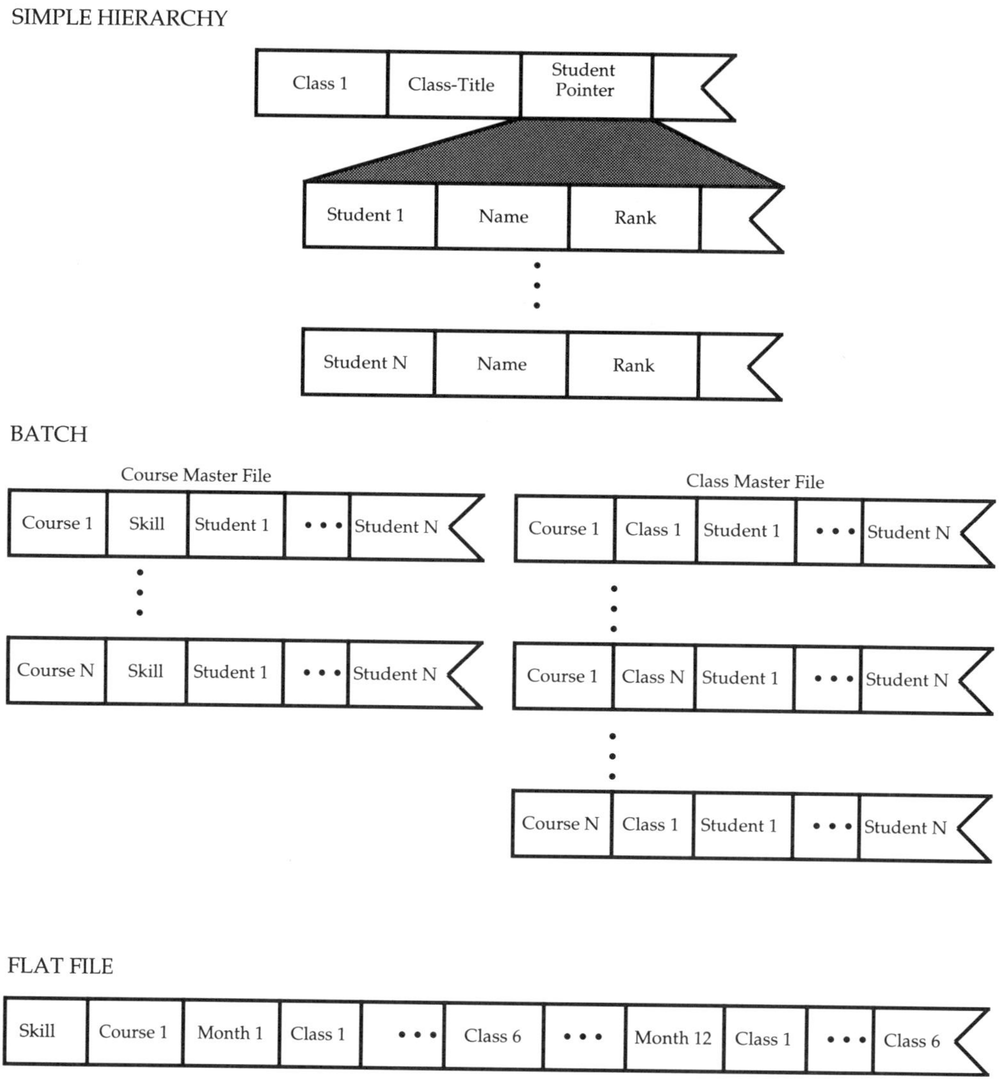

# References

## CHAPTER 1


1. Jay Galbraith, Designing Complex Organizations (Reading, MA: Addison-Wesley Publishing Co., 1973), p. 5.

2. David M. Kroenke and Kathleen A. Dolan, Business Computer Systems (Santa Cruz, CA: Mitchell Publishing Co., 1987), pp. 34-44.

3. Philip J. Gill, "On-Line Transaction Processing," Computerworld (September 29, 1986), p. 43.

4. Ibid.

5. James Martin, An Information Systems Manifesto (Englewood Cliffs, NJ: Prentice-Hall, Inc., 1984), p. 10.

6. Ibid.

7. "Missing Computer Software," Business Week, (September 1, 1989), p. 44.

8. "He Was An Idea Sparker," Datamation (March 1980), p. 55.

9. Phillip Ein-Dor, "Grosch's Law Re-Revisited: CPU Power and the Cost of Computation:, Communications of the ACM (February, 1985), p. 149.

10. Robert I. Benjamin, "Managing Through a Decade of Discontinuity," Information Systems News (August 22, 1983), p. 20.

11. Henry C. Lucas, Jr., "Utilizing Information Technology: Guidelines for Managers," Sloan Management Review (Summer 1986), p. 25.

13. Lucas, Ibid, p. 42.

14. Martin Healey, "What is a Workstation," Datamation (Jan. 15, 1987), pp. 55-57.

15. Robert M. Alloway and Judith A. Quillard, "Users Managers' Systems Needs," MIS Quarterly (June 1983), pp. 35-39.


## CHAPTER 2


1. Charles Wiseman, Strategy and Computers (Homewood, Ill.: Dow-Jones-Irwin, 1985), pp. 5-7.

2. Annual Report McKesson Corp., 1983

3. Wiseman, Ibid., pp. 5-7.

4. Michael E. Porter and Victor E. Miller, "How Information Gives You Competitive Advantage," Harvard Business Review (July-August 1985), p. 150.

5. Harold S. Bott, Jacque H. Pasino and Jeff Hamilton, "How to Make a Strategic Move with Information Systems," Information WEEK (May 26, 1986), pp. 30-52.

6. Donald A. Marchand and Forest W. Horton, Jr., Infotrends (New York: John Wiley and Sons, Incl, 1986), pp. 76-80.

7. James I. Cash, Jr. and Ben R. Konsynski, "IS Redraws Competitive Boundaries," Harvard Business Review (March-April 1985), p. 134.

8. Peter Petre, "How To Keep Customers Happy Captives," Fortune (September 2, 1985), p. 44.

9. Cash and Konsynski, Ibid., p. 135.

10. Paul A. Strassman, Information Payoff (New York: The Free Press, 1985), p. 131.

11. Ibid.

12. Petre, Ibid., p. 32.

13. George Schussel, "Application Development in the 5th Generation," Datamation (November 15, 1987), p. 102.

14. Duncan G. Copeland and James L. McKenney, "Airline Reservation Systems: Lessons from History," MIS Quarterly (September 1988), pp. 367-368.

15. Schussel, Ibid.

16. Bott et al., Ibid., p. 32.

17. Robert H. Hayes and William J. Abernathy, "Managing Our Way to Economic Decline," Harvard Business Review, (July-August 1980), p. 74.

18. James Martin, Strategic Data Planning Methodologies, Englewood Cliffs, NJ: Prentice-Hall, Inc., 1982), p. 1.

19. William J. Doll, "Avenues for Top Management Involvement in Successful MIS Development," MIS Quarterly, (March 1985), p. 21.

## CHAPTER 3

1. John Rockart, "Chief Executives Define Their Own Data Needs," Harvard Business Review, (March-April, 1979), pp. 82-84.

2. Ibid., pp. 86-87.

3. Dennis M. Fitzpatrick and Earl F. Hadden, II, "Information Engineering Based System Development," Database Newsletter, (May/June, 1987), p. 11.

4. Milt Bryce, "The IRM Idea," Datamation, (April 15, 1987), p. 92.

5. Albert L. Lederer and Vijay Sethi, "The Implementation of Strategic Information Systems Planning Methodologies," MIS Quarterly (September 1988), pp. 445-461.

6. Dale L. Goodhue, Judith A. Quillard, and John F. Rockart, "Managing the Data Resource: A Contingency Perspective," MIS Quarterly (September 1988), pp. 377-379.

7. Robert H. Holland, Data Base: The Misused Technology, unpublished paper, p. 1.

## CHAPTER 4

1. Fred R. McFadden, and Jeffrey A. Hoffer, Data Base Management, 2nd Edition (Menlo Park, CA: The Benjamin/Cummings Publishing Co., 1988), p. 20.

2. S. Atre, DATABASE: Structured Techniques for Design, Performance and Management (New York: Wiley-Interscience, 1980), p. 17.

3. McFadden and Hoffer, Ibid.

4. Alan Radding, "RDBMS Show They Can Pull OLTP Weight" Computerworld (February 27, 1989), pp. 63-64.

5. Edith Myers, "Database Machines Take Off" Datamation (May 15, 1985), p. 54.

6. George Schussel, "Application Development in the 5th Generation," Datamation (November 15, 1987), p. 97.

7. "The Genesis of a Database Computer" Computer (November 1984), p. 43.

8. George Schussel, Ibid.

9. "How Relational Architectures Differ" Datamation (November 15, 1988), p. 34.

10. Janis Herter, "3 Directions of PC DBMS," Software Magazine (October, 1989), pp. 63-70.

11. James Martin, Managing the Data-Base Environment (Englewood Cliffs, N.J.: Prentice-Hall, Inc., 1983), p. 13.

## SUPPLEMENT TO CHAPTER 4

1. C. J. Date, "Where SQL Falls Short," Datamation (May 1, 1987), p. 84.

2. Ibid., p. 83.

3. George Schussel, "Application Development in the 5th Generation," Datamation (November 15, 1987), p. 100.

4. Gary Long and Robert Byers, "SQL in Perspective," Data Based Advisor (September 1987), p. 22.

## CHAPTER 5

1. William Durell, "Politics of Data," Computerworld (September 9, 1985), p. 1-25.

2. "Project Methodology Survey," Data Base Newsletter (March-April 1986), pp. 5-7.

3. James Martin, Managing the Data-Base Environment (Englewood Cliffs: Prentice Hall, Inc., 1983), pp. 76-78.

4. V. Venkatakrishnan, "Differences in Dictionaries," Computerworld (March 14, 1988), p. 513.

## CHAPTER 6

1. Powers, Adams and Mills, Computer Information Systems Development: Analysis and Design (Cincinnati: South-Western Publishing Co., 1984), pp. 52-53.

2. Gane and Sarson, Structured Systems Analysis: Tools and Techniques (Englewood Cliffs, N.J.: Prentice-Hall, Inc., 1979), pp. 224-225.

3. The first three generations are from Colter. The 4th Generation is my own interpretation. Mel A. Colter, "A Comparative Examination of Systems Analysis Techniques," MIS Quarterly (March 1984), pp. 51-66.

4. Couger, Colter and Knapp, Advanced System Development/ Feasibility Techniques (New York: John Wiley and Sons, 1982)< p. 51.

5. Capers Jones, Programming Productivity, (New York: McGraw-Hill Book Co., 1986), p. 118.

6. Ibid., p. 114.

## CHAPTER 7

1. James C. Wetherbe, Systems Analysis and Design: Traditional, Structured and Advanced Concepts and Techniques, 2nd Edition (St. Paul: West Publishing Co., 1984), p. 7.

2. James Martin, Application Development Without Programmers (Englewood Cliffs, N.J.: Prentice-Hall, Inc., 1982), p. 2.

3. Steven L. Alter, "How Effective Managers Use Information Systems," Harvard Business Review (November-December, 1976), pp. 97-104.

4. Linda Speckmann, "Joint Application Design at Texas Instruments," Technology Transfer News (Winter 1986/1987), p. 12.

5. Don Leavitt, "Team Techniques in System Development," Datamation (September 15, 1987), p. 82.

6. Allen Gill, "Setting Up Your Own Group Design Session," Datamation (September 15, 1987), p. 88.

7. Beau Sheil, "Power Tools for Programmers," Datamation, (February 1983), p. 132.

8. Bernard H. Board, Application Prototyping (New York: Wiley-Interscience, 1984), p. 35.

9. Adapted from Lee Adamski, "Prototyping," Computerworld (May 6, 1985), pp. 24-25.

10. Gremillian and Pyburn, "Breaking the Systems Development Bottleneck," Harvard Business Review, (March/April, 1983), pp. 130-137.

## SUPPLEMENT TO CHAPTER 7

1. David H. Freeman, "Programming Without Tears," High Technology (April 1986), p. 38.

2. George Schussel, "A Taxonomy for Productivity Software," Data Base Newsletter (September/October 1986), pp. 1-11.

3. Ibid.

4. James Martin and Carma McClure, Diagramming Techniques for Analysts and Programmers (Englewood Cliffs, NJ: Prentice-Hall, Inc., 1985), p. 311.

5. W. W. Dowdell, "What MIS Professionals Need from Their 4GLs," Computerworld (September 29, 1986), p. 61.

6. Elie C. Harel and Ephraim R. McLean, "The Effects of Using Nonprocedural Computer Language on Programmer Productivity" MIS Quarterly, (June 1985), pp. 109-120.

7. Capers Jones, Programming Productivity (New York: McGraw-Hill Book Company, 1986), pp. 160-163.

8. Eberhard E. Rudolph, "Productivity in Computer Application Development" Department of Management Studies - The University of Auckland Working Paper #9 (March 1983), pp. 24-25.

9. James Martin, Fourth Generation Languages Vol. I (Englewood Cliffs, NJ: Prentice-Hall, Inc., 1985), pp. 87-88.

10. Stan Kolodziej, "The Fate of the 4GLs," Computerworld (February 3, 1988), pp. 25-28.

## CHAPTER 8


1. Elliot J. Chikofsky and Burt L. Rubenstein, "Case: Reliability Engineering for Information Systems," IEEE Software (March 1988), p. 11.

2. Jan Synders, "The CASE of the Artful Dodgers," Infosystems (March 1988), p. 28.

3. Ibid.

4. George Schussel, "Application Development in the 5th Generation," Datamation (November 15, 1987), p. 100.

5. Richard Phelps, "New Tools Automate the Development Cycle," Software News (January 1987), pp. 138-141.

6. Edith Myers, "Back-End Tools Seek Front-End Companions," Software Magazine (September 1988), p. 50.

7. Carma McClure, CASE is Software Automation (Englewood Cliffs, N.J.: Prentice-Hall, Inc., 1989), p. 8.

8. Ibid., p. 49.

9. Charlie Backman, "A CASE for Reverse Engineering," Datamation (July 1, 1988), pp. 49-55.

10. William Ulrich, "Re-engineering vs. Reverse Engineering," Software Magazine (September 1988), p. 8.

11. Susan Messenheimer and Carol Weiszmann, "Quality Software Quest," Software Magazine (February 1988), p. 31.

12. McClure, Ibid., pp. 188-190.

13. George Schussel, "Application Development in the 5th Generation," Datamation (November 5, 1987), p. 102.

14. Charles F .Martin, "Second Generation CASE Tools: A Challenge to Vendors," IEEE Software (March 1988), pp. 46-49.

15. McClure, Ibid., p. 202.

16. Ibid., p. 199.


## CHAPTER 9


1. James Martin and Al Hershey, "Software Engineering Depends on Information Engineering," Software News (March 1986), p. 60.

2. James Martin, Information Engineering, Book 1: Introduction (Englewood Cliffs, NJ: Prentice-Hall, Inc., 1989), pp. 101-126.

3. Richard D. Hackathorn and Johngir Karimi, "A Framework for Comparing Information Engineering Methods," MIS Quarterly (June 1988), p. 204.

4. Tony Percy, "What CASE Can't Do Yet," Computerworld (June 20, 1988), p. 60.

5. Thomas Haughey, "Information Engineer: Problems Impeding Acceptance," Database Newsletter (May-June 1988), pp. 8-10.

6. James Martin, An Information Systems Manifesto (Englewood Cliffs, NJ: Prentice-Hall, Inc., 1984), p. 92.

7. Carma McClure, CASE is Software Automation (Englewood Cliffs, NJ: Prentice-Hall, Inc., 1989), p. 86.

8. James Martin and Carma McClure, Diagramming Techniques for Analysts and Programmers (Englewood Cliffs, NJ: Prentice-Hall, Inc., 1985), p. 12. Copyright © 1989, Texas Instruments Incorporated. All rights reserved.

9. Ibid., pp. 329-330.

10. Mel A. Colter, "Evolution of the Structured Methodologies" in Couger, Colter, and Knap, Advanced Development/Feasibility Techniques (New York: John Wiley and Sons, 1982), p. 92.

11. "An Interview With Burt Rubenstein," Database Newsletter (November/ December 1987), p. 17.

12. Martin, Information Engineering: Introduction, (Englewood Cliffs, N.J.: Prentice-Hall, Inc., 1989), pp. 23-25.

## CHAPTER 10

1. Phillip Ein-Dor, "Grosch's Law Revisited: CPU Power and the Cost of Computation," Communications of the ACM, (February 1985), p. 149.

2. Michael Tucker, "Connectivity," Computerworld (April 1, 1987), p. 52.

3. James Hannan, "A Primer on Micro-to-Mainframe Links," Info Systems (February 1986), pp. 32-33.

4. Barry Keating, "Telecommunications: The Ideal and the Reality," Creative Computing (February 1985), p. 102.

5. James Martin, "Micro-to-Mainframe Links," Computer World (January 6, 1986), p. 78.

6. Merv Adrian, "Stalking the Micro to Mainframe Links," Information Center (April 1986), p. 33.

7. Martin, Ibid., p. 79.

8. Gilbert Wai, "Take Your Pick," Byte (July 1989), pp. 218-220.

9. George Schussel, "Application Development in the 5th Generation," Datamation (November 15, 1987), p. 97.

10. Wai, Ibid., p. 220.

11. Henry F. Korth and Abraham Silberschatz, Database System Concepts (New York: McGraw-Hill Book Co., 1986), pp. 404-406.

12. Ibid., p. 406.

13. Fred R. McFadden and Jeffrey A. Hoffer, Data Base Management, 2nd edition (Menlo Park: Benjamin Cummings Publishing Co., 1988), p. 647.

14. Steve Feldman, "Sketches of Distributed DBMS," Computerworld (February 16, 1987), p. S14.


## CHAPTER 11


1. David S. McMaster, "IBM's Token-Ring: What are the Alternatives?" Mini-Micro Systems (September, 1986), p. 114.

2. Harvey Kaufman, "PBX versus LAN," Telecommunications (May, 1986), pp. 92-94.

3. Trends in Information Technology, 3rd Edition, (Chicago: Arthur Andersen, 1987), pp. 9-24.


## CHAPTER 12


1. Robert I. Benjamin, "Information Technology in the 1990's: A Long Range Planning Scenario", MIS Quarterly, (June, 1982), pp. 11-31.

2. John F. Rickert and Laura S. Flannery, "The Management of End User Computing", Communications of the ACM, (October, 1983), pp. 778.

3. Robert Peterson, "Giving End-Users the MIS Seal of Good System Building," Computerworld (June 1, 1987), pp. 83-86.

4. Thomas P. Gerrity and John F. Rockart, "End-User Computing: Are You a Leader or a Loggard," Sloan Management Review (Summer 1986), pp. 28-29.

5. John Naisbitt, Megatrends (New York: Warner Books, Inc., 1982), p. 143.

6. William E. Perry, The Information Center (Englewood Cliffs: Prentice-Hall, Inc., 1987), pp. 4-5.

7. Gerrity and Rockart, Ibid., pp. 26-27.

8. Henry C. Lucas, "Utilizing Information Technology: Guidelines for Managers," Sloan Management Review (Fall, 1986), p. 42.

9. D.G. Dologite, Using Computers (Englewood Cliffs: Prentice-Hall, Inc., 1987), pp. 273-274.

10. Martin Healey, "What is a Workstation,"" Datamation (Jan. 15, 1987), pp 55-57.

11. Lee Gremillion and Philip Pyburn, Computers and Information Systems in Business (New York: McGraw-Hill, 1988), p. 289.

12. Richard L. Nolan, "Managing the Crises in Data Processing," Harvard Business Review (March-April 1979), pp. 115-126.

## CHAPTER 13

1. Peter G. W. Keen and M. S. Scott Morton, Decision Support Systems: An Organizational Perspective, (Reading, Mass.: Addison-Wesley Publishing Company, 1978), p. 86.

2. Ibid., pp. 87-88.

3. Steven Alter, Decision Support Systems: Continuing Practice and Continuing Challenges, (Reading, Mass.: Addison-Wesley Publishing Co., 1980), pp. 110-111.

4. John F. Rockart and Michael E. Treacy, "The CEO Goes On-Line," Harvard Business Review, (January-February, 1982), pp. 82-88.

5. Paul Harmon and David King, Expert Systems (John Wiley and Sons, Inc., 1985), pp. 5-7.

6. Efraim Turban and Paul R. Watkins, "Integrating Expert Systems and Decision Support Systems," MIS Quarterly (June 1986), p. 122.

7. Harmon and King, Ibid., p. 5.

8. Ibid., p. 94.

9. Ibid., p. 58.

10. Dimitris N. Choratas, Applying Expert Systems in Business (New York: McGraw-Hill Book Co., 1987), pp. 191-192.

11. Ibid., p. 210.

12. Ibid., p. 206.

13. Ibid., p. 207.

14. Ibid., pp. 210-211.

15. Robert Poe, "Nissan Drives Toward Parallel Development," Datamation (January 15, 1988), p. 73.

16. Karen Gullo, "Bank of New England Grows Image Minded," Datamation (January 15, 1988), p. 62.


## CHAPTER 14


1. Kalthoff and Lee, Productivity and Records Automation (Englewood Cliffs, N.J., Prentice Hall, 1981), p. 4.

2. John Naisbitt, Megatrends, (New York: Warner Books, 1984), p. 5.

3. B. Uttal, "What's Detaining the Office of the Future," Fortune (May 3, 1982), pp. 176-196.

4. John Helliwell, "Optical Overview, What's Coming in CD-ROMs and WORMs," PC Magazine (October 14, 1986), pp. 149-164.

5. Carolyn Dodson, "CD-ROMs for the Library," Special Libraries (Summer 1987), p. 191.

6. Bruce P. Berra and Nikos B. Trallinos, "Optical Techniques and Data/Knowledge Base Machines," Computer (October 1987), p. 60.

7. Helliwell, p. 161.

8. David Whiledon, "Look at Optical Storage," Computer Decisions (December 1986), p. 59.

9. Philip Elmer-DeWitt, "The World on a Silver Platter," Time (April 11, 1988), p. 52.

10. Whieldon, Ibid.

11. Harry Katzan, Jr., Office Automation: A Managers Guide (New York: American Management Association, 1982), p. 109.

12. Kalthoff and Lee, Ibid., pp. 84-87.

13. Ibid., p. 49.

14. Ibid., p. 80.

15. Ibid., p. 107.

16. Ibid., p. 49.

17. Thomas J. Billesbach, "Applicability of Just-In-Time Techniques in the Administrative Area," (unpublished doctoral dissertation, University of Nebraska, 1987), pp. 7-10.

18. James Martin, An Information Systems Manifesto, Prentice-Hall, p. 225.

19. Jonathan Schlefer, "Office Automation and Bureaucracy," Technology Review, July 1983, pp. 32-40.

20. Martin, Manifesto, p. 226.

## CHAPTER 15

1. Richard Cyert, "Saving the Smokestack Industries," Bell Atlantic Quarterly (Autumn 1985), pp. 17-24.

2. John Merwin, "A Tale of Two Worlds," Forbes (June 16, 1986), pp. 102-103.

3. William G. Stoddard and Nolan G. Rhea, "We Need to Change the Role of MRP in Manufacturing," Material Handling Engineering (July 1985), pp. 104-105.

4. Willie Schatz, "Making CIM Work," Datamation, (December 1, 1988), p. 19.

5. Jean S. Bozman and Alan J. Ryan, "Rethink Before Automating," Computerworld (June 26, 1989), p. 6.

6. William G. Stoddard and Nolan G. Rhea, "People Make Manufacturing Productivity Work," Material Handling Engineering (September 1985), p. 86.

7. Doug Carroll, "Honda Shifts into Higher Gear in USA," USA Today (July 23, 1986), p. 1B.

8. Trends in Information Technology, 3rd Edition (Arthur Andersen and Co., 1987), p. 70.

9. Jeffrey G. Miller and Thomas E. Vollmann, "The Hidden Factory," Harvard Business Review (September-October 1985), pp. 144-146.

10. Richard J. Schoenberger, World Class Manufacturing (New York: The Free Press, 1986), pp. 42-45.

11. Mikell P. Groover and Emory W. Zimmers, Jr., CAD/CAM: Computer-Aided Design and Manufacturing (Englewood Cliffs: Prentice-Hall, Inc., 1984), pp. 61-63.

12. Craig K. Harman and Russ Adams, Reading Between the Lines (Peterborough, NH: North American Technology, Inc.), p. 16.

13. Gene Bylinsky, "A Breakthrough in Automating the Assembly Line," Fortune (May 26, 1987), p. 66.

14. William G. Rankin, "Group Technology and Cellular Manufacturing the Keys to 'CIM', " A Program Guide for CIM Implementation (Society of Manufacturing Engineers, 1987), p. 197.

15. Schatz, Ibid., p. 21.

16. Rankin, Ibid., p. 198.

17. Schoenberger, World Class Manufacturing, p. 45.

18. Ibid., pp. 184-188.

19. Ted Kumpe and Piet T. Bolwijn, "Manufacturing: The New Case for Vertical Integration," Harvard Business Review (March-April 1988), p. 79.

20. Ibid., p. 76.

21. Larry Stevens, "The CIM Connection: Reaching Out to the Shop Floor," Computerworld (May 30, 1988), p. 46.

22. Richard J. Schoenberger, "Frugal Manufacturing," Harvard Business Review (September-October, 1987), p. 96.

23. Trends in Information Technology, p. 86.

24. Timothy N. Warner, "Information Technology as a Competitive Burden," Sloan Management Review (Fall, 1987), p. 60.

## CHAPTER 16

1. Daniel Bell, The Coming of Post-Industrial Society (New York: Basic Books, 1973), p. 14.

2. John Naisbitt, Megatrends (New York: Warner Books, 1984), p. 5.

3. Peter Drucker, The Age of Discontinuity (New York: Harper and Row, 1968), p. 265.

4. Business Week, January 27, 1986, p. 12.

5. Stephen S. Cohen and John Zysman, Manufacturing Matters: The Myth of the Post-Industrial Economy (New York: Basic Books, 1987), pp. xiii-xiv.

6. Herold J. Leavitt and Thomas L. Whisler, "Management in the 1980's," Harvard Business Review (November-December, 1958), pp. 41-48.

7. "The Shrinking of Middle Management," Business Week (April 25, 1983), p. 54.

8. Peter Drucker, "The Coming of the New Organization," Harvard Business Review (January-February 1988), p. 46.

9. Ibid.

10. Ibid., pp. 46-47.

11. John F. Rockert, "The Line Takes the Leadership-IS Management in a Wired Society," Sloan Management Review (Summer 19898), pp. 59-60.

12. Drucker, Ibid., p. 49.

13. Ibid., p. .

14. Dale D. Achabal and Shelby H. McIntyre, "Information Technology is Reshaping Retailing," Journal of Retailing (Winter 1987), pp. 321-324.

15. Jeremy Main, "The Winning Organization," Fortune (September 26, 1988), p. 51.

16. Jean Woodworth, "1988: The Year of the Debit Card?" the Bankers Magazine (July/August 1988), pp. 34-38.

17. Main, Ibid., p. 50.

18. Main, Ibid., pp. 50-51.

20. George Gilder, "The Revitalization of Everything: The Law of the Microcosim," Harvard Business Review (March/April, 1988), p. 57.

21. Christopher Meek, Warner Woodworth, and W. Gibb Dyer, Jr., Managing by the Numbers: Absentee Ownership and the Decline of American Industry (Reading, MA: Addison-Wesley Publishing Co., 1988), p. 106.

22. Norman Jones, "The Hollow Corporation," Business Week (March 3, 1986), p. 57.

23. Meek et al., Ibid., pp. 109-111.

24. "Is Your Computer Secure," Business Week (August 1, 1988), pp. 64-72.

## APPENDIX

1. Martin, James. Managing the Database Environment (Englewood Cliffs, N.J.: Prentice-Hall, 1983), pp. 321-337.

2. Tony Percy, "The Importance of Good Relations," Datamation (December 15, 1984), p. 86.

3. Martin, Managing the Data Base Environment (Prentice-Hall, Inc., Englewood Cliffs, NJ, 1983), p. 203.

4. Percy, Ibid.

5. Martin, Ibid., p. 204.

6. Ibid., pp. 572-574.

7. Mark L. Gillenson, "The Duality of Database Structures and Design Techniques," Communications of the ACM (December 1987),m p. 1058, and C. J. Date, "A Practical Guide to Database Design," Technical Report TR-03.220 IBM, (December 1982), p. 20.

8. William Kent, "A Simple Guide to Five Normal Forms in Relational Database Theory," Communications of the ACM (February 1983), p. 120.

9. S. Atre, Data Base: Structured Techniques for Design, Performance, and Management (New York: John Wiley & Sons, 1980), p. 149N. Also, Martin, Ibid., p. 227.

10. Paul Winsberg, "Smoothing the Data Administration Path," Computerworld (March 14, 1988), p. 515.

# Index

Abstraction, 376
Accessibility, 98
Action Diagram, 283-289
Active Data Dictionary, 152
ADA, 226
Advanced Technology Group, 59
Analog Signal, 329
Analogic Models, 171
Analysis, 172
APL, 224
Application Architecture, 81
Application Certification, 367
Application Generator, 100
Application Specific approach, 86, 143
Applications Backlog, 198
Applications Prototyping, 207
Artificial Intelligence, 393
ASCII, 308
Assembler, 222
Asynchronous Transmission, 308
Attribute, 109, 482
Auditing, 163, 164
Automated Database Modeling, 502
Automated diagramming, 257
Automated Drafting Systems, 438
Automatic Code Generation, 258
Automatic Navigation, 23, 235

Back-End CASE, 252
Bar Coding, 439
Baseband Channel, 340
BASIC, 226
Batch Processing, 8, 9
Baud Rate, 328
Binary Relationship, 478
Boolean, 236
Brackets, 283
Branch, 234
Broadband Channel, 328, 340
Bubble Chart, 482
Bus, 337
Business Area Analysis, 275
Business Modeling
Business Systems Planning (BSP)
By-Product Approach, 73, 74

C, 226
Canonical Synthesis, 499

Cardinalities, 477
CASE 23, 188, 212, 231, 249
Case Selection, 283
CD-ROM, 413
Centralized Database
Changing Organizational Boundaries, 459
Changing Organizational Structures, 457
Chief Information Officer, 69
Clustered database, 320
Coaxial Cable, 338
COBOL, 224
Coding, 172
Commonality, 210
Compilers, 237
Computer Aided Design (CAD), 438
Computer Aided Engineering, 438
Computer Aided Manufacturing (CAM), 439
Computer Aided Process Planning (CAPP), 440
Computer crime, 464
Computer Virus, 466
Computer-Aided Design/Computer-Aided Engineering (CAD/CAE), 438
Computer-Aided Software Engineering (CASE), 188, 212, 231, 249
Concatenated Key, 483
Conceptual Model, 475
Concurrency Control, 320
Concurrent Access Controls, 162
Conditions, 286
Connectivity, 307
Contention (CSMA/CD), 339
Copy Machine, 412
Corporate Culture, 51, 52, 53, 54
Critical Success Factors, 75, 76

Data, 5, 375
Data Administration, 69, 116, 147, 150, 162, 361
Data Administrator, 148, 149
Database, 95
Database Controls, 160, 161
Database Design, 151
Database Designer
Database Machines, 111
Database Manager, 101
Database Management Systems (DBMS), 99
Database Modeling
Database Server, 113, 114, 312
Database Server Architecture, 113
Data Dictionary, 151

Data Driven, 26, 277
Data Element, 110
Data Element Naming Standard, 156, 157
Data Elements, 110
Data Encyclopedia, 156
Data Extraction, 309, 354
Data Files, 95
Data Flow Diagram, 182-185
Data Group, 110, 485
Data Independence, 96, 147
Data Integrity, 95
Data Modeling, 116
Data Redundancy, 147
Data Security, 99, 160-162
Data-Driven Methodology, 277
Decision Support Systems (DSS), 12, 374-376
Decision Support Usage Patterns, 379
Decision Tables, 179-181
Decision Trees, 186
Decomposition, 171
Design, 172
Desktop Publishing, 410
Development Center, 69, 362
Development of Expert Systems, 394
Diagramming Techniques, 171
Dialog, 375
Digital Signal, 329
Direct File Organization, 154
Distributed Database, 316
Distributed Processing, 302

Effectiveness, 8, 47
Efficiency, 8
Electronic Data Interchange (EDI), 416-417
Electronic Filing, 412
Electronic Filing/Records Automation, 412
Electronic Mail/Message Systems, 415-416
Encyclopedia, 292
End-User Certification, 366-368
End-User Computing, 24, 25, 353, 354
Enterprise Model, 73, 82-85
Entity, 78, 107
Entity Relationship Diagram, 476
Entity Subtypes, 480
Entity Supertypes, 481
Erasable Optical Disk, 414
Extended Binary Coded Decimal Interchange Code (EBCDIC), 308
Extended Enterprise, 44-46

Executive Information Systems (EIS), 380-381
Executive Leadership, 55
Executive Steering Committee, 58
Expert Systems, 390-392
Expert Systems Versus Decision Support, 392
Extended Development Period, 48, 49

Factory of the Future, 446-448
Feedback, 5
Fiber Optic Cable, 333, 339
File Processing, 111
File Server, 312, 335
File Transfer, 309
Financial Planning Software, 384-390
First-Normal Form, 494-495
Flexibility, 97, 462
Focused Factories, 435
Foreign Key, 491, 492
FORTRAN, 223
Fourth Generation Languages, 23, 229
Front-End CASE, 252
Full Life-Cycle Coverage, 258
Functional Dependence, 489
Future of Expert Systems, 398

Geometric Modeling, 438
Graphics Language, 101
Group Technology, 435-436

Hierarchical Database Model, 101, 102
Hierarchical Structure, 286

Iconic Models, 171
Image Processing, 411-412
Impact, 211
Implementation, 172
Indexed Sequential File Organization, 154
Information Architecture, 78
Information as a Competitive Weapon, 39
Information Center, 70, 358-363
Information Engineering, 274
Information Engineering Facility (IEF), 290
Information Ethics, 467
Information Middleman, 47
Information Overload, 60
Information Resource Management (IRM), 57, 58, 278
Information Strategy Planning, 143, 275
Information System, 5
Infrastructure, 70

Input/Output Descriptors, 174
Input, 5
Integrated CASE, 253
Integrated Data Dictionary, 101, 186, 228
Integrated Digital Services Network (ISDN), 345
Integration, 6
Intellectual Property Rights, 468
Intelligent Persistance, 50
Interpretor, 237
Inventory Control Systems, 430-431
Islands of Automation, 440
Iteration, 171

JOIN, 106, 108
Joint Application Design, 200
Just-In-Time (JIT), 417, 420

Key-Indicator Approach, 74
Knowledge Worker, 460

Laser Printer, 336, 410
Leased Lines, 328
Linear Programming Packages, 384
Local Area Networks (LANs), 334, 406
Logical Model, 474
Logical User View, 110
Loop, 324

Machinge Language, 221
Magnetic Disks, 20, 21
Maintenance, 27, 28
Maintenance Trap, 197
Management of Technology, 66, 463
Managerial Workstation, 365
Managing End-User Computing, 369
Manufacturing Automation Protocol (MAP), 443
Manufacturing Database, 441
Many-to-Many Relationship, 478
Many-to-One Relationship, 478
Materials Management, 445
Materials Requirements Planning (MRP), 427-430
Methodology, 194, 260
Microprocessor-Based Workstations, 25, 315
Microprocessors, 18, 19, 20
Microwave, 331
Modeling, 171, 375-377
Modularity, 181

N-ARY Relationship, 478
Natural Languages, 393
Network Administration, 346
Network Database Model, 102
Network Gateway, 335
Networking, 25
Non-Procedural Language, 233
Nonmonotonic Reasoning, 394
Normalization, 481
Null Approach, 74

Object Code, 237
Office Automation, 13, 361
On-Line Transaction Processing, 10, 11
Operand, 221
Operation Code, 221-222
Optical Disks, 21, 22, 413-415
Output, 5

Page Composition Software, 410
Partitioned Database, 316
PASCAL, 226
Passive Data Dictonary, 152
Peer-Coupled Network, 302, 303
Personal Computers, 12, 13, 353
Peter Principle, 51
Physical Database Design, 474
PL/1, 225
Polling, 340
Post Industrial Society, 454-457
Premanufacturing, 444
Primary Key, 107, 482
Privacy, 160
Private Telephone Networks, 344
Private-Branch Telephone Exchange (PBX), 341
Procedural Language, 233
Process Control, 445
Process Driven, 26, 277
Product Codes, 46
Productivity of Software Development, 68, 97
Professionalism, 468-470
Program Flowcharts, 175-177
Programmer Productivity, 240
PROJECT, 106
Propogation Delay, 333
Protocol, 308
Protocol Conversion, 309
Prototypes, 60

Prototyping, 171, 207-209
Public Packet Switching Network, 345
Public Telephone Networks, 345

Query Languages, 26, 100, 227, 383

Rapid Iterative Prototyping, 261
Reducing Transactions, 434
Relational Database Model, 94, 103
Repeating Group, 494
Relationship, 477
Repetition, 283
Replicated Database, 319
Report Generator, 100, 229
Repository, 156, 256
Ring Network, 337
Robotics, 393, 437

Satellites, 331-333
Screen Painter, 229
Second-Normal Form, 496
Secondary Key, 483
Security, 311
SELECT, 105, 106
Semi-structured Decision, 377-378
Sequence, 234
Sequential File Organization, 153
Simplification, 376-377, 419, 431
Simulation Languages, 384
Single Point of Contact, 47
Software Development Methodology, 194
Software Engineering, 182, 260, 279
Software Reverse Engineering, 259
Software Upload, 309
Source Code, 237
Source Data Automation, 47
Spreadsheet Software, 381-383
SQL, 107, 123-139
Stand-Alone Personal Computer, 25
Standards, 72, 360
Star Network, 336
Statistical Analysis Software, 384
Structure, 211
Structured Decision, 377-378
Structured English, 186
Structured Methods, 181
Structured Query Language (SQL), 107, 123-139
Subject Database, 78, 79

Subject Database Matrix, 80
Subsystems, 2
Symbolic Models, 171
Synchronous, 308
Synthesis, 171
System Flowcharts, 178, 179
System, 2, 3
Systems Analyst, 170
Systems Design, 276
Systems Engineering, 260
Systems Life Cycle, 172, 173

Table, 109
Task Technology Congruence, 49
Technical Architecture, 81
Terminal Emulation, 309
Terminations, 287, 288
Testing, 172
The Authoritarian Approach, 356
The Extended Enterprise, 45-46
The Free Rein Approach, 357
Third-Normal Form, 497
Three-Tiered Network, 304
Token Passing, 340
Tool, 260
Top Down Process
Top-Down Design, 181
Total Quality Control (TQC), 433
Traditional Systems Life Cycle, 262
Transaction Processing, 8
Transitive Dependence
Transparently-Coupled, 255
Twisted Pair Cable, 338
Two-Tiered Network, 303

Unstructured Decision, 377-378
Upload-Linked, 255
User-Based Development, 209, 368

Validity, 377
Voice Grade Channel, 328

Weak Entity, 480
White Collar Productivity, 404-406
White Collar Workers, 405
Wide-Area Networks, 344
Word Processing, 365, 407-410
World Class Manufacturer (WCM), 427, 443
Write Once Read Many Times (WORM), 414